Contents

INSECT DEVELOPMENT

Previous Symposia of the Royal Entomological Society

SYMPOSIA OF THE ROYAL ENTOMOLOGICAL
SOCIETY OF LONDON: NUMBER EIGHT

Insect Development

EDITED ON BEHALF OF THE SOCIETY BY

P. A. LAWRENCE

PUBLISHED FOR

THE ROYAL ENTOMOLOGICAL SOCIETY

41 QUEEN'S GATE, LONDON SW7

BY

BLACKWELL SCIENTIFIC PUBLICATIONS

OXFORD LONDON EDINBURGH MELBOURNE

© 1976 Blackwell Scientific Publications
Osney Mead, Oxford,
8 John Street, London, WC1
9 Forrest Road, Edinburgh,
P.O. Box 9, North Balwyn, Victoria, Australia

First published 1976

British Library Cataloguing in Publication Data
Insect development—(Royal Entomological
Society. Symposia; No. 8).
Bibl.—Index.
ISBN 0-632-00049-X
1. Lawrence, P A 2. Series.
595.7'03 QL495.5
Insects—Development—Congresses

Distributed in the USA by
Halstead Press, a Division of
John Wiley & Sons Inc
New York

Set by Malvern Typesetting Services Ltd, Malvern, Worcs.
Printed and bound in Great Britain by
Butler and Tanner, Ltd., Frome

Foreword

Developmental biology, after about 30 years in the doldrums, is beginning to move again. New work on insects is one of the main reasons for this fresh start. Insects are easy to keep in the laboratory, and show the results of experiments rapidly. The simple monolayered epithelium means that most cuticular patterns are in two dimensions and therefore easier to analyse. New techniques have been developed to investigate insect eggs. *Drosophila* geneticists are beginning to turn to the problems of embryology.

Although these advances are technical, the real step forward has been a change of attitude towards a more analytical and reductionist approach. Three people have been outstandingly important here: Professors Antonio Garcia-Bellido, Ernst Hadorn and Curt Stern. I would like to dedicate this book to them.

PETER LAWRENCE

Cambridge
November 1975

Acknowledgements

This volume is a record of the eighth Royal Entomological Symposium held in Imperial College, London on 18–19 September 1975. The following firms contributed towards the cost of the meeting and we gratefully acknowledge their help:

Boots Pure Drug Company Ltd
Cadbury-Schweppes Ltd
Imperial Chemical Industries Ltd
May and Baker Ltd
Rentokil Ltd
Shell Research Ltd
Tate and Lyle Ltd
The Wellcome Foundation Ltd

Contents

I. INTRODUCTION: DEVELOPMENT OF THE INSECT EGG

II. IMAGINAL DISCS OF *DROSOPHILA*

III. PATTERN IN LATER DEVELOPMENT

Contributors to Discussions

OWEN K. WILBY *Developmental Biology Building, 124 Observatory Road, Glasgow*

LAWRENCE RAZAVI *32 Eastholm, London*

GABRIEL DOVER *Department of Genetics, University of Cambridge, Milton Road, Cambridge*

J. M. W. SLACK *Department of Biology, Middlesex Hospital Medical School, Cleveland Street, London*

H. HENSON *24 Elmete Avenue, Leeds*

ANON. *Imperial College, University of London*

JAMES B. NARDI *MRC Laboratory of Molecular Biology, Hills Road, Cambridge*

B. J. SELMAN *Department of Agricultural Zoology, School of Agriculture, University of Newcastle upon Tyne*

JOHN SHIRE *Institute of Genetics, University of Glasgow, Glasgow*

GINES MORATA *MRC Laboratory of Molecular Biology, Hills Road, Cambridge*

T. WEIS-FOGH *Late of Department of Zoology, Downing Street, Cambridge*

K. R. WILLISON *4 Nourse Close, Woodeaton, Oxford*

JOHN PALKA *Department of Zoology, University of Cambridge, Cambridge*

VERNON FRENCH *Division of Developmental Biology, National Institute for Medical Research, The Ridgeway, Mill Hill, London.*

G. C. VARLEY *Hope Department of Zoology (Entomology), University Museum, Oxford*

I • Introduction: development of the insect egg

1 • New ways to probe pattern formation and determination in insects

HOWARD A. SCHNEIDERMAN

Center for Pathobiology, University of California, Irvine, California 92717

1. INTRODUCTION

The general problem of developmental biology is to explain how the genetic information present in the fertilized egg is translated to produce a complex multicellular organism with well-defined spatial and temporal patterns of cellular differentiation. In this paper I shall describe some of the ways in which the fruit fly *Drosophila melanogaster* has been a particularly useful organism in which to analyse parts of this problem and why insects in general are receiving such extraordinary attention from developmental biologists. I shall focus especially on experiments in which methods of genetics have been applied to analyse *Drosophila* development and have yielded insights into several general developmental problems that are not yet possible with other systems. The first problem to be dealt with is how cells in a developing organism make commitments. I shall analyse pattern formation, the process by which cells acquire specific fates according to their position in a developing tissue. I shall then examine the role of oogenesis in epigenesis and shall analyse, as far as it is understood, the role of cytoplasmic factors built into the egg by the mother in initiating particular developmental commitments in embryonic cells.

During development there are numerous occasions when cells decide between alternative programmes of development, e.g., whether to be an epidermal cell, a myoblast, or a germ cell. Each commitment is implemented by a series of biochemical events in the cell: an epidermal cell synthesizes cuticular proteins, a myoblast synthesizes muscle proteins, a germ cell synthesizes other sorts of proteins. These cellular commitments appear to be of two basic kinds: *heritable* and *nonheritable* (Schneiderman 1969; Bryant 1974). The commitment to be an epidermal cell, a myoblast, or a primary germ cell is a heritable commitment: the mitotic progeny of epidermal cells are epidermal cells, the mitotic progeny of myoblasts are myoblasts, etc. In *Drosophila* the commitment to belong to a particular imaginal disc is a heritable commitment. In addition to these heritable commitments cells also make nonheritable commitments. For instance, the commitment to be a particular part of an imaginal disc, such as a specific bristle or pattern element, is not heritable. As we shall see it depends on the position of the cell in the disc. Nor is the commitment of an insect epidermal cell to secrete pupal cuticle rather than adult cuticle heritable. It depends upon local hormonal conditions.

3

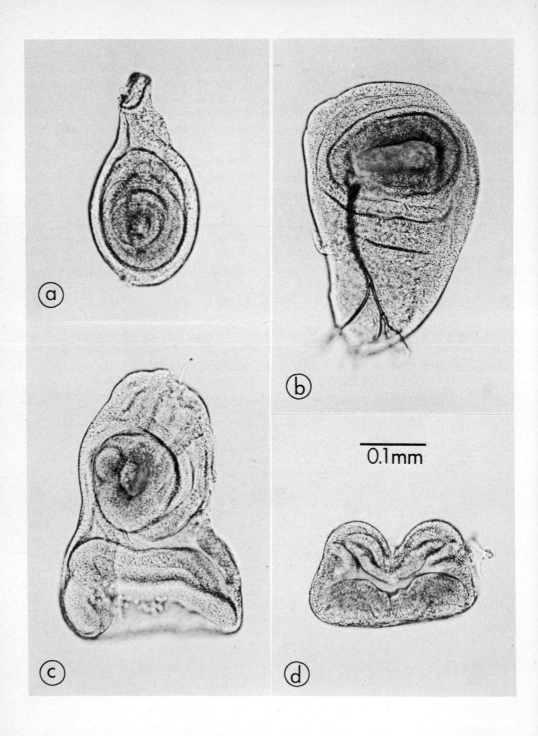

FIG. 1.1. Several of the major imaginal discs of *Drosophila melanogaster* as seen in living, unstained whole mounts. (a) First leg disc; (b) wing disc; (c) eye-antenna disc; (d) genital disc. (From Bryant, 1974.)

2. HERITABLE COMMITMENTS IN IMAGINAL DISC CELLS: DETERMINATION

Imaginal discs are small nests of cells that become physically separated from other tissues early in development and are committed to form parts of the adult integument. In *Drosophila* the entire adult integument except for the abdomen arises from imaginal discs. There are ten pairs of major imaginal discs and a genital disc (Fig. 1.1). Each is characterized by its location in the larva, by its size and shape, and most importantly by the part of the adult that it forms. The integument of the adult head arises from three pairs of discs; the external parts of the adult thorax are formed by three pairs of leg discs, a pair of dorsal prothoracic discs, wing discs, and haltere discs. The genitalia and analia are formed from the genital disc. Each segment of the abdomen is formed from eight small nests of cells called abdominal histoblasts which are continuous with the larval epidermis (Roseland, personal communication).

In *Drosophila,* the imaginal discs are first evident histologically in the late embryo (Laugé 1967) or early larva (Auerbach 1936) as thickenings of the epidermis. Later they become invaginated to form a sac-like structure, attached to the larval epidermis by a stalk. When they are first evident histologically each disc contains between 15 and 60 cells depending on the disc (Fig. 1.2) (M. Madhavan, personal communication). Unlike other epidermal cells, which secrete a cuticle at each larval moult, the imaginal discs do not secrete a cuticle until metamorphosis.

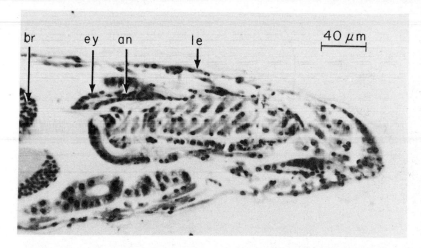

Fig. 1.2. Sagittal section through the anterior region of a 14-hour larva of *D. melanogaster* showing the eye-antenna disc. At this stage the eye portion of the disc and the antenna portion of the disc are each composed of about 40 cells. an, Antenna part of disc; ey, eye part of disc; le, larval epidermis; br, brain. (Courtesy of Dr M. Madhavan.)

The imaginal discs have a remarkably simple organization. They are basically hollow folded sacs that consist of a single layered columnar epithelium. During the four days of larval life the epithelium becomes folded as the discs grow by cell division. Their cells remain undifferentiated, however, and resemble the relatively undifferentiated cells of a young embryo. This state of affairs continues until the onset of metamorphosis at which time the number of cells in an individual disc ranges from a few hundred in the smaller discs to many thousands in the larger ones. At metamorphosis the epithelium of the imaginal discs undergoes a spectacular morphogenetic movement known as eversion, which converts the tightly folded epithelium of the disc into an extended adult structure. The shape of the cells changes from tall columnar to squamous and the kinds of junctions between the cells also change (Poodry & Schneiderman 1970; Fristrom & Fristrom 1975). Differentiation and cuticle synthesis follow, and each disc secretes a specific part of the cuticle of the adult fly such as the leg, antenna, wing, etc. For the most part, the cuticular contributions of individual cells can be recognized. This attribute permits an analysis of the spatial control of patterns of differentiation at the level of single cells and provides a special opportunity to identify the factors that initiate the appearance of different kinds of cells in different parts of a developing organ. Some of the imaginal discs contain presumptive muscle and nerve cells but most of our discussion in this paper concerns the epithelium of the disc which gives rise to cuticular structures.

Imaginal discs can easily be isolated from a larva, cut into fragments and transplanted into another larva where they respond to hormonal stimuli, undergo metamorphosis and differentiate along with the host (Hadorn 1963, 1966a; Ursprung 1967). Alternatively metamorphosis can be stimulated *in vitro* by the addition of an ecdysone to the culture medium (Milner & Sang 1974). Discs or fragments of discs can also be cultured in an adult fly abdomen where hormonal conditions permit them to grow but not to metamorphose (Hadorn 1963, 1966a). At any time the fragments can be extracted from the adult and reimplanted into a larva for metamorphosis.

Such imaginal disc tissue fragments can be subcultured in a series of adult hosts for years (Hadorn 1966a, b). Periodically tissue fragments can be removed, and caused to metamorphose to ascertain their developmental capacity. What usually happens is that tissue derived from a disc fragment continues to metamorphose into structures belonging to the original disc. Thus cultures derived from fragments of a genital disc will usually metamorphose into genital disc derivatives. A few of these cultures have been maintained for many years. For example, some tissue lines derived from a genital disc retained the ability to produce anal plates over several years of culture *in vivo* and hundreds of cell divisions (Hadorn 1966a, b). Experiments of this kind demonstrate that imaginal disc cells convey to their mitotic descendants not only their genetic information but also the decision to use a certain part of that genetic information. In this paper I shall use the term *determination* to denote such a heritable decision. Each imaginal disc has its own particular determination. I recognize that the term determination is sometimes used to encompass both heritable and nonheritable commitments, but evidence will be offered in this paper that some real advantage is gained from separately identifying the two types of commitments.

Occasionally, imaginal disc cells that have been cultured *in vivo* change their determined state and give rise to structures normally formed by a different disc. This phenomenon is known as transdetermination (Hadorn 1966a, b). Once a disc fragment has transdetermined, the mitotic progeny of those transdetermined cells retain the altered determination. One such tissue line derived from a genital disc retained the capacity to differentiate into thorax and wing tissue for 236 subcultures over nine years of culture *in vivo* (approximately 1800 cell generations) (Hadorn 1969 and personal communication). Another transdetermined tissue line derived from an eye-antenna disc retained the capacity to differentiate into parts of the genitalia for more than 120 subcultures over seven years (about 1200 cell divisions) (Gateff & Schneiderman 1974).

Another example of a possible heritable commitment involving imaginal discs has been proposed by Garcia-Bellido and his colleagues (Garcia-Bellido *et al.* 1973; Garcia-Bellido 1975). They have presented evidence that certain groups of cells in imaginal discs that correspond to particular geographical regions of the disc called compartments become defined at a certain time in development. Thereafter each of these compartments seems to represent a separate population of proliferating cells in which the descendants of the cells in one compartment never cross into the other compartment. In the wing, for example, there appears to be an anterior and a posterior compartment which are established early in development. Clones generated after the establishment of the compartment never cross this border in any individuals. No other line drawn on the surface of the wing will have this property, but will be crossed by clones in at least some individuals. In normal development *in situ,* the cells in a compartment seem to convey to their mitotic descendants the commitment to belong to that compartment. There is as yet no clear evidence that compartment boundaries are maintained when fragments of discs are cultured *in vivo* or that the mitotic descendants of cells from one compartment will always belong to that compartment. The possible importance of compartments for normal development have been examined by Crick & Lawrence (1975) and are considered by Lawrence & Morata, Chapter 8, in this volume.

3. Nonheritable commitments in imaginal disc cells: specification

Other kinds of cellular commitments are *not* heritable, but may change at every cell division. Such nonheritable commitments include the decision to be specific structures in a specific part of a disc (such as specific bristles or sensilla). This is readily seen when you cut a disc, such as a wing disc, into two fragments. Each wing disc produces the entire wing and also the dorsal and lateral part of the thorax. If you cause the fragments to metamorphose immediately, each will differentiate those structures that they would have formed *in situ* (Bryant 1975a). From the analysis of such metamorphosed fragments the investigator can construct a fate map or anlage plan of the disc. However, if you transplant the fragments into an adult abdomen and allow them to grow before you cause them to metamorphose, one fragment regenerates the missing parts and metamorphoses into an intact structure whereas the complementary fragment forms a mirror-image duplicate of itself and metamorphoses into mirror-image structures. This has been demonstrated in leg discs, wing discs, haltere discs, and eye-antenna discs (see Bryant 1974, 1975b for review).

In the case of regeneration of a disc fragment, cells which normally form a particular group of bristles or sensilla, undergo extensive mitosis and some of their descendants give rise to other structures in the disc. Clearly the commitment to be a particular *part* of a disc is not passed on by a cell to its mitotic progeny. Imaginal discs are not mosaics of separate anlagen, each determined for forming certain adult structures. Rather, they are endowed with the capacity for extensive epimorphic pattern regulation.

The term *specification* was coined by Bryant (1974) to denote the process by which a cell's position becomes specified in an imaginal disc so that it will produce a particular part of that disc and give rise to a specific bristle, sensillum, etc. As a result of specification a cell becomes committed to differentiate into a specific part of a disc. Specification is not heritable.

4. Differences between Determination and Specification

In addition to being nonheritable, specification in imaginal discs differs in the following fundamental way from determination: the determination of each type of imaginal disc is different, but the specification of spatial patterns in all discs appears to be very similar and possibly identical. The evidence for these statements comes from studies of the homoeotic mutant *Antennapedia* in which various parts of the antenna are transformed into mesothoracic leg structures. In the *Antennapedia* the antenna may have only small regions changed into mesothoracic leg tissue or may be almost completely leg-like. Detailed analysis of these intermediates showed that the replacement of structures was absolutely position-specific; that is, a given part of the antenna, if transformed, would always produce a specific part of the leg (Postlethwait & Schneiderman 1971b). Hence, a correspondence map of the two structures could be drawn (Fig. 1.3). Presumptive leg cells in a part of the antennal disc that normally forms the tip of the antenna will form the claws at the tip of the leg; presumptive leg cells in the third antennal segment will form femur or tibia, etc. The presumptive leg cells become specified according to their

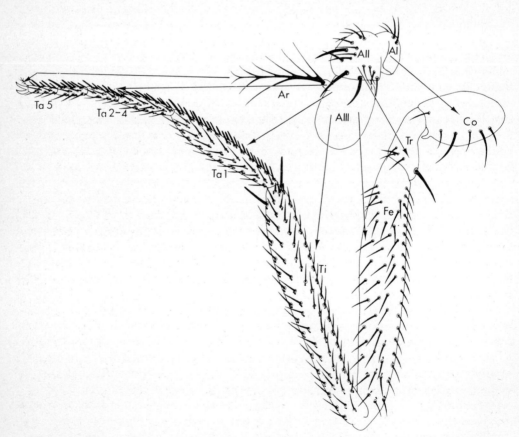

Fig. 1.3. Correspondence map of antennal and leg structures based on position-specific transformations in homoeotic antennae of *Antennapedia*. AI, AII, AIII, first, second and third antennal segments; Ar, arista; Co, coxa; Tr, trochanter; Fe, femur; Ti, tibia; Ta 1-5, first to fifth tarsal segments. (From Postlethwait & Schneiderman, 1971b.)

position in an antennal disc and respond to that specification by differentiating a particular structure. The simplest explanation is that the mechanism for specification of positional information is similar in the antenna and leg discs. The difference between leg cells and antenna cells must be in their response to the same specification, and these differences in response must be a manifestation of their different determined states. (This is analogous to a proximal vertebrate forelimb forming distal forelimb parts when transplanted to the distal part of a hindlimb.)

A second difference between determination and specification in imaginal discs is that maintenance of determination of a group of cells in an imaginal disc is not altered by surrounding cells, whereas the specification of a group of cells may be altered by surrounding cells. Nöthiger (1964) showed that after imaginal dics of genitalia and wing were dissociated and reaggregated, very small groups of genital cells of one genotype may be surrounded by wing cells of another genotype. The wing cells and genital cells did not alter each other's determination. In contrast, Haynie & Bryant (1976) have convincingly demonstrated that specification of a cell within an imaginal disc depends upon its neighbours. They assessed the developmental capacities of two different fragments of the imaginal wing disc, derived from the two ends of the disc, when cultured alone and when cultured together. One fragment was the presumptive notum and the other was the presumptive pleura and ventral wing blade. When two fragments from the same end of two discs were folded together many times with a tungsten needle, cultured together for a week, and then caused to metamorphose, the fragments underwent duplication and produced mirror-image structures, e.g., presumptive notal fragments gave rise to mirror-image notal structures, whereas presumptive pleural and ventral wing blade fragments produced mirror-image pleural and ventral wing blade structures. But when two fragments, suitably marked genetically, from opposite ends of the disc, were folded together and cultured in the same way, and then caused to metamorphose, they were both induced to regenerate structures which normally lie between them and which were never produced by either fragment when cultured alone. The disc fragments underwent intercalary regeneration of the sort reported for cockroach limbs and amphibian limbs (Bohn 1971; Iten & Bryant 1975; French & Bulliere 1975; French 1976). Evidently the developmental fate of the cells in the fragments is a function not only of their lineage but also of their position with respect to other cells. The cells in the mixed fragments engaged in intercellular communication, assessed their mutual positions and then regenerated the structures missing between them. These experiments demonstrate the reality of intercellular communication in positional information and offer a number of ways to analyse the process.

A third difference between determination and specification in imaginal discs is in the number of cells involved in the initiation of these commitments. When imaginal discs first become clonally distinct from the remainder of the embryo they comprise groups of about seven to 20 cells. The determinative events in the embryo that initially establish discs must involve groups of cells at least this large. Similarly, changes in this determined state in transdetermination occur in small groups of cells rather than in individual cells (Gehring 1972). Also compartmentalization occurs in small groups of cells. Once these events have occurred in a group of cells so that all of the cells in the group have a particular developmental commitment, all of the descendants of that group of cells inherit that same commitment. Crick & Lawrence (1975) have coined the term *polyclone* to identify all of the surviving descendants of a small group of cells. Determination, transdetermination, and compartmentalization all appear to be polyclonal. In contrast, specification in imaginal discs may involve single cells since many structures which are specified in discs are made by individual cells, and daughter cells may have different specifications (Bryant 1974).

From this analysis we may conclude that what a cell differentiates into depends on what disc it belongs to (i.e., its determination) and on what exact geographical position it occupies within a disc (i.e., its specification). What it differentiates into may also depend on what compartment it occupies within a disc.

There are mutations which alter the response of imaginal discs to their determination, i.e., homoeotic mutations (see Postlethwait & Schneiderman 1973 for review; also Schubiger & Alpert 1975). *Antennapedia* is such a mutation and there are many others, such as *ophthalmoptera* in which part of the eye is transformed into part of the wing. There are also mutations which can alter spatial patterns within a disc. For example, a mutation denoted *1(1)ts-504* causes duplicated legs, antennae and abdominal tergites (Simpson & Schneiderman 1975). These also appear to be mutations which may affect particular compartments. The mutation *engrailed,* for example, appears to transform part of the posterior compartment of the wing into a mirror-image of the anterior compartment (Morata & Lawrence 1975).

It is of some interest that the responses to determination and specification and perhaps also to compartmentalization are each altered by distinct mutations. This fact emphasizes that Nature distinguishes between these processes. This viewpoint is useful in experimental studies. If a mutation alters a process, then the process is likely to be biologically significant. It is easy when studying an organism to become convinced that a process that we as observers think is important will also be important to the organism. This is not necessarily the case. However, when we study a process that is changed by a mutation, then we can have confidence that the process is not only interesting to the observer, but probably significant to the organism as well.

The foregoing analysis enables us to identify several central problems of insect development. What is the mechanism of specification of positional information in an imaginal disc? When a disc cell divides what factors affect the specification of the daughter cells? How do the cells in the disc communicate with each other to insure that as a disc grows, regenerates, or duplicates, appropriate specification of daughter cells is made? How does determination first become established in embryonic cells and how is it propagated by cell heredity during post-embryonic life? What is the importance of compartments in normal development? Why do polyclones made early in development appear to keep within certain fixed compartment boundaries? To attack these problems a number of experimental approaches have been devised and models have been proposed which we shall now consider.

5. GENETIC MOSAICS

A powerful tool for the analysis of the process of pattern formation in imaginal discs is the use of genetic mosaics, individuals composed of cells of more than one genotype. By using mosaics, the experimenter can follow the fate of the progeny of individual cells or introduce cells with a different genotype into a cell population and study cellular interactions. One of the most useful techniques to produce mosaicism is mitotic recombination induced by X-rays at a selected time in development, usually during the larval stage. The genetic makeup of the animal is designed so that certain mitotic recombinants will be phenotypically different. Mitotic recombination can make single cells in imaginal discs (and elsewhere) homozygous for recessive marker genes while the cells in the rest of the animal are heterozygous. For example, if the animal is doubly heterozygous for the recessive genes y and sn (i.e., $y\ sn^+/y^+sn$), yellow rather than dark brown bristles; $sn,$ singed rather than straight bristles), it will normally display a wild-type phenotype. However, if one of its cells undergoes mitotic recombination then one of the daughter cells might be homozygous *yellow $(y\ sn^+/y\ sn^+)$* and the other homozygous *singed (y^+sn/y^+sn)*. As each cell divides, it will generate a clone of cells, which, after metamorphosis, can be seen as a coherent patch of *yellow* or *singed* bristles, surrounded by wild-type bristles. Thus, X-ray induced mitotic recombination permits the investigator to follow the developmental activities of the descendants of a single cell with great precision. The mechanism of mitotic recombination and some applications are considered by Nöthiger in Chapter 6, in this volume.

Clones of cells arising from mitotic recombination can conveniently be used to study cell lineage, morphogenesis, cell migration, cell division rates and determination, as well as cell interactions and autonomy. For example, clone size in the adult depends on the stage of irradiation, because the number of cell divisions that are to occur before metamorphosis decreases with larval age. Hence, the average clone size following irradiation at various stages can be used to estimate the cell numbers and rates of cell division in the discs at these stages. For example, the leg disc begins its developmental career as a group of about twenty cells in the embryo, and grows throughout larval life with an average cell cycle time of about 15 h, until the time of metamorphosis (Bryant & Schneiderman 1969). The wing and antennal discs grow somewhat faster, with an average doubling time of about 11 h (Bryant 1970; Garcia-Bellido & Merriam 1971a; Postlethwait & Schneiderman 1971a). The abdominal tergites represent an unusual situation, since the abdominal histoblasts do not appear to increase in cell number during larval life, but do show rapid growth during the initial stages of metamorphosis (Garcia-Bellido & Merriam 1971b; Guerra *et al.* 1973). A striking result from the mitotic recombination studies is that in many parts of the adult, clones are markedly nonrandom in shape. The clearest case is that of the leg in which clonally related cells form long narrow strips of tissue often extending over several leg segments (Bryant & Schneiderman 1969). Some clones have been found to be over 100 cells long and only a few cells wide. This indicates that there is a predominantly radial alignment of daughter cells in the developing disc, which may be one of the important factors determining its structure. Similar longitudinal clonal patterns are present in wing discs (Bryant 1970; Garcia-Bellido & Merriam 1971a). Furthermore, the fact that most clones are continuous and have smooth outlines persuades us that there is little individual cell movement in these systems.

Besides mosaics produced by X-ray induced mitotic recombination, there are a variety of genetic ways to produce mosaics, especially gynandromorphs, animals that are mosaics of male and female tissue. In *Drosophila,* gynandromorphs usually arise by the loss of one X-chromosome from one cell line in a zygote that is originally XX (female). Several stocks are available which contain an unstable ring X-chromosome which is spontaneously eliminated in high frequencies at the first nuclear division to give an embryo and ultimately an adult which consists of about half male and half female cells. There are also mutants such as *claret nondisjunction, paternal loss,* or *mitotic loss inducer,* all of which produce X-chromosome loss in the progeny. Mosaicism in gynandromorphs has been used in a variety of novel ways to analyse developmental problems (e.g. Hotta & Benzer 1972; Bryant & Zornetzer 1974).

6. The Effects in Mosaics of Mutations That Reduce Mitotic Rate or Kill Cells

There are a series of dominant mutations called '*Minutes*' (*M*) which are lethal when homozygous. Heterozygous M/M^+ individuals grow slowly and have small bristles. Morata & Ripoll (1975) discovered that *Minute* mutants have a decreased rate of mitosis in imaginal discs. When a clone of normal M^+/M^+ cells is induced in a *Minute* individual by X-ray induced mitotic recombination, the normal imaginal disc cells divide more rapidly than the surrounding *Minute* cells. Slow-growing *Minute* cells can also be formed in a wildtype background. This system permits the possibility of inducing, at any stage in development, cells with different cell-cycle lengths and clones that are larger or smaller than normal. Using this system Garcia-Bellido and his colleagues were able to demonstrate the existence of particular geographical regions of imaginal discs, the compartments mentioned earlier, in which clones of rapidly growing normal cells were confined in a *Minute* animal (Garcia-Bellido *et al.* 1973; Garcia-Bellido 1975; see review by Crick & Lawrence 1975, and Chapter 8 by Lawrence and Morata in this volume).

Recently a temperature-sensitive (ts) cell autonomous mutation has been isolated that reversibly blocks or retards cell growth and mitotic rate (Simpson & Schneiderman, 1976). Temperature-sensitive mutants are conditional mutants which show a normal phenotype at one temperature and a mutant phenotype at another. In this mutant, *1(1)ts-1126,* at 22° C the cells divide normally, whereas at 29° C the cells cease to divide or divide very slowly until they are returned to 22° C. This mutant provides a powerful technique with which to approach developmental problems: by means of genetic mosaicism and temperature-shifts it is possible to arrest the division of large or small local populations of cells in an animal at any stage in development for various periods of time and examine the consequences. Figure 1.4 illustrates the thorax of a gynandromorphic mosaic fly that possessed cells of mutant genotype on the one side and had been exposed to 29° C for a period during development.

Another series of useful mutations that have recently been discovered are ts autonomous cell lethals: the cells are normal at 22° C but die when exposed to 29° C for 24–72 hours (depending on the mutation) (Russell 1974; Arking 1975; Simpson & Schneiderman 1975). By using genetic mosaicism and temperature shifts one can locally manipulate cell death and examine the consequences for development of deleting large or small populations of cells in specific regions. This is particularly useful because the initial events of pattern formation appear to occur in extremely small groups of cells (Wolpert 1969; Bownes 1975a, b) which are beyond the reach of conventional micro-surgery.

The consequences for development of the localized cell death caused by ts cell lethals are noteworthy. For example in *1(1)ts-504* after exposure to the restrictive temperature for 72 hours during larval development, duplicated (and sometimes triplicated) legs, antennae, halteres or wings occur in 57 per cent of the animals examined (Simpson & Schneiderman 1975). In addition, large numbers of deficiencies and alterations in segmentation and bristle patterns could be produced by applying heat pulses at appropriate times. Many of these abnormalities closely resemble those produced by various well-known mutations which indicates that these same mutations probably act by causing cell death in specific regions at specific times. The analysis of the defects and duplications caused by localized cell death provide important clues to the process of pattern formation and to the role of cell death in morphogenesis.

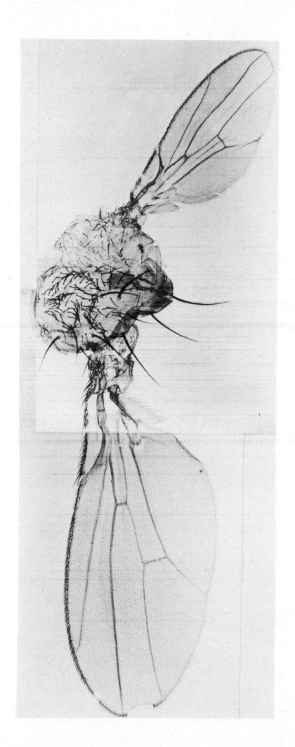

FIG. 1.4. (a) Dorsal mesothorax of a gynandromorph in which the right side of the thorax is male and is comprised of cells of mutant genotype *(l(1)ts-1126 sn³)*, whereas the left side is female and wildtype. This individual was grown at 22°C for 72 hours and then shifted up to 29°C for the remainder of the development. The right wing is considerably smaller than the left wing. (Simpson & Schneiderman 1976.)

7. A NEW MODEL FOR SPECIFICATION

We have already mentioned the finding that regeneration and duplication usually occur from complementary halves of an imaginal disc (Bryant 1974). This observation seems to indicate a general property of these structures and led to the idea of a gradient of positional values within a disc (Bryant 1971, 1974). It was suggested that from any one level on the gradient, growth allows the generation of lower positional values but not higher values. Addition of the same set of positional values to the two halves of the gradient comprises regeneration in one case and duplication in the other. This gradient model accounted well for the behaviour of segments of the wing disc (Bryant 1974) but was shown to be inadequate to account simultaneously for the behaviour of segments, central fragments, and sectors of that disc (Bryant 1975b). For example, it was found that all four 270° sectors regenerate while the complementary 90° sectors duplicate. This result is not explicable in terms of the predictable behaviour of each free edge, since a given edge would have to undergo regeneration under some circumstances and duplication under others.

Recently French, Bryant & Bryant (1976) have made a conceptual breakthrough and devised a new model which accounts for all of these results and for many other features of pattern regeneration in imaginal discs and in many other systems where previously there were no clear unifying principles. Their model accounts for the regulative responses of whole tissues such as imaginal disc fragments in terms of the behaviour of individual interacting cells. It permits the experimenter to predict alteration in the specification of daughter cells in experiments in which normal patterns are made defective and allowed to reform.

To understand their model it is necessary to recognize the distinction which is normally made in studies of pattern formation between an initial event where cells are assigned positional values (positional information) according to their physical location in the tissue, and the subsequent response of the cells (interpretation) in terms of specific cytodifferentiation (Wolpert 1972). This distinction can be justified on the grounds of the separate effects of genetic mutations on the two processes and the finding, discussed in Section 2, that different patterns can apparently result from the same underlying positional value matrix as a result of differences in the interpretation step (see Wolpert 1972; Postlethwait & Schneiderman 1971b, 1973; Bryant 1974).

The model proposes that positional information is specified in terms of polar co-ordinates (Fig. 1.5); one component of positional information is a value corresponding to position on a circle (circumferential sequence) and the second component is the position on a radius (radial sequence). In the *Drosophila* leg disc, the outer circle is the proximal limb boundary and the centre is the distal tip. In the *Drosophila* wing disc, the outer circle is the disc boundary and the centre is a point whose location is known but it is not the distal tip of the wing (Bryant 1975a). Both the radial and circumferential sequences behave according to an intercalation rule; when two nonadjacent positional values are grafted together, growth occurs at the graft junction until the missing positional values are intercalated, then growth ceases. Where experimental evidence is available it indicates that the new tissue arises from both sides of the graft junction. In the circumferential sequence it is assumed that $12=0$ so that the sequence is continuous. This means that there are always two possible ways of connecting any two nonadjacent positional values. One of the stipulations of the model is that when two nonadjacent positional values are brought into contact, intercalation of positional values between

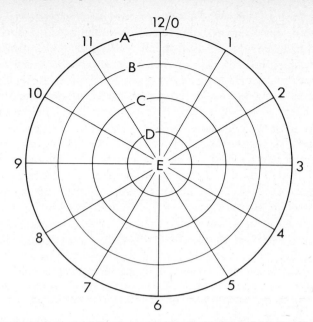

FIG. 1.5. The concept of polar coordinates in a positional information field. Each cell is assumed to have information with respect to its position on a radius (A through E) and its position around the circle (0–12). Positions 12 and 0 are identical, creating a circular sequence. When cells of different values on either axis are in contact, it is assumed that growth occurs to generate the intermediate values, then stops. The field centre (E) in the case of cockroach limbs is the distal tip (Bohn 1971), in the *Drosophila* leg disc it is the presumptive distal tip (Schubiger 1971), and in the *Drosophila* wing disc it has been mapped to a position in the presumptive dorsal wing surface (Bryant 1975a). (From French *et al.* 1976).

them is always by the shortest of the two possible routes.

The radial sequence in addition to following the intercalation rule described above, also behaves according to a transformation rule; when central (distal) or peripheral (proximal) levels are removed, growth occurs to replace all of the levels more central (distal) than the level of the cut. A further stipulation of the model is that in order for distal transformation to occur, a complete circumference must be present at the free edge.

The model can predict the regenerative behaviour of many sorts of fragments of imaginal discs if we assume that the regulative behaviour of a fragment is not merely a function of the independent behaviour of free cut edges, but is the result of interaction between the cut edges after they fuse together during wound healing. Bryant (personal communication) has shown that wound healing occurs very rapidly in imaginal disc fragments, probably before any significant growth has occurred. In the case of 90° and 270° sectors, the two radial cut surfaces seem to heal together in both cases.

The model assumes that regulation occurs in the circumferential direction as a result of the apposition of different circumferential levels. If the apposition of any two levels leads to the intercalation, during growth, of the levels that normally lie between them via the shortest of the two possible circumferential routes, this accounts for regeneration of 270° sectors and duplication of 90° sectors. It also accounts for the behaviour of wing disc segments if we assume that wound closure occurs as in sectors. Again, observations indicate that wing disc segments do show the appropriate type of wound healing. The radial transformation rule means that central fragments should duplicate, which was shown to be the case in the leg disc (Schubiger 1971) and the wing disc (Bryant 1975a).

Other direct evidence of the validity of the proposed model comes from extensive experiments performed by French (personal communication) on cockroach legs. He has found that removal of longitudinal strips of leg epidermis in the cockroach, at any location around the circumference of the leg, results in the regeneration of the removed epidermis and of all those structures which would normally lie between the two longitudinal cut surfaces. French & Bulliere (1975a, b) have also shown that when longitudinal strips of leg epidermis are grafted into a normal leg, growth occurs between the edges of the graft and the host leg. The structures produced by this growth are those that would normally lie between the edge of the host leg and the edge of the graft on the circumference of a normal leg, by the shortest route.

The model accounts in a simple and unified way for the following kinds of developmental and growth regulation in insects:

In the imaginal discs of *Drosophila* it explains regeneration or duplication of segments and sectors of the imaginal wing, leg, eye-antenna, haltere, and genital imaginal discs. The model also accounts for pattern reconstruction by dissociated and reaggregated discs, for growth stimulation in dissociated discs, for the inability to establish tissue lines from small fragments, and for the absence of growth in entire discs and in completely regenerated or duplicated disc fragments (see reviews by Gehring & Nöthiger 1973; Bryant 1974). It also explains the intercalary regeneration observed when fragments derived from the two ends of a wing disc were cultured together (experiments of Haynie & Bryant 1976, discussed in Section 3).

The model also accounts for a vast array of regenerative phenomena involving legs of cockroaches (see Chapter 10 by Bohn, this volume), hemipterans, lepidopterans and spiders, the anal cerci of crickets, and the calipers of earwigs. The phenomena include simple regeneration, regeneration with reversed polarity, and intercalary regeneration following experimental manipulation of the proximo-distal axis, lateral intercalary regeneration, and supernumerary regeneration following experimental manipulation of the antero-posterior and dorsal-ventral axes. The model explains the number, position, orientation, and a symmetry of supernumerary regenerates (see Bryant & Iten 1976 for a discussion of this point). The model also tells us a great deal about the regulation of growth in insects as we shall now see.

8. Pattern Formation and Growth Control

In a paper on homeostasis and insect growth, Wigglesworth (1964) developed the view that growth and pattern formation are closely coupled. He argued that the nonhormonal factors that regulate insect growth are the same factors that regulate pattern and form, and that the capacity for localized growth in normal development is as much an element of body pattern as is a localized capacity for laying down a black pigmented cuticle or a particular type of bristle. To understand the control of growth it is necessary to understand the phenomena of pattern formation and pattern regulation. Although these views were given wide currency they did not evoke verifiable models which explained both pattern regulation and growth regulation.

The model described above provides a clear link between pattern formation and growth control in imaginal discs. It is assumed that growth is stimulated by the apposition of positional values which are ordinarily nonadjacent. Thus, growth during normal development will occur until the pattern is complete, and during culture of a disc fragment growth will occur until either regeneration or duplication is complete. Small fragments of discs will duplicate and then cease to grow, whereas reaggregated fragments will grow until intercalation of positional values is complete. These predictions are all in accord with experimental findings. Recently we have succeeded in culturing tiny fragments of imaginal wing discs in nuclear multiplication stage embryos and recovered them in the adult flies after they had metamorphosed. The tiny fragments never grew into large structures but remained extremely small and metamorphosed into tiny vesicles of wing cuticle (Bownes & Schneiderman, unpublished observations).

What the model means in molecular terms is not yet known. We have yet to learn the physical nature of the positional information field and the mechanism of intercellular communication in development. However, the model identifies a number of new ways by which these questions may be probed.

9. INITIATION OF DETERMINATION IN EMBRYONIC CELLS

The process by which determination is initiated in embryonic cells has puzzled developmental biologists for decades. More than 70 years ago Theodore Boveri devised a hypothesis that focused attention on the cytoplasm of the egg as the locus of factors which initiated determination. Boveri (1902) proposed that genetically equivalent nuclei are specifically programmed by interacting with different cytoplasms localized in the egg. 'When the primitive differences of the cytoplasm . . . are transferred to the cleaved egg without any change . . . they affect the originally equal nuclei *un*equally by unfolding (activating) or suppressing certain nuclear qualities . . . The inequalities of the nuclei, in some cases perhaps of a temporary nature only, lend different potencies to the cytoplasm . . . Thus new cytoplasmic conditions are created which again release, in certain nuclei the activation or suppression of certain qualities thus imprinting on these cells, in turn, a specific character and so on and so on' (p. 93).

Boveri's hypothesis is still viewed with favour by many contemporary students of development, witness the following statement. '(the fertilized egg) . . . is a large cell which contains many different regions of cytoplasm, each destined to promote a certain type of differentiation. During cleavage, many identical nuclei are rapidly formed and these come to occupy different regions of egg cytoplasm . . . A few hours after fertilization, each nucleus is surrounded by a different kind of cytoplasm, which is thought to activate or repress genes, and so lead to the first initial differences between the cells of an embryo' (Gurdon 1974, pp. 87–88). Let us now see to what extent and how cytoplasmic factors are responsible for specifying the fate of the cells of the young *Drosophila* embryo.

The egg of *Drosophila,* like that of most insects, does not undergo cleavage in the usual sense but develops as a *syncytium* (Fig. 1.6). After fertilization, the zygote nucleus undergoes a series of about eight rapid and synchronous divisions, about one every 10 minutes at 25° C. Several hundred nuclei result, each of which has a halo of clear cytoplasm but no cell membrane. After this *nuclear multiplication* or 'cleavage' stage, the nuclei migrate to the peripheral cytoplasm, the so-called periplasm or cortical cytoplasm, where they form a monolayer. The embryo is now called a *syncytial blastoderm.* Four additional divisions occur in the cortical cytoplasm. Then the cell

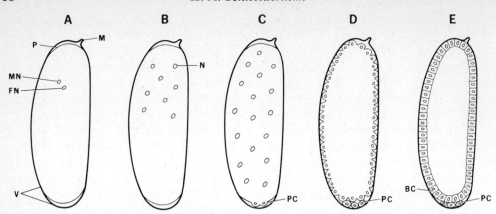

FIG. 1.6. Early embryonic development of *D. melanogaster*. The age of the embryo is indicated for development at 25° C. (A) Fertilized egg, 10 min.; (B) nuclear multiplication stage, 40 min.; (C) beginning of pole cell formation, 90 min.; (D) syncytial blastoderm, 120–50 min.; (E) cellular blastoderm, 180–210 min. M, micropyle; P, plasma membrane; MN, male pronucleus; FN, female pronucleus; V, vitelline membrane; N, nuclei; PC, pole cell; BC, blastoderm cell. (Redrawn from Gehring 1972.)

membranes grow down from the egg surface to separate the nuclei from each other and from the yolk, and about 3500 cells form abruptly and almost simultaneously. This stage is called a *cellular blastoderm*. At about 180 minutes there are some 3500 nuclei on the surface of the blastoderm; the rest of the nuclei stay behind in the interior of the egg. Mitosis ceases when the cellular blastoderm forms but resumes about an hour later when gastrulation occurs (Scriba 1964; Zalokar, personal communication). Prior to cellular blastoderm formation, at about the ninth nuclear division, the first few nuclei that enter the posterior pole of the egg form a small group of large cells called pole cells (Sonnenblick 1950). These are the first cells formed in the embryo and they lie outside of the presumptive blastoderm (Fig. 1.7). They divide until there are about 50, some of which ultimately are carried into the interior of the embryo to form germ cells. Pole cells will be discussed in Section 11 in connection with germ cell determination. The cellular blastoderm stage is followed by germ band formation, gastrulation, and the remainder of embryogenesis. The presumptive imaginal discs are formed in specific locations in embryonic segments. At 25° C the larva hatches about 22 hours after fertilization.

Although the *Drosophila* egg and embryo are small (450μm long, 200 μm in diameter, weight about 13 μg), they can withstand penetration by a micropipette of up to 15 μm in external diameter and therefore of adequate size to permit injections of nuclei, cytoplasm, cells or other materials. A number of injection and transplantation studies have been conducted to ascertain when determination occurred for various embryonic and adult structures. In one series of experiments nuclei of one genotype were withdrawn from the anterior of donor embryos of *Drosophila* at the nuclear multiplication stage when they had about 256 nuclei, and were injected into the posterior pole of host embryos of another genotype at the 32-nuclei stage (Okada *et al.* 1974c). From 812 embryos that were injected, 46 adults emerged. Eight of these adults were cuticular chimeras and in six cases the cuticle of donor phenotype was limited entirely to the terminal segments of the abdomen (Fig. 1.8). In one case the germ cells were shown to be of donor genotype. This result shows that surviving transplanted nuclei develop into structures characteristic of their position in the host, rather than their region of origin in

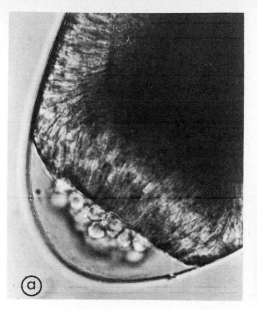 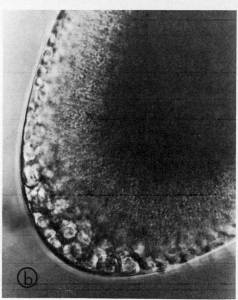

FIG. 1.7. (a) Pole cells of *D. melanogaster* approximately 90 min. after fertilization, at the posterior pole. (b) Subsequently the cells of the blastoderm form behind the pole cells. Here about 210 min. after fertilization, the pole cells are about to move dorsally as the posterior midgut invaginates. (Courtesy of Dr M. Bownes.)

the donor. All donor nuclei were taken from the anterior of the donor embryo, yet when they were injected posteriorly they produced posterior structures. These results strongly support the idea that the nuclei at the stage of nuclear multiplication are multipotent and that they become determined and acquire different fates according to the region of the embryonic cortical cytoplasm which they occupy. The fact that the injected nuclei could support the development of germ cells indicates that the injected nuclei from the nuclear multiplication stage were not merely multipotent but totipotent.

Similar results have been obtained by Zalokar (1971, 1973) and Illmensee (1972, 1973). Illmensee's experiments are of special interest because he injected single nuclei from the nuclear multiplication stage into fertilized eggs and some of these eggs developed into larvae. He also showed that when nuclei from any of five regions of early gastrulae were injected into unfertilized eggs, the eggs would develop, although never to adulthood. However, when he took the presumptive pole cells (which are the future germ cells) of such nuclear-transplanted embryos and implanted them into the posterior pole of host blastoderm eggs, he obtained germ line mosaics (6 of 29 fertile flies). Clearly the gastrulae nuclei are totipotent.

These nuclear transplantation results indicate that the totipotency of insect embryonic nuclei is similar to that of vertebrate embryonic nuclei. During early embryonic development the nuclei have not forfeited any of their talents and can replace an egg nucleus. Recently experiments have been undertaken to test whether the nuclei of determined *Drosophila* cells can be reprogrammed to support embryonic development. The cells employed as donors of nuclei were neuroblasts from the brain of 12-hour-old embryos. These cells are determined to form various parts of the larval and adult brain. The hosts were embryos of another genotype at the nuclear multiplication stage. Several chimeras were obtained (Okada and Schneiderman 1976). This result indicates that

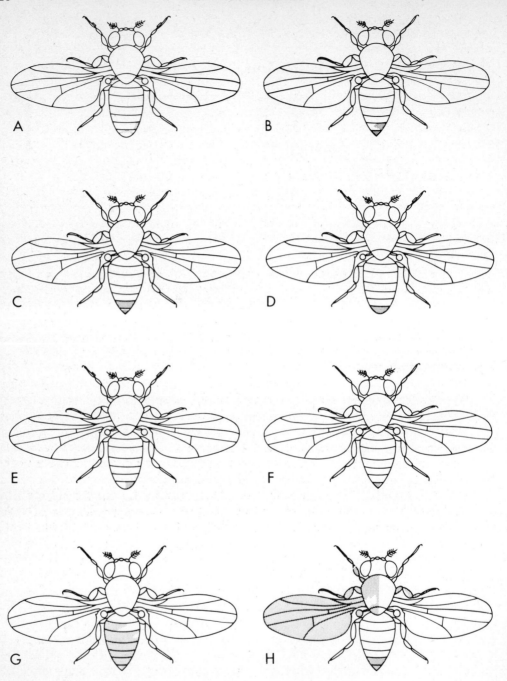

FIG. 1.8. Schematic diagram of dorsal surface of eight chimeric adults resulting from transplantation of nuclei from *mwh e*[11] or *y w spl sn*[3] embryos into *v; bw* embryos. In all cases the nuclei were withdrawn from the anterior of the donor egg and deposited in the posterior of the host egg. The dotted areas represent cuticle with donor phenotype. In six cases the cuticle of donor phenotype was limited entirely to the terminal segments of the abdomen. The fly illustrated in (B) produced progeny which were exclusively of donor phenotype, indicating the presence of donor germ cells. (From Okada *et al*. 1974c.)

the nuclei of determined *Drosophila* cells like those of determined vertebrate cells have not suffered a permanent restriction of their information and can be reprogrammed when they are exposed to egg cytoplasm (Gurdon 1962; Brun & Kobel 1972; also review by Gurdon 1974).

These nuclear transplantation experiments indicate that the nuclei of nuclear multiplication stage embryos are not yet programmed to become parts of particular determined cells. However, by the time cellular blastoderm formation has occurred, i.e., about 3 hours after fertilization, some of the blastoderm cells appear to have become determined to form anterior or posterior segments. This was demonstrated by two kinds of experiments. Chan & Gehring (1971) mixed genetically marked cells from anterior or posterior halves of cellular blastoderm embryos with whole embryos, cultured them in adults and then caused them to metamorphose. Their results showed that the anterior ends of cellular blastoderm stage embryos produce only head and thoracic adult structures whereas the posterior ends produce only thoracic and abdominal structures. In another experiment Illmensee & Mahowald (1974; see also Chapter 4 by Illmensee in this volume) transplanted cells from the anterior end of a blastoderm to the posterior end of another blastoderm which had been genetically marked. The transplanted anterior cells differentiated into head structures which were not integrated with the posterior tissues of the host. These two experiments indicate the establishment of an anterior and a posterior determination in the cellular blastoderm.

In order to learn when the determination to belong to a specific imaginal disc is initiated, clones of genetically marked cells were induced by X-rays at the cellular blastoderm stage (3 hours) (Wieschaus & Gehring 1975). The results revealed that most clones were confined to structures derived from a single disc. However, clones were found extending from the wing into the second leg. This finding indicates that the blastoderm cells that gave rise to these clones had not yet been determined at the time of X-irradiation to belong to a specific disc. A complicating factor in interpreting experiments of this kind is the fact that the X-rays used to induce clones also cause extensive cell death in embryos and imaginal discs (Postlethwait & Schneiderman 1973; Haynie and Bryant, personal communication). It is not yet known whether cell death or other effects caused by X-rays may alter the determination of surviving cells in the cellular blastoderm. In any case, the precise time during development at which the determination to belong to a specific disc occurs has not been ascertained (see Chapter 5 by Gehring in this volume).

10. THE ROLE OF EGG CYTOPLASM LAID DOWN BY THE MOTHER IN INITIATING DETERMINATION

The nuclear transplantation studies suggest that the cortical cytoplasm plays an important role in initiating determination whereas the rest of the egg cytoplasm appears to undo any restrictions that may have been imposed on nuclei as a result of determination. Until nuclei enter the cortical cytoplasm they appear to be totipotent, divide extremely rapidly, and have no nucleoli. But, once they enter the cortical cytoplasm, they come to lie in apparently diverse cytoplasmic surroundings, and become separated into cells. A nucleolus appears, the nuclei divide much more slowly (hours instead of minutes), and the cells become determined. Initially, cells of the blastoderm appear to become determined to belong to anterior or posterior parts of the embryo.

At the same time or perhaps later, some cells become determined to belong to particular discs that form specific parts of the adult integument, e.g. about 20 cells are destined to form each leg and about 9 to form each antenna.

It would be of uncommon interest to discover the molecular nature of the information needed for determination, how it is organized in the cortical cytoplasm of the egg and embryo and how it is established in oogenesis and the early stages of embryonic development. It would also be interesting to identify the interaction of the nuclei with the cortical cytoplasm and discover how the determined state, once initiated, is propagated by cell heredity.

The cortical cytoplasm of the egg is produced during oogenesis under the influence of the maternal genome. Experimenters have examined mutants that have various defects in oogenesis in an effort to discover to what degree the egg cytoplasm laid down by the mother plays a role in determination and in other processes of early embryonic development. A number of mutants in *Drosophila* produce defective eggs incapable of supporting normal embryonic development. These are called maternal effect mutants because the mutant phenotype depends on the genotype of the mother in which the egg is formed. Apparently, the homozygous mother either fails to provide her eggs with a substance indispensible for normal development or forms an egg with an abnormal organization or structure. In some maternal effect mutants the embryos die at various stages of embryonic life: *deep orange (dor)* undergoes abnormal nuclear multiplication, partial blastoderm formation and abnormal gastrulation, whereas *rudimentary (r^9)* has various postgastrula defects (Counce 1956a, b, c). In a few cases the mother produces eggs that give rise to embryos or adults that lack specific structures or organs (see Section 11).

There appear to be two basic types of maternal effect mutants. The eggs of one type can be rescued by being fertilized with a normal sperm. When the sperm introduces a wildtype allele into an egg from a homozygous mutant female, it rescues the egg by supplying the factor omitted by the mother when the egg was formed. The fact that the wildtype sperm can rescue the defective egg means that the missing factor is not needed during oogenesis but during other stages of development. Such a mutant should be rescuable by injecting materials in which the egg was deficient. Another type of maternal effect mutant also produces defective eggs but these cannot be rescued by wildtype sperm and the fertilized egg either fails to develop or develops abnormally. The phenotype of the embryo depends entirely on the maternal genotype and is not affected by the genotype of the embryo itself. It has been suggested that such mutant genes are essential only for oogenesis (Rice & Garen 1975). Such mutants might be rescued by injecting the materials in which the egg was deficient unless the defect was in some essential structural feature of the egg. The analysis of these two kinds of maternal effect mutants provides developmental biologists with a new means of attacking the problem of how the egg cytoplasm controls early embryonic development.

Several attempts have been made to rescue maternal effect mutants by egg injection. An example is *rudimentary (r^9)*, a recessive female sterile mutant which produces abnormal eggs which fail to hatch. If homozygous mutant females (r/r) are mated to hemizygous mutant males (r/Y), the offspring die as embryos after gastrulation. But if heterozygous females ($r/+$) are mated to hemizygous mutant males (r/Y), then all the progeny survive including the homozygous mutant females (r/r). The homozygous mutant mother fails to provide her eggs with a substance indispensible for normal development. Norby (1970) showed by means of nutritional experiments that the defect is in pyrimidine biosynthesis. Thus *rudimentary* larvae require an extrinsic source of pyrimidines.

The eggs of *rudimentary* mothers could be rescued by injecting them at the nuclear multiplication stage with wildtype nuclei and cytoplasm or wildtype cytoplasm alone from unfertilized eggs (Okada *et al.* 1974b). Some eggs injected with 1.5 per cent of egg volume of cytoplasm from unfertilized wildtype eggs were able to complete both embryonic and post-embryonic development and emerged as adults, whereas not a single uninjected control egg was able to complete embryonic development. The eggs of *rudimentary* mothers could also be rescued by injecting each egg with 0.01 μg of pyrimidine nucleosides. The results demonstrate that a pyrimidine deficiency is the cause of abortive embryogenesis. Experiments by Garen & Gehring (1972) with the maternal effect mutation *deep orange* yielded similar results: eggs that received wildtype egg cytoplasm were enabled to develop to late embryonic stages. Therefore, wildtype egg cytoplasm, manufactured under the direction of the maternal genome, contains factors that can repair preblastoderm eggs from *r* or *dor* mothers.

Another maternal effect lethal mutation which has a striking and specific effect on development is called *daughterless (da)* (Bell 1954). Genetically *daughterless* females produce only male offspring; the females die during early development. Recently Bownes *et al.* (1976) have shown that the female eggs of *daughterless* females can be rescued by the injection of cytoplasm from wildtype eggs.

Other examples of maternal effect mutants that alter essential events in embryonic development have been described by Rice & Garen (1975; Rice 1973). These mutants are not rescuable by wildtype sperm. The lethal phenotypes of the embryo depend entirely on the maternal genotypes, a result which indicates that the genes defective in these mutants are essential only for oogenesis and not for any other period of development. Thus, heterozygous embryos from the eggs of homozygous mutant females die, whereas homozygous mutant embryos from the eggs of heterozygous mutant females develop into adults. In one mutant, *mat(3)1,* blastoderm cells do not form, but pole cells do form. The existence of this mutation indicates that there are separate genetic controls in oogenesis for materials needed for blastoderm cell formation and for pole cell formation. In another mutant, *mat(3)3,* blastoderm cells fail to form in certain areas, and embryos develop defects in these particular areas. Evidently, the mother builds into the egg materials that are necessary for blastoderm formation in particular areas. When these materials are not made or are missing from certain regions of the egg, blastoderm formation is incomplete in certain regions.

11. MATERNAL EFFECT MUTANTS AFFECTING SPECIFIC ORGANS

Studies of these various maternal effect mutants permit the conclusion that wildtype mothers provide factors in the egg which are necessary for normal nuclear multiplication, blastoderm formation, gastrulation, primarty organogenesis, and the survival of females. Injection of cytoplasmic factors from eggs laid by wildtype animals can partly repair the damage due to *deep orange* and, in some cases, can completely repair the damage due to *rudimentary* and *daughterless*. There is no evidence, however, that any of these cytoplasmic factors are localized in the cortical cytoplasm or that these mutants have specific effects on determination. However, certain maternal effect mutants do produce eggs that lack localized factors necessary for the normal determination of certain organs.

A well-known example of such a mutant is *grandchildless (gs)* of *Drosophila subobscura*. This autosomal mutation is a 'Zero Population Growth' mutant. Homozygous *(gs/gs)* females are not visibly different from the wildtype. But, when mated to either *gs* or wildtype males, *gs* females produce both sons and daughters that lack germ cells and are therefore sterile (Spurway 1948; Fielding 1967). It has been reported that cleavage nuclei enter the polar cytoplasmic region but that pole cells, the precursors of germ cells, do not form (Gehring 1973). Apparently *gs/gs* females produce eggs which are missing some factors necessary for germ cell formation. A similar effect can be produced by ultraviolet irradiation of the posterior cytoplasm of the egg. This was first done with *Drosophila* in 1931 by Geigy who showed that irradiation of posterior cytoplasm of the *Drosophila melanogaster* egg resulted in adult flies that were completely normal except that their gonads lacked germ cells and consequently the flies were sterile. It was suggested that the UV destroyed germ cell determinants which are localized in the polar cytoplasm. Similar results were obtained in amphibian eggs, where destruction of posterior cytoplasm also leads to the formation of animals which are normal in all respects except that they are sterile (Blackler 1962; Smith 1966).

Recently, experiments were conducted to decide whether the sterility caused by UV irradiation to *Drosophila* eggs was due to UV destroying germ cell determinants or whether UV prevented cells from forming by damaging the posterior of the egg (Okada *et al.* 1974a). If UV acted by destroying localized germ cell determinants, then sterility should be prevented by injecting polar cytoplasm from normal eggs into the posterior pole of irradiated eggs. By precisely timed UV irradiation of the posterior region of newly laid *D. melanogaster* eggs, sterility was produced in 99 per cent of the resulting adults. Such eggs could be rescued by injection of cytoplasm from the posterior pole of unirradiated eggs so that 42 per cent of the animals that survived the injection became fertile (Fig. 1.9; Table 1.1). In contrast, injection of cytoplasm from the anterior pole of unirradiated eggs into the irradiated eggs failed to prevent sterility (Table 1.2). Apparently the polar cytoplasm contains materials not concentrated elsewhere in the cytoplasm that are destroyed by UV and are necessary for germ cell formation. It was also shown that when cytoplasm from the posterior pole was injected in the anterior-lateral region of unirradiated *D. melanogaster* eggs, this led to the formation at the place the posterior cytoplasm was deposited of large cells which closely resemble pole cells (Okada *et al.* 1974a). This result confirms the conclusion that polar cytoplasm contains materials necessary for germ cell formation and that these are the materials destroyed by UV. It is also clear that cytoplasmic injection into eggs can be used both as a bioassay for germ cell determinants and to identify the biochemical nature of the active components. Further experiments revealed that cytoplasm from the posterior pole of the eggs of other species of *Drosophila* such as *D. hydei* and *D. immagrans* could prevent sterility when injected into the posterior pole of *D. melanogaster* eggs (Okada *et al.* 1974a).

Illmensee & Mahowald (1974, 1975) have carried these experiments a decisive step further and demonstrated that the pole cell-like cells formed after transplantation of polar cytoplasm are in fact primordial germ cells. They transplanted cytoplasm from the posterior pole to the anterior of embryos, produced ectopic pole cells and then transplanted these pole cells into the posterior regions of normal host embryos of the same age and of a different genotype. Some of the transplanted ectopic pole cells became germ cells and gave rise to flies with a genotype that showed that the flies had come from the ectopic pole cells. Identification of the molecule or molecules in the posterior pole cytoplasm responsible for germ cell determination remains to be done.

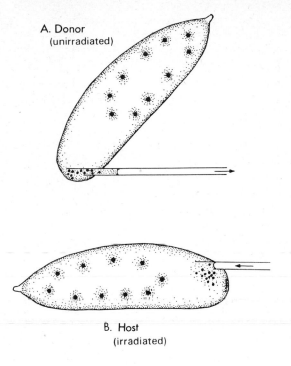

FIG. 1.9. Diagrams showing the design of the polar cytoplasm transplantation experiment. (A) The needle is inserted into the donor egg to remove polar cytoplasm. (B) The polar cytoplasm is then injected into the posterior pole of the irradiated host egg. (From Okada *et al.* 1974a.)

TABLE 1.1 Transplantation of polar cytoplasm of unirradiated eggs into the posterior pole of UV irradiated eggs. (From Okada *et al.* 1974a.)

	Donor *mwh e*[11] (posterior pole)		Host *mwh e*[11] (UV-irradiated for 25 seconds at posterior pole)		Significance
	No. of eggs treated	No. of adults emerged	Sterile adults	Fertile adults	
Experimental	582	50	29 (58%)	21 (42%)	
					$P \ll 0.01$
Control	607	83	82 (99%)	1 (1%)	

TABLE 1.2. Transplantation of cytoplasm from the anterior pole into the posterior pole of UV-irradiated eggs. (From Okada *et. al.*, 1974a.)

	Donor *mwh e*[11] (anterior pole)		Host *mwh e*[11] (UV-irradiated for 25 seconds at posterior pole)		Significance
	No. of eggs treated	No. of adults emerged	Sterile adults	Fertile adults	
Experimental	1093	57	56 (98%)	1 (2%)	
					0.8>*P*>0.9
Control	1005	257	254 (99%)	3 (1%)	

These experiments with polar plasm raise the question of whether the interaction between polar plasm and nuclei to determine germ cells is a simple paradigm of the initiation of determination in other cells by other materials in the egg cytoplasm. Are other determinants localized in the egg? Evidence that the cytoplasm of the egg contains materials other than polar plasm that are responsible for initiation of determination comes from both genetic and experimental procedures. There is a maternal effect mutation called *bicaudal* in which homozygous females produce abnormal eggs (Bull 1966). When mated to any male, the females lay eggs that die due to head abnormalities. The tip of the head is often replaced by the tip of the abdomen and in about one per cent of the cases, the head and thoracic segments are entirely absent and a mirror-image abdomen forms. These phenotypes, caused by the mother's genotype rather than the individual's genotype, indicate that there are factors in the egg that normally determine anterior structures—determinants—and that these anterior determinants are missing, abnormal, or do not function in the eggs of *bicaudal* females.

12. EXPERIMENTAL ALTERATIONS OF DETERMINATION IN EMBRYOS

The occurrence of the maternally inherited mutation *bicaudal* demonstrates that at some stage during oogenesis the polarity of the anterior can be reversed. In more primitive Diptera, notably chironomids, it has been possible to induce this polarity reversal experimentally by several procedures. Centrifugation of nuclear multiplication stage embryos toward one of the poles results in mirror-image double abdomens or mirror-image double heads (Gauss & Sander 1966; Overton & Raab 1967; Yajima 1960, 1970). Ultraviolet irradiation of the anterior pole can also produce double abdomens (Yajima 1964). It can be demonstrated that UV primarily affects the cytoplasm of the egg (a maternally derived component) rather than the nuclei, since irradiation of the anterior 1/8 of the egg *prior* to nuclear immigration yields double abdomens (Kalthoff 1971).

In *Drosophila,* irradiation of the anterior of nuclear multiplication eggs does not produce genuine double abdomens. In general most of the resulting embryos show defective head structures, but 10 per cent of the embryos have just an abdomen, i.e., they have become one large abdomen. The eight abdominal segments spread to the anterior of the egg, and head and thoracic structures are completely absent (Bownes & Kalthoff 1974 and personal communication). It is noteworthy that these embryos form from an almost normal-appearing blastoderm. Apparently, the UV has changed the cortical cytoplasm so that many blastoderm cells acquire a different determination than usual, and a *bicaudal*-like embryo is formed. Once the cellular blastoderm has formed, reorganizations are no longer possible and UV produces only anterior defects. Since it is not possible to completely reverse the polarity of *Drosophila* eggs, as in lower Diptera, it seems that at the time of egg deposition the antero-posterior axis of *Drosophila* is established, and that *Drosophila* passes through a stage when the polarity can still be reversed during oogenesis.

Recent experiments of Herth & Sander (1973) on egg fragments provide further evidence that the determinants for particular embryonic segments are not fixed in the egg during oogenesis but become fixed during embryonic life prior to cellularization of the blastoderm. They used the blowfly *Protophormia* whose eggs are rather large and confirmed their principal results in *Drosophila*. Because the embryonic development of the higher dipterans is rather uniform, conclusions drawn from experiments on *Protophormia* probably hold with some minor modifications for *Drosophila* as well. They fragmented eggs at various stages in embryonic development between oviposition and cellular blastoderm formation by pressing down a blunt razor blade onto the egg. This procedure separated the egg into two fragments but did not cut the vitelline membrane. When they fragmented eggs early in nuclear multiplication, only the most anterior and posterior embryonic segments formed. However when they fragmented later and later, more and more of the middle segments formed. Finally, when they fragmented at the cellular blastoderm stage, the two half embryos that developed contained together all of the segments. These experiments indicate that the anterior and posterior regions of the egg interact during early development and that the determination of middle embryonic segments depends on the interaction of both anterior and posterior factors. Their results indicate that embryonic segmentation is not programmed in either the *Protophormia* or the *Drosophila* egg cortex at oviposition. Instead, the conditions necessary to establish a pattern of segmentation develop during the nuclear multiplication stage and become completed when the blastoderm cellularizes.

Bownes & Sang (1974) and Bownes (1975a, b; 1976) have used micro-cautery and pricking to locally damage *Drosophila* embryos before and after cellularization of the blastoderm. These studies showed that when nuclear multiplication stage embryos were damaged, often a major group of closely associated disc derivatives were missing for example, most of the left side of the thorax. Apparently, loss of part of a nuclear multiplication stage embryo leads to the loss of a large region of the embryo rather than loss of a specific adult structure (the germ cells are an exception). However, after cellularization, destruction of the cells in a particular region was often associated with a defect or a duplication in a specific adult structure. This result indicates that the determinants for specific adult structures such as imaginal discs are not localized in their definitive positions in the egg until after cellularization. This fact may explain why no maternal effect mutants have yet been found which block or alter the determination of a specific disc (Rice 1973).

From the foregoing it seems clear that in *Drosophila,* with the exception of the germ cell determinants and the factors involved in anterior and posterior polarity, determinants for parts of the embryo, larva, and adult are not located in their final position when the egg is laid. They become localized during the first few hours of embryonic development. Initially embryonic segmentation is established. At the same time, polarity within each segment appears to become established. Then dorso-ventral localizations probably become established including the determination to belong to a particular imaginal disc (Wieschaus & Gehring 1975; Steiner, personal communication).

It is worth inquiring about the number of different kinds of determinants that are needed to account for the many different determined tissues found in *Drosophila*. One view is that determinants comprise a rather large group of substances, a few of which are localized in particular parts of the cortical cytoplasm during oogenesis, but most of which become localized during embryonic development. This has been termed by Herth & Sander (1973) a 'qualitative' model for determinants because many qualitatively different determinants are necessary. An alternative view is that concentration gradients of a very few substances, let us denote them as primary determinants, lead to localized differences—a matrix of positional information—all over the cortex and provide a whole range of different nuclear environments. This has been denoted a 'quantitative' type of model for determinants because each region of cortex would not have its own chemically unique cortical determinants but its own unique set of concentrations of a few primary determinants (Herth & Sander 1973; Sander 1960, 1975). There may be only a few primary determinants built into different regions of the egg during oogenesis (e.g., anterior, posterior, and germ cell determinants) (Gehring 1973). The final distribution of these primary determinants in the cortex to establish a matrix of positional information in the embryo might be influenced by early embryonic events such as nuclear multiplication, the invasion of nuclei to form the syncytial blastoderm, and movements of various parts of the egg cytoplasm. For a further analysis of these matters see the chapter by Sander elsewhere in this volume.

13. MAINTENANCE AND PROPAGATION OF THE DETERMINED STATE

Once the process of determination is initiated, the problem remains of how it is maintained during successive cell divisions in the somatic cells of an embryo, a larva, and a mature organism. What factors keep somatic cells such as wing disc cells programmed in a specific direction? Experiments like those of Gurdon (1962 and review 1974) on amphibians indicate that no permanent alterations to somatic cell nuclei have occurred because nuclei of determined cells such as epidermal or intestinal cells when transplanted into enucleated eggs can support embryonic development. The recent experiments of Okada & Schneiderman (1976) with the neuroblast nuclei of *Drosophila* indicate that no permanent alterations have occurred in the nuclei of those determined cells either. The continuity of determination cannot depend upon a single finite supply of a substance which is distributed when the cells divide. Such a supply would be diluted continuously and its effect would disappear. At present the mechanism by which determination is maintained is a matter of pure speculation, but several possible mechanisms have been suggested, two of which will be mentioned. One is a chromosomal mechanism which would involve a process analogous to X-chromosome inactivation in man in which some chromosomal organizational feature such as the heterochromatization of part of a chromosome is propagated by cell heredity. Perhaps determination involves some localized change in chromosomal organization that, once initiated by determinants in the egg and embryo, is propagated even though those determinants get diluted out as the cells divide. Another possibility is that determinants may initiate in the cells that they determine, the further production of determinants. If this were true, then the cytoplasm of determined cells such as imaginal disc cells and salivary gland cells should contain materials in their cytoplasm that act on the nuclei and keep the nuclei programmed. When determined cells divide, these cytoplasmic determinants would be shared amongst daughter cells, and as the cell grows they would be replenished. This hypothesis could be tested by transplanting or fusing somatic cell cytoplasm to parts of the cortex of nuclear multiplication stage embryos to learn whether the somatic cell cytoplasm influences the fate of any nuclei that invade it and form cells.

ACKNOWLEDGMENTS

I am indebted to my colleagues in the Center for Pathobiology from whom I have learned so much and with whom it has been a pleasure to work. The following have kindly criticized parts of the typescript or allowed me to cite recent results: P. Bryant, M. Bownes, C. Duranceau, T. Cline, D. Falk, S. Germeraad, J. Haynie, M. Madhavan, M. Okada, C. Roseland and G. Schubiger. Original work described in this paper was partly supported by grants from the National Science Foundation (GB 43075), the National Cancer Institute (CA 12643), and the National Institute of Child Health and Human Development (HD 00347) of the Department of Health, Education and Welfare.

DISCUSSION

Wilby: What moves the nuclei from the middle of the egg out to the cortical cytoplasm?

Schneiderman: It's not fully known. *(See discussion after Sander's paper, ed)*

Gurdon: There is one maternal mutant studied by Garen which inhibits that particular process.

Schneiderman: There are maternal affect mutants that alter the steps that I have described. For instance the 'opposite' of *grandchildless* which makes no blastoderm and only pole cells.

Wolpert: I got the impression that no one knew when determination of the imaginal cells occurred, and I thought this was known. Is this a controversial issue?

Schneiderman: From the evidence that I have seen, the precise time that determination to belong to a particular disc occurs has not been established. Wieschaus and Gehring have shown that it may not be when they become cells, because at that time the descendants of a single cell can belong to two discs, the leg and the wing. Perhaps we shall find out more during this symposium.

Sander: Probably determination of the segments occurs before the determination of the difference between the ventral and the dorsal discs. This appears to be a general rule in insects, that antero-posterior pattern elements are specified earlier than the bilateral symmetry. You can get bilateral twins at a stage when you cannot get anything like twins by cutting the egg transversally.

Gurdon: You emphasize the experimental approaches in your talk. Could you suggest an experimental approach to analyze the information which passes between cells, for example during the regeneration of cut discs. Could you see a way of identifying the messages which pass from one cell to another?

Schneiderman: Well, one could look at discs when they are healing, and see what kinds of junctional connections they establish. We should also like to know the kinetics of this information exchange. Is there an eclipse period when you put two tissues together when they are establishing conversational pathways? Can different discs talk to each other? Can the leg cells communicate positional information to wing cells, resulting in regeneration? Of course, we assume that each would grow and form cells of their own type. We could take a temperature sensitive mutation which arrests cell division. Such mutations exist. Can tissue carrying such a mutation and not dividing, communicate positional information to other cells? These approaches do not tell us the molecules that may be involved. If anyone in this room knows the answer to these questions they should be in Stockholm and not here, because that is a very important question. But they set the stage for that kind of analysis. We have a bio-assay for the molecules! When these tissues stimulate each other in a specific way, we know they are talking to each other, and that I think is very important.

Gurdon: Supposing I gave you a test tube, saying that these were the molecules that told the cells what to do, what is your bio-assay for them?

Schneiderman: First of all, I don't think you could get that test tube! The real philosophical question is, at what point does one adopt a reductionist approach? This is why the field of positional information has not been amongst the most attractive to molecular biologists, because it has not yet been amenable to reductionist approach. We have not yest established the basic rules and I am afraid that I can only speculate about these experiments. However, if you gave me such a test tube, then I should apply those molecules in various ways to imaginal disc fragments cultured *in vitro* and *in vivo,* to see whether the molecules altered the expected programme of differentiation of the regenerating imaginal disc fragments. That would be the bioassay.

Razavi: What is the number of nuclei present in the syncytial stage of the blastoderm?

Schneiderman: About 3,500. These divisions are terrifically rapid, taking about ten minutes. Divisions at that rate have not been observed elsewhere amongst animal cells.

Razavi: So the question of intercellular communication would arise at around 3,500 cells?

Schneiderman: Yes, since that is when cells first form.

REFERENCES

ARKING, R. (1975). Temperature-sensitive cell lethal mutants of *Drosophila:* Isolation and characterization. *Genetics* **80**, 519-537

AUERBACH, C. (1936). The development of the legs, wings and halteres in wild-type and some mutant strains of *Drosophila melanogaster. Trans. Roy. Soc. Edinburgh,* **58**, 787-815.

BELL, A. E. (1954). A gene in *Drosophila melanogaster* that produces all male progeny. *Genetics* **39**, 958.

BLACKLER, A. W. (1962). Transfer of primordial germ-cells between two subspecies of *Xenopus laevis. J. Embryol. exp. Morph.* **10**, 641-651.

BOHN, H. (1971). Interkalare Regeneration und Segmentale Gradienten bei den Extremitäten von *Leucophaea* —Larven (Blattaria) III. Die Herkunft des interkalarvan Regenerates. *Wilhelm Roux Arch. Entwmech. Org.* **167**, 209-221.

BOVERI, TH. (1902). Über mehrpolige Mitosen als Mittel zur Analyse des Zellkerns. Verhandlungen der physikalisch-medizinischen Gesellschaft zu Würzburg. *Neue Folge*, **35**, 67-90 (Translated in *Foundations of Experimental Embryology* (B. H. Willier & J. M. Oppenheimer, eds.). Prentice-Hall, Englewood Cliffs, New Jersey, 1964).

BOWNES, M. (1975a). Adult deficiencies and duplications of head and thoracic structures resulting from microcautery of blastoderm stage *Drosophila* embryos. *J. Embryol. exp. Morphol.* **34**, 33-54.

BOWNES, M. (1975b). Larval and adult abdominal defects resulting from microcautery of blastoderm stage *Drosophila* embryos. *J. exp. Zool.* (in press).

BOWNES, M. (1976). Defective development after puncturing the periplasm of nuclear multiplication stage *Drosophila* eggs. *Dev. Biol.*, (in press).

BOWNES, M. & KALTHOFF, K. (1974). Embryonic defects in *Drosophila* eggs after partial UV irradiation at different wavelengths. *J. Embryol. exp. Morph.*, **32**, 329-345.

BOWNES, M. & SANG, J. H. (1974). Experimental manipulations of early *Drosophila* embryos. I. Adult and embryonic defects resulting from microcautery at nuclear multiplication and blastoderm stages. *J. Embyol. exp. Morph.*, **32**, 253-273

BOWNES, M., CLINE, T. W. & SCHNEIDERMAN, H. A. (1976). Daughters from *daughterless* mothers—rescuing a female-lethal maternal effect by cytoplasmic transplantation in *Drosophila* embryos. *Dev. Biol.* (submitted).

BRUN, R. B. & KOBEL, H. R. (1972). Des grenouilles metamorphosées obtenues par transplantation nucleaire a partir du prosencephale et de l'épiderme larvaire de *Xenopus laevis*. *Rev. Suisse Zool.*, **79**, 961-965.

BRYANT, P. J. (1970). Cell lineage relationships in the imaginal wing disc of *Drosophila melanogaster*. *Dev. Biol.*, **22**, 389-411.

BRYANT, P. J. (1971). Regeneration and duplication following operations *in situ* on the imaginal discs of *Drosophila melanogaster*. *Dev. Biol.*, **26**, 637-651.

BRYANT, P. J. (1974). Determination and pattern formation in the imaginal discs of *Drosophila Curr. Topics Dev. Biol.*, **8**, 41-80.

BRYANT, P. J. (1975a). Pattern formation in the imaginal wing disc of *Drosophila melanogaster:* Fate map, regeneration and duplication. *J. exp. Zool.*, **193**, 49-78.

BRYANT, P. J. (1975b). Regeneration and duplication in imaginal discs. *In Cell Patterning*, pp. 71-93. *Ciba Found. Symp.*, **29**.

BRYANT, P. J. & SCHNEIDERMAN, H. A. (1969). Cell lineage, growth, and determination in the imaginal leg discs of *Drosophilia melanogaster Dev. Biol.*, **20**, 263-290.

BRYANT, P. J. & ZORNETZER, M. (1973). Mosaic analysis of lethal mutations in *Drosophila*. *Genetics*, **75**, 623-637.

BRYANT, S, V, & ITEN, L. E. (1976). Supernumerary limbs in amphibians: Experimental production in *Notophthalmus viridescens* and a new interpretation of their formation. *Dev. Biol.*, (in press)

BULL, A. L. (116). *Bicaudal* a genetic factor which affects the polarity of the embryo in *Drosophila melanogaster*. *J. exp. Zool.*, **161**, 221-242.

CHAN, L.-N. & GEHRING, W. (1971). Determination of blastoderm cells in *Drosophila melanogaster*. *Proc. natn. Acad. Sci. USA*, **68**, 2217-2221.

COUNCE, S. J. (1965a). Studies on female-sterility genes in *Drosophila melanogaster*. I. The effects of the gene *deep orange* on embryonic development. *Z. Indukt. Abstamm Vererbungsl.*, **87**, 443-461.

COUNCE, S. J. (1956b). Studies on female-sterility genes in *Drosophila melanogaster*. II. The effects of the gene *fused* on embryonic development. *Z. Indukt. Abstamm. Vererbungsl*, **87**, 462-481.

COUNCE, S. J. (1956c). Studies on female-sterility genes in *Drosophila melanogaster*. III. The effects of the gene *rudimentary* on embryonic development. *Z. Indukt. Abstamm. Vererbungsl.*, **87**, 482-492.

COUNCE, S. J. (1973). The causal analysis of insect embryogenesis. Developmental Systems: Insects, Vol. 2 (C. H. Waddington & S. Counce-Niklas, eds.), 1-156. Academic Press, New York.

CRICK, F. H. C. & LAWRENCE, P. A. (1975). Compartments and polyclones in insect development. *Science*, **189**, 340-347.

FIELDING, C. J. (1967). Developmental genetics of the mutant *grandchildless* of *Drosophila subobscura*. *J. Embryol exp. Morph.*, **17**, 375-385.

FRENCH, V. (1976). Leg regeneration in the cockroach, *Blatella germanica*. II. Regeneration from a non-congruent tibial graft/host junction. *J. Embryol exp. Morph.*, (in press).

FRENCH, V., BRYANT, P. J. & BRYANT, S. V. (1976). A model for pattern regulation in epimorphic fields. *Science*, (in press).

FRENCH, V. & BULLIERE, D. (1975a). Nouvelles données sur la determination de la position des cellules épidermiques sur un appendice de Blatte. *C. R. Acad. Sci. Paris*, **280**, 53-56.

FRENCH, V. & BULLIERE, D. (1975b). Étude de la determination de la positiondes cellules: ordonnance des cellules autour d'un appendice de Blatte; demonstration du concept de géneratrice. *C. R. Acad. Sci. Paris*, **280**, 295-298.

FRISTROM, D. & FRISTROM, J. W. (1975). The mechanism of evagination of imaginal discs of *Drosophila melanogaster. Dev. Biol.*, **43**, 1-23.

GARCIA—BELLIDO, A. (1975). Genetic control of wing disc development in *Drosophila. In Cell Patterning*, pp. 161-177. Ciba Foundation Symposium *29*.

GARCIA—BELLIDO, A. & MERRIAM, J. R. (1971a). Parameters of the wing imaginal disc development of *Drosophila melanogaster. Dev. Biol.*, **24**, 61-87.

GARCIA—BELLIDO, A. & MERRIAM, J. R. (1971b). Clonal parameters of tergite development in *Drosophila. Dev. Biol.*, **26**, 264-276.

GARCIA—BELLIDO, A., RIPOLL, P. & MORATA, G. (1973). Developmental compartmentalization of the wing disc of *Drosophila. Nat. New Biol.*, **245**, 251-253.

GAREN, A. & GEHRING, W. (1972). Repair of the lethal developmental defect in *deep orange* embryos of *Drosophila* by injection of normal egg cytoplasm. *Proc. natn. Acad. Sci. USA*, **69**, 2982-2985.

GATEFF, E. A., AKAI, H. & SCHNEIDERMAN, H. A. (1974). Correlations between developmental capacity, histology, and fine structure of tissue sublines derived from the eye-antenna imaginal disc of *Drosophila melanogaster. Wilhelm Roux Arch. Entw Mech. Org.*, **176**, 89-123.

GATEFF, E. & SCHNEIDERMAN, H. A. (1974). Developmental capacities of benign and malignant neoplasms of *Drosophila. Wilhelm Roux Arch. Entw Mech. Org.*, **176**, 23-65.

GAUSS, U. & SANDER, K. (1966). Stadienabhängigkeit embryonaler Doppelbildungen von *Chironomus th. thummi. Naturwissenschaften*, **53**, 182-183.

GEHRING, W. (1972). The stability of the determined state in cultures of imaginal discs in *Drosophila. In Results and Problems in Cell differentiation*, V. (H. Ursprung & R. Nöthiger, eds.), pp. 35-58. Springer, Germany.

GEHRING, W. (1973). Genetic control of determination in the *Drosophila* embryo. *In Genetic Mechanisms of Development* (F. H. Ruddle, ed.), pp. 103-128. *Symp. Soc. Develop. Biol.*, **31**.

GEHRING, W. & NÖTHIGER, R. (1973). The imaginal discs of *Drosophila. In Developmental Systems: Insects*, Vol. 2 (C. H. Waddington & S. Counce-Niklas, eds.). Academic Press, New York.

GEHRING, W. & SCHUBIGER, G. (1975). Expression of homeotic mutation in duplicated and regenerated antennae of *Drosophila melanogaster. J. embryol exp. Morph.*, **33**, 459-469.

GEIGY, R. (1931). Erzeugung rein imaginaler Defekte durch ultraviolette Eibestrahlung bei *Drosophila melanogaster. Wilhelm Roux' Arch. Entw Mech. Org.*, **125**, 406-447.

GUERRA, M., POSTLETHWAIT, J. H. & SCHNEIDERMAN, H. A. (1973). The development of the imaginal abdomen of *Drosophila melanogaster. Dev. Biol.*, **32**, 361-372.

GURDON, J. B. (1962). Adult frogs derived from the nuclei of single somatic cells. *Dev. Biol.*, **4**, 256-273.

GURDON, J. B. (1974). *The Control of Gene Expression in Animal Development*, 160 pp. Harvard University Press, Cambridge.

HADORN, E. (1963). Differenzierungsleistungen wiederholt fragmentierter Teilstücke männlicher Genitalscheiben von *Drosophila melanogaster* nach Kultur *in vivo. Dev. Biol.*, **7**, 617-629.

HADORN, E. (1966a). Konstanz, Wechsel und Typus der Determination und Differenzierung in Zellen auf männlichen Genitalanlagen von *Drosophila melanogaster* nach Dauerkultur *in vivo. Dev. Biol.*, **13**, 424-509.

HADORN, E. (1966b). Dynamics of determination. *Symp. Soc. Develop. Biol.*, **25**, 85-104.

HADORN, E. (1969). Proliferation and dynamics of cell heredity in blastema cultures of *Drosophila. Nat. Cancer Inst. Monogr.*, **31**, 351-364.

HAYNIE, J. & BRYANT, P. J. (1976). Intercalary regeneration in the imaginal wing disc of *Drosophila melanogaster. Nature, Lond.*, **259**, 659-662.

HERTH, W. & SANDER, K. (1973). Mode and timing of body pattern formation (regionalization) in the early embryonic development of cyclorrhaphic dipterans *(Protophormia, Drosophila). Wilhelm Roux Arch. Entw Mech. Org.*, **172**, 1-27.

HOTTA, Y. & BENZER, S. (1972). Mapping behaviour in *Drosophila* mosaics. *Nature, Lond.*, **240**, 527-535.

ILLMENSEE, K. (1972). Developmental potencies of nuclei from cleavage, preblastoderm, and syncytial blastoderm transplanted into unfertilized eggs of *Drosophila melanogaster. Wilhelm Roux Arch. Entw Mech. Org.*, **170**, 267-298.

ILLMENSEE, K. (1973). The potentialities of transplanted early gastrula nuclei of *Drosophila melanogaster*. Production of their imago descendants by germ-line transplantation. *Wilhelm Roux Arch. Entw Mech. Org.*, **171**, 331-343.

ILLMENSEE, K. & MAHOWALD, A. P. (1974). Transplantation of posterior polar plasm in *Drosophila*. Induction of germ cells at the anterior pole of the egg. *Proc. natn. Acad. Sci. USA*, **7**, 1016–1020.

ILLMENSEE, K. & MAHOWALD, A. P. (1975). The autonomous function of germ plasm in a somatic region of the *Drosophila* egg. *Expl. Cell Res.* (in press).

ITEN, L. E. & BRYANT, S. V. (1975). The interaction between the blastema and stump in the establishment of the anterior-posterior and proximo-distal organization of the limb regenerate. *Dev. Biol.*, **44**, 119–147.

KALTHOFF, K. (1971). Position of targets and period of competence for UV-induction of the malformation 'double abdomen' in the egg of *Smittia* spec. (Diptera, Chironomidae). *Wilhelm Roux Arch. Entw Mech. Org.*, **168**, 63–84.

KAMBYSELLIS, M. P. & SCHNEIDER, I. (1975). *In vitro* development of insect cells. Effects of ecdysone on neonatal larval cells. *Dev. Biol.*, **44**, 198–203.

LAUGÉ, G. (1967). Origine et croissance du disque génital de *Drosophila melanogaster* Meig. *C. N. Acad. Sci. Paris*, **265**, 814–817.

MILNER, M. J. & SANG, J. H. (1974). Relative activities of α-ecdysone and β-ecdysone for the differentiation *in vitro* of *Drosophila melanogaster* imaginal discs. *Cell*, **3**, 141–143.

MORATA, G. & LAWRENCE, P. A. (1975). Control of compartment development by the *engrailed* gene in *Drosophila. Nature, Lond.*, **255**, 614–617.

MORATA, G. & RIPOLL, P. (1975), *Minutes:* mutants of *Drosophila* autonomously affecting cell division rate. *Dev. Biol.*, **42**, 211–221.

NØRBY, S. (1970). A specific nutritional requirement for pyrimidines in *rudimentary* mutants of *Drosophila melanogaster. Hereditas*, **66**, 205–214.

NÖTHIGER, R. (1964). Differenzierungsleistungen in Kombinaten, hergestellt aus Imaginalscheiben verschiedener Arten, Geschlechter und Körpersegmente von *Drosophila. Wilhelm Roux Arch. Entw Mech. Org.*, **155**, 269–301.

NÖTHIGER, R. (1972). The larval development of imaginal discs. In *Results and Problems in Cell Differentiation, V.*, (H. Ursprung & R. Nöthiger, eds.), pp. 1–34. Springer, Germany.

OKADA, M., KLEINMAN, I. A. & SCHNEIDERMAN, H. A. (1974a). Restoration of fertility in sterilized *Drosophila* eggs by transplantation of polar cytoplasm. *Dev. Biol.*, **37**, 43–54.

OKADA, M., KLEINMAN, I. A. & SCHNEIDERMAN, H. A. (1974b). Repair of a genetically-caused defect in oogenesis in *Drosophila melanogaster* by transplantation of cytoplasm from wild-type eggs and by injection of pyrimidine nucleosides. *Dev. Biol.*, **37**, 55–62.

OKADA, M., KLEINMAN, I. A. & SCHNEIDERMAN, H. A. (1974c). Chimeric *Drosophila* adults produced by transplantation of nuclei into specific regions of fertilized eggs. *Dev. Biol.*, **39**, 286–294.

OKADA, M. & SCHEIDERMAN, H. A. (1976). Evidence for multipotency of embryonic neuroblast nuclei transplanted into *Drosophila* embryos. *Wilhelm Roux Arch. Entw Mech. Org.* (submitted).

OVERTON, J. & RAAB, M. (1967). The development and fine structure of centrifuged eggs of *Chironomus thummi. Dev. Biol.*, **15**, 271–287.

POODRY, C. A. & SCHNEIDERMAN, H. A. (1970). The ultrastructure of the developing leg of *Drosophila melanogaster. Wilhelm Roux Arch. Entw Mech. Org.*, **166**, 1–44.

POSTLETHWAIT, J. H. & SCHNEIDERMAN, H. A. (1971a). A clonal analysis of development in *Drosophila melanogaster*: Morphogenesis, determination, and growth in the wild-type antenna. *Dev. Biol*, **24**, 477–519.

POSTLETHWAIT, J. H. & SCHNEIDERMAN, H. A. (1971b). Pattern formation and determination in the antenna of the homoeotic mutant *Antennapedia* of *Drosophila melanogaster. Dev. Biol.*, **25**, 606–640.

POSTLETHWAIT, J. H. & SCHNEIDERMAN, H. A. (1973). Developmental genetics of *Drosophila* imaginal discs. *Ann. Rev. Genet.*, **7**, 381–433.

POULSON, D. (1950). Histogenesis, organogenesis and differentiation in the embryo of *Drosophila melanogaster* Meigen. In *The Biology of Drosophila* (M. Demerec, ed.), pp. 168–274. Hafner, New York.

RICE, T. B. (1973). Isolation and characterization of maternal-effect mutants: An approach to the study of early determination in *Drosophila melanogaster*. Ph.D. Thesis, Yale University.

RICE, T. B. & GAREN, A. (1975). Localized defects of blastoderm formation in maternal effect mutants of *Drosophila Dev. Biol.*, **43**, 277–286.

RUSSELL, M. (1974). Pattern formation in imaginal discs of a temperature-sensitive cell lethal mutant of *Drosophila melanogaster. Dev. Biol.*, **40**, 24–39.

SANDER, K. (1960). Analyse des ooplasmatischen Reaktions systems von *Euscelis plebejus* Fall. (Cicadina) durch Isolieren und Kombinieren von Keimteilen. II. *Wilhelm Roux Arch. Entw Mech. Org.*, **151**, 660–707.

SANDER, K. (1975). Pattern specification in the insect embryo. In *Cell Patterning*, pp. 256–264. *Ciba Found.*

Symp., **29**.

SCHNEIDERMAN, H. A. (1969). Control systems in insect development. In *Biology and the Physical Sciences* (S. Devons, ed.), pp. 186-208. Colombia University Press, New York.

SCHNEIDERMAN, H. A. & BRYANT, P. J. (1971). Genetic analysis of developmental mechanisms in *Drosophila. Nature, Lond.*, **234**, 187-194.

SCHUBIGER, G. (1971). Regeneration, duplication and transdetermination in fragments of the leg disc of *Drosophila melanogaster. Dev. Biol.*, **26**, 277-295.

SCHUBIGER, G. & ALPERT, G. D. (1975). Regeneration and duplication in a temperature-sensitive homoeotic mutant of *Drosophila melanogaster. Dev. Biol.*, **42**, 292-304.

SCRIBA, M. E. L. (1964). Beeinflussing der frühen Embryonalentwicklung von *Drosophila melanogaster* durch Chromasomenabberationen. *Zool. Jb.*, **81**, 435-490.

SIMPSON, P. & SCHNEIDERMAN, H. A. (1975). Isolation of temperature sensitive mutations blocking clone development in *Drosophila melanogaster*, and the effects of a temperature sensitive cell lethal mutation on pattern formation in imaginal discs. *Wilhelm Roux Arch. Entw Mech. Org.*, **178**, 247-275.

SIMPSON, P. & SCHNEIDERMAN, H. A. (1976). A temperature-sensitive mutation that reduces mitotic rate in *Drosophila melanogaster. Wilhelm Roux Arch. Entw Mech. Org.* (in press).

SMITH, L. D. (1966). The role of a 'Germinal plasm' in the formation of primordial germ cells in *Rana pipiens. Dev. Biol.*, **14**, 330-347.

SONNENBLICK, B. P. (1950). The early embryology of *Drosophila melanogaster*. In *Biology of Drosophila* (M. Demerec, ed.), pp. 62-167. John Wiley and Sons, New York.

SPURWAY, H. (1948). Genetics and cytology of *Drosophila subobscura*. IV. An extreme example of delay in gene action, causing sterility. *J. Genet.*, **49**, 126-140.

THIERRY—MEIG, D., MASSON, M. & GANS, M. (1972). Mutant de sterilite a effet retarde de *Drosophila melanogaster. C. r. Acad. Sci, Paris*, **275**, 2751-2754.

URSPRUNG, H. (1962). Einfluss des Wirtsalters auf die Entwicklungsleistung von Sagittälhaften männlicher Genitalscheiben von *Drosophila melanogaster. Dev. Biol.*, **4**, 22-39.

URSPRUNG, H. (1962). *In vivo* culture of *Drosophila* imaginal discs. In *Methods in Developmental Biology* (F. Wilt & N. Wessells, eds.), pp. 485-492. Crowell, New York.

WARN, R. (1975). Restoration of the capacity to form pole cells in UV irradiated *Drosophila* embryos. *J. Embryol exp. Morph.*, **33**, 1003-1011.

WIESCHAUS, E. & GEHRING, W. (1975). Clonal analysis of early development in *Drosophila melanogaster. Experientia*, **31**, 750.

WIGGLESWORTH, V. B. (1964). Homeostasis in insect growth. *Symp. Soc. Exp. Biol.*, **18**, 265-281.

WOLPERT, L. (1969). Positional information and the spatial pattern of cellular differentiation. *J. theor. Biol.*, **25**, 1-47.

WOLPERT, L. (1972). Positional information and pattern formation. *Curr. Topics Devl. Biol.*, **6**, 183-224.

YAJIMA, H. (1960). Studies on embryonic determination of the harlequin fly, *Chironomus dorsalis*. I. Effects of centrifugation and of its combination with constriction and puncturing. *J. Embryol. exp. Morph.*, 8 (Part 2), 198-215.

YAJIMA, H. (1964). Studies on embryonic determination of the harlequin fly, *Chironomus dorsalis*. II. Effects of partial irradiation of the egg by ultraviolet light. *J. Embryol. exp. Morph.*, 12 (Part 1), 89-100.

YAJIMA, H. (1970). Study of the development of the internal organs of the double malformations of *Chironomus dorsalis* by fixed and sectioned materials. *J. Embryol. exp. Morph.*, **24**, 287-303.

YUND, M. A. & FRISTROM, J. W. (1975). Uptake and binding of ß-ecdysone in imaginal discs of *Drosophila melanogaster. Devl. Biol.*, **43**, 287-298.

ZALOKAR, M. (1971). Transplantation of nuclei in *Drosophila melanogaster Proc. natn. Acad. Sci. USA*, **68**, 1539-1541.

ZALOKAR, M. (1973). Transplantation of nuclei into the polar plasm of *Drosophila* eggs. *Devl. Biol.*, **32**, 189-193.

2 • Morphogenetic movements in insect embryogenesis

KLAUS SANDER

Biologisches Institut I (Zoologie),
Katharinenstr. 20, D 78 Freiburg

I. INTRODUCTION

During embryogenesis, insects as most other animals proceed through successive steps of development which superimpose new levels of structural complexity on those established previously. Many such steps embody movements of pre-existing components relative to each other. These are called morphogenetic movements since they more or less directly shape the animal's body. The classical morphogenetic movements of vertebrates such as gastrulation, neurulation, and the formation of embryonic covers, all have their counterparts in insect development. Yet for technical reasons they are much more difficult to study there. Consequently, the morphogenetic movements analysed most intensely in insects are those peculiar to this group, for instance energid migration and blastokinesis; but even with these, present knowledge is far from satisfactory. This article is intended to review relevant research at both the descriptive and the experimental levels. For general background and earlier references, the reader is referred to the recent monographs and reviews by Anderson 1972, Counce 1961, 1972, Garrod 1973, Krause & Sander 1962, Sander 1976, and Trinkaus 1969. A list of the research films shown during the lecture on which this article is based, and of other recent films illustrating morphogenetic movements in insects, will be found at the end of this chapter.

II. AN OUTLINE OF INSECT EMBRYOGENESIS

In insects, the transformation of the fertilized egg cell into a spheroid epithelium comparable to a blastula is rather aberrant (see Wolf 1969, Fullilove & Jacobson 1971). Subdivision of the large and yolky egg cell into daughter cells is delayed until a huge number of daughter nuclei have been produced from the zygote nucleus by a succession of mitotic divisions (*superficial cleavage*). The 'cleavage' nuclei and the surrounding regions of yolk-free cytoplasm which spread through the egg cell are called *cleavage*

*The author is greatly indebted to Dr H. Vollmar, Freiburg, and to Professor G. Krause and Dr R. Wolf, Würzburg, for permission to use their time-lapse films, and figures based on these. Research by the author and his collaborators was supported by grants from the Deutsche Forschungsgemeinschaft, SFB 46.

energids (Fig. 2. 1a). When most energids have become lodged near the surface in rather uniform distribution, infoldings from the egg cell's boundary membrane cut in between the nuclei and separate these and the adjacent portions of cytoplasm from each other and from the central, more yolky part then called the *yolk system*. The latter will become subdivided into large *yolk cells* by *yolk cleavage* much later, if at all.

The superficial layer of cells thus formed is called the *blastoderm*. Soon its cells become distributed unevenly (Fig. 2.1b). This leads to segregation of the blastoderm into the *germ anlage* or embryonic primordium proper (Fig. 2.1c), and the *extraembryonic blastoderm* or prospective embryonic covers, where the cells are less crowded. Differential distribution of blastoderm cells is frequently initiated, and in part accomplished, by movements in the *ooplasm* (egg cytoplasm) which may start much earlier in development.

The series of transformations leading from germ anlage to *germ band* include *gastrulation,* formation of the *embryonic covers,* and *extension* and *metameric segmentation* of the germ band (Fig. 2.1c-e). They are followed by minor movements such as infolding of tracheal pits, fore and hind gut, salivary ducts etc. The germ band represents essentially only the ventral structures of the future body.

The dorsal parts of the larva become established from the lateral margins of the germ band which grow out in dorsal direction around the remnants of the yolk system. They finally meet and fuse in the dorsal midline, and thereby complete the process known as *dorsal closure*. Usually, this process is preceded by changes concerning the embryonic covers. These are best characterized as reversal of the folding and fusing processes of blastodermal epithelia which led to establishment of the *amniotic cavity* (Fig. 2.1d, e). The result is a plain layer of flattened cells provisionally serving to enclose those regions of the yolk system which are not covered by the germ band (see Fig. 2.8b). Dorsal closure occurs roughly halfway between oviposition and hatching. The remaining period of embryonic development is mainly devoted to functional specialization of cells and tissues (*histological differentiation*).

Between germ anlage stage and dorsal closure, the embryo in most hemimetabolans suffers some dramatic changes of position subsumed under the term *blastokinesis*. The tail end of germ anlage or early germ band thereby bends dorsally and starts moving in anterior direction, with the remainder of the germ band (and the prospective amnion) following suit (*anatrepsis,* see Figs. 2.4-6). The resulting reversal of antero-posterior orientation becomes abolished shortly before dorsal closure when the more mature germ band retraces the route it took earlier (*katatrepsis*). Before or during this process, the germ band may undergo *rotation* or temporary torsion with reference to the longitutinal axis, a type of movement observed also in some species lacking anatrepsis and katatrepsis (*Smittia,* Kalthoff & Sander 1968, Kalthoff 1975).

Dorsal closure is the last gross morphogenetic movement during embryogenesis. Yet a different type of movement, less conspicuous than the epithelial movements observed from the blastoderm stage to dorsal closure, may continue far into the remaining stages of embryonic development. This is *migration of individual cells or groups of cells.* As in vertebrates, where this type of migration has been studied extensively (see Trinkaus 1969), the migrating cells must be guided by appropriate signals. Consequently, the phenomena of cell guidance and cell affinity must exist in insects, too, although not much studied so far.

With individual insect species, innumerable variations become superimposed on the basic traits of embryogenesis as outlined here. From this multitude of phenomena, some

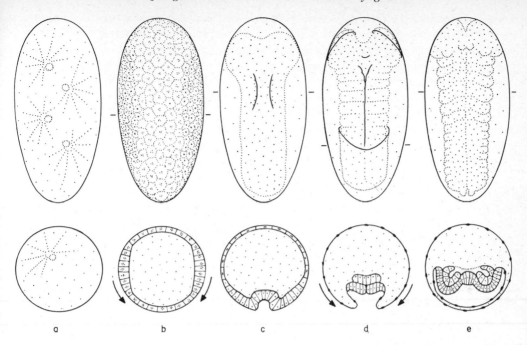

FIG. 2.1. Steps in the early embryogenesis of insects. Top row: Ventral view of egg, anterior end up. Bottom row: diagrammatic cross sections at the levels indicated by bars in top row. (a) Multiplication and migration of nuclei within the ooplasm ('intravitelline cleavage'). (b) Cellularization of the superficial part of the ooplasm. The resulting blastoderm initially consists of uniform cells but soon regional differences in cell density and shape indicate segregation into germ anlage and prospective embryonic covers. The arrows indicate shifting of lateral primordia to produce the germ anlage proper (see (c) and Fig. 2.2). (c) The prospective mesoderm starts to invaginate along the midline of the germ anlage (gastrulation). (d) Germ band after gastrulation, with segment borders (dotted) and amniotic folds forming. The folds shown over head lobes (top) and abdomen approach each other (see arrows at cross section) and finally fuse, thereby closing the amniotic cavity (see (e)). (e) Advanced germ band stage, with appendage buds, transient coelom anlagen, and amniotic cavity (below ventral face of germ band in cross section, see also Fig. 2.8). (Modified from various authors.)

general rules have emerged (Krause 1939, Anderson 1972; see Sander 1976). These cannot be considered here. It is, however, important to note that the examples discussed in the following chapters are not representative of all pterygote insects, and not at all of the Apterygota.

III. MORPHOGENETIC MOVEMENTS PROGRAMMED IN THE EGG CYTOPLASM

The insect egg cell is a highly dynamic structure despite the apparently rather constant shape enforced on it by the egg shell. This has been known in some species for a long time, and recent time-lapse observations have revealed unexpectedly strong movements in several other species. Circumstantial evidence indicates that many movements which occur between oviposition and the germ band stage become programmed much earlier, that is during oogenesis, by proper arrangement in the ooplasm of contractile or sliding molecules, or of structures which subsequently orient these molecules. The capability of the egg cell for local or general contraction is evident from such phenomena as the 'activation reaction' in *Leptinotarsa decemlineata* Say (Haget 1969), the wholesale contraction seen in many species before or during cleavage (and sometimes even in unfertilized eggs, see Counce 1972), and the 'twitching' reaction observed in several species when the egg is approached with a hot needle (Seidel 1929); the occurrence of actomyosin-like contractile complexes was demonstrated in the ooplasm of the cricket by Moser *et al.* (1970.) Of special interest are regional vectorial movements, particularly those involved in shaping the germ anlage (see Seidel 1966, Striebel 1960). Such movements have been studied with the aid of time-lapse films in the cricket *Acheta domesticus*. Sauer (1966, 1973) described meticulously the movements which can be observed under high power at the egg surface. Concomitant changes in the interior were revealed by differential vital staining (Sander & Vollmar 1967). Exposing the growing oocytes to a short pulse of trypan blue injected into the hemolymph of the mother, Vollmar (1972b) obtained eggs in which a discrete layer of yolk equidistant to the oocyte surface was stained; individually, the distance between the stained layer and surface was greater or smaller, reflecting exposure of the oocyte early or late in its development. By comparing changes in stain distribution during embryogenesis (Fig. 2.2), Vollmar was able to show that the stream of superficial ooplasm which carries the blastoderm nuclei towards the site of the prospective germ anlage reduces the thickness of the superficial layers in the anterior egg half (Fig. 2.2c). The loss of material there is compensated for by accumulation of internal material (See Fig. 2.2a, b), apparently propelled anteriorly by some kind of internal peristalsis which provides space for the superficial material moving backwards. The importance of such movements for embryogenesis is stressed by the fact that in the beetle *Atrachya menetriesi* Falderm, anomalies in the aggregation of blastoderm nuclei may lead to formation of multiple embryos (Miya *et al.* 1974).

Cytoplasmic streaming during early cleavage can be very intense (see Wolf & Krause 1971, Bruhns 1974) and may also lead to aggregation of cytoplasm in specific peripheral regions (Reith 1931). Since the genome is probably not very active during this period of rapid mitoses, the conclusion is that the cytoplasm must not only carry the programme, but also the molecules required for performing these movements. Evidence for storage in the ooplasm of relevant molecules needed later in development comes from 'morphogenetic movements' which occur in the absence of functional nuclei. An especially striking example is the excessive extension of the boundary membrane in blocked *Leptinotarsa* eggs at the time when in control eggs this membrane starts to extend and cut in between the prospective blastoderm nuclei (Schnetter 1965). 'Pseudo-cleavage' and formation of a 'pseudo-blastoderm', although clearly differing from the corresponding processes occurring in the presence of functional nuclei, reveal a considerable potential of the ooplasm for defined movements, too (see Schnetter 1965). At least part of this potential should be utilized in normal cleavage also (see below). The coordinated release of such cytoplasmic movements, on the other hand, may depend to a considerable degree not only on the physical presence (Wolf 1969), but also on the physiological activities of nuclei, as evidenced in *Drosophila* by the studies of Kinsey (1967) on development of interspecies hybrids.

IV. MIGRATION OF CLEAVAGE ENERGIDS

Distribution of cleavage energids through the egg cell looks like a random process in some species and stages, while in others at least the crowd of energids as a whole seems to obey rather strict laws. In either case we may note the capacity of energids to move

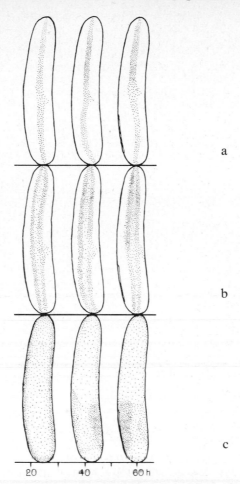

FIG. 2.2. Displacement of trypan blue stained yolk globules (dotted) in cricket eggs during formation of the germ anlage; left side views. Superficial stain (bottom row) becomes concentrated in the posterior egg half, at first dorsolaterally, and then underneath the ventral germ anlage. These changes in stain distribution reflect cytoplasmic streaming involved in shaping the germ anlage. Stain further inside the egg cell (middle and top rows) reveals compensatory shifting of internal material towards the anterior. The stain left in the posterior half moves towards the dorsal side when the ventral germ anlage forms. Time scale refers to hours after oviposition at 23° C. (From Vollmar 1972b.)

over large distances, and their tendency to maintain equal distances between each other and thereby to disperse evenly over a given volume or area. Cytoplasmic streaming, ameboid movements of the nuclei themselves, and the mitotic apparatus all have been invoked as causing energid movements. For discussion of these ideas we refer the reader to the reviews quoted in Section I, and turn instead to a single system analysed recently with considerable ingenuity and success.

In the tiny egg of the gall midge *Wachtliella persicariae* L. the cleavage energids are marked by orange pigmentation so that their location can easily be recognized. Wolf (1973, 1975) projected time-lapse films of cleavage stages on a screen split by a narrow longitudinal cleft; behind this, a drum covered with photosensitive recording paper was

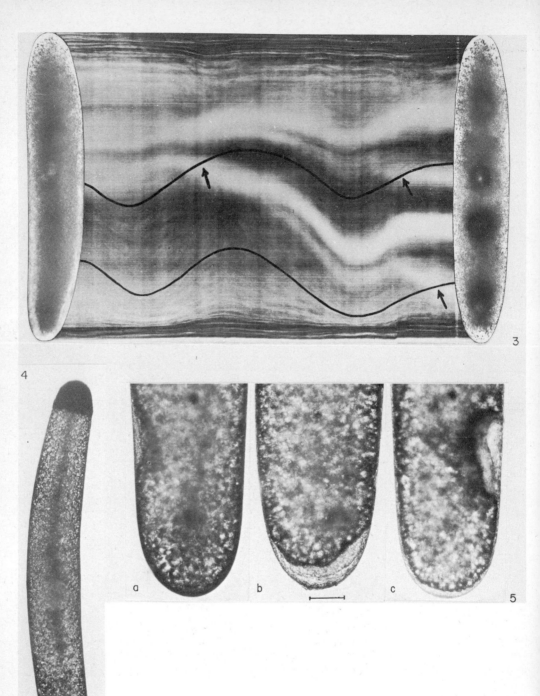

slowly turned. He thus recorded kymographically the longitudinal components of energid migration, and concomitant ooplasmic movements (Fig. 2.3). His technique revealed strikingly that at times the energids move in phase with slow oscillatory movements of the cytoplasm while at other times they do not (arrows in Fig. 2.3). In the latter case the nuclei are apparently being pulled through the cytoplasm by a special organelle derived from the aster of the mitotic apparatus, called the 'migration aster' (Wolf 1973). Its microtubules extend over great distances and may temporarily attach to the oocyte periphery. The locomotory activity of the migration aster, which was proven by several types of experiment, is not yet fully explained. However, time-lapse films of flattened eggs under modified Nomarski optics show small yolk particles being pulled along the microtubules towards the centre of the aster. Some force must therefore act in this direction along the 'rays' of the aster, and the direction of movement of the whole structure may depend on where the longest 'rays' form (Wolf 1973). This is usually the direction away from neighbouring asters, probably because formation of microtubules involves competition for precursor molecules. This would explain the mutual 'repulsion' so strikingly evident in energid movements.

A somewhat different mechanism has been postulated for energid movement in damsel flies. Here, energids appear to be pulled by contractile cytoplasmic strands which become established successively and insert in the egg cell's surface (Hujer 1975).

V. GASTRULATION, EXTENSION AND SEGMENTATION OF GERM BAND, AND FORMATION OF EMBRYONIC COVERS

As pointed out in the introduction, no experimental or ultrastructural investigations comparable to those on vertebrate gastrulation and neurulation have been published so far. It is probably safe to assume that the formation of a typical gastrulation furrow (primitive groove) as observed for example in *Drosophila* must, at the ultrastructural level, involve some of the phenomena described in gastrulation and particularly neurulation of amphibians (see Burnside 1973, Schroeder 1973). For the honey bee, in which the prospective mesoderm is being overgrown by ectoderm rather than folded in, DuPraw (1965) has presented evidence in favour of ameboid movement of the marginal cells which might serve to pull the ectoderm over the mesoderm—a process reminiscent of blastodisc growth in vertebrates (see Trinkaus 1969).

Gastrulation is accompanied or followed by a considerable longitudinal stretching of the incipient germ band. This *'germ band extension'* according to circumstantial evidence, must be due to reshuffling of cells rather than mitotic growth. Although clearly

FIG. 2.3. Kymographic record of movements of marker particles in the ooplasm and of the cleavage nuclei in the gall midge *Wachtliella* from the zygote to the 4-cell stage. The cleavage nuclei are surrounded by pigmented cytoplasm (see inset at the right) which shows as broad white bands on the record. Black curves trace oscillations of ooplasm, arrows indicate phases where nuclei clearly move opposite to ooplasm. Period recorded is 40 min at 23° C, egg length is ca. 400 μm. (From Wolf 1975.)

FIG. 2.4. Egg of the cricket *Oecanthus pellucens* (Scop.) showing the tiny germ anlage at the ventral (convex) egg side (see bar). Length of egg ca. 3 mm. (From Baader 1968.)

FIG. 2.5. Anatrepsis in the cricket *Oecanthus pellucens* (Scop.). (a) Germ anlage as in Fig. 4, age 95 h at room temperature. (b) Germ anlage passes posterior egg pole, age 105 h. (c) Germ anlage located on dorsal egg side at the onset of hibernation (diapause), age 150 h. Calibration bar ca. 0.1 mm. (From Baader 1968.)

a multicellular event (which in the silk worm may occur even in the absence of yolk system and egg shell, see below), the process may in *Drosophila* be guided by cytoplasmic streaming in the underlying yolk system. This view is based on eggs which, due to a genetic defect in the mother, are unable to form blastodermal cell boundaries. The multinucleate egg cell then displays streaming movements which carry the prospective germ cells forward from the posterior egg pole, as does germ band extension in normal development (Rice & Garen 1975).

The mechanisms which shape segment borders and thus cause segmentation of the germ band are also largely unknown. Careful study of mutants which cause failure of this process might yield some relevant information, as should other mutants with respect to gastrulation (see Counce 1972).

The movements shaping the germ band may not be programmed in a direct way during oogenesis, yet their proper execution in most instances appears to depend upon the presence of a rather intact yolk system and/or egg shell (see Haget 1953, Davis *et al.* 1968). However, in the silk worm *Bombyx mori* L., the isolated early germ anlage will become transformed *in vitro* into a typically segmented germ band when supported by a bit of lens paper (Krause & Krause 1964). Starting as a saddle-shaped structure about twice as broad as long it changes within 1–2 days into a typically elongated, narrow germ band. This profound remodelling of shape starting from a single-layered isolated epithelium is amazing to watch in a time-lapse film. The fact that attempts to cultivate the isolated germ anlage in other insect species have failed so far (see Koch 1964, Davis *et al.* 1968) may be indicative of the rather peculiar type of early development represented by the lepidopterans (see Anderson 1972).

Head involution leading to the 'acephalic' maggot of higher dipterans is a specialized and rather dramatic movement subsequent to germ band segmentation (see e.g. Ede & Counce 1956, Schoeller 1964). It is easily disturbed by mutation or experimental interference but its physiology has not yet been analysed in any detail. This is also true for formation of the embryonic covers, *amnion* and *serosa*. The ways by which these are formed in different groups differ as much as does gastrulation (see Anderson 1972). In hemimetabolans, formation of the amniotic cavity frequently is an integrated part of anatrepsis (see below, Fig. 2.6). It may be interesting to note that failure of the embryonic covers to enclose the germ band does not visibly affect morphogenesis in leaf hoppers (where isolated posterior egg parts often lack anatrepsis, see Sander 1959), and in the 'double abdomen' anomaly of chironomids (Kalthoff & Sander 1968); however, the absence of a continuous serosal envelope may render the embryo unable to hatch (see Section IX).

VI. BLASTOKINESIS: ANATREPSIS AND KATATREPSIS

Blastokinesis as described in section II occurs in most hemimetabolans. Anatrepsis is frequently accompanied by a considerable stretching of the germ band and may therefore phylogenetically be related to germ band extension as observed in many holometabolans, where the posterior tip of abdomen is carried far up the dorsal side during germ band extension (see e.g. Went 1972). In some beetles, germ bands defective from anterior cautery may indeed perform a perfect anatrepsis of the immersion type (see below) (Jura 1957, Schnetter 1965).

In species with an inconspicuous germ anlage, anatrepsis may easily be overlooked when it takes place without germ band extension. This happened probably in the case of

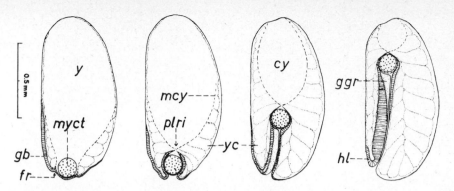

FIG. 2.6. Yolk cleavage and anatrepsis in the leaf hopper *Pyrilla* as reconstructed from sectioned material. For explanation, see text.

cy	uncleaved core of yolk system
fr	furrow
ggr	gastrulation groove in longitudinal section
gb	germ band
mcy	'core membrane'
myct	globular aggregate of microbial symbionts
plri	prominent constriction of core membrane
y	yolk system
yc	yolk cells

(From Sander 1956.)

Oecanthus niveus. This species is said to form the germ anlage with head lobes pointing backwards in the egg, that is to lack anatrepsis (see Warne 1972). However, the tiny germ anlage of the closely related *Oecanthus pellucens* (Scop.) was definitely shown to acquire this position by an extensive anatrepsis prior to hibernation (Baader 1968) (Fig. 2.4, 2.5).

While complete anatrepsis always leads to the same result, that is reversal of position of the embryonic rudiment (see Section II), the ways and mechanisms by which this is achieved may differ considerably. Morphologically, a distinction can be made between species where the posterior tip of germ anlage moves along the serosa (superficial type, e.g. crickets; see Fig. 2.4, 2.5) and species there it moves within the yolk system (immersion type, most hemimetabolans; see Fig. 2.5). In the former case, movement may be related to activities of the most posterior germ anlage cells which appear to 'crawl' on the inner face of the serosa, and drag along the germ band as well as some adjacent yolk cells. The yolk system seems to assist in this movement only as long as the tip of germ anlage moves through the posterior curvature of egg shell and serosa; during this period, pulsating posterior movements in the yolk system may serve to ensure contact between tip and serosa (Vollmar 1972a). With the immersion type of anatrepsis, which requires only a few hours, the invaginating tube consisting of germ band plus amnion must be moved essentially by structures in the yolk system. One possible mechanism has been suggested independently by Sander (1956, 1968a) and Baudisch (1958), based on observations in leaf hoppers and in *Pediculus vestimenti*, De Geer, respectively. In these species, yolk cleavage is very prominent. The yolk cells are huge polygonal columns cut from the yolk system by cell boundaries advancing inward from its surface (Fig. 2.6). The boundaries are apparently being pulled step by step into the

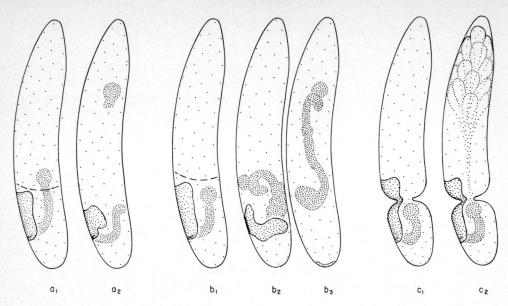

FIG. 2.7. Experiments demonstrating the role of the yolk system in anatrepsis in the leaf hopper *Euscelis*. (a) When yolk system and germ band were separated within the egg shell by squeezing (dashed line in a_1), only the 'posterior' germ band fragment continued to move anteriorly (a_2) (44 out of 44 cases). (b) When the yolk system in front of the germ band was separated (dashed line in b_1), the germ band failed to continue anatrepsis in 18 out of 25 cases (b_2). In 7 cases anatrepsis was resumed after some time so that the germ band reached its normal position (b_3). This shows that anatrepsis is possible despite temporary separation of the yolk system. (c) If anatrepsis is blocked by a bottle neck (incomplete ligature) through which the symbiont mass at the posterior tip of the germ band cannot pass, the yolk cells in the anterior egg region become extremely extended in posterior direction (c_2) and finally are pulled backward while others take up the anteriormost position. This demonstrates longitudinal contraction of structures linking these yolk cells to the tip of the germ anlage. Length of egg ca. 1.1 mm. (After Sander 1968a).

yolky cytoplasm. This is accomplished by a contractile apparatus which in *Euscelis plebejus* Fall. becomes visible in transmitted light as a dark lamella separating the yolk cells from the as yet uncleaved central parts of the yolk system (Sander 1968a). In paraffin sections of eggs of *Pyrilla perpusilla* Walker, a fibrillar layer of cytoplasm is found in the same position. This giant organelle was called 'core membrane' (Sander 1956) since it surrounds the as yet undivided core of the yolk system. Its 3-dimensional shape for most of the time is that of a conical funnel because yolk cleavage starts at the posterior end and gradually spreads in anterior direction (Fig. 2.6a-c). Cytological evidence indicates that the core membrane does not only contract concentrically towards the main egg axis, but also in longitudinal direction. Since the posterior end of the core membrane attaches to the tip of germ anlage, while anteriorly it is anchored in the yolk system and/or serosa (see Sander 1968a), this longitudinal component of contraction must pull the germ band in anterior direction through the cleaving yolks system (Fig. 2.6). Whatever the physiological and ultrastructural details of this mechanism may be, the fact that the germ band is being pulled by forces attaching to its posterior tip was clearly established by experiment (Sander 1968a) (Fig. 2.7).

Anatrepsis is accompanied by yolk cleavage in many other insects. Yet in dragonflies, where its spatio-temporal course (Ando 1962) is very similar to that observed in leaf hoppers and in *Pediculus,* yolk cleavage may be less involved in causing the anatrepsis movement (Vollmar, unpublished data; see also Schanz 1965, Bergmann-Schanz 1970).

Katatrepsis was ascribed by one of the earliest observers (and by many since) to contractions of the serosa which were to pull and/or press the germ band out of the yolk system (Brandt 1869 pp. 15, 28, 29; he called the serosa 'parietales Blatt'). A different mechanism was proposed by Slifer (1932). On the basis of katatrepsis being accomplished halfway even if the embryonic covers failed to rupture and contract, she ascribed the main locomotory effect to undulations of the epithelia which laterally connect germ band and amnion. In the cricket, however, the function of these undulations appears to be subsidiary at best (Mahr 1961; Vollmar, unpublished time-lapse observation). In many other forms, no undulations were observed at all (e.g. leaf hoppers, dragonflies). In these, the main moving force must surely be provided by the contracting serosa.

VII. DORSAL CLOSURE

Nothing is known concerning the forces which cause the lateral margins of the fully developed germ band to extend so as to close the body dorsally (Fig. 2.8a-c). Looking at living embryos and time-lapse films one would guess at a combination of growth, cell rearrangement, cell deformation, and perhaps pulling activities of the contracting embryonic covers. The subsequent incorporation of the conspicuous anterior yolk mass and the concomitant stretching of the larval body in the cricket, should mainly be due to contraction of the serosal cells, which become extremely columnar during this period.

Some hints at the causes of dorsal closure are provided by 'everted' embryos. These result from suppression of katatrepsis in dragonflies (Ando 1955) and leaf hoppers (Sander 1959, 1960). In the absence of katatrepsis the amniotic cavity remains intact and, in these species, becomes lined by the flanks of the germ band. These at the time of dorsal closure grow in ventral instead of dorsal direction, and face the lumen of the cavity with their outer sides which produce the cuticle. Legs and bristles then grow into the amniotic cavity, while the internal organs 'dangle' outside in the space originally occupied by the yolk system (Fig. 2.8d). This type of malformation indicates active extension of the body flanks rather than contraction of embryonic covers as the cause of dorsal closure. Active extension must also occur in the cricket where dorsal closure can be accomplished inside the intact serosa when katatrepsis is prevented by ligature (Sander, unpublished observations). Dorsal closure within the intact serosa was also observed in grass hopper eggs after spontaneous failure of katatrepsis (Slifer 1932), and it is the normal event in some beetles and in the Lepidoptera (see Anderson 1972).

VIII! CELL MIGRATION AND CELL AFFINITY

In vertebrates, migration of individual cells or cell groups over considerable distances is evident in primary germ cells and in the cells deriving from the neural crest (see Trinkaus 1969). Migration to spatially restricted target regions must be guided by appropriate signals if not by chance, and cells arriving at their proper location must be trapped there by cell affinity. These principles are likely to be employed by insects, too. For instance, cell guidance and cell affinity are apparently involved in formation of the mid-gut around the remnants of the yolk after dorsal closure, a process which starts from anterior and posterior primordia in most insects. But the movement itself in this

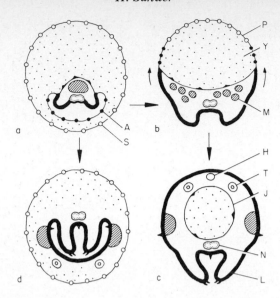

FIG. 2.8. Dorsal closure (a-c) and formation of 'everted' embryo (d). In this malformation, the body flanks instead of growing around the remaining yolk (see arrows in b) extend along the persisting amnion and fuse underneath the ventral side of the germ band. Highly diagrammatical cross sections, based on observations in the leaf hopper *Euscelis*. The bold lines represent the body wall in the different stages of its development. For explanation see text.

A   amnion
H   heart
J   prospective intestine
L   leg
M   mycetocytes (actually located far behind the leg-bearing region shown)
N   nerve chain
P   provisional dorsal closure consisting of retracted amnion and serosa
S   serosa
T   Malpighian tubules
Y   yolk

case is probably epithelial outgrowth. Examples of migration of individual cells or cell groups could probably be found in the primary germ cells of many species for which, however, only descriptive evidence is available so far.

A clear-cut experimental result providing evidence for cell migration and cell affinity is illustrated diagrammatically in Fig. 2.7. It involves specific cell populations which harbour intracellular symbionts. Some insects contain several such cell types, and these appear to develop most astonishing affinities to their respective symbionts during embryogenesis (see Müller 1940, Sander 1968b). In the advanced germ band stage of the leaf hopper *Euscelis,* two types of such cells each harbouring a different type of symbiont are located in a single cluster (hatched in Fig. 2.7a) at the dorsal face of the germ band. After katatrepsis, cells of both types move laterally and aggregate on either side to form a compound mycetome attached to the lateral body wall (Fig. 2.8b, c) (Sander 1959, 1968b, Körner 1969). In everted embryos, the cells as a rule aggregate on the same regions of the body wall (Fig. 2.8d) (Sander 1959). Considering the scrambled-up topography of these embryos, cell affinity must indeed act very efficiently to achieve this result.

IX. EXTRAEMBRYONIC HATCHING DEVICES

For most morphogenetic movements in insect embryos it is easy to name an indispensable function, although each may serve further and less obvious purposes. With formation of embryonic covers and with blastokinesis matters are different, as is evident from the multitude of speculations offered in the literature. It may therefore be worthwhile to point out that the serosa serves a vital function in insect eggs which are deposited inside living plants and produce larvae with specialized mouth parts unsuitable for gnawing. This function is secretion of a serosal cuticle next to the inner face of the egg shell. In dragonflies and hemipterans with endophytic oviposition, the serosal cuticle is indispensible for hatching (Balfour-Browne 1909, Müller 1951, Ch. Davis 1961). When the embryo is ready to hatch, pressure inside this cuticle raises until the egg shell bursts at the anterior end. The serosal cuticle then becomes inflated so as to bulge out anteriorly (Fig. 2.9), and thereby penetrates and re-opens the slot in the plant tissues through which the egg was inserted by the ovipositing female. It is only then that the larva starts to swell and propel itself into the hatching channel thus provided. Finally, the serosal cuticle bursts and the larva (or prolarva in some damsel flies) emerges from the host plant by wriggling movements.

X. SUMMARY AND OUTLOOK

Besides the types of morphogenetic movement found in vertebrates—viz. active deformation of epithelia, rearrangement of cells within epithelia, ameboid movements of cells at the leading margin of migrating or extending epithelia, and migration of single cells or cell groups—insects employ some peculiar modes of movement which are linked to superficial cleavage and to the persistence of a large yolk system besides the actual embryonic primordium until late in development (Section II). These are: (1) Movement of cleavage nuclei by special locomotory cell organelles derived from the asters of the mitotic spindle (Section IV). (2) Movement of nuclei, cells or complete epithelia by cytoplasmic streaming in the adjacent yolk system (Sections III and V). (3) Transportation of the entire embryonic primordium by a giant locomotory organelle in the yolk system (Section VI). (4) Transportation of the well advanced embryo by contraction of extraembryonic epithelia (Section VI). Movements no. 2 to 4 are more pronounced in lower insects; in the higher dipterans they are absent altogether, or replaced by the more 'conventional' types of morphogenetic movement mentioned above for vertebrates.

The experimental studies published so far on morphogenetic movements in insect embryogenesis all employed species in which the movement studied is particularly evident. These species were also selected because of certain technical advantages not found in other forms. Therefore, our knowledge concerning the mechanisms of morphogenetic movements in insects, apart from being rather rudimentary, may also be far from representative. Considering the amazing differences in kind and degree which exist with nearly all steps of embryogenesis between different groups and species of insects, what needs to be done is classification of morphogenetic movements, on a descriptive basis but with physiological questions in mind, and subsequent detailed investigation of representative examples with modern techniques.

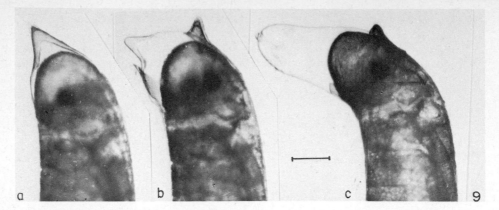

FIG. 2.9. Hatching in the damsel fly *Calopteryx virgo* (L.). a. Anterior 4/10 of egg prior to the onset of hatching. Due to rotation during katatrepsis, the ventral side of the embryo (at the right) faces the dorsal side of the egg shell. b. The egg shell has burst and the serosal cuticle bulges through the cleft. c. The serosal cuticle has become fully inflated and the embryo starts to push its head into the hatching channel (see text). Time required under laboratory conditions for hatching is 4-6 h. Calibration bar ca. 0.1 mm.

DISCUSSION

Gurdon: You gave us a very nice illustration of the extensive movement of cell layers. Are these movements necessary for the normal development of the embryo, and in particular, for cells to differentiate as they normally would? Would I be right in suspecting that they are not essential for differentiation?

Sander: It depends upon which movements you are thinking of. The most striking movement of anatrepsis and katatrepsis of the germ band are not necessary for the formation of the typical body pattern. Indeed, nobody knows what these movements are good for. With respect to gastrulation, I would not share your suspicion, because it has been shown in 2 rather different insect species that the mesoderm, the inner layer, is being programmed in respect to its organ pattern by regional inductive influences from the ectoderm. So if invagination did not occur, the middle plate would perhaps produce mesodermal structures, but it's very likely that it would not produce them in the typical spatial pattern.

Lawrence: I would like to ask you to describe again how the mechanism of nuclear separation works during cleavage.

Sander: What you see is mitotic spindles, each with an aster which becomes attached to the nucleus and extends rapidly a long way into the cytoplasm. If you separate the nucleus from the aster mechanically, and this has been done by Wolf, the nucleus remains where it was and the astor moves. So it is quite clear that the nucleus is being pulled by the aster. Then if you analyse these films very carefully, you see movement of the yolk particles relative to the rays of the aster (which of course probably consists of microtubules). The movements take the form of short centripetal excursions followed by a sudden rebound. There are also movements over quite a long distance. You may assume that the surface of the astral ray is a sort of conveyor belt, which produces a shearing force on particles anchored elastically in the ooplasm. Now the rays differ in length, and note that they are longest in the direction mostly away from other asters. Supposing that per unit length of ray you get a constant amount of force, the resultant force will then be in the direction of the longest rays, and will pull the aster and nucleus in that direction. This is a model that has been evolved essentially by Wolf.

Dover: What determines the orientation of the spindle in the beginning?

Sander: I can only remind you of that last film showing the reconstitution of stratified *Smittia* eggs. It is simply a marvel but everything becomes rearranged and in the end you get a normal embryo. This means there must be very definite signals in the cytoplasm which guide these movements.

Lawrence: But surely the first spindle isn't orientated in any particular direction?

Dover: But the asters must position themselves outside the nucleus in the first place.

Sander: This is done during mitosis, because the asters derive from the mitotic asters, and those by definition are at the opposite ends of the mitotic figure.

Schneiderman: And the axis of the first mitosis, that is random.

Wolpert: Are you quite sure it is pulling and not pushing? Could it be extension of the astral rays which pushes the asters to the opposite side?

Sander: There are several arguments against that, which I cannot really go into at the moment.

APPENDIX: TIME-LAPSE FILMS ON INSECT EMBRYOGENESIS

The following papers (see references) include results based on time-lapse films.
Bergmann-Schanz 1970 (publ. IWF). Bruhns 1974, DuPraw 1965 (publ.), Ede & Counce 1956 (publ.), Fullilove & Jacobson 1971, Hujer 1975, Kalthoff 1975 (publ. IWF), Kinsey 1967, Krause & Krause 1964, Sauer 1966, 1973 (publ. IWF), Schanz 1965, Striebel 1960. Vollmar 1972a, 1972b, Went 1972, Wolf 1969, 1973, 1975 (publ. IWF). Published films are marked (publ.). IWF indicates that films by the respective authors are available from the Institut für den Wissenschaftlichen Film. Nonnenstieg 72, *D 34 Göttingen,* Federal Republic of Germany.

At the symposium, the following time-lapse scenes were shown:

Embryonic development of *Drosophila* (Ede & Counce)

Normal development and formation of 'double abdomen' in *Smittia* (Kalthoff)

Energid migration in *Wachtliella* (Wolf)

Energid migration in *Gryllus bimaculatus* (Vollmar)

Superficial cleavage mitoses in *G. bimaculatus* (Vollmar)

Formation of germ anlage in *Acheta domesticus* after vital staining (Vollmar)

Gastrulation and amniotic fold movement in *Leptinotarsa* (Vollmar)

In vitro- transformation of *Bombyx* germ anlage into germ band (Krause & Krause)

Antrepsis in *Acheta* and *G. bimaculatus* (Vollmar)

Antrepsis in *Euscelis* (Sander)

Katatrepsis in *G. bimaculatus* (Vollmar)

Dorsal closure in *G. bimaculatus* (Vollmar)

Development of *Smittia* egg stratified by centrifugation (Vollmar/Kalthoff)

REFERENCES

ANDERSON, D. T. (1972a). The Development of Hemimetabolous Insects. In *Developmental Systems: Insects* Vol. I, S. J. Counce & C. H. Waddington, eds., pp. 95-163, Academic Press, London and New York.

ANDERSON, D. T. (1972b). The Development of Holometabolous Insects. In *Developmental Systems: Insects* S. J. Counce & C. H. Waddington, eds., Vol. I, pp. 165-242, Academic Press, London and New York.

ANDO, H. (1955). Everted embryos of dragónflies produced by ligation. *Sci. Rep. Tokyo Bunrika Daig.*, Sect. B 8 **119**, 65.

ANDO, H. (1962). The Comparative Embryology of Odonata with Special Reference to a Relict Dragonfly *Epiophlebia superstes*, Selys. *Jap. Soc. for the Promotion of Science*, Tokyo.

BAADER, P. (1968). Entwicklungsgeschichte und Lebensweise der Blütengrille *Oecanthus pellucens* (Scop.). Zulassungsarbeit (thesis), Univ. Freiburg i. Br.

BALFOUR-BROWNE, F. (1909). The Life-History of the Agrionid Dragonfly. *Proc. Zool, Soc.* (1909 part I) London, 253-261.

BAUDISCH, K. (1958). Beiträge zur Zytologie und Embryologie einiger Insektensymbiosen. *Z. Morph. Ökol. Tiere*, **47**, 436-488.

BERGMANN-SCHANZ, G. (1970). Embryonalentwicklung der Libelle *Ischnura elegans*. Begleitveröffentlichung Filme D 928 & D 929, Inst. Wiss. Film, Göttingen.

BRANDT, A. (1869). Beiträge zur Entwicklungsgeschichte der Libelluliden und Hemipteren. *Mém. Acad. St Pétersbourg*, **13**, 1-33.

BRUHNS, E. (1974). Analyse der Ooplasmaströmungen und ihrer strukturellen Grundlagen während der Furchung bei *Pimpla turionellae* L. (Hymenoptera) I. Lichtmikroskopisch-anatomische Veränderungen in der Eiarchitektur koinzident mit Zeitrafferfilm-befunden. Wilhelm Roux Arch. *Entw Mech. Org.*, **174**, 55-89.

BURNSIDE, B. (1973). Microtubules and Microfilaments in Amphibian Neurulation. Amer. Zool. **13**, 989-1006.

COUNCE, S. J. (1961). The Analysis of Insect Embryogenesis. *Ann. Rev. Ent.*, **6**, 295-312.

COUNCE, S. J. (1972). The Causal Analysis of Insect Embryogenesis. In *Developmental Systems: Insects* Vol. II, S. J. Counce & C H. Waddington, eds., pp. 1-156. Academic Press, London and New York.

DAVIS, C. C.(1961). A Study of the Hatching Process in Aquatic Invertebrates II. Hatching in *Ranatra fusca* P. Beauvois (Hemiptera, Nepidae). *Trans. Am. Microscop. Soc.*, **80**, 230-234.

DAVIS, C. W. C., KRAUSE, J. & KRAUSE, G. (1968). Morphogenetic Movements and Segmentation of Posterior Egg Fragments in vitro *(Calliphora erythrocephala* Meig., Diptera). *Wilhelm Roux Arch. Entw Mech. Org.*, **161**, 209-240

DUPRAW, E. J. (1965): The organization of honey bee embryonic cells. I. Microtubules and amoeboid activity. *Devl. Biol.*, **12**, 53-71.

EDE, D. A., COUNCE, S. J. (1956). A cinematographic study of the embryology of *Drosophila melanogaster*. *Wilhelm Roux Arch. Entw Mech. Org.*, **148**, 402-415.

FULLILOVE, S. L., JACOBSON, A. G. (1971). Nuclear Elongation and Cytokinesis in *Drosophila montana*. *Devl. Biol.*, **26**, 560-577

GARROD, D. R. (1973). *Cellular Development*. Chapman and Hall Ltd, London.

HAGET, A. (1953). Analyse expérimentale des facteurs de la morphogenèse chez le coléoptère *Leptinotarsa*. *Bull. biol. Fr. Belg.*, **87**, 123-217.

HAGET, A. (1969). Quelques donnés sur la maturation et l'activation de l'oeuf du Doryphore *(Leptinotarsa decemlineata* Say.) *C.r. Acad. Sc. Paris*, **269**, 2128-2131.

HUJER, H. (1975). Dokumentation zur Funktionsstruktur der Energiden im Entwicklungsprozeß der Eier der Libellen *Platycnemis* und *Ischnura*. *Verh. dt. zool. Ges.*, **67**, 178-183.

JURA, C. (1957). Experimental Studies on the Embryonic Development of the *Melasoma populi* L. (Chrysomelidae, Coleoptera). *Zoologica Pol.*, **8**, 177-199.

KALTHOFF, K. (1975). *Smittia* spec. (Diptera)-Normale Embryonalentwicklung und Aberration des Segmentmusters nach UV-Bestrahlung. Begleitveröffentlichung Film E 2158/1974, Inst. Wiss. Film, Göttingen.

KALTHOFF, K., SANDER, K. (1968). Der Entwicklungsgang der Mißbildung 'Doppelabdomen' im partiell UV-bestrahlten Ei von *Smittia parthenogenetica* (Dipt., Chironomidae) *Wilhelm Roux Arch. Entw Mech. Org.*, **161**, 129-146.

KINSEY, J. D. (1967). Studies on an embryonic lethal hybrid in *Drosophila*. *J. Embryol. exp. Morph.*, **17**, 405-423.

KOCH, P. (1964). In vitro-Kultur und entwicklungsphysiologische Ergebnisse an Embryonen der

Stabheuschrecke *Carausius morosus* Br. *Wilhelm Roux Arch. Entw Mech. Org.,* 155, 459-593.

KÖRNER, K. H. (1969). Die embryonale Entwicklung der symbiontenführenden Organe von *Euscelis plebejus* Fall. (Homoptera-Cicadina). *Oecologica* (Berl.), 2, 319-346.

KRAUSE, G. (1939). Die Eitypen der Insekten. *Biol. Zbl.,* 59, 495-536.

KRAUSE, G. und KRAUSE, J. (1964). Schichtenbau und Segmentierung junger Keimanlagen von *Bombyx mori* L. (Lepidoptera) in vitro ohne Dottersystem. *Wilhelm Roux Arch. Entw Mech. Org.,* 155, 451-510.

KRAUSE, G., SANDER, K. (1962). Ooplasmatic Reaction Systems in Insect Embryogenesis. *Adv. Morphogenesis,* 2, 259-303.

MAHR, E. (1961). Bewegungssysteme in der Embryonalentwicklung von *Gryllus domesticus. Wilhelm Roux Arch. Entw Mech. Org.,* 152, 662-724.

MIYA, K., KOBAYASHI, Y. (1974). The embryonic development of *Atrachya menetriesi* Faldermann (Coleoptera, Chrysomelidae) II. Analysis of early development by ligation and low temperature treatment. *J. Fac. Agric. Iwate Univ.,* 12, 39-55.

MOSER, J. G., BODE, H. J., NÜNEMANN, H., COLLATZ, S., FELDHEGE, A. und HERZFELD, A. (1970). Differenzierung des Actomyosinsystems während der Morphogenese der Hausgrille, *Acheta domesticus* L. *Verh. dt. zool. Ges.,* 64, 56-60.

MÜLLER, H. J. (1940). Die Symbiose der Fulgoroiden (Homoptera Cicadina). *Zoologica* (Stuttgart), 36, Heft 98, 1-220.

MÜLLER, H. J. (1951). Über das Schlüpfen der Zikaden (Homoptera auchenorrhyncha) aus dem Ei. *Zoologica* (Stuttgart), 37, Heft 103, 1-41.

REITH, F. (1931). Versuche über die Determination der Keimanlage bei *Camponotus ligniperda. Z. wiss. Zool.,* 139, 664-734.

RICE, T. B., GAREN, A. (1975). Localized defects of blastoderm formation in maternal effect mutants of *Drosophila. Devl. Biol.,* 43, 277-286.

SANDER, K. (1956). The early embryology of *Pyrilla perpusilla* Walker (Homoptera), including some observations on the later development. Aligarh, M. U. Publ., Zool. Ser., *IV,* 1-61.

SANDER, K. (1959). Analyse des Ooplasmatischen Reaktionssystems von *Euscelis plebejus* Fall. (Cicadina) durch Isolieren und Kombinieren von Keimteilen. I. Die Differenzierungsleistungen vorderer und hinterer Eiteile. *Wilhelm Roux Arch. Entw Mech. Org.,* 151, 430-497.

SANDER, K. (1960). Analyse des ooplasmatischen Reaktionssystems von *Euscelis plebejus* Fall. (Cicadina) durch Isolieren und Kombinieren von Keimteilen. II. Die Differenzierungsleistungen nach Verlagern von Hinterpolmaterial. *Wilhelm Roux Arch. Entw Mech. Org.,* 151, 660-707.

SANDER, K. (1968a). Mechanismen der Keimeseinrollung (Anatrepsis) im Insekten-Ei. *Zool. Anz. Suppl.,* 31, 81-89.

SANDER, K. (1968b). Entwicklungsphysiologische Untersuchungen am embryonalen Mycetom von *Euscelis plebejus* F. (Homoptera, Cicadina). I. Ausschaltung und abnorme Kombination einzelner Komponenten des symbiontischen Systems. *Devl. Biol.* 17, 16-38.

SANDER, K. (1976). Specification of the basic body pattern in insect embryogenesis. *Adv. Insect Physiol. 12* (in press).

SANDER, K., VOLLMAR, H. (1967). Vital staining of insect eggs by incorporation of trypan blue. *Nature* (Lond.), 216, 174-175.

SAUER, H. W. (1966). Zeitraffer-Mikro-Film-Analyse embryonaler Differenzierungsphasen von *Gryllus domesticus. Z. Morph. Ökol. Tiere,* 56, 143-251.

SAUER, H. W. (1973). Entwicklungsvorgänge im Ei der Grille *Acheta domestica* (L.) Begleitveröffentlichung Film D 1118/1973, Inst. Wiss. Film, Göttingen.

SEIDEL, F. (1929). Untersuchungen über das Bildungsprinzip der Keimanlage im Ei der Libelle *Platycnemis pennipes*, I-IV. *Wilhelm Roux Arch. Entw Mech. Org.,* 119, 322-440.

SEIDEL, F. (1966). Das Eisystem der Insekten und die Dynamik seiner Aktivierung. *Zool. Anz. Suppl.,* 29, 166-187.

SLIFER, E. H. (1932). Insect development. III. Blastokinesis in the living grasshopper egg. *Biol. Zbl.,* 52, 223-229.

SCHANZ, G. (1965). Entwicklungsvorgänge im Ei der Libelle *Ischnura elegans* und Experimente zur Frage ihrer Aktivierung. Eine Mikro-Zeitraffer-Film-Analyse. Dissertation, Universität Marburg Lahn.

SCHNETTER, W. (1965). Experimente zur Analyse der morphogenetischen Funktion der Ooplasmabestandteile in der Embryonalentwicklung des Kartoffelkäfers *(Leptinotarsa decemlineata* Say.) *Wilhelm Roux Arch. Entw Mech. Org.,* 155, 637-692.

SCHOELLER, J. (1964). Recherches descriptives et expérimentales sur la céphalogenèse de *Calliphora erythrocephala* (Meigen), au cours des dévelopments embryonnaire et postembryonnaire. *Archs. Zool. exp. gén.,* 103, 1-216.

SCHROEDER, T. E. (1973). Cell constriction: contractile role of microfilaments in division and development. *Am. Zool.*, **13**, 949-960.

STRIEBEL, H. (1960). Zur Embryonalentwicklung der Termiten. *Acta trop.*, **17**, 193-260.

TRINKAUS, J. P. (1969). *Cells into Organs. The Forces that Shape the Embryo.* Prentice Hall, Englewood Cliffs/New Jersey.

VOLLMAR, H. (1972a). Die Einrollbewegung (Anatrepsis) des Keimstreifs im Ei von *Acheta domesticus* (Orthopteroidea, Gryllidae) *Wilhelm Roux Arch. Entw Mech. Org.*, **170**, 135-151.

VOLLMAR, H. (1972b). Frühembryonale Gestaltungsbewegungen im vitalgefärbten Dotter-Entoplasma-System intakter und fragmentierter Eier von *Acheta domesticus* L. (Orthopteroidea). *Wilhelm Roux Arch. Entw Mech. Org.*, **171**, 288-243.

WARNE, A. C. (1972). Embryonic development and the systematics of the Tettigoniidae (Orthoptera: Saltatoria). *Int. J. Insect Morphl. Embryol.* **1**, 267-287.

WENT, D. F. (1972). Zeitrafferfilmanalyse der Embryonalentwicklung in vitro der vivipar paedogenetischen Gallmücke *Heteropeza pygmaea. Wilhelm Roux Arch. Entw Mech. Org.*, **170**, 13-47.

WOLF, R. (1969). Kinematik und Feinstruktur plasmatischer Faktorenbereiche des Eies von *Wachtliella persicariae* L. (Diptera). I. Teil: Das Verhalten ooplasmatischer Teilsysteme im normalen Ei. *Wilhelm Roux Arch. Entw Mech. Org.*, **162**, 121-160.

WOLF, R. (1973). Kausalmechanismen der Kernbewegung und -teilung während der frühen Furchung im Ei der Gallmücke *(Wachtliella persicariae* L.) I. Kinematische Darstellung des 'Migrationsasters' wandernder Energiden und der Steuerung seiner Aktivität durch den Initialbereich der Furchung. *Wilhelm Roux Arch. Entw Mech. Org.*, **172**, 28-57.

WOLF, R. (1975). Ein neuartiger Migrationsmechanismus bei Furchungskernen auf der Basis des Astersystems. *Verh. dt. zool. Ges.*, **67**, 174-178.

WOLF, R., KRAUSE, G. (1971). Die Ooplasmabewegungen während der Furchung von *Pimpla turionellae* L. (Hymenoptera), eine Zeitrafferfilmanalyse. *Wilhelm Roux Arch. Entw Mech. Org.*, **167**, 266-287.

3 • Specification of the antero-posterior body pattern in insect eggs

KLAUS KALTHOFF

*Biologisches Institut I (Zoologie),
Katharinenstr. 20, D 78 Freiburg*

I. BASIC TERMINOLOGY

Insect embryogenesis may be subdivided very coarsely into initial periods of nuclear multiplication and cell proliferation, and subsequent periods of increasingly complex regional differentiation (see Fig. 3.1). After fertilization the nucleus undergoes a series of divisions within the yolk rich endoplasm of the egg. At the end of this period usually referred to as *intravitelline cleavage*, nuclei with jackets of cytoplasm migrate towards the egg surface. When the yolk free periplasm has thus become populated with nuclei, a continuous layer of *blastoderm* cells is formed by infoldings of the boundary membrane (oolemma) of the egg cell. After subsequent cell divisions, part of the blastoderm gives rise to the germ anlage while the remainder will form embryonic covers (amnion and serosa). By processes including gastrulation and segmentation, the germ anlage develops into the *germ band* which already reflects the basic organization of the larval body. Typically, it consists of the procephalon (A), the gnathocephalon (B), the thoracic segments (C), and 8 to 12 abdominal segments (D and E).

The germ band segments and, likewise, the body regions designated as A, B, C, D, and E may be regarded as elements of a basic body *pattern*. The formation of such spatial patterns requires recognizable differences, in structure or alignment, between cells or groups of cells. The *realization* of spatial patterns therefore occurs as cells undergo *differentiation*. Cell differentiation results from specific cell activities which are programmed by cell *determination*. This process is visualized as a stepwise 'instruction' and 'commitment' (see Sander 1976) of cells to carry out specific activities. As long as the underlying molecular mechanisms are unknown, determination has to be defined by operational criteria (Gehring 1973; see also Chapter 5 of this volume) such as the capability of the cells to differentiate autonomously upon transplantation, or their development, after isolation, in accordance with their fate in the whole organism. It is inherent in these definitions that the term 'determination' is used to cover the—as yet unknown—initial steps of differentiation. The initial phase of spatial pattern formation is referred as 'pattern specification'. The pattern is specified as groups of cells are determined differently and in a spatially coordinated manner so as to form different pattern elements.

The study of spatial pattern formation during embryogenesis therefore proceeds along

53

           K. Kalthoff

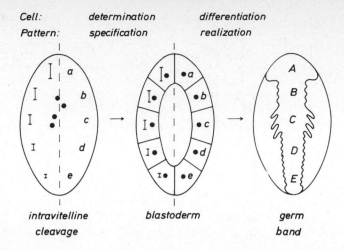

FIG. 3.1. Development of a generalized insect. For description of stages and definition of terms see text. Black discs represent nuclei. Pattern elements A (procephalon), B (gnathocephalon), C (thorax), D and E (abdomen) can be *directly identified* at germ band stage. Cytoplasmic determinants *thought to exist* at earlier stages are represented by small letters a-e (mosaic model), or bars of different lengths (gradient model), see text.

two lines of questions and experiments which are interrelated but basically distinct. One line is along the *time axis* and is mainly concerned with the processes that channel a given group of cells into special activities. The other line is placing the emphasis on the coordination of the developing cellular activities along the *spatial axes* of the embryo. This article will focus the attention on the spatial aspect of the specification of the longitudinal body pattern in insect embryogenesis.

    Polarity is a basic feature of many spatial patterns in organisms. It may be defined as an asymmetry with respect to a spatial axis. The asymmetry allows us to assign a unit vector to the axis under consideration. Polarity reversal then means the reversal of the direction of the assigned unit vector. The polarity of an organism with respect to a spatial axis can be realized in four different ways: (1) Structures located at each end of the spatial axis may be different even though the intermediate part of the body is not polarized (*terminal polarity*, Fig. 3.2a). (2) Reiterated elements of the body may be all polarized in the same direction but otherwise equal (*element polarity*, Fig. 3.2b). (3) A scalar quantity may be distributed along the spatial axis in a gradually decreasing manner, so that its slope defines the polarity (*gradient polarity*, Fig. 3.2c). (4) The polarity of a spatial pattern may be defined by an ordered sequence of qualitatively different pattern elements (*sequence polarity*, Fig. 3.2d). All these types of polarity may be involved in the antero-posterior polarity of the insect embryo.

    With respect to experiments discussed below (Sections V and VI), it is of interest to see that, in an organism with a terminal polarity axis, transplantation of the terminal regions alone would result in a large scale polarity reversal (Fig. 3.2a). By contrast, reversal of element polarity would require rotation of all elements (Fig. 3.2b).

II. THE CONCEPT OF CYTOPLASMIC DETERMINANTS

The differentiation of cells and the ensuing realization of spatial patterns are based upon

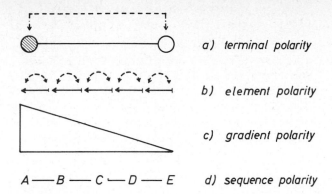

FIG. 3.2. Types of polarity potentially involved in the polarity of insects at different stages of development. Note that in the case (a) a large scale polarity reversal can be achieved by transplantation of the terminal regions alone.

different cell activities which in turn are ascribed to different gene activities. On the other hand, the nuclei in (almost) all cells appear to have the same set of genetic information. This has been shown in *Drosophila* by transplantation of nuclei from germ anlage cells back into unfertilized eggs. Such eggs may give rise to complete embryos with the genetic constitution of the transplanted nucleus (Illmensee 1973; see also Chapter 4 of this volume). The transplanted nuclei must have preserved the full complement of genetic instructions. It is a basic question then to ask how, in a sphere of blastoderm cells which carry identical genetic information, differential gene activities can be realized in spatial order. External physical factors such as gravity or light have little if any influence upon polarity and pattern formation in insect eggs. The agents that channel the cells into different pathways therefore seem to reside in the cells themselves but not in the nuclei.

It is a fundamental concept in developmental biology to ascribe the realization of differential cell activities to cytoplasmic determinants. This concept, as applied to insect embryogenesis, postulates that cytoplasmic determinants are prelocalized in the egg and channel the blastoderm cells in which they become incorporated into different developmental pathways. The way the egg makes the insect is thus related to the way the insect makes the egg. Observations on growing follicles in wild type and mutant *Drosophila* indeed indicate that the anterior pole of the oocyte is determined by influences of the adjacent nurse cells (Gill 1963, 1964; see also Sections VI, VII, and X).

III. GRADIENT VERSUS MOSAIC MODEL

Concerning the number, specificity, and mode of action of the cytoplasmic determinants involved in the specification of the longitudinal segment pattern of an insect, there are two extreme views: (1) Each pattern element may be determined by a special determinant of its own which is located in its proper relative position and differs qualitatively from the determinants of the other pattern elements. If single segments were determined this way, one would have to postulate 5 or 6 qualitatively different determinants for the head segments, 3 for the thorax, and about 10 for the abdominal segments. (2) Alternatively, one might conjecture that only one determinant is distributed in graded amount and that its local level determines the character of the pattern element to be formed there.

These alternative models have been diagrammed in Fig. 3.1 where, for simplicity, only 5 pattern elements (A, B, C, D, E) are distinguished. Each element may be determined by a corresponding determinant of distinct type (a, b, c, d, e) which could enable each egg region, after separation (and maintainance under sufficiently physiological conditions), to develop and differentiate in accordance with its fate in the whole embryo. This type of development is commonly referred to as *mosaic development*. Correspondingly, the prelocalization of a specific cytoplasmic determinant for each pattern element will be termed the *mosaic model* of pattern specification. Alternatively, graded quantities of one type of determinant (bars of different length in Fig. 3.1) might be able to evoke the characters of the different pattern elements in their proper sequence. This model will be referred to as the *gradient model* of pattern specification. With respect to polarity, the mosaic and the gradient model are obviously different in that the mosaic model essentially implies a sequence polarity while the gradient model of pattern specification involves a gradient polarity, which in turn might depend on a terminal polarity.

The applicability of the gradient versus the mosaic model is obviously dependent upon the developmental stage of the organism under study. As determination means the initiation of different cell activities which eventually manifest themselves as visible differences, the mosaic status (according to the operational criterion used for determination) will usually be reached *sometime*. Correspondingly, sequence polarity becomes established sooner or later in higher organisms.

The main concern of this article is the status of the insect egg, with respect to antero-posterior polarity and body pattern specification, at the time soon after deposition. A wealth of relevant data has been produced since the pioneering work of Seidel (1926). The few lines of evidence discussed here have been selected to draw the attention to those experimental systems which may allow the analysis to be taken to the molecular level. A broad review including a thorough re-evaluation of 'classical' work on pattern specification in insect embryogenesis has recently been presented by Sander (1976). For a comprehensive account on the causal analysis of insect embryogenesis, the reader may be referred to the review of Counce (1972).

IV. LACK OF ULTRASTRUCTURAL EVIDENCE FOR CYTOPLASMIC DETERMINANTS OTHER THAN THE OOSOME

The ultrastructure of oocytes and newly deposited eggs has been scrutinized in the search for signs of prelocalized morphogenetic determinants (Okada & Waddington 1959; Zissler & Sander 1973; see also Mahowald 1972). The posterior pole of the eggs of many Coleoptera, Diptera, and Hymenoptera carries basophilic, granular material referred to as the oosome or polar granules. The cells that originate at this site and incorporate the polar granules, are referred to as pole cells. They usually cleave separately before the blastoderm is formed. It has long been known that these cells produce the primary germ cells, although they may give rise to other cell types (see Counce 1972).

The observations on the fate of the pole cells suggest that the oosome acts as a cytoplasmic determinant of the germ cells. This idea was supported by the production of sterile animals after selective destruction or removal of oosome material. However, in the ichneumonid *Pimpla turionellae* fertile animals can develop after removal or X irradiation of the oosome (Günther 1971). Although this case seems clearly exceptional, it still reminds us of the ambiguity which interpretations of embryonic defects are always subject to (see below). It was a great advance, therefore, when the determination of prospective germ cells by oosome material was positively demonstrated. Okada *et al.* (1974) performed a 'rescue' experiment by sterilizing *Drosophila* eggs by UV irradiation of the posterior pole, and then restoring the fertility by transplantation of cytoplasm from the posterior pole of unirradiated eggs. Illmensee and Mahowald (1974) transferred posterior polar plasm from *Drosophila* eggs at early cleavage stages to the anterior tip of host eggs of the same age. This caused, in the presumptive somatic region, the formation of 'pole cells' which, after transplantation into the posterior region of a second host, gave rise to progeny with the genetic label of the first host (see Chapter 4 of this volume).

Besides the oosome, the ultrastructure of insect oocytes does not reveal any signs of cytoplasmic determinants. The accumulation of mitochondria at the anterior pole of newly laid *Smittia* eggs (Zissler & Sander 1973) has suggested a rôle for these organelles in the establishment of the antero-posterior polarity. Later experiments, however, have not corroborated this idea (Kalthoff *et al.* 1975). Biochemical and immunological techniques have also been applied to screen fragments of cricket eggs for differences in their protein components (Koch & Heinig 1968; Nünemann & Moser 1970). Regional differences have indeed been found, but due to the lack of appropriate bioassays, none of the factors showing uneven distributions has been tested for morphogenetic activity.

V. PATTERN SPECIFICATION BY POSTERIOR EGG MATERIAL IN *EUSCELIS*

Due to the lack of ultrastructural or direct biochemical evidence for cytoplasmic determinants other than the oosome, the case for such determinants is almost entirely based upon results of experimental interference with the development of insect eggs. Such experiments often cause defects, such as the lack of parts of the body. However, results of this type at best allow the construction of fate maps. They provide no evidence for the existence of cytoplasmic determinants because it is impossible to prove strictly why a part of an embryo has *not* formed. This difficulty does not exist in experiments that channel development into abnormal but positively defined pathways.

Experiments which positively demonstrate the involvement of posterior determinants in the specification of the longitudinal body pattern were carried out by Sander (1960) with eggs of the leaf hopper, *Euscelis plebejus*. The posterior pole region of these eggs carries a cluster of symbiotic bacteria which can be used as a visible marker to indicate the position of posterior pole material and can be pushed anteriorly by invaginating the egg with a blunt needle. In combination with transverse fragmentation of the egg, such translocation experiments have clearly demonstrated a key rôle of posterior pole material in specification of the basic body pattern of *Euscelis*.

Anterior fragments of *Euscelis* eggs, after fragmentation during cleavage stages, produce only head structures or no embryonic parts at all (Fig. 3.3b, c). They become capable, however, of forming complete embryos if posterior pole material is shifted anteriorly before fragmentation (Fig. 3.3d$_2$, g). This dramatic increase in morphogenetic capacity must be ascribed to the presence of the posterior pole material moved to the anterior fragment. Complete embryos may even form in the anterior fragment if the posterior pole material, after having been present from late cleavage to early germ

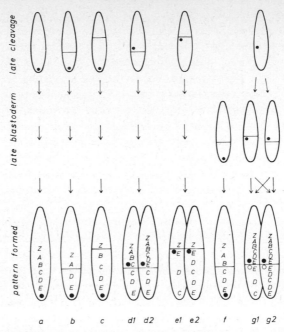

FIG. 3.3. Combined egg fragmentation and translocation of posterior pole material in *Euscelis* (after Sander 1960, 1975). Anterior pole up, stages of operation indicated at left. Horizontal bar in outline of egg symbolizes fragmentation at the respective level, black disc represents the symbiont ball indicating the position of posterior pole material before and after translocation. The patterns formed are symbolized by letters as defined in Fig. 3.1, Z represents the posterior limit of 'extraembryonic' material. The indicated patterns represent typical results identified at the germ band stage some days later. The symbols at the upper and lower ends of each series indicate the approximate location of the precursor cells for the respective pattern elements in the blastoderm, as inferred from direct observation of the developing germ band. The remaining symbols have been distributed evenly in between. The germ band regions next to the plane of separation or mirror symmetry (e.g. region C in Fig. d and in the mirror duplications e_2 and g_2) may not be complete (e.g. one or two thoracic segments may be missing from C).

anlage stages, is later separated from the anterior fragment (Fig. 3.3g). In the posterior fragment, this type of operation causes the formation of a posterior partial germ band with reversed polarity (EDC) or an aberrant pattern with two sets of posterior segments joined in mirror image symmetry (EDCDE). The formation of 2 supernumerary abdominal ends in the middle of the egg (Fig. 3.3g) must also be ascribed to some action of the translocated posterior egg material.

For a further characterization of the posterior pole material, it is important to realize two features of its action: First, the posterior pole material when provided to an anterior fragment will not always cause this fragment to form a complete germ band (Fig. 3.3d$_2$) but may sometimes increase the morphogenetic potential there only to a sub-maximal degree. In such cases, the posterior pole material does not cause supernumerary formation of the terminal abdominal segments that are normally formed in its vicinity. Instead, segments of the middle region are added (Figs. 3.3b, 3.3d$_1$). Second, the length of a given set of segments may vary by a factor of more than 2 (e.g. CDE in Figs. 3.3e$_1$, 3.3g$_1$, and 3.3g$_2$). These characteristics suggest that the posterior pole material does not produce a sequence of segment specific determinants but instead initiates a gradient of one determinant, the local level of which would cause the respective blastoderm cells to form different segments. The results diagrammed in Fig. 3 could then be ascribed to changes in level and/or slope of such a gradient (Sander 1960, 1961).

Experiments to characterize the active fraction of the transplanted posterior material in *Euscelis* eggs are now under way. To exert its influence in the anterior fragment, it must become located close to the oolemma (Franz 1972). Schwemmler (1974) proposed that the symbiotic bacteria cooperate, in the specification of the body pattern, with ion binding proteins in the egg cortex. This hypothesis is mainly based upon the occurrence of embryos with reduced or missing abdomens ('head embryos') in eggs with small or missing symbiont balls. Such eggs result from administration of tetracycline to the mothers. However, Sander and co-workers found that the formation of head embryos was not strictly correlated to the size of the symbiont ball but rather to damage inflicted upon the egg during collection (Sander 1974). Recent evidence indicates that the antibacterial agent directly or indirectly causes some adverse effect on the posterior follicle cells so that an abnormal chorion is formed there (Sander, personal communication).

Translocation of polar egg material, in combination with fragmentation, was also carried out in eggs of the bean weevil, *Bruchidius obtectus,* by Jung and Krause (1967). They found complete embryos in anterior fragments after invagination of posterior egg material (9 cases) as well as in posterior fragments after invagination of anterior egg material (4 cases). In control fragments without invaginated material from the opposite pole, complete embryos were never observed. These results again indicate that components located near both the anterior and the posterior egg pole are indispensable for the specification of the normal segment pattern. Jung and Krause could not identify these components but tended to exclude the circumpolar ectoplasm as a carrier of the active fractions. Increased numbers of segments in anterior fragments after translocation of posterior pole material were also found in *Pimpla* eggs (Achtelig & Krause 1971).

VI. ANTERIOR DETERMINANTS IN DIPTERAN EGGS

While *Euscelis* eggs are especially suitable to demonstrate the action of posterior cytoplasmic determinants, the involvement of anterior egg components in pattern specification is most evident in dipteran eggs. Eggs of chironomid midges have an apparent predisposition to produce, upon various types of experimental interference, abnormal embryos with longitudinal pattern mirroring. Such cases were first described by Yajima (1960, 1964) who observed, after centrifugation or partial UV irradiation of *Chironomus dorsalis* eggs, mirror image duplications of the abdomen without head and thoracic segments ('double abdomens') and, conversely, Janus type heads without thoracic and abdominal segments ('double heads'). With the letters assigned to the body regions in Fig. 1, these double heads and double abdomens may be symbolized as ABBA and EDDE, respectively. Thus, in each of these aberrant segment patterns, the polarity of a considerable part of the antero-posterior axis is reversed, and pattern elements are replaced by elements that normally are formed only in the other egg half. Both types of aberrant pattern, after appropriate treatment of the eggs, are perfectly symmetrical in their external and internal morphology except that germ cells are found only in the posterior part of the double abdomens and double heads (Yajima 1970). Asymmetrical segment patterns with more segments in one part of the double head or double abdomens were obtained after oblique centrifugation (Yajima, 1960). After UV irradiation, defective embryos were also observed (Yajima, 1964).

A 'genocopy' of the double abdomens in *Chironomus dorsalis* was found in the *bicaudal* mutant syndrome of *Drosophila melanogaster* (Bull 1966). Some of these abnormal embryos also develop the terminal segments of a second abdomen in mirror-image symmetry to the terminal segments of the normal abdomen. The two abdomens may be symmetrical with four or five segments at each end of the egg or have more abdominal segments at the normal posterior end than at the reversed end. The reversed posterior ends appear to have normal spiracles, hindgut, and Malpighian tubules but no germ cells. With respect to the concept of prelocalized cytoplasmic determinants, it is important that in the *bicaudal* mutant the *maternal* genotype is the controlling factor. Therefore the abnormalities must be ascribed to a defective oogenetic condition. Unfortunately, the most extreme type of pattern aberration, i.e. the more or less symmetric *bicaudal,* was produced at very low frequency, and no successful attempts to obtain a similar mutant with higher penetrance have been reported so far. Attempts to produce double abdomens experimentally in a wild type strain of *Drosophila melanogaster* have also failed (Bownes & Kalthoff 1974).

In a terrestrial chironomid midge of the genus *Smittia,* double abdomens can be produced by several unrelated types of experimental interference including UV irradiation of the anterior pole region (Kalthoff & Sander 1968), centrifugation (Kalthoff, unpublished) and puncture of the egg at the anterior pole (Schmidt *et al.* 1975). It is hard to conceive that all these procedures could *de novo* generate specific determinants for the formation of an abdominal end. Much more likely, the different methods have in common the *removal* or inactivation of crucial anterior egg components. This view is strongly supported by the photoreversibility of the UV induction of double abdomens. Irradiation with visible light after UV markedly increases the yield of normal embryos at the cost of double abdomens (Kalthoff 1973). Visible light is effective only after but not before UV, and has to be received by the same egg area. This phenomenon is known as 'photoreactivation' and is commonly ascribed to a light dependent, enzymatic *repair* of UV damage to nucleic acids (see section VII). After UV irradiation at early stages of development, the light dependent respecification of the normal body pattern can be delayed for several hours (Kalthoff *et al.* 1975). It seems therefore that double abdomen formation does not result from the release of unspecific UV photoproducts, but from the inactivation of a specific anterior determinant.

A bistable system which is switched by the presence or absence of a crucial component thus appears to be involved in the specification of the basic body pattern in *Smittia* eggs. Bistable control circuits may also operate in the determination and trans-determination of imaginal discs (Kauffmann 1973), and in the genetic control of compartmentalization during embryonic development (Garcia-Bellido, 1975; see also Chapter 8 of this volume). For instance, the posterior compartment of the *Drosophila* wing resembles a mirror image of the anterior compartment of the wing in flies mutant for the homeotic gene *engrailed* (Morata & Lawrence 1975).

The development of double abdomens in *Smittia* does not involve cell death to any extent that could be observed in a high quality time lapse film. Rather, the anterior abdomen is apparently made from cells that normally form head and thorax. Actually, the double abdomen germ anlage develops by fusion of two separate layers of thick blastoderm which originate from the pole regions (Kalthoff 1975). Thus pattern specification may occur independently in each half of the double abdomen germ anlage. The two abdomens in the egg develop in strict symmetry and synchrony unless one partner is handicapped by lack of space (Kalthoff & Sander 1968). The formation of the anterior abdomen does not even require interaction with the anterior egg half as can be proved by combined fragmentation and UV irradiation (Sander unpublished). These results demonstrate that potentially the conditions (designated as p and p' in Fig. 3.4) resulting in the formation of an abdomen exist not only in the posterior but also in the anterior egg half. The determinant p', however, is not expressed as long as the anterior determinant (designated as a in Fig. 3.4) is active at the proper site and time. This interpretation implies that elimination of a by UV or removal does not cause the concomitant elimination of p' (see also Section IX).

The model for longitudinal polarity and basic pattern specification in *Smittia* as diagrammed in Fig. 3.4 may also apply to *Drosophila* oocytes: The *bicaudal* embryos may result from the absence or inactive state of an anterior determinant like a in *Smittia*, since the overwhelming majority of mutations causes *defective* conditions. Potentially relevant data that are not accounted for in the model is the production of double heads by UV irradiation of posterior egg regions in *Chironomus dorsalis* as observed by Yajima (1964). However, the frequency of double heads in his experiments was rather low (about 6 per cent), and double heads are sometimes hard to distinguish from extreme posterior defects. At any rate, my attempts to reproduce this result by UV irradiation of *Smittia* and *Chironomus tentans* eggs have completely failed so far. Double heads were found after centrifugation of *Chironomus thummi* and *Smittia* eggs (Gauss & Sander 1966; Overton & Raab 1967; Kalthoff unpublished), but not with the strict dependence on the orientation of the eggs in the centrifuge as described by Yajima (1960). Therefore Yajima's results appear rather exceptional.

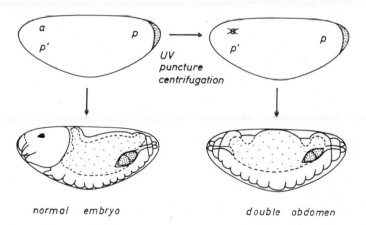

normal   embryo   double   abdomen

FIG. 3.4. Diagrammatic representation of double abdomen induction in *Smittia* eggs by UV irradiation of the anterior pole region (Kalthoff, 1971b), puncture at the anterior pole (Schmidt *et al.* 1975), or centrifugation with the long egg axis parallel to the centrifugal force (Kalthoff, unpublished). All these types of interference are thought to inactivate or remove an anterior determinant designated as a. This is thought to cooperate with another determinant p' in the anterior pole region, so as to enable the formation of head and thorax. Upon inactivation or removal of a, p' is assumed to cause abdomen formation in the anterior egg half, as the formation of the normal abdomen is ascribed to the posterior determinant p in the posterior egg half (see also Fig. 3.7). Note that the germ cells (shaded) are present only in the posterior part of the double abdomen.

VII. CLUES AS TO THE NATURE OF THE ANTERIOR DETERMINANT IN *SMITTIA*

An effort is being made to characterize the origin, localization, and biochemical nature of the anterior determinant in the *Smittia* egg. This is greatly facilitated because UV irradiation under appropriate conditions causes double abdomen formation in virtually every treated egg. The dependence of the double abdomen yield upon the irradiated egg area indicates that the bulk of the anterior determinant is localized in the anterior pole region (Kalthoff 1971b). This is corroborated by the formation of double abdomens after puncturing the eggs at the anterior pole (Schmidt *et al.* 1975). The anterior determinant is apparently deposited in the oocyte during oogenesis since double abdomens can be induced with full yield immediately after egg deposition (Kalthoff 1971b). These results suggest that the anterior determinant originates from the nurse cell adjacent to the anterior pole of the oocyte during oogenesis.

The localization of the anterior determinant is extranuclear because the yield of double abdomens after UV irradiation is independent of the presence or absence of nuclei in the irradiated egg region (Kalthoff 1971b). Moreover, UV irradiation of centrifuged eggs shows that the anterior determinant is contained in the clear cytoplasmic fraction. Within this fraction, the anterior determinant is apparently *not* stratified under conditions causing stratification of both mitochondria and endoplasmic reticulum (Hanel 1975).

To obtain a hint of the biochemical nature of the anterior determinant, an action spectrum for the UV induction of double abdomens was determined (Fig. 3.5a). This has been computed from dose-response curves obtained with monochromatic UV of different wavelengths. Transmittance spectra of the egg chorion and egg homogenate (Fig. 3.5b) were also determined to correct for wavelength-dependent shielding of the effective targets. The two action spectra shown in Fig. 3.5a take into account wavelength dependent shielding under two alternative assumptions: Random distribution of the targets in the irradiated anterior egg quarter yields the filled circles whereas exclusive localization in a 5 μm thick layer of ectoplasm yields the open circles (see Kalthoff 1973). Regardless of these different assumptions, the maximum efficiency per incident quantum is found between 280 and 285 nm, indicating a protein moiety in the effective targets. A minor peak is also found at 265 nm, hinting at a nucleic acid.

Further independent evidence for the involvement of a nucleic acid is the photoreversibility of the UV induction of double abdomens. Photoreversal is defined as the mitigation of UV effects by subsequent irradiation with light of longer wavelength. Photoreversal after UV induction of double abdomens, by its wavelength dependence, temperature dependence, and dose rate saturation, indicates that the underlying molecular mechanism belongs to the well known type of 'direct photoreactivation' (Kalthoff 1973). This is commonly ascribed to light dependent, enzymatic splitting of UV induced pyrimidine dimers in nucleic acids (Cook 1970).

From the data on localization, and presumable biochemical nature of the effective targets of UV induction of double abdomens, masked messenger RNA appears as a strong candidate for the anterior determinant in the *Smittia* egg. This hypothesis is consistent with two further lines of evidence. (1) Subribosomal ribonucleoprotein particles are apparently transferred from nurse cells to oocytes in insects with meroistic oogenesis (Duspiva *et al.* 1973; Winter 1974). (2) The effective targets for the UV induction of double abdomens appear metabolically inactive until blastoderm

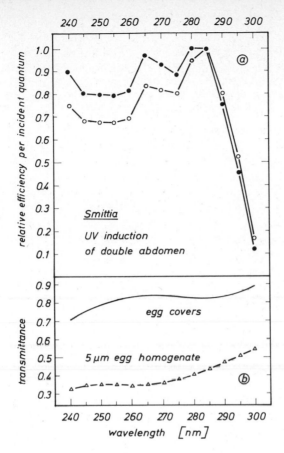

Fig. 3.5. (a) Action spectrum for UV induction of double abdomens in *Smittia* eggs. The relative efficiency per incident quantum was determined at each wavelength, assuming target localization throughout the irradiated anterior egg quarter (●) or only within a superficial layer of periplasm (o). Peaks at 285 and 265 nm indicate a nucleic acid-protein complex as the effective target.
(b) Transmittance of egg covers and a 5 μm layer of egg homogenate from *Smittia* eggs. Data from Kalthoff (1973).

formation. Before this stage, UV irradiation at different stages results in a fairly constant yield of double abdomens (Kalthoff 1971b). Moreover, after early UV irradiation, photoreverting illumination can be delayed without much detriment to its efficiency until the deadline for double abdomen induction, i.e. around blastoderm formation (Kalthoff *et al.* 1975). The results obtained so far are thus compatible with the idea that the anterior determinant in the *Smittia* egg involves masked mRNA which is provided to the oocyte during oogenesis but inactive until blastoderm formation. Upon activation at this stage, the antero-posterior polarity becomes firmly established and the longitudinal body pattern specified. If the masked messenger is inactivated or removed, double abdomens develop. This resembles the action of homeotic mutations in *Drosophila* which are also able to switch morphogenesis into abnormal but well-defined pathways, probably by regulation of other genes rather than the synthesis of enzymes or structural proteins for other cell activities (Garcia-Bellido 1975).

VIII. THE GAP PHENOMENON—NEGATIVE REGULATION

The experiments described in sections V to VII have exploited specific advantages of *Smittia* and *Euscelis* eggs. One may ask whether the conclusions drawn from experiments with one of these eggs also apply to the other, or even to a larger variety of eggs. There is no direct answer to this question: *Euscelis* eggs just do not produce double abdomens upon UV irradiation of the anterior pole, and *Smittia* eggs do not permit controlled translocation of posterior egg material.

However, there is one set of clear cut experimental results which has been observed in eggs from a variety of insects including *Bruchidius* (Coleoptera), *Euscelis* (Cicadina), *Smittia* (Orthorapha), and *Protophormia* (Cyclorapha) (see Herth & Sander 1973). Eggs from all these insects, upon transverse fragmentation, display the 'gap phenomenon' which may be characterized as follows. From some stage of development onwards, the segments formed in the anterior and posterior fragment add up to the complete germ band (Fig. 3.3f). If separated before this particular stage, some segments are usually missing next to the site of separation so that the segment pattern is interrupted by a 'gap'. *Which* segments fail to appear, depends statistically upon the level of fragmentation (Fig. 3.3b,c). The *number* of segments which fail to appear decreases with increasing age at fragmentation (Fig. 3.6). In *Euscelis* eggs, fragments were allowed to reunite after separation; the frequency of complete germ band patterns then decreases with increasing duration of separation (Sander 1975).

Insect eggs of different species have to reach different stages of development before the segments formed in complementary anterior and posterior fragments add up to the complete pattern (Fig. 3.6). While in *Protophormia* the gap vanishes after an early blastoderm stage, *Smittia* embryos upon fragmentation at a later blastoderm stage still have an average of one segment missing. In *Bruchidius* and *Euscelis* the gap persists until fragmentation at early germ anlage stages.

The gap phenomenon observed after *transverse* fragmentation of insect eggs differs from the text book type of regulation as found upon separation of sea urchin or amphibian blastomeres after the first cleavages. Such blastomeres may give rise to dwarfed but otherwise normal embryos provided certain cytoplasmic components, e.g. gray crescent material in amphibians or animal *plus* vegetative material in sea urchins, are contained in the isolated blastomere. It was an intriguing question, therefore, to ask if *longitudinal* fragments of insect eggs could give rise to complete embryos. This question could not be answered as long as insect eggs were fragmented by ligation. Using a novel technique of fragmentation by a blunted razor blade, Sander (1971) was able to separate left from right, and dorsal from ventral halves of *Euscelis* eggs. After fragmentation in either plane, complete bilateral embryos developed in both fragments of several eggs. Bilateral germ bands were also found after median splitting of the germ-anlage in *Tachycines* and *Bombyx* (Krause & Krause 1957, 1965).

Thus insect eggs do display classical regulation after *longitudinal* fragmentation as opposed to the development of incomplete germ bands after *transverse* fragmentation. It would be misleading, however, to consider the latter case as a *mosaic development* since this is defined as *development of parts according to their fates in the intact system*. It is inherent in the gap phenomenon that transverse fragments of insect eggs, after early separation, produce *less* segments than they would have achieved within the whole embryo. As Sander (1971) has pointed out, this could be termed *negative regulation* as opposed to *positive regulation* when a fragment deviates from its fate in the intact system

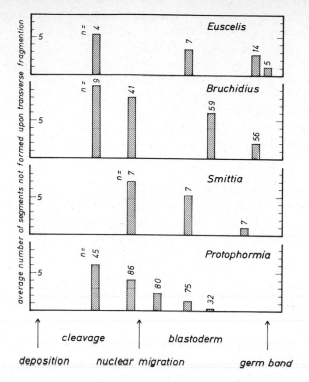

FIG. 3.6. Schematic representation of the 'gap phenomenon' resulting from transverse fragmentation of insect eggs, based upon data from Jung (1966), Herth & Sander (1973), and Sander (1975). The average number of segments missing from both fragments generally decreases with increasing age of the embryo at fragmentation. However, the gap phenomenon vanishes at earlier stages of development in more evolved insect species (Sections VII and X). The numbers of eggs (n) quoted account only for those eggs which have formed identifiable segments in *both* fragments. These results are statistically supported by larger numbers of eggs with partial germ bands in one fragment only.

towards a *more complete* embryo or organ.

The interpretation of the gap phenomenon is crucial since it is found in several insect species from different orders. The phenomenon might be ascribed to some damage by the fragmentation procedure to prelocalized determinants for the missing segments. Young eggs then would have to be more sensitive to such damage than eggs at more advanced stages. However, this interpretation is at variance with the following results. Removal of the separating razor blade after fragmentation, despite the additional stress, leads to the development of complete embryos (Sander 1975). Similarly, translocation of polar material before fragmentation, despite the additional stress, causes the formation of more complete or fully normal patterns (Section V). A reasonable interpretation of the gap phenomenon which is also in line with the mode of action of the posterior determinant in *Euscelis* eggs was put forward some time ago by Sander (1960, 1961). According to this hypothesis the longitudinal body pattern in insects is specified under the control of anterior and posterior determinants which are thought to originate from egg material near the respective terminal egg regions. These determinants may become established as antagonistic gradients; their relative levels may determine the prospective fates of the cells in the different egg areas. Spreading of these determinants with increasing age of the embryo could then account for the gap phenomenon. The anterior fragment, at an early stage of development, would have received less of the posterior determinant than the same fragment has at a later stage. Conversely, the posterior fragment would receive more of the anterior determinant with increasing time before separation, enabling it to form some more anterior pattern elements.

The classical distinction between regulative and mosaic development thus appears to be a matter of time (see also Counce 1961). To judge from the different stages of development to which the gap phenomenon persists in different insect species (Fig. 3.6), regulative development gives way to mosaic development sooner or later. It may be emphasized that eggs of cycloraphan dipterans which are frequently regarded as strict mosaic eggs (Anderson, 1966) also display negative regulation through intravitelline cleavage until early blastoderm stages. This has been demonstrated by Herth & Sander (1973) in an extensive series of fragmentation experiments with *Protophormia* eggs (see Fig. 3.6). The comparatively early cessation of the regulative capacity in these eggs will be reconsidered together with their extreme degree of 'prefabrication' during oogenesis (Section X). The state of determination in *Drosophila* blastoderm cells seems also similar in egg fragments and in isolated cells. The latter, when prepared from either anterior or posterior egg halves and cultivated *in vivo*, produce only head and thoracic, or abdominal and thoracic structures, respectively (Chan & Gehring 1971).

IX. THREE CYTOPLASMIC DETERMINANTS—DIFFERENT MODES OF ACTION

There is evidence for three cytoplasmic determinants in insect eggs: the oosome which acts as a germ cell determinant, a posterior determinant other than the oosome, and an anterior determinant. The latter are involved in the specification of the basic longitudinal pattern in the somatic part of the body. The evidence for these determinants is based upon results of experimental interference with the development of eggs from several insect species. The search for the biochemical nature of the determinants is in a rudimentary state. The main concern is therefore still centered on the formal aspects of their action. Little is known so far, even on a formal level, about the specification of the transverse body pattern (see Sander 1976).

The oosome has been recognized for many decades and, somewhat unfortunately, has served as a paradigm for cytoplasmic determinants in general. The germ cell case, however, is peculiar in several respects (see Sander 1975): The germ cells tend to segregate early and preserve a full chromosome complement in species which eliminate a number of chromosomes from their somatic cells. While pattern specification in the somatic part of the body obviously initiates specialized cell activities, the germ cells have to be kept in a nonspecialized state as they will give rise to all types of cells in the future embryo. Consistent with this fundamental difference, the determination of the germ cells is clearly dissociated from the specification of the basic body segment pattern. Double abdomens induced by mutation, centrifugation, or UV irradiation carry germ cells only in the original abdomen (Bull 1966; Yajima 1970; Gollub 1970). Conversely, mutations or experimental treatment affecting the oosome do not affect the segment pattern as well (Achtelıg & Krause 1971; Counce 1972; Gehring 1973; Okada *et al.* 1974). Thus the oosome conveys an exceptional message for the formation of particular cells, and there is no indication that this special case of cell determination is a paradigm for pattern specification in the somatic part of the body.

In striking contrast to the limited determinative range of the oosome, the anterior and posterior determinants as characterized in Sections V to VII exert their influence far beyond the polar egg regions from which they appear to originate. Their mode of action, together with the gap phenomenon, shall now be reconsidered with respect to the gradient versus mosaic model of pattern specification (Section III, Fig. 3.1). It is crucial to such a discussion that the stage of development and the level of resolution of pattern elements are well defined. I have implied in the mosaic model that the body regions designated as A,B,C,D,E in Fig. 3.1, or smaller pattern elements, are each determined by a determinant of its own. I will also confine the discussion to the status soon after egg deposition and according to the lines of evidence reviewed here. If qualitatively different cytoplasmic determinants (a–e in Fig. 3.1) were prelocalized in mosaic fashion in the *Euscelis* egg, one should expect, after providing posterior pole material to an anterior fragment, the formation of patterns such as ABE. However, such patterns with gaps in the normal sequence of elements have never been observed under these conditions. Instead, complete patterns, or partial patterns like ABC were found. If *Smittia* eggs had a prelocalized determinant for each pattern element, UV irradiation or puncturing at the anterior pole should result in patterns like XBCDE. Such patterns (with X standing for defective head structures) have indeed been found upon UV irradiation *after blastoderm formation*. This result indicates that the egg may *then* have reached a mosaic state. By contrast, such patterns are *not* formed upon UV irradiation *before* blastoderm formation; either the normal pattern or double abdomens are found instead. It must be concluded that neither the *Euscelis* nor the *Smittia* egg are in a mosaic state before blastoderm formation. The gap phenomenon (Section VIII) provides further evidence that other insect eggs as well cannot be described adequately by the mosaic model until later stages of their development.

The gradient model of pattern specification as put forward by Sander (1960, 1961) provides a basis for a formal understanding of most of the data reviewed here. According to this model, egg components localized near the anterior and posterior poles set up gradients of cytoplasmic determinants, e.g. concentration gradients of diffusible substances. Pattern specification is then regarded as a function of the local levels of these determinants. This model readily explains the cases of large scale polarity reversal in *Smittia* and *Euscelis* eggs (sections V and VI) which demonstrate that the polarity of these eggs at early stages is of the terminal polarity type (Fig. 3.2). The polar egg components which constitute this rudimentary polarity are thought to set up the gradients of determinants which specify the visible pattern with its inherent sequence polarity.

The gradient model was earlier proposed to account for the basic body pattern formation in sea urchins (Runnstroem 1929) and it has proved its heuristic value in many systems (see Waddington 1966; Lawrence 1970; Wolpert 1971). In insect embryogenesis, the idea that the longitudinal body pattern is specified under the control of anterior and posterior determinants can in fact be used as a unifying concept to explain, in a formal way, a large body of data. This includes also results interpreted by Seidel and his followers in terms of more detailed determinants spreading from a differentiation centre located in the prospective thorax (see Seidel 1961, for review, and Sander 1976, for critical reinterpretation). However, as Sander emphasizes, the gradient model is a gross *formal* concept which may require adaptations to match specific results. For instance, the double abdomens in *Smittia* eggs are invariably symmetrical regardless of the applied UV dose, size of irradiated area, and other experimental parameters

(Sander & Kalthoff unpublished). This is hard to understand if the UV irradiation acts *directly* upon a determinant specifying the body pattern by a *rather rigid* spatial distribution. The dilemma may be resolved by allowing major dynamic properties in the shapes of morphogenetic gradients; this could in fact explain the formation of symmetrical double abdomens after treatment of only a small polar egg region (Meinhardt & Gierer 1974).

Another attempt to reconcile the *Smittia* data with the general concept of graded anterior and posterior determinants may start from the following assumption. The anterior determinant (*a* in Fig. 3.4) may act *indirectly* by modifying, in an all or nothing fashion, another determinant which is distributed as a gradient. This may be outlined in a highly speculative way as follows. Posterior determinants (*p′* and *p* in Fig. 3.4) may reside normally in the *anterior and posterior,* respectively, pole region of the egg. The rôle of the anterior determinant *a* may be, in the normal egg, to cooperate with *p′* so as to form a product *ap′* (Fig. 3.7). This could then serve as a graded anterior signal which, together with *p*, specifies the normal body pattern. It is implied that *a* cooperates with *p′* but not with *p*. Yet both *p* and *p′* are thought to be 'understood' as posterior determinants by the reacting cells. If *a* is then inactivated or removed, a symmetrical double abdomen will be formed. The model implies that UV irradiation and other types of interference causing double abdomen formation act upon *a* but leave *p′* essentially unaffected. Moreover, the cooperation of *a* and *p′* should not occur before blastoderm formation since repair of UV damage to *a* can be delayed until this stage (Kalthoff *et al.* 1975). This would explain why *a* is apparently inactive until blastoderm formation (Section VII) whereas the number of missing segments, upon transverse fragmentation, seems to decrease also before this stage (Fig. 3.6). A result not readily covered by this model is the reduction in the yield of double abdomens, after UV irradiation of the anterior egg quarter, by irradiation of posterior egg regions (Kalthoff, 1971a). This effect is accompanied, however, by developmental delay which in turn may allow temperature and stage dependent repair processes that are not understood (Kalthoff, 1971c). In any case the speculative modification discussed here may show that the gradient model allows further sophistication. This will become almost inevitable if it becomes possible to take the analysis of pattern specification to a molecular level.

X. RELEVANCE OF SOME PHYLOGENETIC TRENDS IN INSECT OOGENESIS AND EMBRYOGENESIS TO PATTERN SPECIFICATION

The vast variety of insect species is reflected in different modes of oogenesis and embryogenesis. This suggests that the formation of the basic body pattern may be different in different groups of insects. Krause (1939) has classified insect embryos as short germ, long germ and semilong germ types. In the short germ type (e.g. the gryllid orthopteran *Tachycines*) the germ anlage essentially represents the procephalon and a budding zone which, subsequent to the germ anlage stage, gives rise to all other segments. This type of germ anlage, as a rule, is also very small as compared to the egg size. By contrast, in the long germ type (e.g. *Drosophila*) the different body regions are represented proportionally to their dimensions in the future germ band. Little or no differential growth occurs, and the germ anlage is usually as long as the egg. Between these extremes, intermediate cases (referred to as semilong germ types) exist where some anterior segments appear to be represented in proportion to the procephalon, while the remaining posterior segments originate from a growth zone (e.g. *Euscelis, Acheta*).

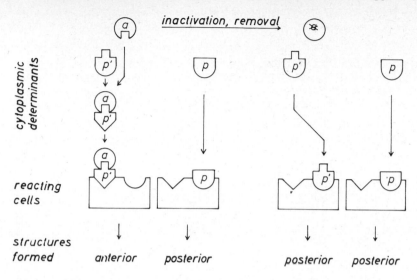

FIG. 3.7. Speculative scheme showing putative interaction of anterior determinant *a*, posterior determinants *p* and *p'*, and reacting cells in *Smittia* eggs (see also Fig. 3.4). In the normal egg, cooperation of *a* and *p'* leads to the signal *ap'* causing formation of anterior structures. No cooperation occurs between *a* and *p*. By inactivation or removal of *a*, cooperation of *a* and *p'* can be prevented. Both *p* and *p'* are then 'understood' as signals causing formation of posterior structures. Both *p* and *p'* might be set up as gradients from egg components located in the anterior and posterior pole region, respectively.

As a rule, the relative amount of clear cytoplasm, and in particular periplasm, increases from short germ to long germ type. This is correlated to a considerable decrease in the time required for embryonic development from about a month in *Acheta* down to one day in *Drosophila* (see Table 3.1). At the same time, the rate of oogenesis is

TABLE 3.1

Germ type	short germ	long germ
Relative amount of clear cytoplasm	small	large
Rate of oogenesis	low	high
Rate of embryogenesis	low	high
Type of oogenesis	panoistic	meroistic
DNA content per haploid genome	high	low
RNA content of deposited egg	low	high
Duration of regulative capacity	long	short
Origin of posterior segments	budding zone	part of germ anlage
Rôle of anterior determinants	not demonstrated	demonstrated

also considerably higher in insects with long germ embryos. The apparent basis for both rapid oogenesis and rapid embryogenesis is the meroistic type of oogenesis which allows the rapid transfer of large stores of RNA and other material to the oocyte within a short time. In the panoistic type of ovary, RNA is synthesized for the oocyte by the oocyte nucleus and possibly some by the follicle cells. In meroistic ovaries the oocyte nucleus is nearly inactive and practically all of the RNA synthesis occurs in the trophocytes or nurse cells, respectively. These cells usually originate from the germ line and become highly polyploid (Mahowald 1972). As the oocyte nucleus is thus relieved of RNA synthesis, the DNA content per haploid genome tends to decrease from species with panoistic to species with meroistic oogenesis (Bier 1970). At the same time, the RNA concentration in eggs from the latter is much higher (Jäckle & Kalthoff unpublished).

The evolutionary trend thus seems to favour an increasing degree of 'prefabrication' of the embryo already during oogenesis. The principal advantages apparently include (1) an increase in the number of generations per season and/or the capacity to populate biotopes with only short periods of sufficiently high temperature, (2) reduction in time of the immobile stage between oviposition and hatching, and (3) a greater phylogenic potential due to a genome with low redundance (Bier 1970). The evolution of the specification of the basic body pattern seems to fit this trend (see Table 3.1). With respect to mosaic versus regulative development, short germ embryos display a considerable capacity for regulation which persists until germ anlage stages. Such regulative capacities are unknown in most higher insects (see Sander 1976). As exemplified by the gap phenomenon (Section VIII), the ability for negative regulation upon transverse fragmentation vanishes, from primitive to evolved types, at increasingly earlier stages of development. In short germ embryos, the basic body pattern may *not* be specified by the position of the prospective pattern elements in gradients or other spatial coordinate systems in the whole egg. Rather, a temporal sequence of functional states in the budding zone may be translated into the ensuing spatial pattern. Such a model has been derived by Summerbell *et al.* (1973) from their results of transplantation experiments with chick wing buds. However, building an embryo by successive growth from a budding zone is obviously more time consuming than simultaneous segregation and subsequent segmentation of the germ anlage over its full length. For an efficient *in situ* specification of an extended segment pattern, the oriented transfer of material from nurse cells to oocytes may have provided a new basis (see Sander 1976).

The contribution of trophocytes or nurse cells to the material stored in the oocyte indeed appears to have great impact on the specification of the body segment pattern of the embryo. This is suggested by the production of double abdomens in dipteran eggs upon removal or inactivation of anterior egg material (Section VI, Fig. 3.4). A correlation of the antero-posterior axis of the developing egg to the nurse cell-oocyte axis was also found in a *Drosophila* mutant with abnormal follicles (Gill 1963, 1964). The involvement of anterior determinants in pattern specification is further indicated in several non-dipteran eggs by the partial segment patterns produced by posterior fragments upon separation. After separation at later stages of development, an increasing capacity to form partial posterior patterns has been observed in several species with meroistic oogenesis but not in species with panoistic oogenesis such as *Acheta* (Sander *et al.* 1970). A speculation as to how the new anterior determinants may have cooperated with pre-existing mechanisms also involved in the specification of the posterior segment pattern has been outlined in Section IX.

XI. SUMMARY

In the insect embryo, procephalon, gnathocephalon, thorax, and abdomen are regarded as elements of a basic longitudinal body pattern. The specification of this pattern and its polarity require the epigenetic action of cytoplasmic determinants which are transferred to the egg during oogenesis.

Three cytoplasmic determinants have been revealed which display different modes of action. (1) The oosome found in many Diptera, Hymenoptera, and Coleoptera acts as a germ cell determinant. Its action is clearly dissociated, however, from pattern specification in the somatic part of the body. In contrast to the limited determinative range of the oosome, other prelocalized egg components exert a specifying influence far beyond their immediate vicinity. (2) Translocation of posterior pole material may cause polarity reversal and/or the formation of supernumerary segments in fragmented eggs of the leaf hopper, *Euscelis*. Results of such experiments are at variance with a 'mosaic' model of pattern specification in which many qualitatively different determinants account each for one pattern element. Rather, the translocated posterior pole material seems to set up a *gradient of one determinant* which, by slope and local level, specifies the polarity and the basic body pattern. (3) In eggs of chironomid midges, the aberrant pattern 'double abdomen' is found upon centrifigation as well as UV irradiation or puncturing near the anterior pole. The anterior determinant apparently inactivated or removed by these operations seems to involve a nucleic acid-protein complex. It is contained in the clear cytoplasmic fraction but apparently not associated with mitochondria or endoplasmic reticulum. Masked messenger RNA may be involved which, by action or nonaction, could cause major changes in the gene regulatory network.

The evolution of basic body pattern specification seems to fit a trend towards increasing 'prefabrication' of the insect embryo during embryogenesis. As a rule, regulative capacities are greater and persist longer in the development of primitive species. In insects with meroistic oogenesis, the transfer of RNA and other material from nurse cells to oocytes may have provided a new basis which allowed the prelocalization of anterior determinants. Their contribution to pattern specification may have used, however, pre-existing mechanisms also involved in the specification of the abdominal segment pattern.

ACKNOWLEDGEMENTS

I wish to thank Professor K. Sander and Dr P. A. Lawrence for stimulating discussions and critically reading the manuscript. My research work was supported by the Deutsche Forschungsgemeinschaft, SFB 46.

DISCUSSION

Slack: Why do you think that the action spectrum indicates destruction of gradient substances; because if cells absorb radiation at 260 and 280, and nucleic acids or proteins are damaged, this is likely to have a non-specific effect. Thus interference with almost any aspect of metabolism could produce the result that you observed. This is confirmed in part by the similar result when mechanical stimuli are used. This suggests to me the use of UV might also be non-specific.

Kalthoff: First, I would like to say that the UV irradiation does not kill or inactivate the cells in the irradiated egg region, at least not to a degree which can be seen in the light microscope, or observed in timelapse movies. The anterior abdomen is apparently made from cells which would normally make the head and thorax. Thus the UV irradiation apparently interferes not with the life of the cells, but with the morphogenetic programme. The next problem is, why do I think that the irradiation is specific and does not cause the production of toxic metabolites, or something like that. I have not mentioned that the effect of ultraviolet irradiation is repairable, by a process which seems to involve the light dependent action of a repair enzyme. This is known in micro-organisms as photoreactivation, and is a process which specifically repairs UV damage to nucleic acids. If the irradiation had just produced some radicals, I could not see a way of the light repairing the damage, so that the egg is made normal again.

Gurdon: Would it help to say what classes of molecules you think are eliminated by those experiments? Do you really feel that they suggest that it can only be protein or RNA, or a combination?

Kalthoff: We have not done large scale screening to eliminate classes of molecules. I think that the action spectrum is positive evidence for a nucleic acid-protein complex. The only components that we think we have ruled out are ATP, and mitochondria.

Gehring: When you irradiated centrifuged eggs, did you get double abdomens by irradiation outside the head regions? It would be nice if you could demonstrate that you could get the absence of a head structure, even if you irradiated targets which were not in a region of the head, but had been moved by the centrifugation to another region.

Kalthoff: That's what we hoped. We hoped that we would be able to stratify the targets, and thereby identify them. But the results just did not fit with this hope, and when we looked at the electron micrographs, we found that even the ribosomes were not stratified, and therefore we assume that smaller particles would not have been stratified either.

When we irradiate in the clear cytoplasm region, the irradiation of centrifuged eggs is much more efficient than the irradiation of the same region in non-centrifuged eggs. This observation gives us the idea that the yolk shields the effective targets in the egg, and if targets have been displaced, it is not because they have been stratified by the centrifugation, but because they have been displaced by the yolk and the lipid.

Henson: Could you please tell me how you got the *Smittia* eggs? The *Smittia* species that I have worked on are parasitic on mayflies, and I could never find the eggs.

Kalthoff: These animals were not caught in the field, but were obtained as a laboratory strain from Professor Bauer in Tübingen, who was using it for translocation of the chromosomal material. I started this work on *Chironomus thummi* and *tentans*, because Yajima had used a *Chironomus* species in his centrifugation studies. *Smittia* is much easier to breed in the laboratory, and also gives much clearer results. This species of *Smittia* feeds on nettle powder. The species has not been determined.

Sander: I think you might be interested in the way we originally got *Smittia*. A paper was published by Waddington and a co-worker on *Smittia*, and since I was interested in getting a chironomid which is easy to rear in the laboratory, I wrote to Waddington. At that time I was in Tübingen, and he wrote back and told me that it was Professor Bauer next door to me from whom he had the stock!

Gurdon: Am I right that *bicaudal*, the mutant, has a very low penetrance?

Kalthoff: The mutant phenotype has a whole syndrome, and the most extreme form is the symmetrical type, and this occurred with a frequency of less than 1 per cent.

Schneiderman: In 10 per cent of the cases you would get the tip of the abdomen forming in the most anterior part.

REFERENCES

ACHTELIG, M. & KRAUSE, G. (1971). Experimente am ungefurchten Ei von *Pimpla turionellae* L. (Hymenoptera) zur Funktionsanalyse des Oosombereichs. *Wilh. Roux Arch. Entw Mech. Org.*, **167**, 164–182.

ANDERSON, D. T. (1966). The comparative embryology of the Diptera. *Ann. Rev. Ent.*, **11**, 23–46.

BIER, K. H. (1970). Oogenesetypen bei Insekten und Vertebraten und ihre Bedeutung für die Embryogenese und Phylogenese. *Zool. Anz. Suppl.*, **33**, 7–29.

BOWNES, M. & KALTHOFF, K. (1974). Embryonic defects in *Drosophila* eggs after partial UV irradiation at different wavelengths. *J. Embryol. exp. Morph.*, **31**, 329–345.

BULL, A. L. (1966). Bicaudal, a genetic factor which affects the polarity of the embryo in *Drosophila melanogaster*. *J. exp. Zool.*, **161**, 221–242.

CHAN, L.-N. & GEHRING, W. (1971). Determination of blastoderm cells in *Drosophila melanogaster*. *Proc. natn. Acad. Sci. USA*, **68**, 2217–2221.

COOK, J. S. (1970), Photoreactivation in animal cells. In: *Photophysiology* Vol. V, A. C. Giese ed., pp. 191–223, Acad. Press, London/New York.

COUNCE, S. J. (1961). The analysis of insect embryogenesis. *Ann. Rev. Ent.*, **6**, 295–312.

COUNCE, S. J. (1972). Causal analysis of insect embryogenesis. In: *Developmental Systems* Vol. II, Edited by Counce, S. J. and Waddington, C. H., pp. 1–156, Academic Press. London/New York.

DUSPIVA, F., SCHELLER, K., WEISS, D. & WINTER, H. (1973). Ribonucleinsäuresynthese in der teletrophmeroistischen Ovariole von *Dysdercus intermedius* Dist. (Heteroptera, Pyrrhoc.) *Wilh. Roux Arch. Entw Mech. Org.*, **172**, 83–130.

FRANZ, D. (1972). Der Einfluss des Abstands zwischen verlagertem Hinterpolmaterial und Eioberfläche auf das embryonale Segmentmuster von *Euscelis plebejus*. *Fak. für Biol. d. Univ. Freiburg*, Staatsexamensarbeit.

GARCIA-BELLIDO, A. (1975). Genetic control of wing disc development in *Drosophila*. In: *Cell Patterning* (Ciba Foundation Symposium 29), pp. 241–263. ASP, Amsterdam.

GAUSS, U. & SANDER, K. (1966). Stadienabhängigkeit embryonaler Doppelbildungen von *Chironomus th. thummi*. *Naturwiss.*, **53**, 182.

GEHRING, W. J. (1973). Genetic control of determination in the *Drosophila* embryo. In: *Genetic Mechanisms of Development* (Edited by Ruddle, F. H.), pp. 103–128. Academic Press, London/New York.

GILL, K. S. (1963). Developmental genetic studies on oogenesis in *Drosophila melanogaster*. *J. exp. Zool.*, **152**, 251–277.

GILL, K. S. (1964). Epigenetics of the promorphology of the egg in *Drosophila melanogaster*. *J. exp. Zool.*, **155**, 91–104.

GOLLUB, G. (1970). Zur Verteilung der Urgeschlechtszellen in Doppelabdomina von *Smittia parthenogenetica*. *Fak. f. Biologie d. Univ. Freiburg*, Staatsexamensarbeit.

GÜNTHER, J. (1971). Entwicklungsfähigkeit, Geschlechtsverhältnis und Fertilität von *Pimpla turionellae* (Hymenoptera, Ichneumonidae) nach Röntgenbestrahlung oder Abschnürung des Eihinterpols. *Zool. Jb. Anat.*, **88**, 1–46.

HANEL, P. (1975). Kombinierte Zentrifugations- und Strahlenstichexperimente zur Analyse der räumlichen Musterbildung im Ei von *Smittia spec.* (Chironomidae, Diptera). *Fak. f. Biologie d. Univ. Freiburg*, Staatsexamensarbeit.

HERTH, W. & SANDER, K. (1973). Mode and timing of pattern formation (regionalization) in the early embryonic development of cyclorrhapic dipterans (Protophormia, Drosophila). *Wilh. Roux Arch. Entw Mech. org.*, **172**, 1–27.

ILLMENSEE, K. (1973). The potentialities of transplanted early gastrula nuclei of *Drosophila melanogaster*. Production of their imago descendants by germ-line transplantation. *Wilh. Roux Arch. Entw Mech. Org.*, **171**, 331–343.

ILLMENSEE, K. & MAHOWALD, A. P. (1974). Transplantation of posterior polar plasm in *Drosophila*. Induction of germ cells at the anterior pole of the egg. *Proc. natn. Acad. Sci. USA*, **71**, 1016–1020.

JUNG, E. (1966). Untersuchungen am Ei des Speisebohnenkäfers *Bruchidius obtectus* Say (Coleoptera) II. Entwicklungsphysiologische Ergebnisse der Schnürexperimente. *Wilh. Roux Arch. Entw Mech. Org.*, **157**, 320–392.

JUNG, E. & KRAUSE, G. (1967). Experimente mit Verlagerung polnahen Eimaterials zur Analyse der Bedingungen für die metamere Gliederung des Embryos von *Bruchidius* (Coleoptera). *Wilh. Roux Arch. Entw Mech. Org.*, **159**, 89–126.

KALTHOFF, K. (1971a). Reversionsmöglichkeiten der Entwicklung zur Mißbildung 'Doppelabdomen' im UV-bestrahlten Ei von *Smittia spec.* (Dipt. Chironomidae). *Zool. Anz. Suppl.*, **34**, 61–65.

KALTHOFF, K. (1971b). Position of targets and period of competence for UV induction of the malformation 'double abdomen' in the egg of *Smittia* spec. (Diptera, Chironomidae). *Wilh. Roux Arch. Entw Mech. Org.*, **168**, 63–84.

KALTHOFF, K. (1971c). Q_{10}-values of normal developmental rate and the effect of temperature upon the frequency of the malformation 'double abdomen' in UV irradiated eggs of *Smittia* spec. (Diptera Chironomidae) *Wilh. Roux Arch. Entw Mech. Org.*, **168**, 85–96.

KALTHOFF, K. (1973). Action spectra for UV induction and photoreversal of a switch in the developmental program of the egg of an insect *(Smittia)*. *Photochem. Photobiol.*, **18**, 355–364.

KALTHOFF, K. (1975). *Smittia* spec. (Diptera). Normale Embryonalentwicklung. Aberration des Segment-musters nach UV-Bestrahlung. *Encyclop. Cinematograph*, (Göttingen) Film E 2158/1974.

KALTHOFF, K. & SANDER, K. (1968). Der Entwicklungsgang der Mißbildung 'Doppelabdomen' im partiell UV-bestrahlten Ei von *Smittia parthenogenetica* (Dipt. Chironomidae). *Wilh. Roux Arch. Entw Mech. Org.*, **161**, 129–146.

KALTHOFF, K., KANDLER-SINGER, I., SCHMIDT, O., ZISSLER, D. and VERSEN, G. (1975). Mitochondria and polarity in the egg of *Smittia* (Diptera, Chironomidae): UV irradiation, respiration measurements, ATP determinations, and application of inhibitors. *Wilh. Roux Arch. Entw Mech. Org.*, **178**, 99–121.

KAUFFMAN, S. (1973). Control circuits for determination and transdetermination. *Science*, **181**, 310–318.

KOCH, P. & HEINIG, S. (1968). Die räumliche Verteilung der Proteine in Feld- und Hausgrilleneiern. *Wilh. Roux Arch. Antw Mech. Org.*, **161**, 241–248.

KRAUSE, G. (1939). Die Eitypen der Insekten. *Biol. Zbl.*, **59**, 495–536.

KRAUSE, G. & KRAUSE, J. (1957). Die Regulation der Embryonalanlage von *Tachycines* (Saltatoria) im Schnittversuch. *Zool. Jb. Abt. Anat. u. Ontog.*, **75**, 481–550.

KRAUSE, G. & KRAUSE, J. (1965). Über das Vermögen median durschnittener Keimanlagen von *Bombyx mori* L. sich in ovo und sich ohne Dottersystem in vitro zwillingsartig zu entwickeln. *Z. Naturf.*, **20b**, 334–339.

LAWRENCE, P. A. (1970). Polarity and patterns in the postembryonic development of insects. *Adv. Insect Physiol.*, **7**, 197–266.

MAHOWALD, A. P. (1972). Oogenesis. In: *Developmental Systems: Insects* Vol I, S. J. Counce & C. H. Waddington eds., pp. 1–49, Academic Press, London/New York.

MEINHARDT, H. & GIERER, A. (1974). Applications of a theory of biological pattern formation based on lateral inhibition. *J. Cell Sci.*, **15**, 321–346.

MORATA, G. & LAWRENCE, P. (1975). Control of compartment development by the *engrailed* gene in *Drosophila*. *Nature, Lond.*, **255**, 614–617.

NÜNEMANN, H. & MOSER, J. G. (1970). Isolierung und immunelektrophoretische Charakterisierung von Proteinen aus Teilen einzelner Eier der Hausgrille *Acheta domesticus*. *Zool. Anz. Suppl.*, **33**, 113–120.

OKADA, E. & WADDINGTON, C. H. (1959). The submicroscopic structure of the *Drosophila* egg. *J. Embryol. exp. Morph.*, **7**, 583–597.

OKADA, M., KLEINMAN, A. & SCHNEIDERMAN, H. A. (1974). Restoration of fertility in sterilized *Drosophila* eggs by transplantation of polar cytoplasm. *Devl. Biol.*, **37**, 43–54.

OVERTON, J. & RAAB, M. (1967). The development and fine structure of centrifuged eggs of *Chironomus thummi*. *Devl. Biol.*, **15**, 271–287.

RUNNSTRÖM, J. (1929). Über Selbstdifferenzierung und Induktion bei dem Seeigelkeim. *Wilhelm Roux Arch. Entw Mech. Org.*, **117**, 123–145.

SANDER, K. (1960). Analyse des ooplasmatischen Reaktionssystems von *Euscelis plebejus* Fall. (Cicadina) durch Isolieren und Kombinieren von Keimteilen. II. Mitteilung: Die Differenzierungsleistungen nach Verlagern von Hinterpolmaterial. *Wilh. Roux Arch. Entw Mech. Org.*, **151**, 660–707.

SANDER, K. (1961). New experiments concerning the ooplasmic reaction system of *Euscelis plebejus* (Cicadina). In: *Symposium on Germ Cells and Development*, Inst. Intern. d'Embryol. Pallanza, pp. 338–353.

SANDER, K. (1971). Pattern formation in longitudinal halves of leaf hopper eggs (Homoptera) and some remarks on the definition of 'embryonic regulation'. *Wilh. Roux Arch. Entw Mech. Org.*, **167**, 336–352.

SANDER, K. (1974). Beeinflussen symbiontische Bakterien die Embryonalentwicklung von Insekten? *Umschau*, **74**, 619.

SANDER, K. (1975). Pattern specification in the insect embryo. In: *Cell patterning* (Ciba Foundation symposium 29), pp. 241–263. *ASP*, Amsterdam.

SANDER, K. (1976). Specification of the basic body pattern in insect embryogenesis. Adv. Insect Physiol. **12** (in press.)

SANDER, K., HERTH, W. & VOLLMAR, H. (1970). Abwandlungen des metameren Organisationsmusters in fragmentierten und abnormen Insekteneiern. *Zool. Anz. Suppl.*, **33**, 46–52.

SCHMIDT, O., ZISSLER, D., SANDER, K. & KALTHOFF, K. (1975). Switch in pattern formation after puncturing the anterior pole of *Smittia* eggs (Chironomidae, Diptera) *Devl Biol.*, **46**, 216–221.

SCHWEMMLER, W. (1974). Endosymbionts: factors of egg pattern formation. *J. Insect Physiol.*, **20**, 1447–1474.

SEIDEL, F. (1926). Die Determinierung der Keimanlage bei Insekten I. *Biol. Zbl.*, **46**, 321–343.

SEIDEL, F. (1961). Entwicklungsphysiologische Zentren im Eisystem der Insekten. *Zool. Anz. Suppl.*, **24**, 121–142.

SUMMERBELL, D., LEWIS, J. H. & WOLPERT, L. (1973). Positional information in chick limb morphogenesis. *Nature, Lond.*, **244**, 492–496.

WADDINGTON, C. H. (1966). Fields and gradients. In: *Major Problems in Developmental Biology* (Edited by Locke, M.), pp. 105–124. Academic Press, London/New York.

WINTER, H. (1974). Ribonukleoprotein-Partikel aus dem telotroph-meroistischen Ovar von *Dysdercus intermedius* Dist. (Heteroptera, Pyrrhoc.) und ihr Verhalten im zellfreien Proteinsynthesesystem. *Wilhelm Roux Arch. EntwMech. Org.*, **175**, 103–127.

WOLPERT, L. (1971). Positional information and pattern formation *Curr. Topics Devl. Biol.*, **6**, 183–224.

YAJIMA, H. (1960). Studies on embryonic determination of the harlequin-fly, *Chironomus dorsalis* I. Effects of centrifugation and of its combination with constriction and puncturing. *J. Embryol. exp. Morph.*, **8**, 198–215.

YAJIMA, H. (1964). Studies on embryonic determination of the harlequin-fly, *Chironomus dorsalis* II. Effects of partial irradiation of the egg by ultraviolet light. *J. Embryol. exp. Morph.*, **12**, 89–100.

YAJIMA, H. (1970). Study of the development of the internal organs of the double malformations of *Chironomus dorsalis* by fixed and sectioned materials. *J. Embryol. exp. Morph.*, **24**, 287–303.

ZISSLER, D. & SANDER, K. (1973). The cytoplasmatic architecture of the egg cell of *Smittia* spec. I. Anterior and posterior pole regions. *Wilh. Roux Arch. EntwMech. Org.*, **172**, 175–186.

Notes added in proof

In *Drosophila* eggs, 'dicephalic' embryos were found as spontaneous pattern abberations (Lohs-Schardin, M. & Sander, K., *Wilh. Roux Arch. EntwMech. Org.*, in press). They resemble the 'double cephalons' produced by UV or centrifugation in *Chironomus* eggs (Yajima 1970).

The anterior determinants in *Smittia* eggs appear to include a ribonucleic acid moiety since double abdomens can be produced by application of RNase to the anterior pole region (Kandler-Singer, I. & Kalthoff, K., unpublished).

4 • Nuclear and cytoplasmic transplantation in *Drosophila**

KARL ILLMENSEE

Institute for Cancer Research, Fox Chase, Philadelphia, Pennsylvania 19111

NUCLEAR TRANSPLANTATION

Although a method for transplanting nuclei in the protozoan *Amoeba* (Comandon & de Fonbrune 1939) has been known for some time, it was not until 1952 that Briggs & King reported successful nuclear transplantations in the frog *Rana pipiens,* thereby opening up a new field in developmental biology of higher organisms. Subsequently, their technique of transplanting a nucleus from a somatic cell back into an unfertilized egg has been extensively applied to several other amphibian species (reviewed by Gurdon 1964). It soon became apparent that such a bioassay system would provide new ways of attacking some of the long-standing problems in biology, among which belong the following: Are there changes in potentiality of nuclei during the course of development? Do nuclei become determined for a certain developmental fate and, if so, how and when does it happen in the organism? Is this 'programme', whatever its molecular nature may be, irreversibly restricting the nuclei to cell lineage-specific pathways? Does a difference in nuclear potential between soma and germ line exist?

Besides the tremendous advantages of Amphibia as the source of convenient experimental material for microinjection which had been widely and effectively employed during the past two decades to study nucleocytoplasmic interactions in development (reviewed by Gurdon 1974), the lack of a well-investigated genetic background amenable to gene manipulation and the long life cycle of these animals make it difficult to gain insight into the genetic mechanisms underlying differentiation and cellular diversification. In this respect, the most promising higher organism from a genetic point of view appears to be the fruit fly *Drosophila melanogaster.* The first attempts to introduce wildtype nuclei from early embryos into genetically marked, unfertilized eggs of this species, however, happened to be rather discouraging inasmuch as only a small number of defective embryos and larvae developed after nuclear transplantation (Geyer-Duszyńska 1967; Illmensee 1968). Improved results from serial nuclear transfers in which nuclei from the defective embryos were successively reinjected into unfertilized eggs indicated that the transplanted nuclei probably did not cause the early developmental standstill. However, since no flies developed, the question still remained: are the transplanted nuclei actually able to promote differentiation of

* This article is dedicated to Robert Briggs.

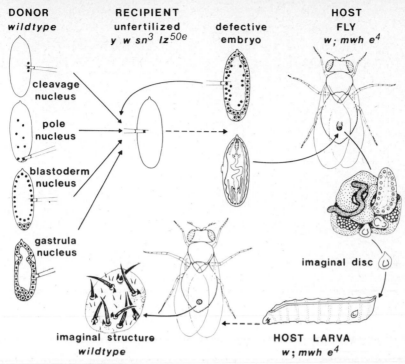

DONOR
wildtype

RECIPIENT
unfertilized
y w sn³ lz⁵⁰ᵉ

defective
embryo

HOST
FLY
w; mwh e⁴

cleavage
nucleus

pole
nucleus

blastoderm
nucleus

gastrula
nucleus

imaginal disc

imaginal structure
wildtype

HOST LARVA
w; mwh e⁴

FIG. 4.1. Procedure for testing the developmental potential of embryonic nuclei. Single nuclei from different regions and at various developmental stages of embryos were transplanted into unfertilized eggs. After the donor nucleus had multiplied and populated the egg, some of the resulting embryos served as nuclear donors for further transplantations into unfertilized eggs. The remaining embryos were implanted into the abdominal cavity of host flies. During this *in vivo* culture, the implants developed further into disorganized larval structures including imaginal discs, the precursors of adult cuticle. These discs were then injected into larvae where they differentiated into imaginal cuticular structures during host metamorphosis. The three kinds of recipients and hosts carried several marker genes in order to distinguish them phenotypically from the wildtype structures derived from the transplanted nuclei. (Modified from Illmensee 1972.)

imaginal structures? By culturing the nuclear-transplant embryos in the abdomen of host flies (Hadorn *et al.* 1968), in which they developed further into disorganized larvae with imaginal discs (the precursors for fly cuticle), it was then possible to implant these discs into genetically different larvae (Fig. 4.1). There they differentiated during host metamorphosis into virtually all cuticular adult structures, thus indicating that the transplanted embryonic nuclei up to the blastoderm stage still possessed the full potential for imaginal development (Illmensee 1971, 1972; Schubiger & Schneiderman 1971). This has recently been confirmed in a transplantation series with nuclei from blastoderm cells in which a few of the nuclear-transplant embryos actually developed into fertile flies, finally proving the totipotency of individual blastoderm nuclei (Fig. 4.2). Developmental flexibility of these nuclei was also convincingly concluded from implantations into *fertilized* eggs. Anterior blastoderm nuclei transplanted to the posterior pole of genetically marked cleavage embryos became integrated and differentiated into posterior structures of the fly cuticle or into germ cells, whereas posterior nuclei transferred to the anterior tip of the embryo participated in forming anterior cuticular structures in mosaic flies (Zalokar 1971, 1973; Okada *et al.* 1974c).

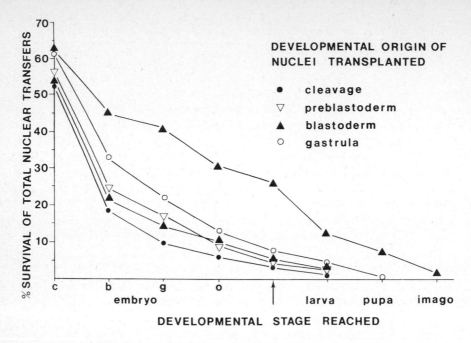

Fig. 4.2. Comparison of nuclear-transplant survival and development with respect to nuclear origin. Single nuclei from different embryonic stages (cleavage to gastrulation) were injected into unfertilized eggs. The various kinds of donor nuclei were equally effective in promoting development. The increased survival rate and development of about 2 per cent of the transplants to the imaginal stage were obtained in a recent series with blastoderm nuclei, that was probably due to technical improvements. c = cleavage; b = blastoderm; g = gastrula; o = organogenesis. The arrow marks the hatching period of the larva. (Summarized from Illmensee (1972, 1973) including unpublished data.)

The same conclusion can be drawn from interspecific nuclear transplantations in *Drosophila* (Santamaria 1975).

In contrast, as soon as cells have been established during blastogenesis, developmental restrictions occurred at the *cellular* level along the anteroposterior axis of the *Drosophila* embryo; i.e., anterior blastoderm cells after *in vivo* culture differentiated exclusively into anterior structures of the fly cuticle and posterior cells gave rise only to posterior structures (Chan & Gehring 1971). Since nuclear transplantations, on the other hand, had revealed that at least some of the blastoderm nuclei remain totipotent, nuclei of early gastrula cells from five different regions in the embryo were subsequently tested for their capacity to initiate development of unfertilized eggs in order to learn whether the nuclei like the cells from a more advanced stage may have undergone loss of developmental potential as ontogeny proceeded. Determination at the *nuclear* and even at the *chromosomal* level could be proved or disproved from the extent to which these eggs developed. All five kinds of transplanted nuclei were equally effective in promoting development. Fertile flies, genetic descendants of the various donor nuclei, could be produced via the germ line in two ways: (1) pole cells of nuclear-transplant blastoderm embryos and (2) gonads from nuclear-transplant larvae were implanted into genetically marked embryos and larvae, respectively. In both instances gametes developed normally from the transplants as could be recognized from the phenotype of their progeny. By means of suitable crosses with partners carrying inversion-stabilized chromosomes to prevent recombination between the nuclear-transplant chromosomes and the chromosomes from the mating partner, it was possible to obtain clones of flies each derived from the original chromosomes of a single gastrula nucleus (Illmensee 1973). This demonstrates that, in principle, a genetic analysis of a somatic nucleus for revealing recessive mutations can be carried out in approximately four weeks in *Drosophila* as compared to 3–4 years in Amphibia (Fischberg *et al.* 1963). For the time being, then, it can be concluded that gastrula nuclei which exhibited the same developmental capacity as the nuclei from earlier embryonic stages (Fig. 4.2) have not become irreversibly restricted for a distinct pathway and, in fact, may still possess the full potentiality of a zygote nucleus. Since the cells and not the nuclei appear determined at this early embryonic stage, the determinative information has to reside in the cytoplasm. Further evidence for this will be provided in the section dealing with cytoplasmic transplantation. At the present time, however, nothing is known in molecular terms about the putative determinative factors localized in the egg cytoplasm nor do we yet understand as to when and how such epigenetic information interacts with the nuclear genome in controlling gene expression and maintaining cell lineage-specific commitments in the developing organism.

In recent years, successful attempts at establishing *in vitro* cell lines from *Drosophila* embryos (Echalier & Ohanessian 1970; Schneider 1972; Mosna & Dolfini 1972; Kuroda 1974; Dübendorfer *et al.* 1975) opened up a new source for nuclear transplantation in this genetically well-defined organism. If nuclei from cultured cells were capable of promoting development at least to the blastoderm stage, one could then hope to clonally propagate their genome in the germ line via pole cell transfer, as mentioned above, and thereby analyse *in vivo* the developmental and genetic potential of nuclei from *in vitro* cultured cells. For as yet unknown reasons, however, none of the 173 unfertilized eggs that had been injected with single nuclei from five different cell lines (kindly supplied by Drs I. Schneider and G. Echalier) showed any signs of development. One possible explanation for the failure to initiate the first developmental processes might be the inability of these nuclei to switch quickly enough to the rapid mitotic cycle, typical of early embryogenesis. This has frequently been observed after transplantation of nuclei from cultured cells in Amphibia (Gurdon & Laskey 1970; Kobel *et al.* 1973; Gurdon *et al.* 1975).

In a subsequent series, the *in vitro* cultured-cell nuclei were therefore injected into cleavage embryos, thus allowing them to adapt gradually to the different cytoplasmic environment and eventually becoming integrated into cells during blastoderm formation. Injections of nuclei into the *posterior* region of the genetically marked recipient embryos should favour their segregation into pole cells, the primordial germ cells, and consequently their appearance in the germ line. The results of these transplantations (Table 4.1) show that only nuclei from cell lines 1 and 52–84 were capable of bringing about development of larval and also adult tissues. Although a relatively small number of nuclei had actually been tested, it seems that nuclei from line 1 more frequently gave rise to larval tissues whereas nuclei from line 52–84 differentiated preferentially into adult structures. Presumably this may reflect different embryonic origins of these two cell lines and/or selection during *in vitro* culture as has recently been attempted to verify at the molecular level (Debec 1974). Both kinds of nuclei participated less frequently in development and produced much smaller patches of tissue, when compared with contributions derived from normal blastoderm nuclei.

TABLE 4.1. Developmental fate of single nuclei from *in vitro* cultured cells after transplantation into fertilized *y sn³ mal* eggs at the cleavage stage.

Source of donor-cell nuclei	No. of nuclear transfers	No. of *y sn³ mal* animals developed				
		Larvae		Flies		
		Total	Mosaics with tissues derived from donor nuclei (%)	Total	Mosaics with tissues derived from donor nuclei (%)	
Line 1	205	53	8	(15.1)	95	6	(6.3)
Line 2	201	65	3	(4.6)	82	—	—
Line 3	160	54	—	—	62	—	—
Line K	142	28	—	—	71	3	(4.2)
Line 52-84	190	43	2	(4.7)	87	9	(10.3)
Blastoderm	123	37	9	(24.3)	49	15	(30.6)

Cell lines 1, 2, and 3 originating from 21 h-old embryos in 1969 were kindly supplied by Dr I. Schneider. Cell lines K established from 9 h-old embryos in 1968 and cell line 52-84, a subclone of K isolated in 1973, were obtained from Dr G. Echalier. Blastoderm nuclei were collected from the mid-lateral region of wildtype embryos at the blastoderm stage.

Furthermore, no progeny from the cultured-cell nuclei could be recovered although from the total number of nuclear-transplant survivors and the frequency of somatic mosaicism obtained one might have expected at least a few flies with mosaic gonads. Once again, it may well be that the potential of these nuclei became somewhat restricted during the long *in vitro* period. Further extensive transplantations with nuclei from short-term cell lines are necessary to cope with the problem of establishing nuclei from cultured cells in the germ line of the living organism. Nevertheless, for the time being after almost five years in culture, some nuclei still functioned normally *in vivo* and were able to participate in forming various kinds of somatic tissues such as gut, fat body, Malpighian tubes, and adult cuticular structures (Table 4.2). The fact that even chromosomes of the cultured-cell nuclei became polytene as observed in cells of the Malpighian tubes is of particular importance inasmuch as it may allow cytogenetic finemapping of somatic mutations. Tissue contributions derived from the transplanted nuclei could be either visualized histochemically by testing for aldehyde oxidase activity or distinguished morphologically from the genetically marked *y sn³ mal* recipients (Fig. 4.3). It is worth mentioning that the hitherto unknown phenotype of the cell lines has been revealed *in situ*. The cuticular structures originating from nuclei of line 1 clearly exhibited the wild phenotype whereas those structures from lines K and 52-84 consistently showed deviations from the normal bristle pattern similar to the *Minute* phenotype. The latter probably results from the haplo-4 chromosomal constitution of these two cell lines which occurred during culture. In principle, therefore, it is feasible to provide a developmental and genetic test system for *in vitro* cultured cells via nuclear transplantation in *Drosophila*.

TABLE 4.2. Larval and adult tissues containing contributions from single nuclei of *in vitro* cultured cells after transplantation to the posterior region of *y sn³ mal* cleavage embryos.

| Source of nucleus transplanted | No. of animals with mosaic tissues (from Table 4.1) | | | | | | | | | | | | | |
| | Larvae | | | | Flies | | | | | | | | | |
	Gut	Fat body	Malpighian tubes	Hypoderm	Gut	Fat body	Malpighian tubes	Thorax	Abdomen	Genitalia	Germ line	Thorax & Abdomen	Abdomen & Genitalia	Abdomen & Genitalia & Germ line
Line 1	3	1	2	2	2	–	1	1	1	–	–	–	1	–
Line 2	1	–	–	2	1	–	–	1	–	–	–	–	–	–
Line K	–	–	–	–	1	1	1	–	1	–	–	–	1	–
Line 52–84	1	–	1	1	1	1	1	–	3	–	–	1	2	–
Blastoderm	2	2	2	3	2	1	2	–	2	1	2	1	1	3

Mosaicism in these animals was detected histochemically and morphologically by using genetically marked embryos as recipients for nuclear implantation (see text for details).

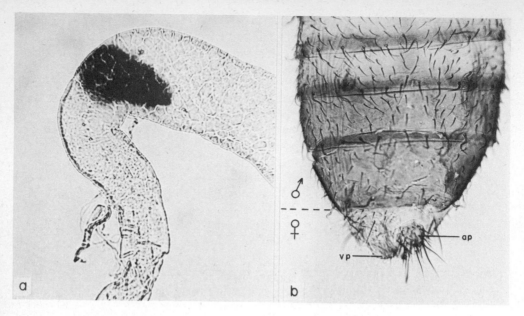

FIG. 4.3. Somatic mosaicism of larval and adult tissues resulting from nuclei of *in vitro* cultured cells after transplantation to the posterior region of fertilized *y sn³ mal* eggs. (a) Larval posterior midgut. A cluster of about 35 intensively stained cells reveals histochemically its clonal origin from a transplanted nucleus of Schneider's cell line 1. The positive staining reaction results from the presence of aldehyde oxidase in these cells, whereas the unstained cells of the host do not express this enzyme due to the mutant gene *maroonlike (mal)*. X 100. (b) Abdomen of a gynandromorphic fly which developed from a male embryo into which a female nucleus of Echalier's line 52-84 had been injected during the late cleavage stage. All the cuticular structures of this male show phenotypically the marker genes *yellow (y)* and *singed (sn³)*, except for the 8th abdominal segment and the following posterior ones. In this female area, as can be seen from the vaginal plate (vp) and anal plates (ap), the slightly pale appearance of the cuticle, deviations from the normal bristle pattern, and the formation of only one vaginal plate may be due to the haplo-4 chromosomal constitution of the transplanted nucleus cryptically expressing a *Minute* phenotype. X 75.

Cytoplasmic Transplantation

For almost a century one of the long-standing problems in developmental biology has been the question of whether there is a morphogenetic architecture built into the egg. The results of cell lineage studies on annelid, nematode, mollusk, ascidian, and insect embryos (reviewed by Davidson 1968) strongly support the idea that very early in embryogenesis a 'precocious segregation' of morphogenetic potential takes place resulting in the partitioning of localized cytoplasmic information of the egg into stem cells for future developmental pathways. Attempts have recently been made towards an understanding of morphogenetic patterns in molecular terms by establishing a relationship between differential segregation of egg cytoplasm and the appearance of specific proteins (Whittaker 1973; Newrock & Raff 1975; Graziosi & Roberts 1975). The biochemical search for cytoplasmic determinants, however, faces the difficulties of finding differences at the molecular level that are causally related to morphogenetic events and of analysing how these cytoplasmic factors interact with discrete portions of the genome to establish cell lineage-specific patterns of gene expression during the course of development.

A promising approach to elucidating the localization phenomenon employs those mutations which might be regarded as 'variations' affecting the morphogenetic 'theme' of the egg. Recent efforts in selecting for maternally inherited mutants with distinctive alterations during oogenesis or early embryogenesis in *Drosophila* (Fielding 1967; Thierry-Mieg *et al.* 1972; Bakken 1973; Rice & Garen 1975) and in the axolotl (reviewed by Briggs 1973), indicate that it is feasible to genetically dissect morphogenesis in higher organisms. An additional means of searching for localized developmental potential utilizes genetic lesions of the egg cytoplasm which can be 'repaired' by injection of cytoplasm from normal eggs; furthermore, this approach provides a system for the possible identification of morphogenetic factors that are being supplied by the injected material. Recent transplantation experiments have already successfully shown that it is possible to rescue genetically defective embryos in the axolotl (Briggs & Cassens 1966; Briggs 1972) and in *Drosophila* (Garen & Gehring 1972; Okada *et al.* 1974b) by injected wildtype cytoplasm.

Probably the most conspicuous example for a cell lineage originating from a particular cytoplasmic region of the egg is demonstrated by the precocious segregation of the germ line in nematodes, amphibians, and insects (reviewed by Beams & Kessel 1974; Eddy 1975). Ablaton studies and ultraviolet irradiations on *Rana* or *Xenopus* eggs (e.g. Bounoure *et al.* 1954; Buehr & Blackler 1970; Züst & Dixon 1975) and *Drosophila* eggs (e.g. Geigy 1931; Warn 1972; Graziosi & Micali 1974) have shown that after removing or destroying the vegetal hemisphere of the frog egg or the posterior pole of the insect egg, no germ cells were formed. Injection of vegetal cytoplasm from normal *Rana* eggs into the vegetal hemisphere of UV-treated eggs could restore the formation of primordial germ cells (Smith 1966). This kind of experiment has recently been repeated successfully in insects by injecting posterior polar plasm from normal *Drosophila* eggs into the posterior region of UV-irradiated eggs (Okada *et al.* 1974a; Warn 1975). Clearly, some developmental information necessary for initiating the germ line has to be located in the cytoplasm of the *Rana* and *Drosophila* egg. In these homotopic transplantation studies, however, it has not been shown that 'germ-cell determinants' *per se* are already present in the egg. Demonstrating the presence of such determinants requires a test for (1) functional autonomy regardless of their position in the egg, and (2) functional specificity, i.e. development of germ cells that give rise to offspring.

Functional autonomy of this particular cytoplasm of the *Drosophila* egg has been tested in heterotopic transplantations. In collaboration with Dr A. P. Mahowald at Indiana University, we injected posterior polar plasm from *fertilized* eggs into the anterior or ventral region of normal cleavage embryos (Illmensee & Mahowald 1974, 1976). With this approach, the determinative potential of polar cytoplasm (or eventually its component elements) can be assayed in non-irradiated areas of the egg and in regions with a distinctive somatic fate (Poulson 1950). Characteristic cytoplasmic constituents, the polar granules, served as a suitable morphological marker to identify and trace the polar cytoplasm following transplantation. These conspicuous subcellular organelles are exclusively located in a 5-μm thick narrow band of cortical cytoplasm at the posterior pole of the egg where they become segregated into a small number of cells, the pole cells (Mahowald 1962). Our ultrastructural analysis revealed that immediately after nuclei migrated into the injected cytoplasm, several cells formed and separated from the remaining embryo just as the pole cells normally bud off at the posterior tip of the egg.

Such an early segregation of pole cells prior to blastoderm formation, even in ectopic egg regions, reflects the morphogenetic autonomy of the posterior cytoplasm. Another characteristic finding was the occurrence of round dense structures, termed nuclear bodies, in anterior as well as in ventral nuclei which had been exposed to the transplanted polar plasm. Their appearance was viewed as a further confirmation at the morphological level that following transplantation the polar cytoplasm still retained its capacity to determine the formation of pole cells (Fig. 4.4). The nuclear bodies which normally would not appear in any of the blastoderm nuclei but only in nuclei of pole cells may signal a specific physiological response of those nuclei subjected to the posterior cytoplasm. At present, however, the nature of this nucleocytoplasmic interaction remains unknown.

The occurrence of cells which contain transferred posterior cytoplasm and which resemble morphologically normal pole cells is not in itself sufficient evidence for the determinative qualities of this particular cytoplasm. The critical test is to ascertain whether or not an experimentally induced pole cell is capable of developing into functional germ cells and giving rise to offspring. Besides the impediment that a pole cell induced at the anterior tip of the embryo is not likely to reach the gonads, it is more important to realize that any progeny descending from this pole cell would not be detected phenotypically among the offspring of the cytoplasmic recipient since the nuclear marker genes in the induced pole cells and in the normal pole cells of the recipient embryo are identical. Cytoplasmic markers, on the other hand, that would allow us to discriminate in genetic terms between the injected polar plasm and cytoplasm of the recipient embryo are not known in *Drosophila*. Consequently, the induced pole cells have to be inserted among the pole cells of genetically different embryos where they migrate together with the host pole cells into the gonads in which their possible contribution to the germ line can be elucidated. Several such heterotopic cell transfers were made from each *mwh e*⁴ embryo to different *y sn*³ *mal* blastoderm hosts in order to ensure that most of the induced pole cells would be transplanted to the posterior pole of host embryos (Fig. 4.5). Flies developing from these hosts were test-mated to *y sn*³ *mal* or *mwh e*⁴ partners and their offspring scored phenotypically for the *mwh e*⁴ marker genes. About 3 per cent of the flies, females and males, proved to be germ-line mosaics (Table 4.3). The progeny test revealed that their gonads produced functional gametes carrying either the *y sn*³ *mal* or *mwh e*⁴ genotype. The latter ones derived from anterior or ventral cells with transferred posterior polar plasm, thus demonstrating that this particular cytoplasm encloses germ-cell determinants which retain their specific determinative ability after transplantation to somatic regions of the egg.

In addition to the genetic test, it was possible to detect germ-line mosaicism in flies histochemically by assaying for aldehyde oxidase activity. When the enzyme test was

FIG. 4.4. Electron micrograph of the mid-ventral peripheral region of a blastoderm embryo into which 10 pl of posterior polar cytoplasm (equivalent to the volume of 20 pole cells) had been implanted near the vitelline membrane (VM) during the early cleavage stage. Nuclei (N) which migrated into this slightly denser cytoplasm show the nuclear bodies (nb). About half the amount of transplanted polar plasm containing the polar granules (pg) is segregated into 10 'pole' cells (PC) of which four are present in this section. The adjacent blastoderm cells (BC) are not yet fully formed, as can be seen from the position of the cleavage furrows (arrows) progressing into the embryo. Thus the early segregation of experimentally induced pole cells at the ventral side as well as the anterior tip of the egg reflects what normally occurs at the posterior pole and demonstrates the morphogenetic autonomy of the posterior polar plasm. X 9,500.

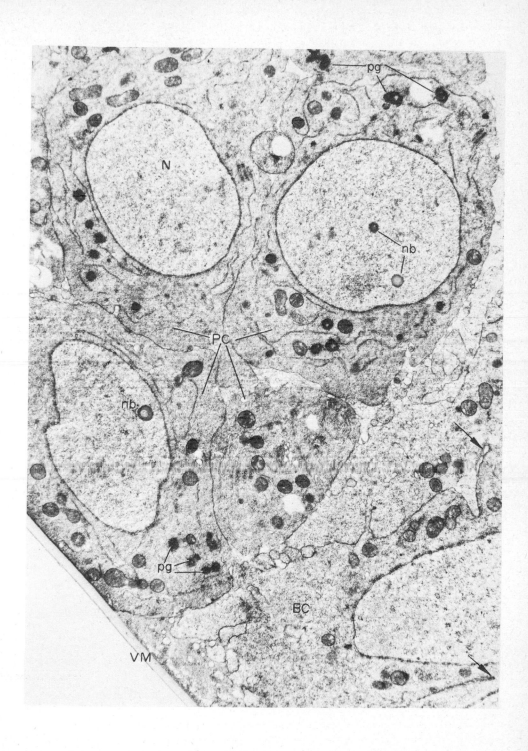

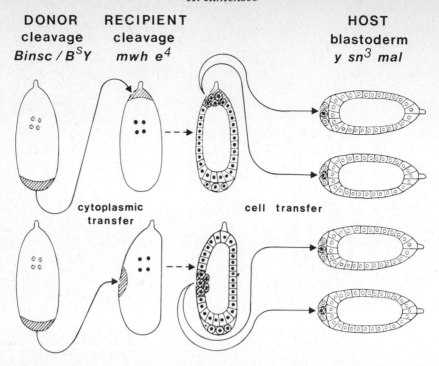

DONOR　RECIPIENT　　　　　　　　HOST
cleavage　cleavage　　　　　　blastoderm
$Binsc / B^S Y$　$mwh\ e^4$　　　　　　$y\ sn^3\ mal$

cytoplasmic
transfer

cell transfer

FIG. 4.5. Schematic illustration of an *in vivo* approach to assay for the capacity of cytoplasm from the posterior pole of the egg to induce germ-cell formation. It consists of two manipulations: (1) injection of posterior polar plasm into the anterior or ventral region of early cleavage embryos to test its autonomous inductive ability to form pole cells, the primordial germ cells, and (2) transplantation of the induced pole cells to the posterior region of blastoderm embryos. The implanted cells together with the host pole cells will eventually reach the gonads and contribute, if functional, to the reproductive line. The cytoplasmic donors were genetically marked with the dominant mutant *Bar (Binsc/B^s Y)* in order to detect any undesirable co-transfer of nuclei together with the polar plasm. The blastoderm host embryos carried the *y sn^3 mal* genes to distinguish their germ cells from those *mwh e^4* germ cells derived from cytoplasmic transfers. The experimentally induced cells, when left in the embryo into which polar plasm had been injected, would not be recognizable as induced germ cells since their nuclei originated from the recipient embryo, thus bearing the same genome as all the other nuclei of the recipient. Therefore, the cells containing transplanted polar plasm were cycled through the germ line of genetically different embryos. (Modified from Illmensee & Mahowald 1974.)

applied to the *y sn^3 mal* flies with implanted cells, those females with a phenotypically mixed progeny also exhibited stained germ cells among their own unstained ones in the ovaries (Fig. 4.6a, c). Apart from their germ-line potential, some of the induced 'pole' cells participated in forming larval and adult midgut tissue, as has been visualized histochemically (Fig. 4.6b). This agrees well with earlier observations that after preventing pole cell formation by UV damage to the posterior pole of the egg, not only are the gonads devoid of germ cells but also are the cuprophilic cells of the larval midgut either missing or significantly reduced in number (Poulson & Waterhouse 1960). Since we tested, however, histochemically for position rather than for function of these integrated cells, we cannot exclude the possibility that they may represent some of the presumptive germ cells which happened to be trapped in the gut during their migration to the gonads.

TABLE 4.3. Test for functional autonomy and specificity of posterior polar plasm. This particular cytoplasm from *Binsc*/*B^{S}Y* or wildtype cleavage embryos was injected into the anterior or ventral region of *mwh e⁴* cleavage embryos and the cells formed at these two injection sites were transplanted to the posterior pole of *y sn³ mal* blastoderm embryos. (Data from Illmensee & Mahowald 1974, 1976).

Site of polar plasm injection	No. of polar plasm transplants	*mwh e⁴* embryos from which cells were taken	*y sn³ mal* embryos to which cells were transplanted	No. of *y sn³ mal* flies developed		
				Total	Germ line mosaics	(%)
Anterior	184	53	228	125	4	(3.2)
Ventral	219	46	194	109	3	(2.8)
Control transfers[a]						
1		61	179	83	—	—
2		75	190	122	—	—

[a] In the controls, anterior (1) or mid-ventral (2) cells from non-injected *mwh e⁴* blastoderm embryos were transplanted to the posterior pole of *y sn³ mal* blastoderm hosts.

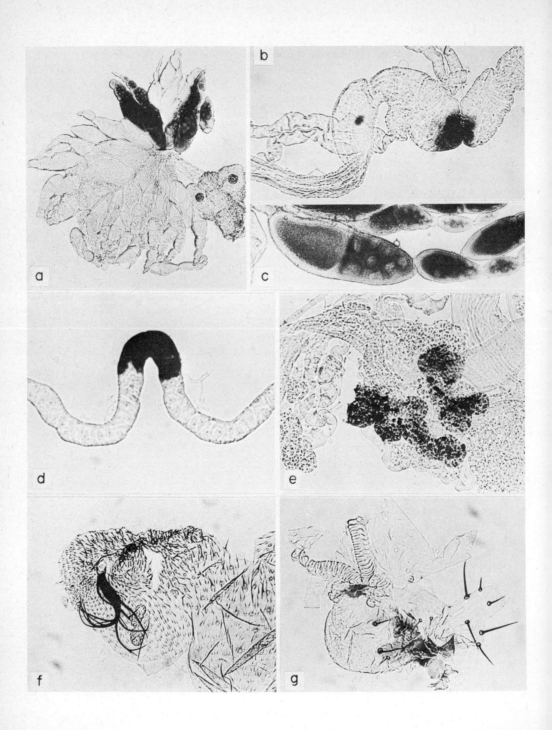

Because of the close association between the experimentally induced pole cells and the anterior or ventral blastoderm cells it is not possible during cell transplantation to distinguish clearly between cells containing transferred polar plasm and normal blastoderm cells formed near the injection site. It is thus likely that some of the latter cells have also been transplanted to the posterior pole of host embryos. In order to determine if they would be able to contribute to the germ line when juxtaposed to normal pole cells, anterior and ventral blastoderm cells from non-injected *mwh e⁴* embryos were implanted into the posterior region of *y sn³ mal* embryos at the same developmental stage. In these controls, germ-line mosaics did not appear (Table 4.3). None of the developing *y sn³ mal* flies produced *mwh e⁴* descendants among their own progeny or showed any aldehyde oxidase positive staining reaction in their gonads. A possible objection, that the transplanted blastoderm cells might degenerate in ectopic egg positions, can be answered by the fact that some of the ventral cells became integrated into larval and adult tissues (Fig. 4.6d, e) and anterior cells differentiated autonomously during metamorphosis into anterior structures of the fly cuticle (Fig. 4.6f, g). Thus it is clear that both kinds of blastoderm cells are able to survive in the posterior region of the embryo and develop into somatic structures but do not contribute to the germ line. During the course of our study, it soon became apparent that this *in vivo* cloning technique provides a unique opportunity to analyse the developmental fate and determinative state of individual blastoderm cells. Without intending to present here detailed information on this subject, it is worth mentioning that single blastoderm cells from several other regions of the embryo when transplanted to homotopic positions formed integrated mosaics but in heterotopic transfers differentiated separately into adult structures specific for the region from which they originated; i.e., posterior blastoderm cells developed into abdominal and genital cuticular structures after transplantation to the anterior tip of the embryo and did not participate in forming head cuticle. It seems reasonable to conclude that at least some of the blastoderm cells are already determined for a certain somatic fate. From the variety and number of structures and tissues clonally arising from a blastoderm cell it is also possible to explore the degree and flexibility of determination at the blastoderm stage. Whether or not somatic determinative events result from cytoplasmic information localized at the egg periphery and segregated into cells during blastogenesis, comparable to germ-cell determination, remains to be seen.

FIG. 4.6. Developmental fate of experimentally induced pole cells (a-c) and normal anterior or ventral blastoderm cells (d-g) after transplantation to the posterior pole of *y sn³ mal* blastoderm hosts. In (a-c) induced cells were collected from the mid-ventral site of *mwh e⁴* blastoderm embryos into which posterior polar cytoplasm had been injected during early cleavage; in (d-g) normal cells derived from the anterior and ventral region of non-injected *mwh e⁴* blastoderm embryos. In (a-e) mosaicism in various adult tissues was revealed by aldehyde oxidase histochemistry. The *mwh e⁴* cells normally express this enzyme, whereas the *y sn³ mal* cells of the host do not. (a) Mosaic ovary with induced germ cells (stained) together with host germ cells (unstained). The other ovary originated entirely from the female host. X 30. (b) Posterior midgut with three cells and a cluster of about 20 cells derived from an experimental pole cell. X 50. (c) Higher magnification of an ovariole in which stained oocytes and nurse cells, derivatives of an induced pole cell, are surrounded by host follicle cells. X 100. (d) Malpighian tube (X 100) and (e) fat body (X 75) in which clusters of about 15 stained cells that derived from ventral blastoderm cells became integrated into adult tissue of two different hosts. (f) Distal area of the antenna. X 175. (g) Mouthparts of the proboscis region. X 125. These antennal and labial structures of the fly cuticle, each clonally originated from a single anterior blastoderm cell, did not integrate into the hosts' tissues but differentiated autonomously in the abdominal cavities. Pigmentation (*e⁴*) and morphology (*mwh*) of the cuticular structures allowed their genotypic identification.

The presence of germ-cell determinants in the posterior cytoplasm of *Drosophila* cleavage embryos poses two closely related questions: (1) is fertilization necessary for the polar plasm to be functional, and (2) at what time during development does this particular cytoplasm acquire its specificity to determine germ cells? Following transplantation to the anterior tip of early cleavage embryos, posterior cytoplasm of *unfertilized* eggs was capable of inducing morphologically normal pole cells which proved to differentiate into functional eggs or spermatozoa after transfer to genetically marked host embryos. About 5 per cent of the developing flies produced some progeny that originated from the induced pole cells. Germ-line mosaicism in those flies could also be detected by aldehyde oxidase histochemistry (Illmensee *et al.* 1976). These results show that fertilization is not required for the posterior polar plasm to become functional in germ-cell determination.

In order to analyse the ontogeny of germ plasm, we transplanted posterior cytoplasm from *oocytes* at different developmental stages (Fig. 4.7 and Table 4.4) to the anterior pole of cleavage embryos and then studied histologically some of these embryos for the formation of pole cells at the site of injection. As in our previous studies, the polar granules served as a morphological marker to identify the transplanted cytoplasm. Since they first appear during mid-vitellogenesis of the oocyte at stage 10 (Mahowald 1962), this was the youngest stage used. Our study should also reveal whether the occurrence of these granules during oogenesis coincides with the presence of functional polar plasm. This is of interest since the polar granules become segregated into the future germ cells and, therefore, are thought to be involved in germ-cell determination. Polar cytoplasm from oocytes of stage 13 and 14 was found to be integrated into several anterior cells that

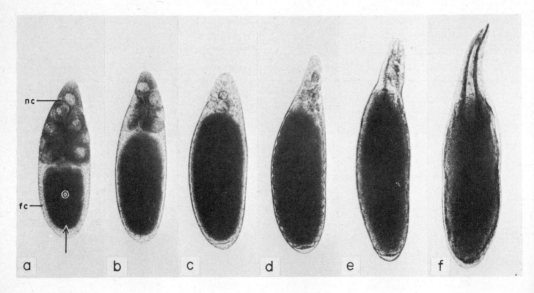

FIG. 4.7. Living egg chambers at different developmental stages whose oocytes served as donors for polar plasm transplants. (The arrow indicates area of the oocyte from which posterior cytoplasm has been collected). Oogenesis from stage 10 up to its completion at stage 14 encompasses a 10 h period during which the oocyte (o) increases rapidly in volume predominantly at the expense of the nurse cells (nc). The surrounding follicle cells (fc) are involved in the formation of the various egg coverings. (a) stage 10; (b) stage 11; (c) early stage 12; (d) late stage 12; (e) stage 13; (f) stage 14. (For a detailed description of stages see King 1970.) X 100.

TABLE 4.4. Ontogeny of posterior polar plasm. This cytoplasm from oocytes at different developmental stages was injected into the anterior region of $mwh\ e^4$ cleavage embryos and the cells formed at the injection site were transplanted to the posterior pole of $y\ sn^3\ mal$ blastoderm hosts. (Data from Illmensee et al. 1976).

Source of polar plasm	No. of polar plasm injections	$mwh\ e^4$ embryos from which cells were taken	$y\ sn^3\ mal$ embryos to which cells were transplanted	No. of $y\ sn^3\ mal$ flies developed		
				Total	No. with $mwh\ e^4$ cells in germ line	(%)
Oocyte						
stage 14	170	42	126	79	3	(3.8)
stage 13	235	50	211	107	5	(4.6)
stage 12	362	104	290	155	—	—
stage 11	154	58	145	67	—	—
stage 10	259	87	241	117	—	—
Control transfers						
1[a]		109	157	72	—	—
2[b]		91	136	74	16	(21.6)

[a] Anterior blastoderm cells from non-injected embryos.
[b] Pole cells from the posterior pole of normal blastoderm embryos.

resembled pole cells in their ultrastructural features. The formation of such cells, however, could not be detected in embryos injected with polar plasm from oogenetic stages 10 to 12. What are the differences between stage 12 and 13 oocytes which can account for the distinct physiological changes of the posterior cytoplasm? Cytochemical (Yao 1949, 1950; King 1960; Gill 1964) and ultrastructural (Cummings and King 1969; Mahowald 1972) studies have not given any clues. Certainly, the principle event during the terminal stages of oogenesis is the breakdown of the nurse chamber and the contribution of its contents to the oocyte during stages 11 and 12 (Bier 1963; King 1970). A reasonable explanation for the failure of stage 12 polar plasm to be functional may be that all of the constituents of the polar plasm have not yet been formed and localized at the posterior pole of the oocyte.

Although the posterior cytoplasm from oocytes at stage 13 and 14 had revealed its inductive ability to form pole cells its role in germ-cell determination still needed to be proven. This can be achieved by transferring the induced pole cells to genetically different host embryos and searching for germ-line mosaics. Viable offspring was obtained from germ cells induced with stage 13 and 14 ooplasm. However, no functional germ cells were recovered with polar plasm transplants from oogenetic stages 10 to 12 (Table 4.4). As in earlier transfers, anterior blastoderm cells did not contribute to the germ line but once again differentiated into anterior cuticular structures of the fly. While our ontogenetic analysis of posterior polar plasm shows that prior to egg maturation this cytoplasm has already acquired its germ-line determinative ability, it is the first demonstration that specific developmental information stored in the cytoplasm can be traced back to a particular region of the oocyte.

Since in all our polar plasm transfers peripheral cytoplasm including cortical material has been used, we cannot determine whether the cytoplasm *in toto* or a distinct cytoplasmic component is responsible for the specific developmental effect. By isolating and characterizing biochemically and genetically subcellular constituents it should be possible to analyse their role in germ-cell determination. The heterotopic transplantation technique will serve as a critical *in vivo* assay to test the biological activity of cytoplasmic factors and to reveal their morphogenetic specificity.

PROSPECTIVES

Nuclear transplantation in *Drosophila* may promise to be a useful tool for revealing nucleocytoplasmic interactions during development of a higher organism that is amenable to genetic analysis as well. It should soon become possible to extend this technique to nuclei from later developmental stages and specialized tissue types in order to gain more insight into the mechanisms underlying determination and differentiation. In this respect, nuclei from *in vitro* cultured cell lines which recently were found able to participate in forming genetically mosaic flies are of particular interest inasmuch as they may enable developmental, biochemical, and genetic analyses of somatic mutations induced *in vitro* and studied *in vivo*. Cytoplasmic transplantation as a bioassay for the localization and characterization of determinants in the egg in conjunction with certain mutants which cause distinctive abnormalities in egg organization would provide an additional means to search for specific morphogenetic factors and to elucidate their function during development. Since we now know where germ cells are determined in the *Drosophila* egg, genes clonally derived from a plasmid system can be introduced via microinjection into this region in order to study transformation, vertical versus horizontal transmission, and phenotypic expression of genetic material in the organism. In addition, gene repair analysis would be feasible utilizing mutant embryos as recipients.

DISCUSSION

Sander: I would like to discuss how we interpret somatic defects obtained after puncturing eggs. There are two possible interpretations of these defects, one is that you destroy information by destroying that particular region of the egg. The other possibility is that you destroy the capacity of cells to react to the instructing signals which arrive afterwards. In both these cases, you will get the same defect. The first interpretation would favour a mosaic egg in which the information has already been spatially ordered, the second interpretation would be compatible with our idea that the somatic pattern is being established epigenetically. In this view, signals spread through the oocyte; of course the cells have to react to these signals in order to produce the different structures, and if you kill or incapacitate the cells, then they cannot respond to the signals. I should add that of course I believe in the germ cell determinant as it has been explained, but I do not believe in somatic determinants of a high specificity.

Illmensee: Yes, these are the problems which people like Bownes and Sang face, when they create defects in the embryo. I would say that this is not only destroying a region of the egg, but also removing something. Many larvae which survive from punctured embryos show alterations in their segmentation which might cause the loss of a wing, for example. This may be due to the inability of the epidermis to fold properly, which then results in wing disc deficiency. A possible way to demonstrate specific determinants would be to transplant somatic cytoplasm to ectopic egg regions, wait until cells are formed, and then test these cells in another region for their developmental capacity.

Gurdon: In my view, as regards the question as to whether there are specific determinants in the egg cytoplasm, all we can do so far is to eliminate the very extreme possibilities. I think nobody believes any longer that an egg is a structure which has individual determinants all mapped out, each one being qualitatively peculiar to a particular type of further development, such as muscle, nerve, and so on. That is no longer considered to be a reasonable hypothesis. Conversely, I think no one would take the view that the egg has absolutely no information in it. It is obvious that pole plasm exists, and there is evidence, as we have seen, that some other determinants exist in some form or another.

Schneiderman: Would you agree that there is evidence that during early stages of embryonic development, some of these determinants become localized? In short, they are not in their final positions when the egg is laid, and that is really the substantial conclusion from several of the arguments presented today.

Gurdon: Yes, some degree of further localization must of course take place.

Kalthoff: I think two points are important in this discussion of the mosaic versus the gradient model. One is the level of resolution. How fine is the pattern? For example, if there are only two pattern elements, one at the anterior and the other at the posterior end, then the egg would be a mosaic, because we have an anterior and a posterior determinant. If we create as many elements as there are segments, which would mean some 18 pattern elements, there seems not to be any evidence for 18 qualitatively different determinants. The second point. There is good evidence that soon after egg deposition, we have few determinants which interact and may then create conditions that are equivalent to a mosaic, but this mosaic system is actually established later. So the distinction between the mosaic model and the gradient model when applied to developing eggs, is partly a matter of time. The time when this system switches towards a mosaic is different in different insect species, and as a rule the more evolved, the earlier it will reach a mosaic state.

Gurdon: I think everyone would agree that we need an assay or some other experimental procedure by which these determinants, whether they are early ones or late ones, can be identified.

REFERENCES

BAKKEN, A. H. (1973). A cytological and genetic study of oognesis in *Drosophila melanogaster*. *Devl. Biol.,* **33,** 100-122.

BEAMS, H. W. & KESSEL, R. G. (1974). The problem of germ cell determinants. *Int. Rev. Cytol.,* **39,** 413-479.

BIER, K.-H. (1963). Autoradiographische Untersuchungen über die Leistungen des Follikelepithels und der Nährzellen bei der Dotterbildung and Eiweissynthese im Fliegenovar. *Wilhelm Roux Arch. Entw Mech. Org.,* **154,** 522-575.

BOUNOURE, L., AUBRY, R. & HUCK, M.-L. (1954). Nouvelles recherches expérimentales sur les origines de la lignée reproductrice chez la Grenouille rousse. *J. Embryol. exp. Morph.,* **2,** 245-263.

BRIGGS, R. (1972). Further studies on the maternal effect of the *o* gene in the Mexican axolotl. *J. exp. Zool.,* **181,** 271-280.

BRIGGS, R. (1973). Developmental genetics of the axolotl. *Genetic Mechanisms of Development* ed. F. Ruddle, pp. 169-199, 31st Symp. Soc. Develop. Biol., Academic Press, New York.

BRIGGS, R. & CASSENS, G. (1966). Accumulation in the oocyte nucleus of a gene product essential for embryonic development beyond gastrulation. *Proc. natn. Acad. Sci. USA,* **55,** 1103-1109.

BRIGGS, R. & KING, T. J. (1952). Transplantation of living nuclei from blastula cells into enucleated frogs' eggs. *Proc. natn. Acad. Sci. USA,* **38,** 455-463.

BUEHR, M. L. & BLACKLER, A. W. (1970). Sterility and partial sterility in the South African clawed toad following the pricking of the egg. *J. Embryol. exp. Morph.,* **23,** 375-384.

CHAN, L.-N. & GEHRING, W. J. (1971). Determination of blastoderm cells in *Drosophila melanogaster*. *Proc. natn. Acad. Sci. USA,* **68,** 2217-2221.

COMANDON, J. & DE FONBRUNE, P. (1939). Greffe nucléaire totale, simple ou multiple, chez une Amibe. *C. r. Soc. Biol. Paris,* **130,** 744-748.

CUMMINGS, M. R. & KING, R. C. (1969). The cytology of the vitellogenetic stages of oogenesis in *Drosophila melanogaster*. I. General staging characteristics. *J. Morph.,* **128,** 427-442.

DAVIDSON, E. H. (1968). *Gene Activity in Early Development*. Academic Press, New York.

DEBEC, A. (1974). Isozymic patterns and functional states of *in vitro* cultured cell lines of *Drosophila melanogaster*. *Wilhelm Roux Arch. Entw Mech. Org.,* **174,** 1-19.

DÜBENDORFER, A., SHIELDS, G. & SANG, J. H. (1975). Development and differentiation *in vitro* of *Drosophila* imaginal disc cells from dissociated early embryos. *J. Embryol. exp. Morph.,* **33,** 487-498.

EDDY, E. M. (1975). Germ plasm and the differentiation of the germ cell line. *Int. rev. Cytol.,* **43,** 229-280.

ECHALIER, G. & OHANESSIAN, A. (1970). *In vitro* culture of *Drosophila melanogaster* embryonic cells. *In Vitro,* **6,** 162-172.

FIELDING, C. F. (1967). Developmental genetics of the mutant *grandchildless* of *Drosophila subobscura*. *J. Embryol. exp. Morph.,* **17,** 375-384.

FISCHBERG, M., BLACKLER, A. W., UEHLINGER, V., REYNAUD, J., DROIN, A. & STOCK, J. (1963). Nucleo-cytoplasmic control of development. *Genetics Today*, pp. 187-198. Pergamon Press, Oxford.

GAREN, A. & GEHRING, W. J. (1972). Repair of the lethal developmental defect in *deep orange* embryos of *Drosophila* by injecting egg cytoplasm. *Proc. natn. Acad. Sci. USA,* **69,** 2982-2985.

GEIGY, R. (1931). Action de l'ultra-violet sur le pôle germinal dans l'oeuf de *Drosophila melanogaster* (castration et mutabilité). *Rev. Suisse Zool.,* **38,** 187-288.

GEYER-DUSZYŃSKA, I. (1967). Experiments on nuclear transplantation in *Drosophila melanogaster*. *Rev. Suisse Zool.,* **74,** 614-615.

GILL, K. S. (1964). Epigenetics of the promorphology of the egg in *Drosophila melanogaster. J. exp. Zool.*, **155**, 91-104.

GRAZIOSI, G. & MICALI, F. (1974). Differential responses to ultraviolet irradiation of the polar cytoplasm of *Drosophila* eggs. *Wilhelm Roux Arch. Entw Mech. Org.*, **175**, 1-11.

GRAZIOSI, G. & ROBERTS, D. B. (1975). Molecular anisotropy of the early *Drosophila* embryo. *Nature, Lond.*, **258**, 157-159.

GURDON, J. B. (1964). The transplantation of living cell nuclei. *Adv. Morphogen.*, **4**, 1-43.

GURDON, J. B. (1974). *The Control of Gene Expression in Animal Development*. Harvard University Press, Cambridge.

GURDON, J. B. & LASKEY, R. A. (1970). Methods of transplanting nuclei from single cultured cells to unfertilized frogs' eggs. *J. Embryol. exp. Morph.*, **24**, 249-255.

GURDON, J. B., LASKEY, R. A. & REEVES, O. R. (1975). The developmental capacity of nuclei transplanted from keratinized skin cells of adult frogs. *J. Embryol. exp. Morph.*, **34**, 93-112.

HADORN, E., HÜRLIMANN, R., MINDEK, G., SCHUBIGER, G. & STAUB, M. Entwicklungsleistungen embryonaler Blasteme von *Drosophila* nach Kultur im Adultwirt. *Rev. Suisse Zool.*, **75**, 557-569.

ILLMENSEE, K. (1968). Transplantation of embryonic nuclei into unfertilized eggs of *Drosophila melanogaster. Nature, Lond.*, **219**, 1268-1269.

ILLMENSEE, K. (1970). Imaginal structures after nuclear transplantation in *Drosophila melanogaster. Naturwiss*, **57**, 550-551.

ILLMENSEE, K. (1972). Developmental potencies of nuclei from cleavage, preblastoderm, and syncytial blastoderm transplanted into unfertilized eggs of *Drosophila melanogaster. Wilhelm Roux Arch. Entw Mech. Org.*, **170**, 267-298.

ILLMENSEE, K. (1973). The potentialities of transplanted early gastrula nuclei of *Drosophila melanogaster*. Production of their imago descendants by germ-line transplantation. *Wilhelm Roux Arch. Entw Mech. Org.*, **171**, 331-343.

ILLMENSEE, K. & MAHOWALD, A. P. (1974). Transplantation of posterior polar plasm in *Drosophila*. Induction of germ cells at the anterior pole of the egg. *Proc. natn. Acad. Sci. USA*, **71**, 1016-1020.

ILLMENSEE, K. & MAHOWALD, A. P. (1976). The autonomous function of germ plasm in a somatic region of the *Drosophila* egg. *Exp. Cell Res.*, **97**, 127-140.

ILLMENSEE, K., MAHOWALD, A. P. & LOOMIS, M. R. (1976). The ontogeny of germ plasm during oogenesis in *Drosophila. Devl. Biol.* In press.

KING, R. C. (1960). Oogenesis in adult *Drosophila melanogaster*. IX. Studies on the cytochemistry and ultrastructure of developing oocytes. *Growth*, **24**, 265-323.

KING, R. C. (1970). *Ovarian Development in Drosophila melanogaster*, Academic Press, New York.

KOBEL, H. R., BRUN, R. B. & FISCHBERG, M. (1973). Nuclear transplantation with melanophores, ciliated epidermal cells, and the established cell-line A-8 in *Xenopus laevis. J. Embryol. exp. Morph.*, **29**, 539-547.

KURODA, Y. (1974). Studies on *Drosophila* embryonic cells *in vitro*. I. Characteristics of cell types in culture. *Devl. Growth Diff.*, **16**, 55-66.

MAHOWALD, A. P. (1962). Fine structure of pole cells and polar granules in *Drosophila melanogaster. J. exp. Zool.*, **151**, 201-215.

MAHOWALD, A. P. (1971). Polar granules of *Drosophila*. III. The continuity of polar granules during the life cycle of *Drosophila. J. exp. Zool.*, **176**, 329-344.

MAHOWALD, A. P. (1972). Oogenesis, *Developmental System. Insects* eds. S. Counce & C. Waddington, Vol. I, pp. 1-47. Academic Press, New York.

MOSNA, G. & DOLFINI, S. (1972). Morphological and chromosomal characterization of three continuous cell lines of *Drosophila melanogaster. Chromosoma*, **38**, 1-9.

NEWROCK, K. M. & RAFF, R. A. (1975). Polar lobe specific regulation of translation in embryos of *Ilyanassa obsoleta. Devl. Biol.*, **42**, 242-261.

OKADA, M., KLEINMAN, I. A. & SCHNEIDERMAN, H. A. (1974a). Restoration of fertility in sterilized *Drosophila* eggs by transplantation of polar cytoplasm. *Devl. Biol.*, **37**, 43-54.

OKADA, M., KLEINMAN, I. A. & SCHNEIDERMAN, H. A. (1976b). Repair of a genetically caused defect in oogenesis in *Drosophila melanogaster* by transplantation of cytoplasm from wild-type eggs and by injection of pyrimidine nucleosides. *Devl. Biol.*, **37**, 55-62.

OKADA, M., KLEINMAN, I. A. & SCHNEIDERMAN, H. A. (1974c). Chimeric *Drosophila* adults produced by transplantation of nuclei into specific regions of fertilized eggs. *Devl. Biol.*, **39**, 286-294.

POULSON, D. F. (1950). Histogenesis, organogenesis, and differentiation in the embryo of *Drosophila melanogaster* Meigen. *Biology of Drosophila* ed. M. Demerec, pp. 168-274. Wiley, New York.

POULSON, D. F. & WATERHOUSE, D. F. (1960). Experimental studies on pole cells and midgut differentiation in Diptera. *Australian J. Biol. Sci.*, **13**, 541-567.

RICE, T. B. & GAREN, A. (1975). Localized defects of blastoderm formation in maternal effect mutants of *Drosophila. Devl..Biol.*, **43**, 277-286.

SANTAMARIA, P. (1975). Transplantation of nuclei between eggs of different species of *Drosophila. Wilhelm Roux Arch. Entw Mech. Org.*, **178**, 89-98.

SCHNEIDER, I. (1972). Cell lines derived from late embryonic stages of *Drosophila melanogaster. J. Embryol. exp. Morphol.*, **27**, 353-365.

SCHUBIGER, M. & SCHNEIDERMAN, H. A. (1971). Nuclear transplantation in *Drosophila melanogaster. Nature, Lond.*, **230**, 185-186.

SMITH, L. D. (1966). The role of 'germinal plasm' in the formation of primordial germ cells in *Rana pipiens. Devl. Biol.*, **14**, 330-347.

THIERRY-MIEG, D., MASSON, M. & GANS, M. (1972). Mutant de stérilité à effet retardé de *Drosophila melanogaster. C. r. Acad. Sci. Paris*, **275**, 2751-2754.

WARN, R. (1972). Manipulation of the pole plasm of *Drosophila melanogaster. Acta Embryol. Exp. Suppl.*, 415-427.

WARN, R. (1975). Restoration of the capacity to form pole cells in UV-irradiated *Drosophila* embryos. *J. Embryol. exp. Morph.*, **33**, 1003-1011.

WHITTAKER, J. R. (1973). Segregation during ascidian embryogenesis of egg cytoplasmic information for tissue-specific enzyme development. *Proc. natn. Acad. Sci. USA*, **70**, 2096-2100.

YAO, T. (1949). Cytochemical studies on the embryonic development of *Drosophila melanogaster*. I. Protein sulphydryl groups and nucleic acids. *Q. J. microsc. Sci.*, **90**, 401-409.

YAO, T. (1950). Cytochemical studies on the embryonic development of *Drosophila melanogaster*. II. Alkaline and acid phosphatases. *Q. J. microsc. Sci.*, **91**, 79-88.

ZALOKAR, M. (1971). Transplantation of nuclei in *Drosophila melanogaster. Proc. natn. Acad. Sci. USA*, **68**, 1539-1541.

ZALOKAR, M. (1973). Transplantation of nuclei into the polar plasm of *Drosophila* eggs. *Devl. Biol.*, **32**, 189-193.

ZÜST, B. & DIXON, K. E. (1975). The effect of UV irradiation of the vegetal pole of *Xenopus laevis* eggs on the presumptive primordial germ cells. *J. Embryol. exp. Morph.*, **34**, 209-220.

II • Imaginal discs of Drosophila

5 • Determination of primordial disc cells and the hypothesis of stepwise determination

WALTER J. GEHRING*

Biozentrum
University of Basel, Switzerland

Gynandromorphs and other genetic mosaics can be used to determine the number and location of primordial cells in the embryo (Garcia-Bellido & Merriam 1969; Hotta & Benzer 1972 and 1973; Janning 1974a and b). One type of gynandromorph occurs frequently in *Drosophila* stocks carrying the unstable ring-X chromosome, $In(1)w^{vC}$ (Hall *et al.* 1976). Loss of this chromosome in female zygotes which carry the unstable ring-X and a normal rod-shaped X-chromosome, leads to the formation of XX/XO mosaics. The XO cells are phenotypically male, and if the rod-X chromosome is appropriately marked, the male cells can be recognized in any kind of tissue. In gynandromorphs arising from such zygotes, the male and female cells are not freely intermingled, but instead they occupy large continuous areas. Since the ratio of male to female cells is roughly one to one, the chromosome elimination is assumed to occur during the first nuclear division. The orientation of the boundary between the cells of the two genotypes (XX and XO) is largely random. On the adult cuticle it tends to follow the longitudinal midline and the segmental borders, which is merely a consequence of the fact that the adult fly is 'constructed' from discrete groups of cells, the imaginal discs. In general, there are two pairs of discs, a dorsal and a ventral pair, for each segment and these clusters of cells are separated by other kinds of cells which do not participate in forming the adult cuticle (Gehring & Nöthiger 1973). For example, the head capsule with the two compound eyes, the antennae and the palps is formed by a pair of eye-antennal discs. During metamorphosis the two eye-antennal discs, which previously have been separated by other cells, come into contact, and each disc gives rise to one lateral half of the head capsule. As a consequence, the boundary between the cells of the two genotypes in many cases follows the longitudinal midline of the head rather precisely. Otherwise, the orientation of this boundary is largely random and depends upon events in early embryogenesis. It is known from cytological studies that the orientation of the first mitotic spindle is random (Parks 1936). From the distribution of male and female areas in the adult gynandromorphs, it can be inferred that relatively little mixing occurs during the nuclear divisions at the early syncytial stages and during the following migration of the nuclei into the cortical cytoplasm, where they form a monolayer of cells, the blastoderm. Therefore, the boundary between male and female cells is randomly oriented on the blastoderm surface. As pointed out by Sturtevant (1929), the probability of the boundary passing between two blastoderm cells is

99

proportional to their distance apart. Since the location of a cell in the blastoderm largely decides its developmental fate, i.e. its cell lineage (Geigy 1931; Hathaway & Selman 1961; Bownes & Kalthoff 1974; Bownes & Sang 1974) the genotypic boundary in the adult reflects the boundary at the blastoderm stage and allows the mapping of the primordial cells on the blastoderm. The frequency of the boundary passing between two cells in the adult, is a measure for the distance between their primordial cells in the blastoderm. A frequency of 1 per cent is defined as 1 sturt unit (Hotta & Benzer 1972). By calculating these frequencies and triangulation, fate maps reflecting the location of the primordial cells can be constructed (Garcia-Bellido & Merriam 1969; Hotta & Benzer, 1972; Ripoll 1972; Janning 1974a and b; Gelbart 1974; Baker 1975; Wieschaus & Gehring 1976a; Gehring, Wieschaus & Holliger 1976). The frequency (f) of mosaicism for a given structure depends upon the size of its primordium. Assuming a circular shape, the radius (r) of the primordium can be calculated using the formula $r = f/\pi$ (Hotta & Benzer 1972). At present there is no precise way to relate sturt distances to cell diameters, but the size of the primordia can roughly be estimated from the ratio of XX to XO cells, if one assumes that the extent of proliferation is the same in all cells of a given primordium. In this case the reciprocal of the smallest fraction of genetically marked cells (XX or XO) gives a minimum estimate for the number of primordial cells. For example, the smallest genetically marked areas in a large sample of gynandromorphs covered approximately 1/13 of the cells derived from the eye-antennal disc indicating that at least 13 cells give rise to this disc (Garcia-Bellido & Merriam 1969). These gynandromorph studies show that each disc is derived from a cluster of primordial cells which can be mapped to a specific position on the blastoderm. A detailed analysis of the thoracic discs indicates that their primordial cells map closely together and probably occupy adjacent areas in the blastoderm (Wieschaus & Gehring 1976a), but the centres of the primordia map to distinctly different sites. For all the discs examined, a group of primordial cells was found rather than a single cell, indicating that the discs are *not clonal in origin*.

The mapping procedure is based upon the assumption that the location of a cell in the blastoderm largely decides its developmental fate. At present we do not know, how precise this relationship really is, but our recent data suggest that the cell lineage relationships are not absolutely fixed. As pointed out clearly by Hotta and Benzer (1973), one would expect the measured distance between two primordial cells which are very close to each other on the blastoderm to be larger than the true distance, if the cell lineage involves some indeterminacy. Such an *'expansion'* of the map over short sturt distances has in fact been observed when 'fine-structure maps' of the leg discs were constructed (Wieschaus & Gehring 1976a). It turned out that the distances between different leg segments were significantly larger than distances within a given leg segment, so that they had to be 'compressed' to fit them into a planar map. This observation can be explained if one assumes that the cell lineage of the leg disc is not absolutely fixed. This interpretation is in fact supported by cell lineage studies using X-ray induced mitotic recombination (Tokunaga & Stern 1965; Bryant & Schneiderman 1969). Whether this map 'expansion' also applies to interdisc distances is at present unknown.

The developmental fate of a cell is largely decided by its location on the blastoderm. However, this does not imply anything about the time at which the *determination* to form a particular structure becomes established, which could occur later in development. The state of determination of blastoderm cells has been tested in dissociation-reaggregation

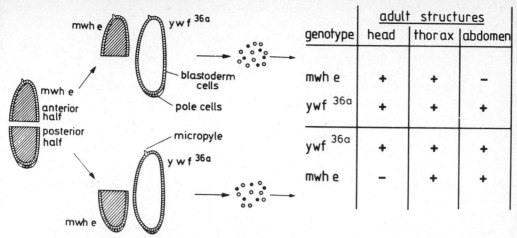

FIG. 5.1. Experimental analysis of the state of determination of primordial disc cells at the blastoderm stage. Genetically marked blastoderm embryos are cut into half and separately intermixed with whole embryos carrying different genetic markers, subsequently the embryos are dissociated into single cells, reaggregated and cultured *in vivo*. Following metamorphosis in a host larva, the kinds of adult structures shown on the right were recovered. Marker genes: *mwh multiple wing hairs, e ebony, y yellow, w white, f³⁶ᵃforked* (after Chan & Gehring, 1971).

experiments using *in vivo* culturing methods (Chan & Gehring 1971). Dissociated and reaggregated blastoderm cells complete their development when cultured first in an adult host and subsequently in a larva, and give rise, for example, to adult epidermal structures. By intermixing cells from bisected blastoderms with genetically marked cells from whole blastoderms (Fig. 5.1), the developmental potential of the cells from anterior and posterior halves could be tested. The cells from whole embryos serve as an internal control and can form epidermal structures from all parts of the body. However, the cells from the anterior half are restricted to form epidermal structures of the head and thorax and cannot produce abdominal structures, whereas the cells from the posterior half-blastoderm are determined for abdominal and thoracic structures and cannot give rise to head structures. These results clearly indicate that the blastoderm cells are determined at least for anterior versus posterior properties and that they are not totipotent.

The *specificity of determination of individual blastoderm cells* was analysed by means of genetic mosaics (Wieschaus & Gehring 1976b). In particular, we were interested to find out whether a single, genetically marked blastoderm cell could give rise to structures derived from two imaginal discs, or whether the clones were confined to a single disc. In order to ask this question in a meaningful way, one has to know the location of the primordial cells in the blastoderm. Gynandromorph studies (Wieschaus & Gehring 1976a) mentioned previously indicated that the wing and the three leg discs form a cluster of closely associated primordial cells in the blastoderm, and therefore, it seemed reasonable to look for clones overlapping two different discs in this area. Marked single cells were obtained by X-ray induced mitotic recombination in heterozygous blastoderm embryos (3.2 h after egg deposition), and the resulting clones were analysed in the adult cuticular structures. Seven out of 31 clones covering the appropriate area, were found to overlap structures derived from the wing and second leg disc. Since in these cases the genetically marked cell still can give rise to two imaginal discs, we can conclude that these blastoderm cells are not yet disc-specifically determined. However, no clones overlapping the first and second, or the second and third leg disc were found, which might suggest a segment-specific determination. Further experiments are needed to test this hypothesis. After irradiation at 7 h and 10 h of embryogenesis no more clones overlapping two discs were found in the thoracic region.

Overlapping clones were also found in the head region derived from the eye-antennal disc. The eye-antennal disc, is a compound structure consisting of two morphologically distinct parts, the eye 'disc' and the antennal 'disc'. The eye disc gives rise to the compound eye and one half of the head capsule, the antennal disc contains the anlagen for the antenna and the palpus (Schläpfer, 1963; Gehring 1966). Clones of genetically marked cells overlapping structures from both the eye and antennal disc were found frequently after irradiation at 3, 7 and 10 h of embryogenesis (Fig. 5.2), which indicates that the determination for eye versus antenna has not yet taken place.

However, the dissociation-reaggregation experiments showed that the anterior blastoderm cells cannot give rise to abdominal or genital structures. Therefore, the primordial cells for the eye-antennal disc are determined at least for forming anterior structures, but the 'decision' to form either eye or antennal cells has not yet been made.

A variety of different experiments indicate that in the eye-antennal disc of a 'mature' third instar larva the differential determination segregating eye-forming from antenna-forming cells has taken place. When the disc is cut into defined fragments, each fragment can give rise to a specific set of structures, and the anlagen for the various structures have been mapped within the disc (Gehring 1966; Ouweneel 1970). In dissociation-reaggregation experiments in which cells from the antennal part of the disc were intermixed with genetically marked wing disc cells, it was shown that the antennal cells differentiate autonomously, and did not produce wing nor eye structures (Gehring, 1966), indicating that they are determined. The analogous dissociation-reaggregation experiment has not been carried out for the eye part but the fragmentation experiments argue strongly for determination of the eye-forming cells as well. In fact, it has been

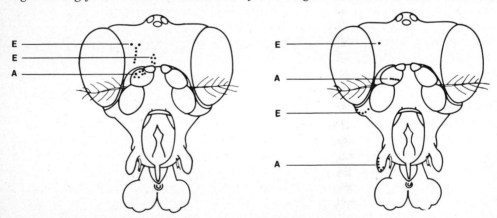

FIG. 5.2. Clones of genetically marked cells induced at the blastoderm stage.
Blastoderm embryos heterozygous for the marker genes *yellow, white* and *forked* (*ywf*[36a]) were given a dose of 1100 r of X-rays, to induce homozygous single cells by mitotic recombination. In the course of development, these genetically marked cells proliferate and give rise to a clone which can be recognized as a patch of marked tissue on the adult fly. The genetically marked bristles are indicated as black dots. The two clones shown, overlap structures which are derived from the eye disc (E) and the antennal disc (A) (after Wieschaus & Gehring, unpubl.).

shown recently, that the cells of the eye and antennal part are not only determined differentially, but are differentiated biochemically with respect to the enzyme aldehyde oxidase (Janning 1973; Conscience-Egli 1974). The activity of this enzyme can be demonstrated by histo-chemical staining of the disc (Fig. 5.3a). Using this reaction, aldehyde oxidase can be demonstrated in the antennal disc whereas the eye disc is virtually lacking this activity. This is not just due to permeability differences, since the same pattern is observed in frozen sections (Conscience-Egli 1974). Furthermore, *aldox*[nl] and *mal* mutants which lack the enzyme activity, give no histochemical staining for aldehyde oxidase, indicating the specifity of the reaction. Therefore, we can conclude that the cells of the eye and antennal disc are not only determined differentially, but they also show some biochemical differentiation.

Recently, we have looked into the question of when in development these histochemical differentiations first appear (Gehring unpublished). During the first larval instar the disc consists of just a few cells, and no histochemical staining for aldehyde oxidase is observed, although other tissues show intense staining (Fig. 5.3d). In the eye-antennal disc of the early second instar a weak staining in the antennal part is observed (Fig. 5.3c) and by the middle of the second instar the reaction has become quite strong (Fig. 5.3b). It is not clear, whether the time at which the reaction first appears, coincides with the time of determination of antennal cells since there are not enough data available for the early larval stages. Postlethwait and Schneiderman (1971) have analysed clones of genetically marked cells obtained by X-ray induced mitotic recombination. They found clones overlapping both the eye and antennal disc after irradiation of newly hatched larvae, whereas irradiation at 36 h yielded no overlapping clones; but the number of clones examined (five) is too small to allow any definite conclusions. However, the more conclusive test would be a dissociation-reaggregation experiment using cells from these early larval stages.

From these considerations it follows clearly that determination occurs sequentially in steps. At the blastoderm stage primordial cells for the eye-antennal disc are still capable of forming both eye and antennal disc cells, but no disc cells from the abdominal region. In a subsequent step, which occurs at some time before the late third instar, the alternative decision for eye versus antennal disc has been made. Future studies are likely to reveal further steps of determination.

The *concept* of a *stepwise determination* has also been proposed for vertebrate development (see Hadorn 1965). For example, the blastula ectoderm in amphibians still has the capacity of forming both epidermal and neural tissue. Following primary induction these capacities are segregated and the cells of the neural plate are determined for neural structures. In a second step the different types of neural and epidermal structures are determined. However, in vertebrates the evidence is largely based upon experiments involving tissues rather than cells, which makes their interpretation more difficult. In *Drosophila* where determination can be analysed at the cellular level, the evidence is strongly in favour of stepwise determination.

On the basis of the reviewed experiments two models for *Drosophila* development are very likely to be incorrect. The first one is an extreme *mosaic model* in which it is assumed that the adult structures are determined in great detail as early as the blastoderm stage. This model is in conflict with our data on the cell lineage of blastoderm cells, which indicate that the decision for the eye versus antenna, and wing versus second leg is not made at this stage. The other model would assume that *determination* is *labile* until the onset of metamorphosis when the cells finally

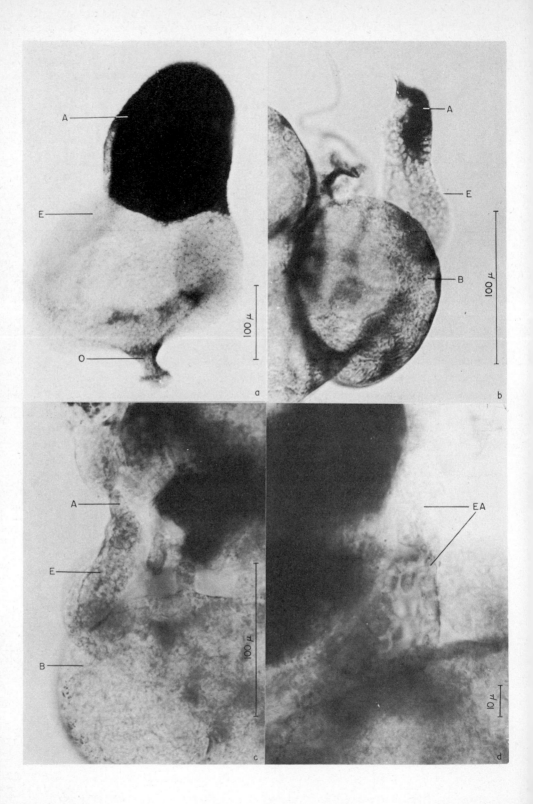

differentiate under the influence of ecdysone. The dissociation-reaggregation experiments of blastoderm cells argue strongly against such a model. It can be shown that the cells are strictly determined and retain their determination during *in vivo* culture. However, at the blastoderm stage the spectrum of developmental pathways open to a given cell is larger than it is later in development when further determinative steps have occurred. The experimental data are most adequately described by a *model of stepwise determination*.

ACKNOWLEDGEMENTS

This work has been supported by Grant GB-17627 from the US National Science Foundation and by the Kanton of Basel-Stadt which is gratefully acknowledged. I would like to thank Dr Eric Wieschaus for his contributions to this paper, and Mrs Erika Wenger for her assistance in preparing the manuscript.

DISCUSSION

Unknown lady: Would it be possible to put the dissociated cells back into an embryo? Although they are determined, would they, if put back into an embryonic environment, become dedetermined?

Gehring: Illmensee has reported briefly his very nice experiment where he takes an anterior blastoderm cell and transplants it to posterior location of a differently marked embryo. These transplanted cells always differentiate anterior structures, even in the posterior location. Moreover, the anterior structures arising from the anterior cell do not integrate into the posterior tissues, strongly suggesting that the cells have different surface properties.

Schneiderman: It might be worth adding that even small fragments of dissociated mature imaginal discs when put back into blastoderm or cleavage embryos, do not get reprogrammed. You can recover small numbers of these cells in the adult, and this has been done with the wing disc, when you get vesicles of wing structures. This shows that the environment of the egg, although it may be programming the nuclei, does not seem to be able to reprogramme imaginal disc cells.

Lawrence: Could you say then that the determined state resides in single cells or in groups of cells, but not in nuclei?

Gehring: Not really, because the nuclei and the cells are in different states.

Lawrence: But the operational criteria for determination must be used, and by those criteria nuclei are not determined and cells are.

Gehring: Yes, but of course in this case the nucleus is an open system, where you can readily exchange components, whereas the cell has a membrane around it.

Lawrence: This may be why the nucleus is not determined and the cell is.

FIG. 5.3. Aldehyde oxidase activity in the developing eye-antennal disc. Eye-antennal discs of various larval stages were dissected and stained for aldehyde oxidase activity according to the procedure of Dickinson (1971) except that dimethylamino benzaldehyde was used as a substrate. a) late third larval instar. The cells of the antennal disc (A) are strongly positive, whereas very little or no activity is detected in the eye disc (E). O = optic stalk. b) Middle second instar. Antennal disc cells show a characteristic pattern of strong activity. B = brain. c) Early second instar. Earliest stage, when some activity was detected in the antennal disc cells. d) First larval instar. The eye-antennal disc (EA) consists of just a few cells showing no aldehyde oxidase activity, although some of the surrounding tissues exhibit a positive reaction (Gehring, unpublished).

Wolpert: By the operational criteria that you gave, you would have to agree with Dr Lawrence that the nucleus was not determined.

Nöthiger: You described the aldox activity, which is so clearly shown in nearly every single cell of the antennal disc. You are, I hope, not invoking the hypothesis that aldehyde dehydrogenase has anything to do with determination?

Gehring: No, we use it as a biochemical marker, indicating some differentiation which is probably the product of a determinative event, but may have nothing to do with determination itself.

Nardi: Do you know whether the boundary that you demonstrate by your cytochemical marker actually corresponds with the boundary between determined eye cells and determined antennal cells?

Gehring: This is shown by fragmentation experiments. You cut discs at various levels, and implant these discs into mature larvae, you find that the borderline between the eye and the antenna cells coincides with the line as defined by staining. There is a spot in the antennal cells which does not stain for aldehyde oxidase. In the wing disc, the situation is much more complex, and you have a very specific staining pattern with stain in the middle of the disc, and unstained material at the edges. In the case of the wing disc, it is not clearly established where the staining patterns fall in relation to the final differentiations.

Schneiderman: You discovered some years ago that the eye part of the antenna disc would invariably regenerate the antennal part, but in your discussion you speak of the two as being almost separate discs, separate determinations. How can that be, when regeneration experiments show that the antenna is just part of the eye disc?

Gehring: When you culture cells in the fragmentation experiment, you can show that the antennal cells do not regenerate the eye cells, so that they must be differently determined, and they are even biochemically different. There are other differences that you can demonstrate by cell aggregation experiments. You can call that intra-disc determination. This would defeat your ruling that intra-disc determination is non-heritable, because according to all criteria, we know the eye antenna difference is heritable. But as I say, heritable is relative. It depends upon the experimental system to which the cells are subjected. The cells have of course a complete genome, and when you culture them, they can trans-determine to wing cells, or leg cells.

Schneiderman: But if an experiment should be performed in which presumptive antennal cells gave rise to eye cells, repeatedly and consistently, then you would consider altering your view. For instance, if you mixed eye and antennal cells, genetically marked, and could show that some of those antennal cells gave rise to eye cells, then you might alter your view. This experiment has not been done, it is hypothetical.

Gehring: No, I think the cleanest test is when you mix the isolated cells and do not allow for additional divisions. Because when you allow for additional divisions, you get the cells to show up a much larger spectrum of different activities.

Ashburner: Do regenerated antennal cells that have come from a fragmented eye disc show the aldox boundary?

Gehring: We are just in the process of doing that experiment.

Wolpert: Can you just remind us, for general information. It always worries me when you talk about eye and antenna. We give names to parts of animals but maybe *Drosophila* does not name them that way. What is the difference in the cell types, between the eye and the antenna. Do they have many cell types in common?

Gehring: The antenna is mostly cuticle, with hairs. It has a large number of specific sensilla, which occur nowhere else on the body. The eye disc is biochemically mostly very different, because of the presence of the ommatidia, which are very special cell types. At the ultrastructural level, you begin to see in the late disc, clusters of cells representing the forming ommatidia. So even at the morphological level you begin to see the first signs of differentiation.

Wolpert: Let's make quite sure. You can go by regeneration from eye to antenna, but never from antenna to eye.

Slack: Would you agree that the situation in the eye disc is very similar to that in the leg disc, with respect to directions of regeneration?

Gehring: Yes, the discs behave very similarly in these respects, as Schneiderman has pointed out. You can consider the eye-antennal disc as two discs, or as one disc. There is no argument strongly in favour of one view or the other. In evolution, they may have come from two different discs.

REFERENCES

BAKER, B. (1975). Paternal loss *(pal):* a meiotic mutant in *Drosophila melanogaster* causing loss of paternal chromosomes. *Genetics,* **80**, 267–296.

BOWNES, M., & KALTHOFF, K. (1974). Embryonic defects in *Drosophila* eggs after partial UV irradiation at different wavelengths. *J. Embryol. exp. Morph.,* **31**, 329–345.

BOWNES, M., & SANG, J. (1974). Experimental manipulation of early *Drosophila* embryos. I. Adult and embryonic defects resulting from microcautery at nuclear multiplication and blastoderm stages. *J. Embryol. exp. Morph.,* **32**, 253–272.

BRYANT, P., & SCHNEIDERMAN, H. (1969). Cell lineage, growth and determination in the imaginal leg disc of *Drosophila melanogaster. Devl. Biol.,* **20**, 263–290.

CHAN, L.-N. & GEHRING, W. (1971). Determination of blastoderm cells in *Drosophila melanogaster. Proc. natn. Acad. Sci.* (USA), **68**, 2217–2221.

CONSCIENCE-EGLI, M. (1974). Histochemische, elektrophoretische und genetische Untersuchungen an einigen Enzymen während der Entwicklung von *Drosophila melanogaster*. Dissertation N. 5243. Eidgenössische Technische Hochschule, Zürich, Switzerland.

DICKINSON, W. (1971). Aldehyde Oxidase in *Drosophila melanogaster:* A system for genetic studies on developmental regulation. *Devl. Biol.,* **26**, 77–86.

GARCIA-BELLIDO, A., & MERRIAM, J. (1969). Cell lineage of the imaginal discs in *Drosophila* gynandromorphs. *J. exp. Zool.,* **170**, 61–76.

GEHRING, W. (1966). Uebertragung und Aenderung der Determinationsqualitäten in Antennenscheiben-Kulturen von *Drosophila melanogaster. J. Embryol. exp. Morph.,* **15**, 77–111.

GEHRING, W., & NÖTHIGER, R. (1973). The imaginal discs of *Drosophila*. In *Developmental Systems: Insects* (Vol. 2), C. H. Waddington & S. Counce-Nicklas, eds., New York, Academic Press.

GEHRING, W., WIESCHAUS, E. & HOLLIGER, M. (1976). Gynandromorph mapping of gonads and pole cells. *J. Embryol. exp. Morph.* (in press).

GEIGY, R. (1931). Erzeugung rein imaginaler Defekte durch ultraviolette Eibestrahlung bei *Drosophila melanogaster. Wilhelm Roux Arch. Entw Mech. Org.,* **125**, 406–447.

GELBART, W. (1974). A new mutant controlling mitotic chromosome disjunction in *Drosophila melanogaster. Genetics,* **76**, 51–63.

HADORN, E. (1965). Problems of determination and transdetermination. *Brookhaven Symp. Biol.,* **18**, 148–161.

HALL, J., GELBART, W. & KANKEL, D. (1976). Mosaic systems. In *Genetics and Biology of Drosophila,* E. Novitski & M. Ashburner, eds., London, Academic Press.

HATHAWAY, D., & SELMAN, G. (1961). Certain aspects of cell lineage and morphogenesis studied in embryos of *Drosophila melanogaster* with an ultra violet microbeam. *J. Embryol. exp. Morph.,* **9**, 310–325.

HOTTA, Y., & BENZER, S. (1972). Mapping of behaviour in *Drosophila* mosaics. *Nature,* **240**, 527–535.

HOTTA, Y., & BENZER, S. (1973). Mapping of behaviour in *Drosophila* mosaics. In: *Genetic Mechanisms of Development* F. Ruddle, ed., New York, Academic Press.

JANNING, W. (1973). Distribution of aldehyde oxidase activity in imaginal discs of *Drosophila melanogaster*. *Drosoph. Inf. Serv.*, **50**, 151.

JANNING, W. (1974a). Entwicklungsgenetische Untersuchungen an Gynandern von *Drosophila melanogaster*. I. Die inneren Organe der Imago. *Wilhelm Roux Arch. EntwMech. Org.*, **174**, 313-332.

JANNING, W. (1974b). Entwicklungsgenetische Untersuchungen an Gynandern von *Drosophila melanogaster*. II. Der morphogenetische Anlageplan. *Wilhelm Roux Arch. Entw Mech. Org.*, **174**, 349-359.

OUWENEEL, W. (1970). Normal and abnormal determination in the imaginal discs of *Drosophila*, with special reference to the eye disc. *Acta Embr. Exp.*, *1970*, 95-119.

PARKS, H. (1936). Cleavage patterns in *Drosophila* and mosaic formation. *Ann. Ent. Soc. Am.*, **29**, 350-392.

POSTLETHWAIT, J., & SCHNEIDERMAN, H. (1971). A clonal analysis of development in *Drosophila melanogaster:* Morphogenesis, determination and growth in the wild-type antenna. *Devl. Biol.*, **24**, 477-519.

RIPOLL, P. (1972). The embryonic organization of the imaginal wing disc of *Drosophila melanogaster*. *Wilhelm Roux Arch. EntwMech. Org.*, **169**, 200-215.

SCHLÄPFER, T. (1963). Der Einfluss des adulten Wirtsmilieus auf die Entwicklung von larvalen Augenantennen-Imaginalscheiben von *Drosophila melanogaster*. *Wilhelm Roux Arch. Entw Mech. Org.*, **154**, 378-404.

STURTEVANT, A. (1929). The claret mutant type of *Drosophila simulans:* A study of chromosome elimination and of cell-lineage. *Z. wiss. Zool.*, **135**, 323-356.

TOKUNAGA, C., & STERN, C. (1965). The developmental autonomy of extra sex combs in *Drosophila melanogaster*. *Devl. Biol.*, **11**, 50-81.

WIESCHAUS, E. & GEHRING, W. (1976a). Gynandromorph analysis of the thoracic disc primordial in *Drosophila melanogaster*. *Wilhelm Roux Arch. Entw Mech. Org.* (in press)

WIESCHAUS, E. & GEHRING, W. (1976b). Clonal analysis of primordial disc cells in the early embryo of *Drosophila melanogaster*. *Devl. Biol.* (in press)

6 • Clonal analysis in imaginal discs

R. NÖTHIGER

University of Zürich, Switzerland

INTRODUCTION

For a long time *blastemas* and *fields* dominated our discussion and ideas on development. The *cells as units of development* were almost non-existent. The pioneering experiments by Curt Stern (1956) and Hans Becker (1957) with *Drosophila* opened the way for an *analysis of development at the cellular level* in this organism. The principle was to construct *genetic mosaics* of a defined composition, and to study the developmental capacities of *clones of cells*.

We will concentrate our discussion on the *imaginal discs* of *Drosophila* (pertinent literature references for this article may be found in Nöthiger, 1972). They consist of a single-layered epithelium of small cells, thrown into characteristic folds. In the early embryo a small number of precursor cells is set aside to form the various disc primordia. These then grow by cell division throughout the larval period and become determined for particular adult structures. Under the influence of ecdysone, metamorphosis sets in, the cells stop dividing, and imaginal differentiation takes place whereby each disc contributes a well defined part of the adult fly. Numerous experiments have shown that at this time each disc consists of a mosaic of different districts whose cells are determined to form specific structures of the adult fly.

Imaginal discs of *Drosophila* render themselves a favourable system for an analysis of development at the cellular level. This is possibly due to the wealth of genetic variants and techniques that are available, and to the fact that bristles and trichomes, which cover the surface of the fly, are derivatives of a *single cell* of a disc. Mutations that express themselves autonomously in cells (= cell marker mutations) are used to mark and trace a single cell and its clonal descendants. The recessive mutations *yellow* (bristles and body colour pale instead of dark), *white* (ommatidia without pigment), *forked* (bristles and trichomes gnarled instead of straight), *multiple wing hairs* (two to five trichomes per cell instead of just one) are some examples that are most widely used.

Clonal analysis can provide information about when and how new developmental programmes become established within a previously homogeneous population of cells. Furthermore, we can estimate the number of cells engaged in making a particular developmental decision, and we can evaluate the stability of such decisions.

MITOTIC RECOMBINATION

The technique of mitotic recombination allows us to initiate in a *heterozygous larva a homozygous clone* of genetically marked cells at any time during the proliferation phase of the imaginal discs. The process is diagrammatically illustrated in Fig. 6.1. The frequency of spontaneous mitotic recombination is very low. It can be significantly increased if a dividing population of cells is treated with X-rays. The exchange of chromatids which must take place in the four-strand stage of the cell cycle occurs in males as well as in females. Upon proper segregation of the chromosomes two homozygous daughter cells are produced. Each of them will now develop into a clone that is genetically different from its heterozygous neighbouring cells. If proper cell marker mutations are used, the resulting animal will be mosaic and show a patch (= clone) of mutant tissue.

Three characteristics of a clone are informative:

i its *size* will reflect the number of cells present in the disc at the time of clone induction. Clone size is dependent on the number of cell divisions that occurred between initiation of the clone and imaginal differentiation when cell divisions cease. The final number of cells (N) that a mature disc reaches at the end of larval development is fixed and constant for each type of disc. Therefore, the ratio $\frac{N}{x_t}$ (where x_t is the average size of clones induced at time t) gives the number of cells present in the growing disc at time t;

ii its *shape* will provide information about morphogenetic processes;

iii its *range or extent* will reveal developmental capacities and restrictions of the ancestor cell of the clone (the clone mother cell), depending on whether the descendants of a clone can give rise to two structures A and B, or whether they remain confined to either A or B.

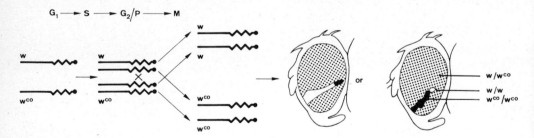

FIG. 6.1. Mitotic recombination in the X chromosome of *Drosophila*. Proper segregation leads to two homozygous cells and hence clones in the eye. *w* and *w^co* are different alleles of the *white*-locus. Note the *shape* of the clones and the difference in *size* between clones in the anterior and clones in the posterior eye region. G_1, G_2, S, P, M; phases of the cell cycle (from Nöthinger, 1972).

GROWTH PARAMETERS OF IMAGINAL DISCS

Induction of mitotic recombination at various times during embryonic and larval development allows us to estimate the number of cells present in each disc at a particular time of development. The formula and the logics for this calculation are given in the preceding section. We may mention here that the procedure assumes that each cell of a disc contributes, on average, the same fraction of the adult disc derivatives.

Data for all major discs are now available. Each disc starts from a small and characteristic number (some 10 to 40) of precursor cells in the embryo. They grow exponentially as the cells divide with a constant doubling time of about 10 hours. The abdominal histoblasts are an exception since their cells remain quiescent throughout the larval period, but then undergo a burst of rapid divisions around puparium formation. But the technique of mitotic recombination can also detect finer regional differences: clones in the anterior region of the eye are consistently bigger than in the posterior region (Fig. 6.1). Similar regional differences are found in other discs, e.g. in the wing disc, showing that growth of discs must be subjected to delicate regional control mechanisms.

Autonomous mitotic rates are exhibited by the cells of a clone that has been rendered homozygous for a mutation causing rapid cell divisions (Morata & Ripoll 1975). As a result these cells outgrow their slow neighbours. Such a clone contributes much more towards the adult structure, e.g. a wing, than the descendants of the clone mother cell would normally do. Nevertheless, the adult structure is normal in size and shape.

This shows that normal development is well buffered against disturbances such as changes in the rate of cell proliferation. We furthermore see that cells can apparently replace each other which is an example of classical regulation.

Normal adult structures are also formed when imaginal discs of second instar larvae are treated with heavy doses of X-rays (4000 R). A careful clonal analysis by Schweizer (1972) revealed that the irradiated discs were severely damaged; but that there was sufficient time until metamorphosis to allow for extensive cell divisions to compensate for the loss. This proliferation became apparent in extra large clones whose size was dose-dependent. This process of cell division restored the organization of the disc to normal. Abnormalities could be produced by irradiating older larvae where there was not enough time for additional proliferation until metamorphosis.

These mosaics, like the ones produced by Morata & Ripoll (1975), provide important insights into developmental phenomena such as regulation and determination.

DEVELOPMENTAL CAPACITIES AND RESTRICTIONS

Two fundamentally different ways can be envisaged that may lead to the mosaic of differently determined districts in a mature disc. First, all the cells of a disc may be equivalent until the beginning of metamorphosis when each is assigned its specific role. Alternatively, the cells may progressively acquire more and more specific developmental programmes as their number increases during the larval period.

Clonal analysis reveals that nature has chosen the second possibility. Fig. 6.2 shows a clone of *yellow* bristles on the external genitalia of a male. It overlaps the three structures clasper, lateral plate and genital arch. This indicates that the clone was initiated before the developmental segregation into these three pathways had taken place. Clones induced at later times will become more and more restricted to fewer and more specific structures, e.g. remain confined to the lateral plate or to the clasper. The early hints to such a process of *progressive developmental restrictions* have recently become much better substantiated (see Lawrence and Morata, this volume).

The same clone reveals another interesting feature, namely that developmental decisions are taken by *groups of cells*. Since the *yellow* patch is a clone and was induced prior to determination of claspers and lateral plates, the fact that these two cuticular elements are themselves mosaic for *yellow* and wildtype shows that each cannot derive from a single cell. It appears that at a given time of development a defined number of cells decide to embark on a particular pathway of development.

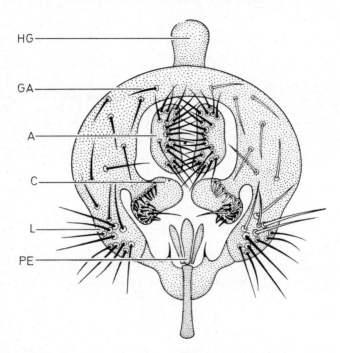

FIG. 6.2. Male genitalia with a clone of *yellow* cells (white bristles), induced in the 2nα ιιstar. The clone overlaps the clasper (C), lateral plate (L) and genital arch (GA), these cuticular structures being mosaic for *yellow* and *wildtype* (black bristles). A: anal plates; HG: hind gut; PE: penis apparatus (from Nöthiger 1972).

REGENERATION

Clonal analysis can also be applied to the phenomenon of *regeneration* in order to ask some specific questions: (i) How many cells are involved in forming the regenerate? (ii) Which cell types serve as the source of regeneration? (iii) Do cells maintain and reproduce their developmental programme during regeneration?

An imaginal disc of a mature larva can be cut in half. Each of the two pieces will form a regenerate (or duplicate) if enough time is provided for cell divisions to take place. Clones can be induced in the stem piece, and clonal relationships may then be studied after regeneration and metamorphosis. In an experiment with the genital disc we induced clones in the stem piece just prior to cutting. Comparing sizes and frequencies of such clones on the stem piece and on the regenerate we find that clones in the regenerate are less frequent but bigger than in the stem piece (Fig. 6.3). This points to a small, but rapidly dividing group of cells from which the regenerated structures are built. In the case of the genital disc there may be as few as two or three cells giving rise to some hundred or more cells of the regenerated half of the genital apparatus. Apparently, the new half is being built up through rapid cell divisions while the cells of the old half remain more or less quiescent.

Although induced at the end of larval development in a mature disc, the clones on the regenerate overlap different cuticular elements, such as clasper and lateral plate, suggesting that developmental programmes are being changed and patterns newly established during regeneration. We arrive at this conclusion because claspers, lateral plates and genital arch belong to separate cell lineages at the end of the third larval instar.

On the other hand, anal plates and genitalia (claspers, lateral plates, genital arch) appear to represent two very different populations of cells whose representatives cannot take over each other's roles: Clones never extended from anal plates into genitalia, but remained confined to either analia or genitalia, even during regeneration.

Clones that extend from the stem piece into the regenerate (Fig. 6.3) show a consistent relationship between the lateral plate of the 'old' side and the clasper and lateral plate of the 'new' side. This points to a specific region or group of cells—the presumptive lateral plate—that are capable of regeneration. Again these cells exhibit a large degree of autonomy in their rate of division and acquisition of developmental programmes.

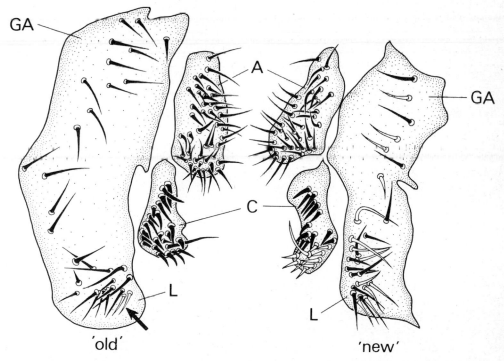

FIG. 6.3. Cell lineage relationships after regeneration in a male genital disc. Clone induced in late 3rd instar just prior to cutting the disc in half. A: anal plates; 'old': stem piece; 'new': regenerated half. Clasper (C), lateral plate (L) and genital arch (GA) of the 'new' side share a common cell pool as indicated by the overlapping clone. Note clone size on 'old' v. 'new' side. The cells of the presumptive lateral plate may be the source of the regenerate: clones frequently appear to originate from L of the 'old' side (arrow points to two yellow bristles on 'old' side).

MORPHOGENETIC MUTANTS

We know a number of mutations that cause morphogenetic alterations. Most prominent among them are the so-called *homoeotic mutations*. They lead to a substitution of one developmental programme by another, e.g. antenna is replaced by leg, eye by wing, etc. It is important to find out when and how these mutations act. A way to tackle this problem is to construct morphogenetic mosaics, i.e. animals consisting mostly of heterozygous wildtype cells with a clone of cells homozygous for the morphogenetic mutation. For this purpose a morphogenetic mutation is coupled with a cell marker mutation on the same chromosome arm. Mitotic recombination in a heterozygous animal will lead to a cell and later on to a clone homozygous for both the morphogenetic and the cell marker mutation. The latter is used as a label or tracer to signal the presence of cells homozygous for the morphogenetic mutant in which we are interested. (In Fig. 6.1 the reader can 'do' this by placing a recessive morphogenetic mutation close to *w* (the cell marker mutation) on one chromosome arm, and the corresponding dominant wildtype allele next to w^{co} on the other arm.)

Morphogenetic mosaics can provide answers to a number of intriguing questions: How will a small number of cells—our clone—differentiate when its developmental programme is different from that of the surrounding cells?—Does it matter when in development and where in the disc the clone is induced?—Are the wildtype alleles of the homoeotic mutations needed continuously, or just at a given time in development?—How do homoeotic genes control development?

We now induce homozygous clones at different times of development. The result is fascinating in two respects: (i) All morphogenetic mutations tested so far show *cell autonomy,* i.e. the homozygous clone differentiated into a small island of homoeotic tissue according to its own genetic constitution. This indicates that a cell's genotype determines its differentiation irrespective of surrounding cells of a different genotype and developmental programme. This was true independent of the time of clone induction. Since the homoeotic genotype already determines the number of precursor cells that initiate a disc, we may conclude that the wildtype allele is functioning continuously throughout development. Only very late in development do we find that a small clone differentiates according to the genotype of the heterozygous clone mother cell, presumably due to some gene product still being around and active after a few cell divisions. (ii) With homoeotic mutations the characteristics of the homoeotic structures differentiated by a clone in a non-homoeotic background depend on the *position* of the homozygous clone. Whereas the genotype determines the general homoeotic quality, the position of the clone provides information as to the region-specificity of the differentiated bristle pattern. This is best illustrated by an example provided by Morata & Garcia-Bellido (unpubl.). The homoeotic mutations of the *bithorax* series (*bx*) transform the metathorax into a second mesothorax. If the clone happens to lie at the anterior margin of the haltere (= metathoracic appendix) it differentiates an anterior margin of the wing (= mesothoracic appendix); in the proximal region of the haltere it differentiates proximal wing structures, such as the costa.

The cells of a clone are apparently provided with some sort of positional information (Wolpert 1969), which appears to be identical in the meso- and metathorax, because metathoracic as well as mesothoracic cells can read it. This positional information may be based on the ontogenetic history of the clone in terms of numbers and nature of developmental decisions undergone so far (see Lawrence & Morata p. 135). A cell in the anterior-dorsal-proximal-marginal region may have taken the same developmental decisions, i.e. the same selector genes (Garcia-Bellido 1975) switched on or off, in the meta- as well as in the mesothorax, except for the one at the *bx*-locus which distinguishes meta- from mesothorax. This hypothesis assumes that the same switching mechanisms are at work in all the discs of an animal. If this were true we could hope to understand the basic genetic mechanisms controlling development.

OUTLOOK

Clonal analysis has helped to elucidate a number of developmental phenomena. Its main contribution was to emphasize the role of the individual cells as units of development, and to allow a quantitative evaluation of the cellular parameters of development. Further insights are to be expected if clonal analysis is applied in an even more sophisticated manner to problems of pattern formation, cell communication and regulation.

DISCUSSION

Kalthoff: I would like to comment on the technique of mitotic recombination. The results of Schweizer showed very dramatically that the size of the clone depends on the X-ray dose. Doesn't this throw into doubt the value of this technique for estimating the number of founder cells?

Nöthiger: The answer is yes, but we don't care! I would like to be less apocalyptic and say that when you use a much lower dose than Schweizer used, say 500 to 1,000 r, you cannot measure any differences in clone size, so within that range we are safe. Of course, we are still only getting an estimate. I have never said that we know exactly how many cells there are. We know it is 30 or 40 cells, and not 300.

Schneiderman: I think there is good evidence from experiments by John Hainey and Bryant (unpublished) that doses even as low as 500 r kill cells, and 1,000 r kill more.

Whittle: It is true that when you use gynanders to determine the number of cells in a disc, you do get figures which correspond well with the estimates made by mitotic recombination? The production of the gynander, we believe has not been associated with cell death.

Nöthiger: We can do a Poisson, and we find that the data fit a Poisson distribution, so all give comparable results. In the wing disc, for instance, the estimates go from about 20 to about 40, depending on the technique we use.

Wilby: What is the probability of crossing over occurring in two adjacent cells? Or in two cells, the progeny of which come to lie together, giving the appearance of a single clone?

Nöthiger: We can do a Poisson, and we find that the data fit a Poisson distribution, so the probability of two cells simultaneously undergoing mitotic recombination which happen to lie together, is very low. Obviously, you can have two hits in one disc, if you irradiate late, when the number of cells in the disc is larger.

Lawrence: Just to give people an idea of the frequency if you irradiate early at blastoderm stage, you get the order of one clone in 50 to a 100 wings.

Nöthiger: You may state it differently. Because mitotic recombination is a cellular event, with 1,000 r the frequency of hits is about 1 in some hundreds of cells.

Wolpert: I would like to make a general comment, referring back to our problems of yesterday. It seems to me overwhelmingly clear now that whatever determination there is in the egg, however mosaic or gradient it is, there is an enormous amount of interaction at the later stages. It is a great pleasure for those of us who work on vertebrates to find the insect people joining the fold. I think it is very interesting that the sort of comments that you would make about the discs having the same kind of positional information, but the interpretation being altered by earlier events, are very similar to the arguments that we could make about the forelimb and the hind limb.

Selman: Is cell determination of imaginal disc cells in pupae made by the same process as cellular determination in the embryo?

Nöthiger: In the pupa, when imaginal differentiation begins, except for the two last differential divisions in the cell producing the bristles, no more cell divisions occur. So I would say at that time there is no more determination, and the whole pattern is fixed. In my view determination starts in the embryo and goes on progressively from more general to more specific qualities until imaginal differentiation begins. I would say that the computer card of the cells' instructions is written during larval development, and is being printed out when imaginal differentiation occurs.

Selman: In other words, you are imagining this as just a delayed programme.

Wolpert: Imaginal discs are just a way of packaging things, while larval development continues.

Schneiderman: You said, I quote 'developmental decisions are changed', then you said 'I believe in progressive developmental decisions taken by groups of cells, and that these decisions are clonally maintained afterwards'. Do you believe that during regeneration, the normal progressive developmental decisions can be altered—because during regeneration things are just very different from normal?

Nöthiger: The way you asked, I can say yes I believe it, but I don't know.

Schneiderman: I was really asking for an opinion, because opinions affect the way you do experiments.

Gurdon: Can I come back to the point made by Wolpert, when he said that intercellular communication is very important in development. I wonder if it will be useful to distinguish morphogenesis and the arrangement of cells from cell differentiation; that is the type of differentiation that single cells display? I wonder if it is really true that cell differentiation, as distinct from the arrangement of cells, depends on intercellular communication? I would only agree with Professor Wolpert that intercellular communication is important with respect to the arrangement of the cells to form observable structures like wing or leg, but not in respect of whether a cell becomes one type of cell or another.

Wolpert: No, that is part of the reason why I asked Dr Gehring what cell types there are in the eye and the antenna. In the early blastoderm a single cell can give rise to any of the cells in either the antenna or the eye, so it is quite impossible for early determination of cell type to occur at that early stage. Is that an answer to your question? Are you suggesting that cell type may be determined at an early stage but not pattern? I think that is very unlikely.

Gehring: On this matter, whether embryonic determination is really the same as later determination, I think there is a very basic difference. The early stages are syncytial, and when the blastoderm forms, the cells can take up, for example, macromolecules very easily, and incorporate them, but at later stages it is much more difficult to imagine large molecules carrying information being exchanged from cell to cell. So the situation, early and late, may indeed be different.

Nöthiger: In the case of later determination events, the cells have a proper envelope. We are asked how certain genes are switched on and off, and we believe that in an antennal disc or wing disc different genes are at work. Wouldn't you imagine that there must be molecules, either produced or taken up by the cells, which switch the genes on or off?

Gehring: But it is a very basic difference, whether these are small or large molecules. Large molecules can directly interact with genes; small molecules usually don't, because they don't have the specificity.

Nöthiger: I would like it to be the same mechanism, the same general kinds of molecules at both stages, but of course nobody knows the answer.

Schneiderman: In human beings, X chromosome inactivation in females, which occurs early in their embryonic development, is propagated clonally. Does anybody know the kinds of mechanisms that maintain that kind of chromosomal change from cell generation to cell generation? I am not proposing that as a model for what determination is, but it is a similar kind of process.

REFERENCES

BECKER, H. J. (1957). Röntgenmosaikflecken und Defektmutationen am Auge von *Drosophila* und die Entwicklungsphysiologie des Auges. *Z. Vererb-Lehre*, **88**, 333-373.

GARCIA-BELLIDO, A. (1975). Genetic control of wing disc development in *Drosophila*. *Ciba Foundation Symp*. **29**, 161-182.

MORATA, G., RIPOLI, P. (1975). *Minutes*: mutants of *drosophila* autonomously affecting cell division rate. *Devl. Biol.*, **42**, 211-221.

NÖTHIGER, R. (1972). The larval development of imaginal disks. In *Results and Problems in Cell Differentiation* Vol. 5, 1-34, Springer Verlag Berlin-Heidelberg-New York.

SCHWEIZER, P. (1972). Wirkung von Röntgenstrahlen auf die Entwicklung der männlichen Genitalprimordien von *Drosophila melanogaster* und Untersuchung von Erholungsvorgängen durch Zellklon-Analyse. *Biophysik*, **8**, 158-188.

STERN, C. (1956). Genetic mechanisms in the localized initiation of differentiation. *Cold Spring Harb. Symp. quant. Biol.*, **21**, 375-382.

WOLPERT, L. (1969). Positional information and the spatial pattern of cellular differentiation. *J. theor. Biol.*, **25**, 1-47.

ACKNOWLEDGEMENTS

The experimental part of this work was supported by the Swiss National Science Foundation grant in 3.081.73.

7 • Mutations affecting the development of the wing

J. R. S. WHITTLE

School of Biological Sciences, The University of Sussex

INTRODUCTION

The interest in investigating mutations affecting a morphogenetic process is that the methodology of genetics will contribute to an increased understanding of the process itself, as well as provide material for analysis. Recent reviews on the genetics of imaginal discs in *Drosophila melanogaster* suggest that this is occurring (Garcia-Bellido 1972, Postlethwait & Schneiderman 1973). The wing disc in particular has recently been the focus of attention in the developmental biology of *Drosophila*. The origin and the clonal history of the structures of the wing have been defined (Bryant 1970, Garcia-Bellido & Merriam 1971, Ripoll 1972) and the dynamic nature of the specification that occurs during larval life has revealed previously unsuspected complexity and flexibility in the organization of imaginal discs (Bryant 1975). Formation of the wing in *Drosophila* is thus an excellent case study which will serve as a paradigm for an examination of the progress, the prospects and the problems of genetic analysis applied to development, and perhaps can even show the misconceptions that genetics may engender when applied to development. The basic questions that must be borne in mind are how is morphogenesis of the wing related to the functioning of genes in the wing imaginal disc, and how do the specific structures like veins, edge bristles and sensilla arise during morphogenesis. Towards this end, this paper has been organized in the following sections:

The biochemical basis of the *rudimentary* mutant.

Homoeotic mutations involving wing tissue.

Mutations causing duplication in the wing.

Cell death and wing morphogenesis.

The interpretation of 'wing mutants'.

Genetic variation affecting wing venation.

Gene interaction in the analysis of the wing.

Future directions in genetic analysis of the wing.

Conclusions.

Wright (1970) has called the common approach of developmental geneticists the classical one and he has encapsulated the classical approach in a number of generalizations. Individual genes apparently have pleiotropic or manifold action, genes show cell or tissue and temporal specificity in their effects and their phenotypic effects are modifiable by environmental factors as well as by the rest of the genome. Lindsley and Grell (1968) list 222 mutations, of which 132 are still available, as those which affect the appearance of the wing in some way. Even supposing that this list were a complete catalogue of genes, of all mutations which affect wing, (which it patently is not since new genes are still being defined) this list may not tell us the true complexity of the genetic programme for making a wing. Firstly, it is unsatisfactory to claim that we can derive more than a series of descriptions from these phenotypes. Secondly, such a simplistic approach neglects the fact that development is a homeostatic or canalized process so that the phenotypes reflect the accommodation of the system to a failure in one unit (a gene) rather than the straightforward subtraction of the contribution of that gene. Thirdly, one must be wary of the age-old trap that the terminology used to describe the genes, usually a name reflecting the phenotype of the defect caused by the gene abnormality, does not interfere with one's understanding of gene action at a level other than description of the whole wing. In other words we must avoid the one gene—one character fallacy. As will be mentioned later, it is even possible that this daunting list of 'wing mutations' is misleading us about the complexity of genetic activity involved in wing morphogenesis, and that the situation might be simpler. In this paper I shall attempt to assess and defend the position of genetics as a forceful methodology and philosophy in understanding development, as instanced by a consideration of genes affecting wing development.

THE BIOCHEMICAL BASIS OF THE RUDIMENTARY MUTATION

The recessive mutation rudimentary (*r*) is one of the earliest known mutants affecting the wing (Morgan 1910). Rudimentary homozygotes have small or rudimentary wings and homozygous *r/r* females lay eggs which are inviable unless the zygotic nucleus they contain after fertilization contains a normal copy of that gene. It was recently discovered that this female-sterility of *rudimentary* could be relieved by added pyrimidines in the diet. (Bahn *et al.* 1971). This clue has meant that the study of this gene has been transformed from being a complex genetic problem to a situation in which it is fairly certain what the primary gene product is, and at the same time the complex genetics (Carlson 1971) has become capable of resolution. Figure 7.1 summarizes knowledge of *rudimentary*. The series of seven genetic complementation groups into which *r* alleles fall has been correlated to a pattern of loss of activity of the three initial enzymes in the biosynthesis of pyrimidines. The relationship between the number of copies of the *r+* gene and the specific activity of these enzymes suggest that rudimentary is the structural gene for these three enzymes (Nórby 1973 for refs). Nutritional growth tests and biochemical essays have together contributed to this picture (Jarry & Falk 1974: Norby 1973, Rawls & Fristrom, 1975) and it is possible to restore egg fertility to eggs laid by *r/r* females by injection of pyrimidines (Okada, Kleinman & Schneiderman, 1974). However, despite the link established between a morphological phenotype and a basic biochemical defect, and the possible resolution of the complementation data, the major question now arises as to how pyrimidine metabolism is related to wing morphogenesis in particular. It has been suggested that wing growth might make stringent demands upon uridine for UDP galactose for use in chitin synthesis, so that a lesion in the supply

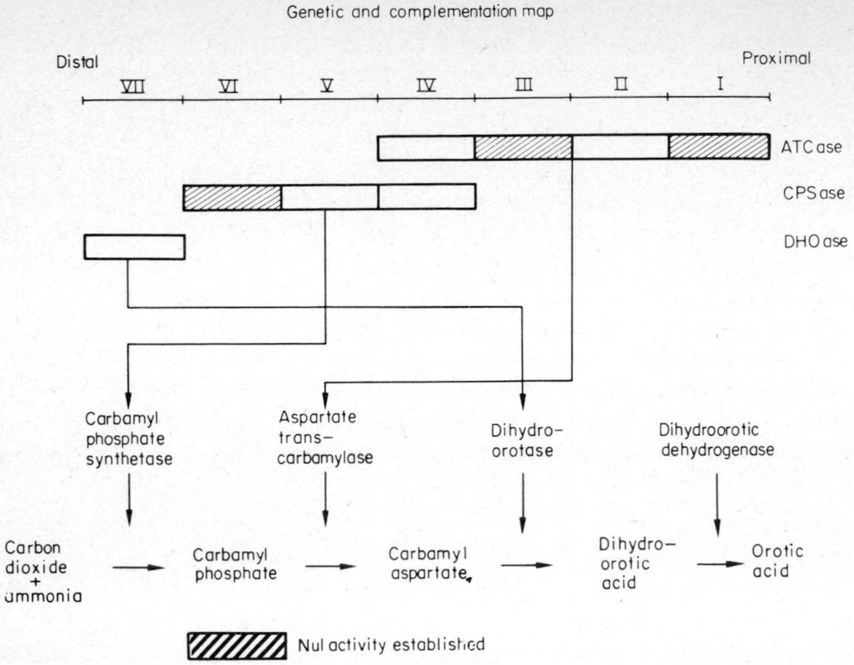

Genetic and complementation map

FIG. 7.1. The genetic and biochemical relationships of the rudimentary gene in *Drosophila melanogaster*.

appears as a limiting factor in wing cell growth. Even the verification of this hypothesis would still leave the question open as to how the particular change in wing shape occurs, and whether it reflects premature cessation of cell division or cell death. But the knowledge derived from this analysis of *rudimentary* so far should undoubtedly prompt specific investigation in this area.

HOMOEOTIC MUTATIONS INVOLVING WING TISSUE

Amongst the most intriguing and tantalizing mutations in *Drosophila* are those called homoeotics. These are a class of mutations which show transformations of areas in particular imaginal disc derivatives to those recognizable and characteristic of another disc (Ouweneel 1976). Table 7.1 lists the presently known homoeotic mutations involving wing tissue whether the wing is the site of transformation or whether wing tissue is formed in another area. The transformation is always in a particular direction and the details of the transformed structure relate quite specifically to the topology of the 'host' disc structures as if both transformed and untransformed cells were responding to common positional cues. (Wolpert 1972). Imaginal disc cells in *Drosophila* are determined to particular developmental fates early in embryonic life (Gehring, p. 101). They show a cell-heredity in their commitment to the formation of derivatives of a particular disc long before they exhibit any obvious outward sign of cellular differentiation. From what has been said so far, homoeotic mutations could represent either upsets in determination or failure in the perpetuation of the given state through cell divisions, or even the failure in competence to differentiate correctly.

TABLE 7.1 Homoeotic mutations involving wing tissue

bx	bithorax	anterior haltere	→ anterior wing
pbx	post bithorax	posterior haltere	→ posterior wing
bxd	bithoraxoid	1st abdominal	→ haltere
Cbx	Contrabithorax	wing	→ haltere
Ubx	Ultrabithorax	haltere	→ wing
en	engrailed	posterior wing	→ anterior wing
Hm	Haltere mimic	wing	→ haltere
Hx	Hexaptera	humerus	→wing
opht	ophthalmoptera	eye	→ wing
Opt^G	Opthalmoptera	eye	→ wing
pod	podoptera	wing	→ thorax
Pw	Pointed wing	antenna	→ wing
ttr	tetraptera	haltere	→ wing

Genetic mosaics have been constructed so that cells homozygous for a recessive mutation causing the transformation haltere to leg are produced at different developmental ages in a background of cells of heterozygous genotype, through removal of the normal allele by somatic crossing-over (see Nöthiger, p. 110). In this manner it has been found that for the genes of the bithorax complex (see Table 7.1) up until late larval life, such changes in genotype of the cells of the haltere disc will lead to homoeotic transformations to wing (Lewis 1964, Morata, G. in preparation). This shows firstly that the expression of this gene is cell-autonomous since the clone does exhibit the transformation, although embedded in a haltere disc and derived ancestrally from 'haltere' cells. In addition one must conclude that the normal copy of the gene which is removed by somatic crossing-over would continue to exert its effect at least to the age at which the clones no longer show transformation to 'wingness'. Such a result argues that the bithorax complex is associated with the cell heredity of a determination event which does not permit the formation of wing structures in the haltere in other words of sustaining determination to 'haltere' in these cells. There is little evidence either way as to whether the bithorax complex is also involved in the setting up of the determinative events in the blastoderm surface.

The homoeotic mutation *ophthalmoptera (Ophth)* (Table 7.1) is interesting because the mutation is only detectable when potentiated by a mutation in one of several other genes (*eyeless* or *loboid*) themselves not homoeotics (Ouweneel 1969 and 1970). The mutation *engrailed* (Table 7.1) is included there since it causes a clear intra-disc change and may, therefore, be considered analogous to the between-disc homoeotic mutations. The posterior part of the wing blade of *engrailed* homozygotes shows an incomplete mirror-image of the structures of the anterior wing; the venation resembles that of the anterior wing and triple row bristles characteristic of the anterior margin are found along the posterior wing margin (Garcia-Bellido & Santamaria 1972). The transformation is incomplete and is localized in patches. Mosaic analysis of *en*/*en* clones in wings of *en*/*en+* genotype suggests that the expression of this transformation is cell-autonomous; presumptive posterior cells will then form structures characteristic of the anterior wing.

The genes of the bithorax complex and *engrailed* have been interpreted by Garcia-Bellido as possibly representing part of a binary network of genes ('selector genes') which sustain determination events through cell proliferation in larval life until metamorphosis (Garcia-Bellido 1975). The analysis of clones growing at different rates in the normal wing, which are produced by somatic crossing-over in heterozygotes for *Minute* mutations, has led to the concept of compartments defined by the parts of a disc that such clones can encompass (Garcia-Bellido, Ripoll & Morata 1973, Crick & Lawrence 1975) and it is suggested that the gene *engrailed* forms part of the mechanism for maintaining the compartment distinction. Recent experiments with *engrailed* substantiate this hypothesis (Morata & Lawrence 1975 and Lawrence & Morata, p. 143).

MUTATIONS CAUSING DUPLICATIONS IN THE WING

Imaginal discs show properties of regeneration and duplication given suitable culture conditions, if they are bisected or damaged (Bryant 1975 and references therein). This discovery has led to a reappraisal of several mutations which produced wing phenotypes that appeared to be duplications. It was thought that these mutations could be reinterpreted as acting via the production of localized cell death or cell stasis. Duplications of the notum area in *vestigial* flies have been noted by Waddington (1953). Fristrom (1968) showed that there was widespread cell death in the wing of this mutant. The mutant *apterous-blot* normally causes a reduction in wing size and severe blistering, but the venation and organization of the wing margin in the occasional wing which is not blistered indicate that these wings may include duplications of the anterior wing (Waddington 1939, and Whittle, unpublished). Cellular degeneration has been reported in the allele *apterous-xasta* at this locus by Fristrom (1969). It is interesting to note the very different explanations for the mirror-image duplications caused by *engrailed* and that produced by *apterous-blot,* since they suggest that similar phenotypes can be formed by very different underlying cell behaviour, either normal growth as a 'copy' of the anterior wing (*engrailed*) or as proliferation from cells surrounding an area of necrosis. Although both mutations have revealed the existence of important constraints on the developmental behaviour of cells in the wing, the cellular interactions that result in the topology of the adult wing are as yet still unclear.

The mutation *scalloped (scl/^{VCl})* forms mirror-image thoracic duplications and the development of this phenotype is accompanied by cell death in the area of the wing blade (Vyse & James 1972, James, quoted in Bryant 1974). The recessive mutation *tufted (tuf)* in certain genetic backgrounds forms small duplications in the wing blade involving the proximal part of the triple row adjacent to the costa region (Whittle, unpublished). Double heterozygotes for two recessive second chromosome lethals, *1(2)cos$_1$* and *1(2)cos$_2$* (together denoted as costal (*Cos*) in a previous report (Whittle, 1974) cause large duplications in the costa region of the wing blade (Fig. 7.2). (Whittle, manuscript submitted). It has been possible to describe the clonal dynamics of this duplication event using genetic mosaics. Analysis of the size and frequency of clones found within the duplicate compared with those in the remainder of the wing reveal that there are few cells contributing to this duplication prior to 72 hours after egg deposition. Clones induced before that age in this area are few and significantly smaller than expected in normal growth (Fig. 7.3), but clonal growth in the rest of the wing is normal. The picture of cell proliferation derived from this analysis would be consistent with the effects of local cell death in the presumptive costa area. Whilst this analysis portrays the clonal dynamics of the duplication event, the basic problem is thus transferred to that of understanding the mechanism specifying the local cellular response resulting in the duplication.

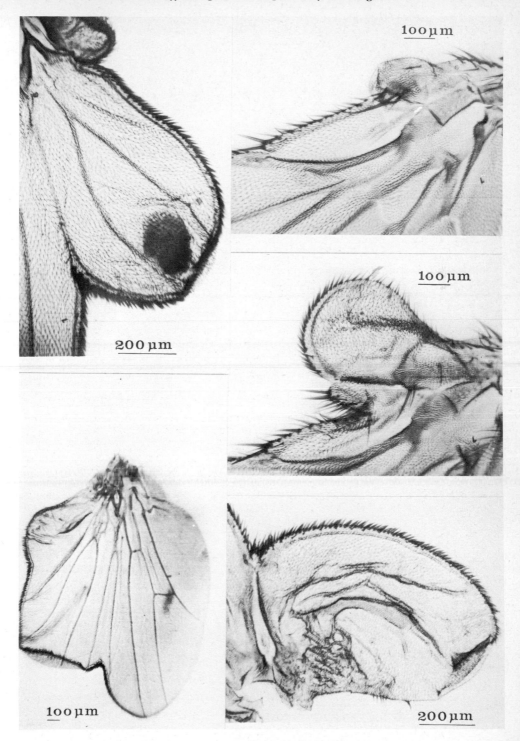

FIG. 7.2. Wings from flies of genotype *l(2)cos₁ l(2)cos₂/++* showing duplications of the costa region.

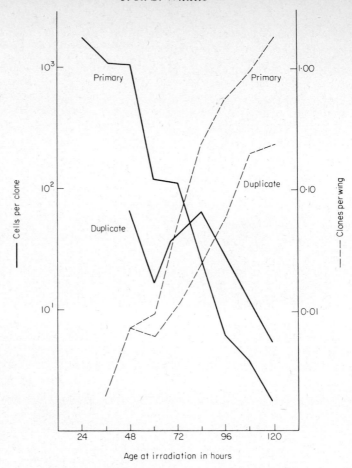

FIG. 7.3. The size and frequency of clones induced by somatic crossing-over in wings of genotype *1(2)cos₁ 1(2)cos₂/++*.

CELL DEATH AND WING MORPHOGENESIS

The description of clonal growth in the wing disc (Bryant 1970, Garcia-Bellido & Merriam 1971) in terms of exponential growth, the coherence of clonal derivatives as a patch and the limited deviation of clone sizes from 2^n has led to the view that widespread or considerable cell death during normal wing morphogenesis would be inconsistent with these data. Cell death is certainly a concomitant of the development of certain mutant phenotypes (Fristrom 1968, 1969, Spreij 1971 and those referred to above). Santamaria (in preparation) has very elegantly examined the deviations from regular clonal growth and the cell autonomy of expression of several such mutants in the wing using genetic mosaics. Bryant (1975) discusses the role of 'programmed' cell death in wing morphogenesis as an interpretation of the discrepancies between the topology of the gynander fate map, the imaginal disc transplantation fate map and clonal analysis. In particular he suggests that the clear dorso-ventral separation of clones at the wing margin might reflect a narrow marginal zone of cell death and that the series of mutations that show nicks or scalloping along the wing margin (including *Beadex,*

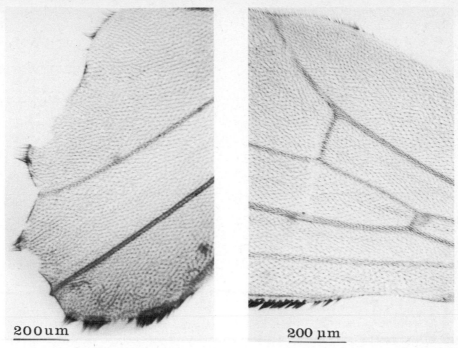

FIG. 7.4. Wings of the mutations *Chopped (Chp)* on the X-chromosome and of *Margin (Mar)* on chromosome 3 showing scalloping.

Beaded, cut and *Lyra*) represent a further extension of this zone of death. This would have to be reconciled with the large number of mutations both dominant and recessive with effects on the wing margin. Fig. 7.4 shows two new mutations of this class, *Chopped (Chp)* and *Margin (Mar)*. One has to suggest that the cells close to the death zone are perhaps labile to other metabolic lesions which could result in their death too. This would explain the number of genes apparently involved in maintenance of the integrity of the wing margin. Alternatively the cells of the wing margin, at the extremity of the 'pouch' in the disc may be generally less tolerant of deviations from the normal diploid genome. Partial aneuploids and deficiencies (for example, *Lyra*) might then lead to cell death at a stage when restitution by proliferation is no longer possible. This reasoning might also explain the other curious observation that the mutant *Margin* is lethal in double heterozygotes with *Lyra* or *Beaded* yet maps separately from them.

The relationship between local cell death and disc development is being pursued using cell-autonomous temperature-sensitive lethal mutations (Russell 1974, Arking 1975, Simpson & Schneiderman 1975). They provide a genetic scalpel with which to engineer local cell death by creating clones of the homozygous mutation with somatic crossing-over at the permissive temperature and subsequently killing them by later transfer to the restrictive temperature. The phenotype of *lethal(1)ts726* of Russell after heat shock has included a wing very similar to that of the double lethal heterozygote *1(2)cos$_1$ 1(2)cos$_2$/++* (Russell, personal communication).

THE INTERPRETATION OF 'WING MUTANTS'

This discussion of the interpretation of the role of genes in which mutations produce scalloping or duplication, possibly via localized cell death, illustrates the possible pitfalls of looking too closely at the wing for the clue to their basic developmental role. The classical genetic approach is to describe the function of the normal gene by reference to the changes produced by a mutation in that gene. But the value of this practice depends largely on the level at which the description is made. If, as is common, the gene is named after the phenotype of the mutant in morphological terms, it is important not to be trapped by this 'naming of parts' (Reed, 1962) into an explanation merely at that hierarchical level. It is not entirely helpful, for example, to define the contribution of a gene by saying that it normally prevents cell death in a particular area of a disc. It may be more heuristic to establish correlated changes at a different level as has been achieved for *rudimentary*. On the other hand, the description of *engrailed* as a selector (loc. cit) has encouraged investigation yielding a new description in terms of the behaviour of clones in the wing and most valuable of all, suggests that the biochemistry and cell-surface biology of such cell-heredity phenomena warrant attention (Crick & Lawrence 1975).

Wing mutations are so called because their obvious effect must have been noticed initially in the wing but a penalty could be paid for concentrating attention too closely on the one disc. Solely because the extent of morphological effects is limited to wing derivatives is insufficient evidence on which to presume that the activity of that gene is confined to that disc; one could only claim that if by judicious construction of genetic mosaics in which both copies of the gene were absent from a clone, there was no change. It is also very difficult to explain why a mutation with dominant effect on the wing (for example, *Beaded*) should be a zygotic lethal as a recessive unless it exerts effects outside the wing disc. If the lethality were confined to the wing disc because the gene really was disc-specific in its action, then one might expect to see flies lacking the dorsal mesothorax or pupal death at a late stage where the wing disc derivatives contribute to the formation of the adult hypodermis. Instead, however, the lethal phase of such loci is often at an early stage. The change in larval phenotype in *Ubx/Ubx* larvae observed by Lewis (1964), in which he reports duplication of larval structures in the same manner that the mutation transforms the metathoracic segments of the adult, makes clear the point that the *Ubx*[+]gene is active in cells other than those of the dorsal mesothoracic disc. There is a simple genetic explanation for recessive lethality associated with a dominant morphological effect and that is that the mutation is a deletion spanning several genes. The morphological effect might then be a consequence of the change in gene dosage for one of the deleted genes and the lethality could be the result of the homozygous deletion of a neighbouring gene. Genetic analysis by reversion and by selecting new mutations allelic to the lethality associated with the gene could resolve this question.

GENETIC VARIATION AFFECTING WING VENATION

Considerable genetic variation affecting the venation in the wing of *Drosophila* has been described. In addition to the many genes in which mutations produce clear-cut phenotypic differences with good penetrance (for example, *plexus,* which causes extra networks of veins to appear, and *veinlet* in which veins L3, L4 and L5 do not extend to the wing margin, see Lindsley & Grell 1968), polygenic variation affecting venation is well described (Milkman 1970) and the specificity of the interaction between polygenic modifiers of mutations with large phenotypic substitution effects has also been analysed (Thompson 1974 and references therein). Thompson has discussed the phenotypes of various mutants and polygenic modifiers in terms of a 'subthreshold vein pattern model' which is a topographical representation of the probability of vein formation at various points on the wing blade. As he implies, it will be important to relate this model to the cytological and physiological processes concerned in vein formation so that the way in which these many genes impinge on the process resulting in vein formation can be understood.

GENE INTERACTION IN THE ANALYSIS OF THE WING

Very understandably, geneticists interested in development have usually chosen fully penetrant mutations for their analysis and have preferred to examine mutations singly. Nevertheless there are indications, in addition to the evidence of polygenic variation, that some mutations can only be detected in the presence of other specific mutations. The homoeotic effect, *tumorous head* (Postlethwait, Bryant & Schubiger 1972) and *ophthalmoptera* (Ouweneel 1970) both require two mutations in combination before the phenotype appears. Waddington (1943) has described interactions between various recessive 2nd chromosome mutations affecting the leg. The costal wing duplication referred to earlier forms if the genotype is heterozygous for both lethal mutations $1(2)cos_1$ and $1(2)cos_2$. Neither heterozygous lethal alone produces any change in the wing. Deliberate selection for mutations which produce the duplication in combination with one of the two lethals shows that $1(2)cos_2$ can be replaced by one of several other mutations. The conclusion that can be drawn here is that some mutations will only be detected if they are induced and screened in genotypes already carrying other mutations.

FUTURE DIRECTIONS IN GENETIC ANALYSIS OF THE WING

Certain of the limitations upon the use of genetics in the analysis of development through the recovery and analysis of mutations affecting the wing have already been mentioned. It is now fair to stress the approaches discussed in this paper where genetics does seem to be making headway. Morphogenetic mosaics, in other words genetic mosaics for mutations affecting wing development, provide valuable information on the time and the particular cell population in which lesions in that gene are critical. It is a small but important step to extend the use of genetic mosaics to discover in what tissues particular genes in the form of their normal alles are not required at all, by using deficiencies in mosaics. Morata has been able to investigate the effect of the removal of the functioning bithorax complex of genes from the genome of cells in the wing (Morata, in preparation). Genetic mosaics for mutations are an important tool in carrying out selective operations during growth. The induction of a clone homozygous for a conditional cell-autonomous lethal by somatic crossing-over permits one to carry out fine scale operations of cell removal. Further mutations as material for developmental analysis may be revealed if it is recognized that some mutations may only be expressed in the presence of other pre-existing mutations in the genome. A rather more systematic but slightly different way of exploring the role of the genome has recently emerged (Lindsley & Sandler *et al.* 1972) which takes advantage of the highly developed chromosome manipulations possible in *Drosophila* in order to construct and examine genotypes haploid for small parts of their genome. This is a method to detect and locate recessive mutations, to study gene dosage effects and investigate the difference between individual gene effects and cumulative effects of partial aneuploidy. The successful resolution of *rudimentary* as a complex locus involving pyrimidine biosynthesis makes the direct search for biochemical mutations concerned with specific processes (for example, Sparrow 1974) perhaps a better approach than the attempt to 'work back' to the biochemistry starting with morphological mutants. Finally it appears that the wing may become a useful and sensitive bio-assay system for the examination of the cellular parameters of determination and differentiation by examining the effect of various environmental modifications upon the behaviour of known mutants affecting the wing.

CONCLUSIONS

In conclusion, the range of mutations affecting the wing of *Drosophila* has been briefly reviewed and the opportunity taken to reassess the methodology and thinking that lies behind the use of genetics and mutations in analysing a developmental process. A number of constraints and shortcomings of this approach have been raised and I have attempted to indicate the profitable avenues along which genetics will continue to contribute to an analytical account of development.

ACKNOWLEDGEMENTS

I gratefully acknowledge receipt of a grant from the Science Research Council in support of my own work, and the able assistance of Miss Jill Rich and Miss Chris Ashley.

DISCUSSION

Kalthoff: Is *rudimentary* cell autonomous; for example, if you make a clone covering half the wing?

Whittle: I believe the only studies on the cell autonomy of this mutant have been done with gynanders, where it behaves autonomously.

Wolpert: Of your 232 wing mutants, could you classify them a bit for us? How many of them are systematic effects, affecting every organ in the body, how many of them affect cell differentiation, for example the bristles, and how many of them are unique to the wing?

Whittle: I don't think I could even give you an order of magnitude answer. Some of the mutants certainly affect structures other than the wing, and so there is a certain danger if you look at one particular process rather than describing genes in terms of their general role in development. One has to remove the genes from a tissue, perhaps as a result of somatic recombination, to prove that a gene is not required in the tissue.

To give an example, if you look at *Ultrabithorax*, normally you study its affects on the haltere segment, but if you look at the larvae of *Ultrabithorax* homozygous survivors, you find transformations affecting the first abdominal segment, showing that the *Ultrabithorax* gene works outside the haltere disc.

Schneiderman: Professor Wolpert, you were one of the first people to point out that pattern formation occurs in very small populations of cells, populations which are too small to be amenable to conventional microsurgery. One of the beauties of somatic recombination, particularly temperature sensitive cell lethals, is that you can perform genetic microsurgeries at very specific stages in development, and destroy larger or smaller clones and examine the consequences. So these experiments have turned out to be a very powerful tool.

Shire: Dr Whittle has given us a very clearcut account of the cautions of using genetics in the analysis of development, and I would like to point out, as a geneticist, that a number of mosaic experiments described in the last 24 hours all depend on having some useful symbol genetic markers, like *yellow* for instance.

Wolpert: On behalf of all embryologists, I would like to thank the geneticists.

Lawrence: I would like to make a general remark about the large number of mutations affecting a particular region of the wing, that is the notching mutations which cause scalloping of the wing margins. These can either be interpreted because many genetic programmes are required to make that region (as you tend to interpret it), or alternatively one could say that it is a sensitive region, so sensitive that a large number of genetic lesions, which produce non-specific damage, show up particularly there.

Whittle: I would agree with you, and in fact the latter explanation is the one I prefer. It is possible that one can use the wing imaginal disc as a sort of bioassay system, to investigate general affects on morphogenesis. For example, one can now use clonal analysis, plus other environmental agencies, in the wing disc to study the effects of particular mutations.

Wilby: Are there mutants in a completely different class which have a specific affect on the pattern on the wing disc?

Whittle: Yes. I would quote particularly the homeotic mutations, the mutation *engrailed* is another example, although it doesn't only affect the wings, it affects also the prothoracic leg disc. This mutation seems to be a much better choice for the study of the process than for example the scalloping mutants.

Wilby: My feeling is that the homeotic mutants relate to transdetermination phenomena, so that there is more than one way the cells can interpret a given pattern of positional information. The *engrailed* looks very similar to the double abdomens syndrome, described by Kalthoff. It looks to me like a cell death and regeneration, leading to the duplication. Is there any correlation between the mirror image symmetry due to *engrailed,* and the mirror image symmetry of a regenerating wing disc? So I still think we need a mutant which changes the actual positional information within a disc.

Morata: I think this question can be answered, because the *engrailed* mutation is cell autonomous in small patches of cells. So you cannot explain the *engrailed* phenotype by gross regeneration.

Lees: Is *rudimentary* anything like the *dumpy* mutations? It looks similar in the picture.

Whittle: Yes, it has a similar phenotype in the wing.

Lees: Then in regards to your first proposition, Waddington showed many years ago that *dumpy* mutants probably arise from over-contraction of the wing membranes during the time when they contract from an inflated phase. One would suggest that either something might be wrong with the haemolymph pressure, or with the contractivity of the membranes. I merely wanted to suggest that the time might be right to work back a little from the other end towards these primary biochemical events. It might not be quite so hopeless as you implied.

Whittle: I didn't want to state a hopeless case, I just wanted to emphasize caution. There are a large number of mutations affecting venation in the wings, which are worth studying. But we need to know much more about the mechanics of folding and vein formation before we can understand how these mutants work.

Wolpert: Could I just echo those remarks, that your criticisms Dr Whittle are that we are not really studying the developmental processes. I think that the real point, that is what the geneticists have to begin to do, is to do some embryology. A cruel statement by the chairman.

REFERENCES

ARKING, R. (1975). Temperature-sensitive cell-lethal mutants of *Drosophila:* isolation and characterization. *Genetics,* **80,** 519-537.

BAHN, E., NØRBY, S. and SICK, K. (1971). Inter allelic complementation for pyrimidine requirement in rudimentary mutants of *Drosophila melanogaster. Hereditas,* **69,** 187-192.

BRYANT, P. J. (1970). Cell lineage relationships in the imaginal wing disc of *Drosophila melanogaster. Devl. Biol.,* **22,** 389-411.

BRYANT, P. J. (1974). Determination and pattern formation in the imaginal discs of *Drosophila. Current topics in Devl. Biol.,* (A. A. Moscona and A. Monroy, eds.), **8,** 41-80.

BRYANT, P. J. (1975). Pattern formation in the imaginal wing disc of *Drosophila melanogaster*: Fate map, regeneration and duplication. *J. exp. Zool.,* **193,** 49-78.

CARLSON, P. (1971). A genetic analysis of the *rudimentary* locus of *Drosophila melanogaster Genet. Res.,* **17,** 53-81.

CRICK, F. H. and LAWRENCE, P. A. (1975). Compartments and polyclones in insect development. *Science,* **189,** 340-347.

FRISTROM, D. (1968). Cellular degeneration in living development of the mutant *vestigial* of *Drosophila melanogaster. J. cell. Biol.,* **39,** 488-491.

FRISTROM, D. (1969). Cellular degeneration in the production of some mutant phenotypes in *Drosophila melanogaster. Molec. gen. Genet.,* **103,** 363-379.

GARCIA-BELLIDO, A. (1972). Pattern formation in imaginal discs. In *The Biology of Imaginal Disks,* Vol. 5, *Results and Problems in Cell Differentiation,* eds. H. Ursprung and R. Nöthiger, Springer-Verlag, Berlin, pp. 59-91.

GARCIA-BELLIDO, A. (1975). Genetic control of wing disc development in *Drosophila* in *Cell Patterning,* Ciba Foundation Symposium **29,** 71-93.

GARCIA-BELLIDO, A. and MERRIAM, J. R. (1971). Parameters of the wing imaginal disc development of *Drosophila melanogaster. Devl. Biol.,* **24,** 61-87.

GARCIA-BELLIDO, A., RIPOLL, P. and MORATA, G. (1973). Developmental compartmentalization of the wing disc of *Drosophila. Nature New Biol.,* **245,** 251-253.

GARCIA-BELLIDO, A. and SANTAMARIA, P. (1972). Developmental analysis of the wing disc in the mutant engrailed of *Drosophila melanogaster Genetics,* **72,** 87-104.

JARRY, B. and FALK, D. (1974). Functional diversity within the rudimentary locus of *Drosophila melanogaster. Molec. gen. Genet.,* **135,** 113-122.

LEWIS, E. B. (1964). Genetic control and regulation of developmental pathways. *Symp. Soc. Devl. Biol.,* **23,** 231-252.

LINDSLEY, D. L. and GRELL, E. H. (1968). Genetic variations of *Drosophila* melanogaster. *Carnegie Instn. Washington Publ.,* 627.

LINDSLEY, D. L., SANDLER, L., BAKER, B. S., CARPENTER, A. T. C., DENELL, R. E., HALL, J. C., JACOBS, P. A., MIKLOS, G. L. G., DAVIS, B. K., GETHMANN, R. C., HARDY, R. W., HESSLER, A., MILLER, S. M., NOZAWA, H., PARRY, D. W., GOULD-SOMERO, M. (1972). Segmental aneuploidy and the genetic gross structure of the *Drosophila* genome. *Genetics,* **71,** 157-184.

MILKMAN, R. (1970). The genetic basis of natural variation in *Drosophila melanogaster Adv. Genet.*, **15**, 55-114.

MORATA, G. and LAWRENCE, P. A. (1975). Control of compartment development by the engrailed gene in *Drosophila. Nature, Lond.*, **255**, 614-617.

MORGAN, T. H. (1910). The method of inheritance of two sex-limited characters in the same animal. *Proc. Soc. exp. Biol. Med.*, **8**, 17-19.

NØRBY, S. (1973). The biochemical genetics of rudimentary mutants of *Drosophila melanogaster* I. Aspartate carbamoyl transferase levels in complementing and non-complementing strains. *Hereditas*, **73**, 11-16.

OKADA, M., KLEINMAN, I. A., SCHNEIDERMAN, H. A. (1974). Repair of a genetically caused defect in oogenesis in *Drosophila melanogaster* by transplantation of cytoplasm from wild-type eggs and by injection of pyrimidine nucleosides. *Devl. Biol.*, **37**, 55-62.

OUWENEEL, W. J. (1969). Morphology and development of loboid-ophthalmoptera, a homoeotic strain in *Drosophila melanogaster. Wilhelm Roux Arch. Entw Mech. Org.*, **164**, 1-14.

OUWENEEL, W. J. (1970). Genetic analysis of loboid-opthalmoptera, a homoeotic strain in *Drosophila* melanogaster *Genetica*, **41**, 1-20.

OUWENEEL, W. J. (1976). Developmental genetics of homoesis. *Adv. Genetics* (in press).

POSTLETHWAIT, J. H., BRYANT, P. J., SCHUBIGER, G. (1972). The homoeotic effect of 'tumerous head' in *Drosophila melanogaster. Devl. Biol.*, **29**, 337-342.

POSTLETHWAIT, J. H. and SCHNEIDERMAN, H. A. (1973). Developmental genetics of *Drosophila* imaginal discs. *Ann. Rev. Genetics*, **7**, 381-434.

RAWLS, J. M. and FRISTROM, J. W. (1975). A complex genetic locus that controls the first three steps of pyrimidine biosynthesis in *Drosophila. Nat.*, **255**, 738-740.

REED, H. (1972). Lessons of the war, in *The Penguin Book of Contemporaty Verse*, selected by K. Allott. Penguin Books, Harmondsworth.

RIPOLL, P. (1972). The embryonic organization of the imaginal wing disc of *Drosophila melanogaster. Wilhelm Roux Arch. Entw Mech. org.*, **169**, 200-215.

RUSSELL, M. A. (1974). Pattern formation in the imaginal discs of a temperature-sensitive cell-lethal mutant of *Drosophila melanogaster. Devl. Biol.*, **40**, 24-39.

SIMPSON, P. and SCHNEIDERMAN, H. A. (1975). Temperature-sensitive cell autonomous mutations in *Drosophila*. I. Isolation by use of somatic recombination. *Wilhelm Roux Arch. Entw Mech. Org.*, **178**, 233-245.

SPARROW, J. (1974). The use of alpha-methyl Dopa to select for mutants affecting cuticle development in *Drosophila melanogaster. Heredity*, **33**, 142.

SPREIJ, T. E. (1971). Cell death during the development of the imaginal discs of *Calliphora* erythrocephala. *Neth. J. Zool.*, **21**, 221-264.

THOMPSON, Jr., J. N. (1974). Studies on the nature and function of polygenic loci in *Drosophila*. II. The sub-threshold wing vein pattern revealed in selection experiments. *Heredity*, **33**, 389-401.

VYSE, J. and JAMES, A. (1972). New mutant. *Drosoph. Inf. Serv.*, **49**, 39.

WADDINGTON, C. H. (1939). Preliminary notes on the development of the wings in normal and mutant strains of *Drosophila. Proc. natn. Acad. Sci. USA.* **25**, 299-307.

WADDINGTON, C. H. (1940). The genetic control of wing development in *Drosophila. J. Genet.*, **41**, 75-139.

WADDINGTON, C. H. (1943). The development of some 'leg genes' in *Drosophila. J. Genet.*, **45**, 29-43.

WHITTLE, J. R. S. (1974). *Costal*: a mutant producing duplications in the wing of *Drosophila. Heredity*, **33**, 139.

WOLPERT, L. (1972). *Current Topics in Developmental Biology*. Vol. 6. A. A. Moscona and A. Monroy, eds. Academic Press, New York, pp. 183-224.

WRIGHT, T. R. F. (1970. The genetics of embryogenesis in *Drosophila. Advan. Genet.*, **15**, 262-395.

8 • The compartment hypothesis

P. A. LAWRENCE AND G. MORATA

MRC Laboratory of Molecular Biology,
Hills Road, Cambridge, CB2 2QH, England

We still know very little about the way one-dimensional genetic information is used in the construction of a three-dimensional organism. How is the size, shape and pattern of structures controlled? Insects are particularly well suited to a study of these problems, partly because so much is known of the genetics of *Drosophila,* and partly because insect cuticle is secreted by a single layer of cells. In recent years these two features have been exploited in studies of the lineage of cells secreting cuticular structures. In particular it has been discovered that the insect body is subdivided into units, termed *compartments* (Garcia-Bellido, Ripoll & Morata 1973), each under independent genetic control so that the development of pattern in each is somewhat autonomous. In this essay we first describe the ideas, which we can call the compartment hypothesis, and then continue with a piecemeal examination of the evidence supporting the main structure of the hypothesis. For clarity we will overstate the ideas, the strength or weakness of the evidence upon which they are based should become apparent. We intend to illustrate their importance by showing how they provide a conceptual framework for the clarification of several major problems in developmental biology.

THE COMPARTMENT HYPOTHESIS

The mature insect can be divided up into regions (compartments) which have borders in precisely the same place in all individuals. *Compartments are characterized by the lineage of their constituent cells,* that is their cells are *all* the descendants of a small neighbouring group of cells (and therefore generate a *polyclone*, Crick & Lawrence 1975) which was set aside at a much earlier stage of development. The founder cells of the polyclone are not closely related to each other in any particular way; for example they have not recently descended from a single progenitor cell. The descendants of each cell of the original polyclone will populate different regions of the adult compartment in different individuals, but together the polyclone will always construct the same region, the compartment, in all individuals. This means that the compartment border is a line with special properties; because, after a critical time when the two neighbouring polyclones are established, all the progeny of any cell, in all individuals, will either be on one side of it or the other. Thus cells marked after this time generate clones which may define the line but never cross it.

132

A polyclone can become subdivided; a group of cells which are exclusively going to form an organ can, after some growth, become subdivided into two polyclones, one set of cells generating for example, a precisely defined anterior region of the organ, the remainder forming a precisely defined posterior region.

The polyclones and the compartments they generate are units for the genetic control of development. Special genes, termed *selector genes* because they 'select' a specific developmental programme (Garcia-Bellido 1975), are in combination, responsible for controlling the entire development of a polyclone. For example, when one polyclone is split into two a selector gene may be 'switched on' in one daughter polyclone and 'off' in the sister (Fig. 8.4) the differing states of this gene constituting the only determining difference between the two sister polyclones (Morata & Lawrence, 1975). *The state of activity of the selector gene is permanent and determinative, being propagated by cell heredity.* The maintenance of the determined state thus depends on special controlling genes which are activated initially in a group of cells. This polyclone of cells then passes the state of activity of the selector gene to all its offspring.

One of the roles of the selector genes is to change cell affinities and thereby control cell mixing during growth (Morata & Lawrence, 1975). Two differently determined sets of cells with different selector genes active, each remain as coherent patches, mixing to some extent within the patches but maintaining a well-defined border at the interface where the two populations meet.

It is possible that compartments are not only units for the genetic control of development but also units in pattern formation. *Positional information could be set up independently in compartments,* the borders of positional fields coinciding with compartment borders (Garcia-Bellido 1975; Crick & Lawrence 1975). Specific interactions may be triggered at the border where cells belonging to two differently determined polyclones confront each other. Because of a possible relation between positional gradients and size control (Bohn, 1971; Lawrence, 1973a) it follows that *compartments may be the units for the control of size and shape.*

Finally it is possible that *the compartment hypothesis may have evolutionary significance,* separate units under the independent control of specific selector genes could be the basis of development of diverse segments from identical metamers in the ancestral form (Garcia-Bellido 1975).

We will now go through some of the evidence for the points made in the introduction. The italicized key phrases given there will be repeated as headings for each section.

COMPARTMENTS ARE CHARACTERIZED BY THE LINEAGE OF THEIR CONSTITUENT CELLS

In insects, investigations of cell lineage have depended on being able to genetically mark individual cells in such a way that all their progeny bear the same mark. In the milkweed bug, *Oncopeltus,* it was found that irradiation of aged eggs produced coloured patches of cells in the mature larva, the older the irradiated eggs, the more frequent and smaller the patches; the younger, the rarer and larger (Lawrence 1971; 1973b). Each of these patches must have descended from a single progenitor cell which was altered by the irradiation; all the marked cells therefore constituting a clone. After irradiation of eggs at the cleavage stage, a small proportion of the insects bore a marked clone which was split up into several patches of the altered colour, each containing hundreds to thousands of cells, and the patches being found in several segments of the abdomen

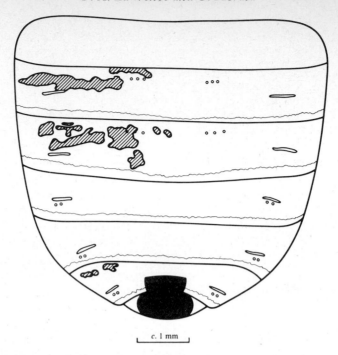

c. 1 mm

FIG. 8.1. A clone (shaded) on the abdomen of a 5th-stage larva of *Oncopeltus*. The clone extends to three different abdominal segments, and was produced by X-irradiation during late cleavage. (After Lawrence 1973b).

(Fig. 8.1), and often on the thorax and head as well. At the end of the blastoderm stage with germ band formation just beginning, (see p. 36) irradiation resulted in clones, which although sometimes split up into patches, were now strictly confined to a single segment (Fig. 8.2). In the abdomen of *Oncopeltus* larvae the segment border is clearly marked by a shape and colour change in the epidermal cells (Lawrence 1975; Lawrence & Green 1975), and when the coloured patch reached this border, it ran along it without crossing it. Within a particular segment the patches were different sizes and shapes in different individuals, showing there was no defined lineage within the segment, but the confinement of clones to single segments suggested that, at the time of irradiation, the formation of segmental polyclones had been completed. Clones also respected a boundary separating the dorsal and ventral parts of the abdomen, which separated each of the segments into four quadrants (left or right, dorsal or ventral).

   Clones produced at that time were on average, one-tenth of the segment quadrant in size, suggesting that there were *about* 10 cells/segment quadrant which were going to make epidermis, at the moment of segmentation (see Nöthiger, p. 110).

   These observations showed that, by the criteria described in the introduction, the segment quadrants are compartments, in that they have precisely defined boundaries, and are made by the descendants of a small group of cells.

   If there were no features marking the intersegmental boundaries it would have been difficult to identify the compartment borders. This problem has been overcome in *Drosophila* by making the marked cell grow more than the other cells so that the clone becomes abnormally large and runs along the compartment border for a long way, displaying it for the investigator. This technique, termed the *Minute* technique (Morata

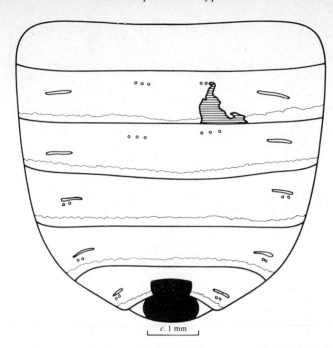

c. 1 mm

FIG. 8.2. The abdomen of an *Oncopeltus* larva, showing a typical clone (shaded) produced by irradiation at the end of the blastoderm stage. The clone is confined to a single segment, and respects the intersegmental boundary. (After Lawrence 1973b).

& Ripoll 1975) uses X-ray induced somatic recombination (p. 110) and depends on making suitable stocks so that as the marker is recombined into the cell, a deleterious allele causing slow growth (a *Minute* allele, Lindsley & Grell 1968) is recombined out. The resulting cell is both homozygous for the marker and for the normally growing wildtype allele of the *Minute* gene. Thanks to this technique a compartment border that runs through the middle of the *Drosophila* wing was recently discovered (Garcia-Bellido, Ripoll & Morata 1973; 1976), even though it had gone unnoticed during earlier and careful clonal analyses of the wing (Bryant, 1970; Garcia-Bellido & Merriam 1971a). This border runs straight through the wing, just anterior to the fourth vein, and its route is not marked by any structural feature at all (Fig. 8.3)—an observation which raises the possibility that compartment boundaries may have been overlooked elsewhere, in other insects and of course in other groups of animals. It is important to note that even when the cells grow much faster and frequently almost fill a compartment, they cannot cross a compartment border. This observation underlines the real nature of the restriction; a cell belonging to a particular polyclone can only contribute to one particular compartment, although which part of the compartment it can generate is not determined.

A POLYCLONE CAN BECOME SUBDIVIDED

In *Drosophila* the wing disc probably begins existence together with the leg disc in a mesothoracic polyclone in the blastoderm, and then becomes subdivided as a separate set of cells a few hours later (Wieschaus & Gehring 1976). It is not clear when it is

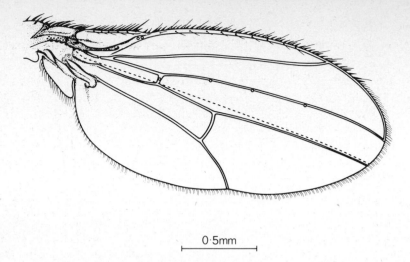

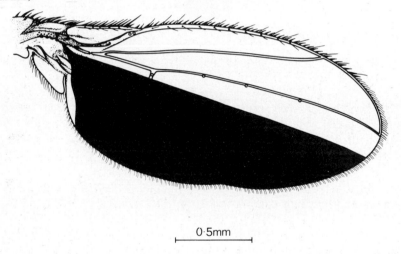

0·5mm

FIG. 8.3a. The wing of *Drosophila* to show the position of the anteroposterior compartment border (dotted line).

0·5mm

FIG. 8.3b. The wing to show a larger posterior *Minute*[+] clone (black) in a *Minute* background. Note how the clone, which extends to both dorsal and ventral surfaces, respects the compartment border. (From Crick & Lawrence 1975).

partitioned into anterior and posterior regions but these are already apparent from a very early stage (Steiner 1975). Garcia-Bellido, Ripoll and Morata (1973, 1976) have described how the anterior and posterior polyclones, both initially including cells destined to form the thoracic notum and the wing appendage, become subdivided so that each polyclone is now split into two, giving a total of four. Two polyclones generate the anterior and posterior parts of the thorax, and two the anterior and posterior parts of the wing. A similar process occurs at about the same time in the first larval stage, to separate dorsal and ventral sets of cells, in each of the four polyclones. There may even be further subdivisions. Fig. 8.4 describes how one set of cells can become subdivided into two separate sets, and the figure suggests this may be done geographically. Other possible mechanisms have been discussed by Crick & Lawrence (1975).

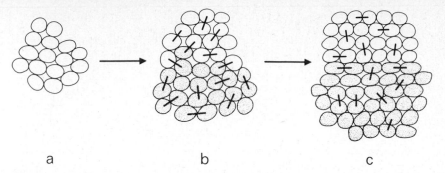

a   b   c

FIG. 8.4. *Hypothetical scheme* to describe how one set of cells can become subdivided into two. At time *a* there is one polyclone. Following some cell division at time *b*, a selector gene is activated in a geographically localized subset of cells. (Shaded.) Some sister cells are allocated to different polyclones by this process which explains why clones produced at time *a* can extend to both daughter polyclones. At time *c* the border between the two polyclones has been straightened, possibly because of the effect of the selector gene on cell affinities. This diagram shows recently divided pairs of sister cells joined by a line.

THE POLYCLONES AND THE COMPARTMENTS THEY GENERATE ARE UNITS FOR THE GENETIC CONTROL OF DEVELOPMENT

This idea, which states that compartment development is under autonomous genetic control, is an important one, which we owe to Garcia-Bellido. The phenotype of a strong *bithorax* allele, in combination with the position of the anteroposterior compartment border of the wing, immediately suggests the idea, because in the *bithorax* mutation it is the anterior wing compartment which appears in place of the anterior haltere (Fig. 8.5). Thus a single mutation can transform an entire compartment, suggesting that in this case the wildtype function of the *bithorax* gene is responsible for determining the development of an anterior haltere.

This idea can be extended to other homoeotic mutations where there are substitutions of one organ by another. For example, we have made a study of *engrailed* (Morata & Lawrence 1975; Lawrence & Morata 1976) a mutation partially transforming the posterior part of the wing so that it has anterior wing characteristics (Garcia-Bellido & Santamaria 1972). We were able to show that the state of the *engrailed* gene (whether mutant or wildtype) is immaterial to all the cells of the anterior compartment, presumably because it is normally inactive in those cells. By contrast, the presence of the wildtype allele is essential for normal development of all the cells of the posterior polyclone, presumably because it is normally active and determinative there. These results strongly support the idea that the different patterns of growth and final differentiation of the anterior and posterior compartments of the wing depend on the state of a single gene which is inactive in the former and active in the latter.

THE STATE OF ACTIVITY OF THE SELECTOR GENE IS PERMANENT AND DETERMINATIVE, BEING PROPAGATED BY CELL HEREDITY

Determination is a progressive restriction of developmental potential, so that with each determinative step, the number of possible fates open to a cell's progeny are reduced. Because of the abundant detail on *Drosophila* cuticle it has been possible to recognize

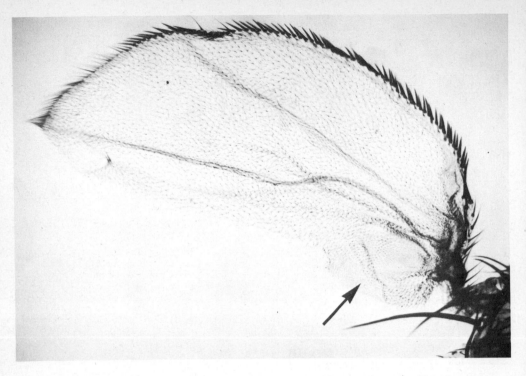

FIG. 8.5. A metathoracic appendage in a fly expressing the *bithorax* phenotype. Note the anterior haltere is missing, and in its place there is a complete anterior wing compartment (compare Fig. 8.3a). The posterior haltere (arrow) is unaffected. The genotype of the fly is bx^3/Ubx^{130}, (Morata & Garcia-Bellido 1975).

even small patches of cuticular structures as being characteristic of a certain region. Using this feature Hadorn's school have been able to map out the progressive narrowing down of prospective fate that occurs during imaginal disc growth. However a theory for this stepwise restriction (Gehring, p. 103) is lacking.

The compartment hypothesis is, in our opinion, very helpful in this difficult area. Steiner (1975) has recently shown that the leg, like the wing, is subdivided into anterior and posterior compartments from around the blastoderm stage. If in a hypothetical example the selector gene *engrailed* is activated at an early stage in the posterior part of the mesothoracic polyclone prior to separation of a dorsal (wing) and ventral (leg) disc, then those cells are thereafter determined, and all their progeny are restricted to make those structures which are within the repertoire, and are characteristic of the pattern, of the posterior leg and wing compartments. If at a later stage another selector gene is switched on, say in the polyclone for the dorsal disc, then those cells are now limited to m. king wing structures and have lost the ability to make leg structures. The combination of states of activity of the two genes determines four different compartments, by what is really a binary code. If 1 signifies the activity of the selector gene and 0 its inactivity, then 00 will specify anterior leg, 01 anterior wing, 10 posterior leg and 11 posterior wing. This combinatorial code is very economical in the use of genetic control units; 3 selector genes specifying 8 states, 4 genes specifying 16, and so on.

We know that the determined state of the cells is dependent not only on the switch—whether the selector gene is active or inactive—but also on some continuous function of the gene. For all homeotic genes so far analysed (*aristapedia* (Postlethwait & Girton 1974) *engrailed* (Garcia-Bellido & Santamaria 1972) *bithorax* (Morata & Garcia-Bellido 1976)) removal of the wildtype allele from a clone of cells results in that clone of cells becoming transformed. For example, we have described how *bithorax* appears to be necessary to determine the development of the anterior haltere—in its absence anterior wing structures are produced in place of the haltere. Removal of the wildtype *bithorax* allele from a cell by somatic recombination results in the transformation of the cell's progeny into wing structures (Morata & Garcia-Bellido 1976). This is a completely cell autonomous process, other cells not being transformed, and all the cells of the clone becoming wing.

These experiments reveal two different aspects of determination; (i) the initial determinative event, where the selector gene is activated or inactivated in a polyclone (ii) the maintenance of the determined state, which depends on the continuous and effective function of the selector gene in all the cells generated in any polyclone where it has been activated. These two aspects can have a completely independent genetic base; the process of switching can be independent of the later function of the activated gene. Clearly, mutations can interfere with this complex process in a number of different ways. Some may alter the determinative switch itself, these will have an early and limited period of effect. Garcia-Bellido has proposed that there may be specific genes (termed 'activator genes') whose products are only required at the time of switching. Clones expressing mutations in such genes produced after the switch could have a wildtype phenotype. There could be mutations in the switch itself so that, for example intermediate amounts of product could be produced in all the cells. There could be mutations in the selector gene so that the product is either completely ineffective, 'leaky' or temperature sensitive. Clones of these types of mutants could express the homeotic phenotype autonomously. In the case of the temperature sensitive mutations, temperature shift experiments can alter the expression of a mutation until late in development. Such experiments do not tell us much about the normal process of determination in wildtype insects, but describe the temperature sensitivity and turnover of the selector gene product in that particular mutant. Thus it has observed (Schubiger & Alpert 1975) that if the antennal disc of a temperature sensitive *aristapedia* mutant was allowed to regenerate, its differentiation could respond to a new ambient temperature, while if undergoing direct metamorphosis without regeneration, it could not. This observation is to be understood, not in terms of a period of lability or 'dedetermination' in the cells, but instead in the case of regeneration simply as a dilution out of a selector gene product which could not be replaced at the restrictive temperature. In the case of direct metamorphosis, there would be no dilution of the effective product.

Thus for the same reason, very late removal of the wildtype allele of a selector gene will not result in homeotic transformation of the clone, because sufficient product of the gene is already present in the cells, resulting in *perdurance* of the wildtype effect (Garcia-Bellido & Merriam 1971b). If these same cells are allowed to divide again in culture then, as expected, the wildtype product is diluted out and homeotic transformation occurs in the clone. (Garcia-Bellido, unpublished results).

Transdetermination (Hadorn 1965) can also be considered in this context. Arguing directly from the frequency and direction of transdeterminations Kauffman (1973; 1975) showed that the relationships between different states, such as 'leg', 'wing' etc., could best be pictured as a net depending on a combinatorial binary code of bistable elements; most common transdeterminations depending on a change of state of a single element, uncommon ones depending on changes in more than one element. It is remarkable that two completely different lines of approach, one based on trans-determination and one based on clonal analysis (Garcia-Bellido 1975) have led to similar models of genetic control of determination. It is also remarkable that both normal determination and transdetermination (Gehring 1967) occur in groups of cells. These considerations, while not advancing our molecular understanding of deter-mination, do suggest that determination is dependent on the activity of a special class of controlling genes. One characterstic of this class is that their state of activity is permanent, being propagated by cell heredity, and another that they are switched on and off in groups of cells. It is worth noting that determination is, in this context, not so much a restriction to specific types of cytodifferentiation, but more a commitment to an area property (Crick & Lawrence 1975).

ONE OF THE ROLES OF THE SELECTOR GENES IS TO CHANGE CELL AFFINITIES AND THEREBY CONTROL CELL MIXING DURING GROWTH

If compartments are to develop autonomously under independent genetic control, it is clear that their cells should not intermingle with those belonging to neighbouring compartments. It has been known for a long time that differently determined cells in *Drosophila,* and of course in other systems (Townes & Holtfreter 1955), remain separated *in situ* and if dissociated and mixed artificially will sort out into separate territories (Nöthiger 1964; Garcia-Bellido 1966). The formation of precisely positioned compartment boundaries during development may partially depend on the differential cell affinities of adjacent polyclones. We have proposed that each selector gene instructs the cells so that they do not mix with other cells having different combinations of selector genes active (Morata & Lawrence 1975; Lawrence & Morata 1976). Thus in the posterior part of the wing the *engrailed* gene will so instruct or 'label' cells that they cannot intermingle with cells of the anterior polyclone and instead form a straight interface with them. This hypothesis predicts that removal of the wildtype allele for *engrailed* in the posterior cells will result in the loss of the 'label' and the cells will now be able to mix with anterior cells. Likewise removal of the wildtype allele for *engrailed* from anterior cells should have no effects on cell affinities—since the gene is inactive there anyway. These experiments have been done and the expected results obtained; thus posterior cells mutant for *engrailed* can cross the compartment border to mix with wildtype anterior cells, while anterior *engrailed* cells cannot cross into posterior wildtype territory (Morata & Lawrence 1975; Lawrence & Morata 1976).

The ontogenetic importance of keeping adjacent compartments separate is clearly seen when several identical compartments are made in the same fly. For example in a fly homozygous for both *bithorax* (which transforms the anterior haltere into anterior wing) and the mutant *wingless* (Sharma 1975) (which in combination with *bithorax* removes the wing and transformed haltere and substitutes each of them with an extra mesonotum) there are four homologous polyclones forming mesonotum on each side of the insect. Instead of forming four well-constructed mesonota, these polyclones fuse together, clones being able to cross from one region to another, and a rather horrible mess results (Fig. 8.6). It follows from this observation that the proper development of a polyclone into a well formed compartment may depend on its being surrounded by the cells of neighbouring and differently 'labelled' polyclones.

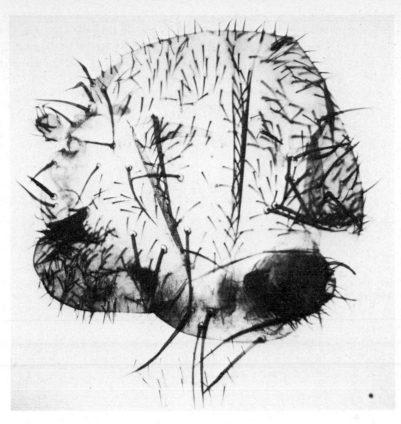

FIG. 8.6. A thoracic conglomerate consisting of 8 mesonota which have fused to varying extents. The genótype of the fly is *wgl/wgl; bx³/Ubx¹³⁰*.

POSITIONAL INFORMATION MAY BE SET UP INDEPENDENTLY IN COMPARTMENTS

Positional information (Wolpert 1969) tells a cell where it is in a developing structure, and there are many experiments suggesting that, in insects and other systems, the information is in the form of some kind of gradient established between defined boundary regions (Locke 1959; Lawrence 1966; Lawrence, Crick & Munro 1972). We do not know what the gradient is; it may, for example, be the concentration of a diffusing molecule (Lawrence 1966; Stumpf 1966), a phase difference between two waves propagated with different velocity (Goodwin & Cohen 1969) or a gradient in cell adhesion (Nardi 1975). We do know that there is a scalar variable in one defined axis, implying a vector and giving position and specifying polarity to the cells. In the abdominal segments the gradient is in the anteroposterior axis, runs from one segment border to the next and is reiterated from segment to segment. By transposing marked cells Marcus (1962; see Lawrence 1971) was able to show that intermediate gradient values form as a result of cell interaction between host and graft, interactions which can explain both pattern changes, and polarity changes near the host-graft border. These experiments suggest that a cell's differentiation and polarity depend more on interaction with its neighbours than on its own ancestry. In short, the establishment of positional information within a field is largely independent of the precise lineage of the constituent cells. Even the segmental boundaries do not have a discrete lineage (Lawrence 1973b). Nevertheless in the abdomen the segmental boundaries have strong organizing properties; when transposed they keep their own positional values and influence other neighbouring cells (Piepho & Marcus 1957; Locke 1960; Stumpf 1967). They are also important in isolating separate fields: a small gap in the intersegmental boundary allows two neighbouring gradients to interact, leading to reversed polarity near the gap (Lawrence 1966) while a large gap results in the fusion of adjacent fields (Lawrence 1970). A cut made through the segmental boundary is followed by much more pattern distortion than a similar cut made elsewhere (Lawrence, Crick & Munro 1972). All these observations suggest that the boundaries of the abdominal segmental gradients coincide at least approximately with the intersegmental boundaries which themselves mark the limits of segmental compartments.

Although each abdominal segment is unique in the details of cuticular pattern, as well as internally, the positional information in different segments is similar, since grafting experiments show that equivalent positions are homologous (Locke 1959). In principle a single axial system of positional information could be used in all compartments, since a cell's differentiation could depend on both its position and its state of determination. Thus when a cell's genetic instructions are changed from say, haltere to wing, either by recombining out an active selector gene or inactivation of a mutant product by temperature shift, the cell responds to the same positional information as if it were in the homologous site in the wing (Morata & Garcia-Bellido 1976).

We have only considered one axis, that is the anteroposterior axis in the abdomen (equivalent to the proximo-distal axis in the legs, Locke 1966) and it has to be admitted that we know even less about the other axes. However, the correspondence of the major axis may well extend to the other axes, giving a homologous 'prepattern' (see Stern 1968) in all discs. Certainly the substitution of posterior with 'anterior' wing in clones of *engrailed* cells (Garcia-Bellido & Santamaria 1972) and haltere by wing in clones of *bithorax* (Morata & Garcia-Bellido 1976) shows that the cells respond appropriate to their coordinates in the two axes. The presence of an anteroposterior compartment border in the wing and the formation of mirror image patterns in the *engrailed* phenotype suggest that the positional information in the anteroposterior axis may change the direction of slope, but not value at the compartment border (Crick & Lawrence 1975).

COMPARTMENTS MAY BE THE UNITS FOR THE CONTROL OF SIZE AND SHAPE

This idea really arises directly from the preceding section, because if there is a relationship between compartments and positional fields, then compartments naturally suggest themselves as units in the control of size and shape (Crick & Lawrence 1975). When two segments of *Oncopeltus* fuse, the combined segment only grows as much as one segment—even though the whole abdomen is distorted as a result (Lawrence 1970). It has been estimated that 1000 r of X-irradiation kills some 50 per cent of the cells in a *Drosophila* wing disc (Haynie & Bryant, personal communication), yet the surviving wing is normal in size and cell number. Likewise the enormous clones produced in *Minute* flies after somatic recombination (Fig. 8.3), which increase more than tenfold the prospective fate of the marked cell, result in a corresponding reduction in growth of the other cells of the compartment, so that the resulting wing is of normal size and shape (Morata & Ripoll 1975). These observations show that the amount of growth is not determined early but can be modified continually to give the correct final dimensions and cell number.

Growth appears to be related to the steepness of the gradient of positional information. When, in the cockroach leg, different gradient values are grafted together growth occurs near the hostgraft border, the amount depending on the difference in gradient value, while the polarity of this intercalary regenerate depends on the sign of the difference. These elegant experiments (Bohn, 1971, p. 174) show a direct correlation between local growth control and positional information.

Just as the gradients are set up between defined boundaries, so the control of growth may reside in the boundaries. For a study of the control of size and shape in the wing of *Drosophila* we have made use of flies that are both *engrailed* and *Minute,* a genetic combination that causes an immense enlargement of the posterior compartment of the wing (Lawrence & Morata 1976). Although *engrailed Minute*[+] flies show a slightly enlarged posterior compartment, *engrailed*[+] *Minute* flies are quite normal. We made marked *engrailed* clones in flies that were *Minute,* to produce the *engrailed Minute* combination in small patches. We found that such patches caused outgrowths in the wing only if they included the posterior margin, where dorsal meets ventral. These outgrowths were much larger than the clone itself, other normal cells outside the patch having been recruited and growing excessively as well (Fig. 8.7). Even if the clone was limited to the dorsal compartment, ventral cells matched the extra growth of the dorsal. By contrast, when the clone was internal in the wing and did not include the posterior border it had no effect on the shape; it had presumably come under the controlling influence of the normal border cells.

It is early days to bring all these observations on growth control together under a unifying hypothesis; they do suggest that more knowledge of the relationship between compartments and gradients is a prerequisite to progress in what is a largely overlooked and fascinating field.

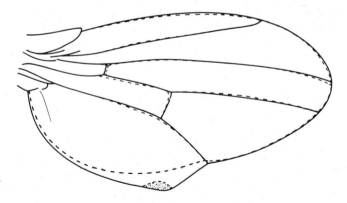

FIG. 8.7. The deformation produced by an *engrailed* clone which touches the posterior margin of the wing. The right wing containing the clone (shaded) is drawn in solid outline, while the left wing is superimposed as a dashed line. Note that the small dorsal clone has produced a large increase in size on both dorsal and ventral wing surfaces. The genotype of the fly is *pwn en/+;M(3)i*[ss]*/mwh jv,* and of the clone is *pwn en/pwn en; M(3)i*[ss]*/mwh jv.* (From Lawrence & Morata 1976).

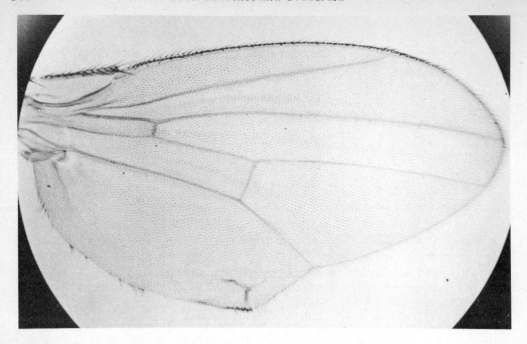

Fig. 8.8. Picture of genetically *Minute* wing bearing an *engrailed* clone in the posterior margin. This produces an outgrowth which is much larger than the clone. (From Lawrence & Morata 1976).

THE COMPARTMENT HYPOTHESIS MAY HAVE EVOLUTIONARY SIGNIFICANCE

Garcia-Bellido (1975) has pointed out how homeotic mutations largely result in transformation back to the same organ—a 'developmental sink', in this case, the mesothorax. Even within the mesothorax, the lack of function of different genes appears to direct the cells back to anterior mesonotum. These points suggest that the activity of selector genes is required to transform groups of cells away from their initial developmental state. This direction of change may also be an evolutionary one—for the progressive acquisition of diversity would go together with the acquisition of diverse control elements. In principle one can see that once a specific selector gene becomes responsible for a small difference between, say, meso and metathorax, natural selection could work on that difference and more and more features could become subsumed under the control of that gene.

Because of the great importance of selector gene function to phenotype, relatively small changes in the activity of their products could have a large effect on the morphology of the fly, suggesting an opportunity for rapid evolutionary changes.

CONCLUSION

In this essay we have attempted to show how helpful the compartment hypothesis is, and reviewed some of the evidence upon which it is based. Clearly more evidence is required if the hypothesis is to become a theory. Nevertheless we believe it promises to reward further study in *Drosophila* and in other experimental systems.

DISCUSSION

Slack: To me, these compartments look similar, at least formally, to embryonic fields in vertebrates, where one also seems to have a succession of subdivisions into fields. But the main difference, at least from your talk, seems to be that in vertebrate embryonic fields a single field may divide up into quite a number of subfields. Consider, for example, primary induction, where you probably segregate six or seven different subfields, such as kidney, limb, somite. Do you think that all compartments subdivisions in insects are binary or have you just picked out experimentally favourable cases which do happen to be binary processes?

Lawrence: You are absolutely right. I think we have heard from Professor Sander about the establishment of segment patterns, and this seems to be something set up in the whole egg. If so, the process cannot be binary because there are many segments. Now in vertebrates you don't have the same criteria. You don't know about the lineage, you don't have the genetic units, so it is not possible unfortunately to compare the two in detail. You are also right that I have picked out specific cases, and that I have overstated the hypothesis in making it only binary. I did that because it is rather elegant, but how far it applies I really do not know. It could happen in the vertebrate leg bud where you see, as you mentioned, antero-posterior determination first and dorso-ventral afterwards. That looks a little binary to me. The number of cells is about right, and the same goes for the vertebrate retina, the number of cells being in the order of tens.

Wigglesworth: I am sure that Peter Lawrence is right, that this is a revolutionary discovery, but some of us getting old in years assimilate a little slowly, and although I am sure that I am suffering from slow assimilation, I can't quite see what it is all about. I can understand compartments in segments, where you have a morphological structure, and I can see why it might be desirable to avoid cellular invasions and so on. But why should you have a compartment cutting clean across the wing, when as you have shown, all the normal processes of differentiation can provide for everything, distribution of sensillae and veins? Why did God make these compartments?

Lawrence: Well it wasn't God, it was evolution, but I think there is an answer to your question. Sure, compartments don't explain everything. Within a compartment, the lineage is not determined, so that the pattern is not strictly dependent only on the compartment itself. But it is a defined region of the wing, and we see the animal is split up into much smaller units. The problem becomes much simpler then, not only for us as observers, but also for the animal to construct itself, and also for evolution to work on the genetic machinery. This means that for the first time we can see the animal as a sum of its parts, which to some extent interact and to some extent are autonomous. Evolution is a very important consideration here. If you have a selector gene which initially has under its control a tiny difference between, say, the metathoracic and the mesothoracic segment, that selector gene can accumulate under its control more and more functions. So that by evolution you can get the independent origin from a simple genetic and physiological framework of two structures, the wing and the haltere. They use the same mechanism.

Weis-Fogh: I do feel that this could be a major breakthrough, and it may interest this society in particular that the line separating the anterior from the posterior part of the wing is a functional line, in all the flying insects that I know of, and is indeed a very important functional division in *Drosophila*. It is the line separating the active wing twisting from the passive elastic part and is of primary importance to the aerodynamics.

Whittle: I wonder if you would comment on the recent interpretation by Bryant that while the compartments set up in the wing are permanent in normal development, they may be crossed during regeneration. Do you have any comments about the ability of these restrictions during regeneration?

Lawrence: Well it is certainly very interesting, and many people are now working to find out how compartments are maintained during regeneration. Does the disc go back to scratch, and start all over again, or are compartments in part inherited during regeneration? The answer to this is really not yet known, but I think we will soon know. However interesting the answer would be, the beauty of this technique and the importance of this type of examination is that it looks at normal development *in situ*. What we really want to know is how is the wing constructed *in situ*. Often regenerates *in vivo* are not the same. They may not make a perfectly normal shaped and sized wing; and one of the things, to go back to Professor Wigglesworth's question, that compartments are good for, is to make a structure of the right scale and containing the right number of cells, in the proper relationship. That is a tricky problem, and that is one of the things the compartments may be for.

Henson: I was intrigued by this idea of a compartment in the wing not conforming to any morphological unit. Is it known whether such morphological units such as leg parts share the same phenomena? Are they compartments or not?

Illmensee: I would like to mention Becker and Baker's (unpublished) work on the eye, where similar compartment boundaries were discovered by the same technique, where there is also an anterior and posterior compartment.

Lawrence: I would like to refer to the work of Steiner (unpublished) on the leg of *Drosophila*, who has also shown that the leg is sub-divided into anterior and posterior compartments, with a very early origin.

Willison: Are the *Minute* wings smaller than normal?

Lawrence: No, the *Minute* wing is of normal size. The *Minute* phenotype is characterized by slow development and small bristles.

Gurdon: Could I refer to the other compartment border, namely the periphery of the wing, which cells don't normally cross over.

Lawrence: After a certain time that is. They do before of course.

Gurdon: Is it not right that one elementary explanation of this could be that during formation of the wing there is a sharp fold in the bag-like structure, which will eventually form the wing, and this could constitute a physical barrier that cells do not like to move over. Then I might extrapolate and suggest that there might be another fold, and if one took the trouble to look one might see it, across the middle of the wing. Has the detailed structure of the forming disc been examined?

Lawrence: The structure has not been examined in detail. What we have is a small patch of cells which suddenly splits up into two patches, so at an early stage a clone can cross and extend to both sides, about one cell division later you suddenly find that a clone is confined to one side or the other, and that is very hard to explain with folding.

Gurdon: Not necessarily, if the tightness of the bend were to increase at that critical stage in development.

Lawrence. Yes. We observe that there is a stage when before anything happens the cells can cross, and afterwards they cannot. We don't know what that something is, but we think it is the surface properties of the cells changing. But a fold could generate this boundary.

Gehring: I would like to add to the criticism made by John Gurdon, when you look at gyndromorphs, you find sharp boundaries between male and female tissue, which definitely now are due to the construction of the flies from separate discs, and they are sharp because we do not see the intervening cells which disappear during development into the interior. My first reaction to the story about compartments was that this must be due to something similar, and I still think that all the evidence, although more is accumulating nicely, still cannot rule out these doubts which I have. So this question as to how the wing is constructed really has to be looked into very carefully.

Lawrence: I am sorry, but I cannot agree with that. You have to tell me when the folding is occurring. Let us suppose, to begin with, that the folding is occurring early, and this fold must be so perfect that all the cells of one kind go on one side of it, and all the cells of the other kind go on the other side. In that case you have to explain to me how small *engrailed* clones very late in development, in a wildtype wing, may cross the boundary. Now let's consider the case where the folding occurs late, and in that case I have to ask you to explain to me how *engrailed* clones in a wildtype wing, but made in the posterior part early in development, can cross all the way into the anterior compartment, and replace structures there. Not displace them, but replace them. So you cannot have your fold early, and you cannot have your fold late.

Gurdon: What I say *engrailed* does is to alter the structure of the sheet.

REFERENCES

BOHN, H. (1971). Interkalare Regeneration and segmentale Gradienten bei den Extremitäten von *Leucophaea*-larven (Blattaria) II. Coxa und Tarsus. *Devl. Biol.,* **23**, 355–379.

BRYANT, P. J. (1970). Cell lineage relationships in the wing imaginal disc of *Drosophila melanogaster. Devl. Biol.,* **22**, 389–411.

CRICK, F. H. C., LAWRENCE, P. A. (1975). Compartments and polyclones in insect development. *Science,* **189**, 340–347.

GARCIA-BELLIDO, A. (1966). Pattern reconstruction by dissociated imaginal disc cells of *Drosophila melanogaster. Devl. Biol.,* **14**, 278–306.

GARCIA-BELLIDO, A. (1975). Genetic control of wing disc development in *Drosophila*. In: 'Cell Patterning' *Ciba Foundation Symposium* No. **29**, pp. 161–182.

GARCIA-BELLIDO, A., MERRIAM, J. R. (1971a). Parameters of wing imaginal disc development of *Drosophila melanogaster. Devl. Biol.,* **24**, 61–87.

GARCIA-BELLIDO, A., MERRIAM, J. R. (1971b). Genetic analysis of cell heredity in imaginal discs of *Drosophila melanogaster. Proc. natn. Acad. Sci. USA,* **68**, 2222–2226.

GARCIA-BELLIDO, A. RIPOLL, P., MORATA, G. (1973). Developmental compartmentalization in the wing disc of *Drosophila*. *Nature New Biology*, **245**, 251-253.

GARCIA-BELLIDO, A., RIPOLL, P., MORATA, G. (1976). Developmental segregations in the dorsal mesothoracic disc of *Drosophila*. *Devl. Biol.*, **48**, 132-149.

GARCIA-BELLIDO, A., SANTAMARIA, P. (1972). Developmental analysis of the wing disc in the mutant *engrailed* of *Drosophila melanogaster*. *Genetics*, **72**, 87-104.

GEHRING, W. (1967). Clonal analysis of determination dynamics in cultures of imaginal discs in *Drosophila melanogaster*. *Devl. Biol.*, **16**, 438-456.

GOODWIN, B., COHEN, M. H. (1969). A phase-shift model for the spatial and temporal organization of living systems. *J. theor. Biol.*, **25**, 49-107.

HADORN, E. (1965). Problems of determination and transdetermination. In: 'Genetic control of differentiation'. *Brookhaven Symp. Biol.*, **18**, 148-161.

KAUFFMAN, S. A. (1973). Control circuits for determination and transdetermination. *Science*, **181**, 310-317.

KAUFFMAN, S. A. (1975). Control circuits for determination and transdetermination: interpreting positional information in a binary epigenetic code. In: 'Cell Patterning' *Ciba Foundation Symposium* No. **29**, pp. 201-221.

LAWRENCE, P. A. (1966). Gradients in the insect segment: the orientation of hairs in the milkweed bug *Oncopeltus fasciatus*. *J. exp. Biol.*, **44**, 607-620.

LAWRENCE, P. A. (1970). Polarity and patterns in the postembryonic development of insects. *Adv. Insect Physiol.*, **7**, 197-266.

LAWRENCE, P. A. (1971). The organization of the insect segment. *Symp. Soc. exp. Biol.*, **25**, 379-392.

LAWRENCE, P. A. (1973a). The development of spatial patterns in the integument of insects. In *Developmental Systems: Insects* Vol. II, S. J. Counce & C. H. Waddington, eds. pp. 157-209.

LAWRENCE, P. A. (1973b). A clonal analysis of segment development in *Oncopeltus* (Hemiptera) *J. Embryol. exp. Morph.* **30**, 681-699.

LAWRENCE, P. A. (1975). The structure and properties of a compartment border: the intersegmental boundary in *Oncopeltus* In: 'Cell Patterning' *Ciba Foundation Symposium* No. **29**, pp. 3-23.

LAWRENCE, P. A., CRICK, F. H. C., MUNRO, M. (1972). A gradient of positional information in an insect, *Rhodnius*. *J. Cell Sci.*, **11**, 815-853.

LAWRENCE, P. A., GREEN, S. M. (1975). The anatomy of a compartment border. *J. Cell Biol.*, **65**, 373-382.

LAWRENCE, P. A., MORATA, G. (1976). Compartments in the wing of *Drosophila*: a study with the *engrailed* gene. *Devl. Biol.* (in press).

LINDSLEY, D. L., GRELL, E. H. (1968). Genetic variations of *Drosophila melanogaster Carnegie Inst. Wash. Publ.* 627.

LOCKE, M. (1959). The cuticular pattern in an insect, *Rhodnius prolixus*. *J. exp. Biol.*, **26**, 459-477.

LOCKE, M. (1960). The cuticular pattern in an insect—the intersegmental membranes. *J. exp. Biol.*, **37**, 389-406.

LOCKE, M. (1966). The cuticular pattern in an insect— the behaviour of grafts in segmented appendages. *J. Insect Physiol.*, **12**, 397-402.

MARCUS, W. (1962). Untersuchungen über die Polarität der Rumpfhaut von Schmetterlingen. *Wilhelm Roux Arch. Entw Mech. Org.*, **134**, 56-102.

MORATA, G., GARCIA-BELLIDO, A. (1976). Developmental analysis of some mutants of the bithorax system of *Drosophila*. *Wilhelm Roux Arch. Entw Mech. Org.* in press.

MORATA, G., LAWRENCE, P. A. (1975). Control of compartment development by the *engrailed* gene of *Drosophila*. *Nature*, **255**, 614-617.

MORATA, G., RIPOLL, P. (1975). *Minutes*: mutants autonomously affecting cell division rate in *Drosophila*. *Devl. Biol.*, **42**, 211-221.

NARDI, J. (1975). *Spatial differentiation in lepidopteran wing epidermis*. Harvard University Ph.D. Thesis.

NÖTHIGER, R. (1964). Differenzierungsleistungen in Kombinaten, hergestellt aus Imaginalscheiben, Verschiedener Arten, Geschlechter und Körpersegmente von *Drosophila*. *Wilhelm Roux Arch., Entw Mech. Org.*, **155**, 269-301.

PIEPHO, H. MARCUS, W. (1957). Wirkungen richtender Factoren bei der Bilding der Schuppen auf dem Schmetterlingsrumpfes. *Biol. Zbl.*, **76**, 23-27.

POSTLETHWAIT, J. H., GIRTON, J. R. (1974). Development in genetic mosaics of *aristapedia*, a homeotic mutant of *Drosophila melanogaster*. *Genetics*, **76**, 767-774.

SCHUBIGER, G., ALPERT, G. D. (1975). Regeneration and duplication in a temperature sensitive homeotic mutant of *Drosophila melanogaster*. *Devl. Biol.*, **42**, 292-304.

SHARMA, R. P. (1975). *Wingless*, a new mutant in *Drosophila melanogaster. Drosoph. Inf. Serv.*, **50**, 134.

STEINER, E. (1975). *Establishment of compartments in the developing leg imaginal discs of Drosophila melanogaster*. University of Zurich Ph.D. Thesis.

STERN, C. (1968). *Genetics mosaics and other essays*. Harvard University Press, Cambridge, Massachusetts.

STUMPF, H. (1966). Uber gefälleabhangige Bildungen des Insektensegmentes. *J. Insect Physiol.*, **12**, 601-617.

STUMPF, H. (1967). Uber den Verlauf eines Schuppenorientierenden Gefälles bei *Galleria mellonella. Wilhelm Roux Arch., Entw Mech. Org.*, **158**, 315-330.

TOWNES, P. L., HOLTFRETER, J. (1955). Directed movement and selective adhesion of embryonic cells. *J. exp. Zool.*, **128**, 53-120.

WIESCHAUS, E., GEHRING, W. (1976). Clonal analysis of primordial disc cells in the early embryo of *Drosophila melanogaster. Devl. Biol.* in Press.

WOLPERT, L. (1969). Positional information and the spatial pattern of cellular differentiation. *J. theor. Biol.*, **25**, 1-47.

III • Pattern in later development

9 • The development of the insect compound eye

P. M. J. SHELTON

Department of Zoology, School of Biological Sciences,
University of Leicester, Leicester LE1 7RH

INTRODUCTION

During development nerve cells are arranged in a predictable and orderly fashion to form networks capable of integrating complex behaviour. How this is done constitutes the ultimate in problems of biological pattern formation. We need to know how the fates of identifiable cells in the nervous system are determined and to what extent their connectivities are rigidly specified.

Mechanisms which could help to explain the development of such intricate patterns can be defined under two broad headings. First, there is the influence of *positional information* whereby cell fate is determined according to relative cell position (Wolpert 1969). Second, there is the role of what we may call *developmental mechanics.* According to the theory of positional information a developing neuron would measure its position with respect to a graded influence between boundaries and respond by developing connections appropriate to this position. Experiments on the development and regeneration of connections in lower vertebrates have been interpreted in this way (Gaze 1970). Developmental mechanics embraces many factors all of which may act differentially in time and space; it includes cell proliferation, cell death, cell movement and cell growth. It emphasizes a programmed sequence of events which favours the connection of particular neurons at particular times. If the sequence is interrupted disruptions in the connectivity pattern are expected. Extremists might argue that either mechanism by itself can explain the development of neural networks. I believe that both mechanisms are likely to have critical roles and that our experimental analysis of neural development should aim to test their relative importance.

The compound eyes of insects offer many advantages for this type of work. Within the vertebrates, visual neurons are organized with considerable order but the crystalline predictability of the compound eye and associated neuropiles defies comparison. It is this predictability which recommends the insect visual system for developmental studies. At the same time the intricacy of connections between neurons excites the imagination. Cajal and Sanchez (1915) examining insect optic neuropiles first demonstrated their incomparable fineness, complexity and precision. Indeed to them vertebrate grey matter seemed gross and rudimentary compared with the delicate structure of dragonfly or bee optic lobe. Recently there has been a renewed interest in the organization of the insect

152

visual system. The Diptera have received particular attention (Boschek 1971; Strausfeld 1971) and in some areas our progress in retinal neuroanatomy has outstripped the progress in neurophysiology. Now that detailed wiring diagrams are emerging it is a logical step to investigate their development.

THE ORGANIZATION OF THE COMPOUND EYE AND ASSOCIATED NEUROPILES

The retina is composed of structural units called ommatidia, each with an identical internal structure. For convenience each ommatidium can be divided into three functional regions. Distally the dioptric apparatus consists of a corneal lens and a crystalline cone. The lens is modified cuticle and the tight packing of ommatidia gives the compound eye its faceted appearance. Next there are the pigment cells which may regulate the entry of light to ommatidia and prevent light rays crossing from one ommatidium to another. Finally there are the retinula cells where sensory transduction takes place. Normally there are eight retinula cells but in bees there are nine (Perrelet 1970; Skrzipek & Skrzipek 1974). The axons of the retinula cells are of two sorts and terminate at different levels within the optic neuropiles (Cajal & Sanchez 1915; Strausfeld & Blest 1970) (Figs. 9.2 and 9.3). Normally six retinula cells have short axons and two have long axons. They terminate in the lamina and medulla neuropiles respectively. The ground plan of the optic lobe is similar for all insects. It consists of three neuropile masses joined by fibre tracts and it joins the retina with the protocerebrum (Fig. 9.1). In sequence moving centrally they are the lamina, medulla and lobula (Bullock & Horridge 1965). With the exception of the fly, the projection of retinula axons to the lamina is uncrossed. In all cases there are chiasmata between the other centres. By tracing axon profiles in serial sections it has been shown that there is an exact topographical projection of the visual fields of receptors upon first the lamina and then the medulla (Horridge & Meinertzhagen 1970a). In the case of the medulla the representation of visual space is inverted because of the chiasma. At the levels of the lamina and the medulla the neurons are organized into optic cartridges with one cartridge for each ommatidium (Fig. 9.4). The projection is perfect for the connection of every single neuron and in the fly it is very nearly perfect even for the exact positions of their synaptic terminals upon particular second order neurons (Horridge & Meinertzhagen 1970b). The detailed structure of the lamina cartridge is best known for fly (Boschek 1971; Strausfeld 1971) where each cartridge is composed of five lamina ganglion cells associated with six short retinula axons, two long retinula fibres which do not form synapses at this level, horizontal cell components and branches of centrifugal fibres whose cell bodies are situated centrally to the lamina. Only in the fly are the detailed interconnections between elements of the cartridge known but other insects possess the same classes of neurons in the lamina (Cajal & Sanchez 1915; Strausfeld & Blest 1970). The structure of the medulla cartridge is almost totally unknown although recent work emphasizes its columnar organization and reveals a superficial similarity to the lamina cartridge (Campos-Ortega & Strausfeld 1972).

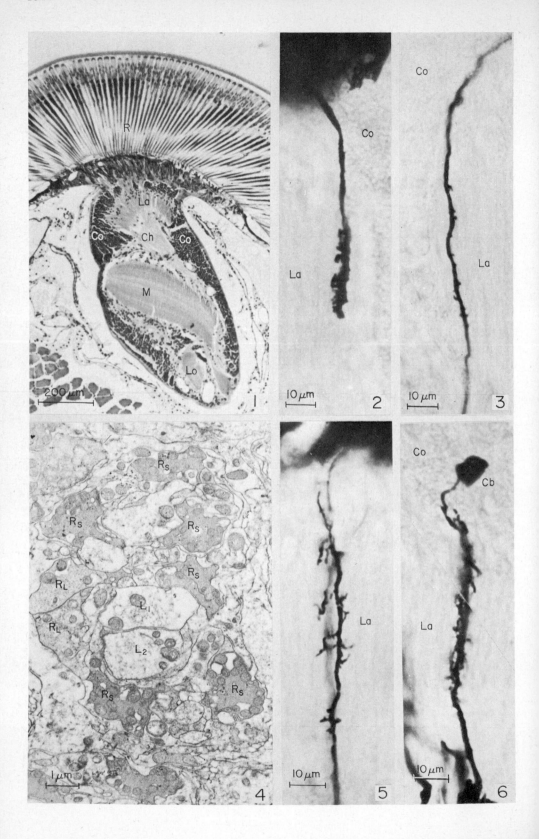

EARLY DEVELOPMENT OF THE EYE FIELD

Initial stages in the differentiation of the retina begin in the dorso-posterior region of the prospective eye field (Umbach 1934). These processes spread out from here in an organizational front which passes across the eye field. If the dorso-posterior portion of the eye is destroyed by cautery prior to the spreading of the front then normal differentiation is inhibited (Wolsky 1949, 1956; White 1963). We know very little about this front but it seems that the advancing eye margin has special properties which enable it to inductively recruit epidermal cells. Transplantation experiments show that unless the prospective eye cells come under the influence of the eye margin ommatidial differentiation will not take place (White 1961). Although much depends on the eye margin the state of determination of the epidermis is also important. Thus in the mosquito *Aedes aegyptii* only epidermis from the prospective eye region is competent to form eye (White 1961). There is a claim that prothoracic epidermis can form ommatidia when placed next to an eye margin in *Periplaneta* (Hyde 1972). However, in *Oncopeltus* it almost certainly cannot (Green & Lawrence 1975) and we have attempted and been unable to repeat these experiments on *Periplaneta* (Anderson & Shelton, unpublished).

The formation of ommatidia seems to involve three processes, these are: recruitment of epidermal cells, their proliferation within the eye margin and the grouping of their division products to form pre-ommatidia (Waddington & Perry 1960). Recruitment has been clearly demonstrated in *Aedes aegyptii* (White 1961), in *Periplaneta americana* (Hyde 1972; Shelton *et al.* in prep.) and in *Oncopeltus fasciatus* (Shelton & Lawrence 1974) by grafting experiments. In each of these cases presumptive eye epidermis with a pigment marker was grafted in front of the advancing eye margin. When incorporated within the retina such grafts are recognizable by their distinctive pigmentation (Figs. 9.7, 9.8, 9.9, 9.10). Little is known about the control of cell division within the advancing eye margin but in *Schistocerca* mitosis reaches a peak during the middle of the intermoult period (Eley, personal communication) and presumably it is affected by levels of insect hormones. In dragonflies both juvenile hormone (Mouze 1971) and ecdysone (Mouze 1972) are required for normal eye development.

The forces which govern cell clustering are totally obscure but almost certainly involve surface adhesion. Dissociated retinal cells from imaginal discs in *Drosophila* sort themselves out from antennal cells and reaggregate to form small groups resembling pre-ommatidia (Kuroda 1970). At this time there is a complex sequence of cell junction

FIG. 9.1. Organization of the retina (R) and optic lobe of *Schistocerca gregaria* as revealed in horizontal section. The neuropile layers are the lamina (La), medulla (M) and the lobula (Lo). There are chiasmata (Ch) between the lamina and medulla and also between the medulla and lobula. The central neuropile area is surrounded by the cell bodies of the lamina and medulla cortices (Co). Stained with haematoxylin and eosin.

FIG. 9.2. Golgi stained preparation of a short retinula ending in the lamina neuropile of *Schistocerca* (La). Co. lamina cortex.

FIG. 9.3. A Golgi stained preparation of *Schistocerca* to show a long retinula axon which passes through the lamina neuropile (La) to the medulla. Co, lamina cortex.

FIG. 9.4. An electron micrograph showing a transverse section through a single optic cartridge in *Schistocerca*. Visible are the profiles of two lamina ganglion cell axons (L_1, L_2), six short retinula endings (R_S) and two long retinula axons (R_L). The other nerve fibres are not yet identified.

FIGS. 9.5 & 9.6. These two Golgi preparations show two types of lamina ganglion cell found in *Schistocerca*. Lateral branches are the sites of interaction of these neurons with incoming retinula fibres and other neurons within the cartridge. Cb, cell body; Co, lamina cortex; La, lamina neuropile.

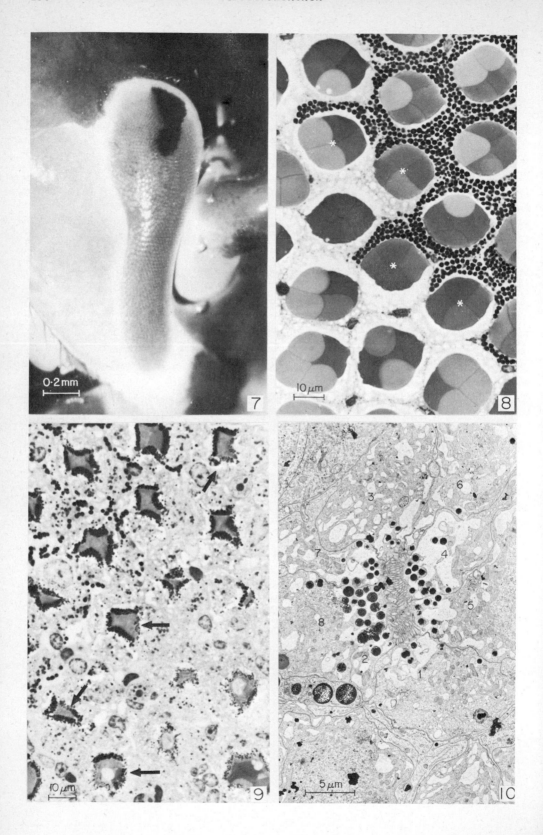

types each of which appears at a particular stage in the development of the cluster (Eley & Shelton in prep.) The types of junction present have been implicated both in surface adhesion and in intercellular communication.

PATTERN FORMATION IN THE RETINA

In terms of pattern, insect eyes can be classified into two groups. The division of eye types is recognizable both in the geometrical arrangement of retinula cells within ommatidia and in the way that retinula cell axons distribute to the second order neurons of the brain. In most insects ommatidia are constructed on the fused rhabdom plan. Here the eight retinula cells within a single ommatidium each contribute a segment (a rhabdomere) to a single central fused rhabdom (Fig. 9.13). As a result retinula cells in a single ommatidium all share the same visual axis. The organizational pattern is exactly reflected in the anatomical distribution of retinula cell axon terminals to the optic lobe. All the retinula axons from a given ommatidium are associated with a single group of second order lamina ganglion cells in a single optic cartridge (Horridge & Meinertzhagen 1970a). Thus the projection is a topographic one in which there is an anatomical representation of the visual field at the brain level.

In Diptera and Hemiptera, ommatidia are built on the open rhabdom plan. Within each ommatidium a small pair of retinula cells contributes to a central fused rhabdom. The retinula cells of the other six have separate rhabdomeres and each has a separate visual axis (Fig. 9.12). Consequently light rays on axis for one retinula cell do not stimulate the other retinula cells within that ommatidium (Kirschfeld 1967). In flies the geometry of the retina is such that different retinula cells in adjacent ommatidia share the same visual axis (Fig. 9.11). The projection of retinula axons to the brain reflects this arrangement. The axons from a *single* ommatidium terminate in *different* optic cartridges while the axons from retinula cells with the same visual axis terminate in the same optic cartridge (Braitenburg 1967; Horridge & Meinertzhagen 1970b). Once again the distribution of optic cartridges forms an anatomical representation of visual space, but in this case it is achieved by a complicated retina-lamina projection which is very different from the simpler projection pattern of fused rhabdom eyes. The existence of two types of ommatidia has caused us to ask whether or not cell fate within the two sorts of ommatidium is determined by the same mechanism and whether or not retinula cell connections are specified in the same way. I shall return to this question later.

FIG. 9.7. A mosaic eye in *Periplaneta americana* showing a patch of tissue with wildtype pigmentation against the background of the *lavender* mutant (Ross *et al.* 1964) host. The donor tissue was epidermis taken from the presumptive eye region and grafted in front of the host's advancing eye margin.

FIG. 9.8. A light micrograph through a mosaic eye at the level of the primary pigment cells. Each ommatidium has two primary pigment cells, one dorsal and one ventral, which surround the four cone cells of the dioptric apparatus. In the ommatidia marked with an asterisk the dorsal cell is derived from the graft and the ventral cell is derived from the host. The differential staining of cone cells is incidental and is not related to cell lineage. 1 μm toluidine blue stained section.

FIG. 9.9. A similar section at the level of the retinula cells. Host and graft cells differ in their ability to synthesize pigment. In four ommatidia (arrows) cells of both types can be seen surrounding the central rhabdom.

FIG. 9.10. An electron micrograph through a mosaic ommatidium to show the cell boundaries between retinula cells. Cells 2 & 8 possess the large wildtype pigment granules, the rest have fewer and smaller *lavender* pigmentation. Cell numbering according to Butler (1971).

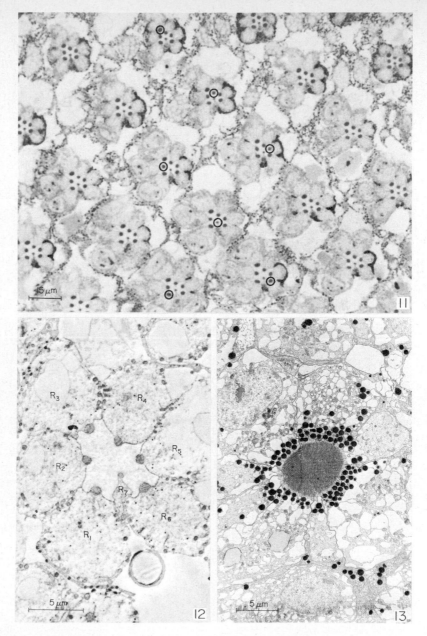

FIG. 9.11. A light micrograph of a 1 μm section of the dorsal quadrant of the left eye of the fly *Calliphora vomitoria* to show retinula cells in adjacent ommatidia that project to the same lamina cartridge. Encircled rhabdomeres have the same visual axis.

FIG. 9.12. An electron micrograph showing the arrangement of retinula cells in a transverse section of an ommatidium in *Calliphora vomitoria*. The central rhabdomere receives contributions from cells R_7 and R_8. The cell body of R_8 is not visible in this section because it is situated at a more proximal level with its cell body between R_1 and R_2.

FIG. 9.13. This electron micrograph of an ommatidium in *Periplaneta americana* illustrates the fused rhabdom pattern of organization. Here, all eight retinula cells contribute to a single fused rhabdom and thus all share the same visual axis.

CELL LINEAGE RELATIONS

In fused rhabdom eyes it was thought that each ommatidium was clonally derived from a single stem cell by a series of determinative cleavages. Histological sections of the ant *Formicina* were interpreted in this way (Bernard 1937), and the findings have been quoted subsequently as a classical example of cell determination by a lineage mechanism (Kühn 1965).

Preliminary reports for *Drosophila* (Diptera) (Benzer 1973) and our own work on *Oncopeltus* (Hemiptera) (Shelton & Lawrance 1974) have shown that ommatidia with open rhabdoms develop quite differently. In *Drosophila* genetic mosaics were generated prior to the formation of the retina. Mosaic eyes developed later in which part of the eye contained wildtype cells which synthesized pigment granules and part of the eye contained cells with a recessive gene which made them pigmentless. According to the cell lineage hypothesis no ommatidium should have contained cells of both types. However, at the junction of the two types of eye tissue, a substantial number of ommatidia contained mixtures of both sorts of cell (Benzer 1973). Our results for *Oncopeltus* were similar. Genetic mosaics were produced by grafting small pieces of epidermis from a red-eyed stock near to the eyes of white-eyed larval hosts. During subsequent retinal growth the donor tissue was incorporated into the eye and could be recognized by its pigmentation and the structure of the retinula cells. At the margins of the graft, ommatidia contained cells of both host and donor phenotypes in a great variety of unpredictable combinations. This demonstrates that the cells forming each ommatidium are normally derived from several unrelated cells and that the retinula and pigment cells are determined by cellular interaction and not by lineage (Shelton & Lawrence 1974). Further, some ommatidia contained only one retinula cell of a different phenotype from the rest; we were able to conclude that cell determination follows the proliferative phase of retinal growth (Shelton & Lawrence 1974). It is not certain when the cells are determined but their fate must depend upon the position they occupy in the cluster of cells which aggregates to form the ommatidium. More recently in *Periplaneta* we have shown that ommatidia with fused rhabdoms develop in a similar way (Shelton *et al.* in prep.) (Figs. 9.8, 9.9 & 9.10).

The compound eye is a regular structure consisting of fixed numbers of cells in a predictable geometrical pattern. It is remarkable that it develops by an interactive mechanism. However, there are considerable advantages to this mode of development. In structures which develop mosaically by a lineage mechanism, errors arising during an early stage of the process may have a drastic effect upon the final pattern. In the nervous system cells are arranged with great precision and it may be significant that nerve cells are grouped together and determined only at the last possible moment.

DETERMINATION OF POLARITY

For the proper functioning of the compound eye it is essential that ommatidia are arranged with consistent polarity across the retina. This is particularly important in Diptera where eye function depends upon a precise geometrical arrangement of receptor cells (Braitenburg 1967; Kirschfeld 1967). In the insect epidermis, hairs, bristles and scales are orientated with respect to postulated gradients of positional information (Lawrence 1973). Similar gradients may provide the basis for the specification of cells in various parts of the brain of lower vertebrates (Wolpert 1969; Gaze 1970). There is some evidence which suggests that retinal polarity in insects is determined in a similar way to bristle orientation (Lawrence & Shelton 1975). By grafting experiments it was shown that the orientation of ommatidia depends partly upon the polarity of the epidermis from which they develop and partly upon the orientation of the host eye. As with bristle patterns, grafts which invert the dorso-ventral axis of the presumptive eye epidermis do not disrupt the orientation of the nascent ommatidia but grafts rotated by 90° or 180° produce altered patterns. The polarity of the epidermis is to some extent conserved in these cases. Significantly ommatidia at the graft/host border take up orientations intermediate between the extremes found in host and graft. We cannot claim that these results provide more evidence for gradients of positional information because for technical reasons we were unable to transpose small grafts up and down the antero-posterior axis. Nevertheless, they demonstrate the need for further experiments of this type and they do emphasize the supracellular nature of the factors which orientate parts of the developing nervous system.

DEVELOPMENT OF THE OPTIC NEUROPILES

There are considerable variations between insects in details of optic lobe development but recent reviews have shown that all conform to the same general pattern (Panov 1960; Edwards 1969; Meinertzhagen 1973, 1975).

The neurons of the lamina, medulla and lobula are derived from neuroblasts of two optic lobe anlagen. The outer optic anlage generates the cells of the lamina and medulla cortices (Fig. 9.19) while the inner optic anlage contributes only the cortex of the posterior lobula (Nordlander & Edwards 1969).

Autoradiographic analysis has shown that the ganglion cells of the lamina and medulla are laid down in a strictly chronological sequence so that retinula cells and ganglion cells connect with neurons of similar ages in the different neuropile layers. This situation arises because both retinal and neuropile expansion proceeds in step from one margin only (Nordlander & Edwards 1969).

In *Danaus plexippus* the behaviour of neuroblasts in the outer optic anlage has been studied in detail (Nordlander & Edwards 1968). Each neuroblast divides asymmetrically to produce another neuroblast and a smaller cell, the ganglion mother cell. The ganglion mother cell then divides an undetermined number of times to produce new ganglion cells which subsequently differentiate into neurons of the optic lobe. Among the differentiating optic ganglion cells, small numbers of degenerating cells are found. A similar situation occurs in the outer optic anlage of *Schistocerca gregaria* (Fig. 9.19). Here, the invading growth cones of the retinula axons establish contact with the newly formed ganglion cells. Pycnotic cells may be those that have failed to receive an input from the periphery.

FORMATION OF NEURAL CONNECTIONS IN THE OPTIC NEUROPILE

GROWTH CONES AND NERVE FIBRE GROWTH

In the crustacean *Daphnia magna* there are only twenty-two ommatidia in a single cyclopic eye. This animal reproduces parthenogenetically and in clonally related individuals the connections within the visual system are absolutely predictable (Macagno *et al.* 1973). By fixing specimens at different stages of development it has been possible to provide a detailed description of eye growth. Not only do ommatidia differentiate in a well defined temporal pattern but their retinula axons seem to grow out in a timed sequence (Lopresti *et al.* 1973). From each ommatidium one fibre, known as the lead axon, grows to the lamina in advance of the other seven. This fibre has an expanded growth cone and makes the initial contact with lamina neuroblasts. The other fibres, known as follower axons, lack growth cones and appear to follow the track of the lead axon by contact guidance.

In insects the situation is much more complicated because the eye consists of thousands of ommatidia. During post-embryonic development of the locust *Schistocerca gregaria* approximately 1200 ommatidia are added during each five day intermoult period (Shelton, unpublished). Since there are eight retinula cells for each ommatidium this means that 9,600 retinula terminals have to make correct connections between moults. In fact, from Golgi preparations I have found that the main period of fibre growth is on the middle three days of the intermoult period. This means that about 3,200 retinula terminals are accurately located every day. We do not know whether such large numbers of connections can be made with precision in the time available by temporal growth sequences alone.

In the butterfly *Pieris brassicae*, Sanchez (1919) described two basic classes of growing axon tip. In the interneuropile tracts the fibre tip is smooth and has a streamlined growth cone but within the neuropile the growth cones are greatly expanded and are covered with filapodia. I have found a similar situation in *Schistocerca*. Fibres in the tracts have no discernible growth cones at all and they appear when the growing axon tips enter the neuropile region (Figs. 9.14, 9.15, 9.16, 9.17 & 9.18). Meinertzhagen (1973) has summarized the phases in the development of expanded growth cones in *Pieris* and has suggested that they form in response to the increased resistance afforded by the more tightly packed neuropile. In *Schistocerca* growing retinula axons first form expanded growth cones as they come into intimate association with the developing ganglion cells in the outer optic anlage (Figs. 9.16, 9.17 and 9.19). In this situation they are entering a region of decreased resistance and it seems likely that the growth cone with associated filapodia is formed to provide an increased area of contact with the second order ganglion cells. The growth cones associated with lead fibres of *Daphnia* may also appear subsequent to the entry into the neuropile. It is not known whether or not the lead fibre possesses an expanded growth cone while it is in the interneuropile tracts. Support for this hypothesis comes from the observation that follower fibres also develop terminal dilations but only when they reach the lamina (Lopresti *et al.* 1973). Many unresolved points remain. It would be interesting to know whether or not the followers from each of the other seven retinula cells always follow the leader in the same sequence and it is not yet clear whether the lead axon is always derived from the same retinula cell. In insects at least, it seems that expanded growth cones form in response to neuropile entry and we have no evidence that axons with such expanded growth cones act as lead fibres.

CONTACT GUIDANCE

When nerve fibres have to traverse great distances in their growth they are often assisted by contact guidance. Thus there is a tendency for fibres to follow the grain of the tissue

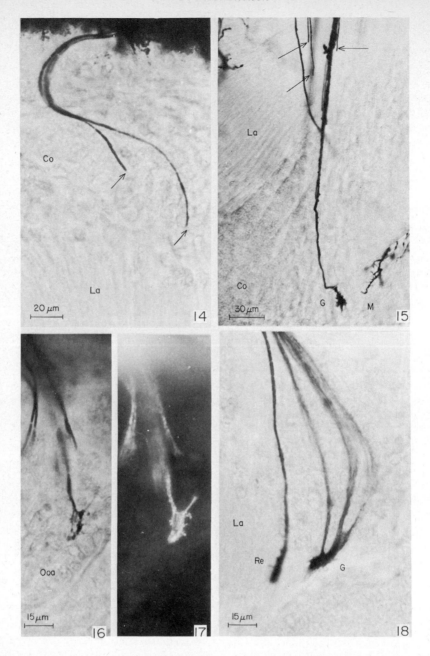

FIG. 9.14. A Golgi stained preparation to show smooth tipped growing retinula axons (arrows) as they approach the lamina neuropile (La) in *Schistocerca gregaria*. Co, lamina cortex.

FIG. 9.15. In this preparation one growing neuron has an expanded growth cone (G) as it enters the developing edge of the medulla neuropile (M). Three others, still in the interneuropile tracts, lack growth cones (arrows). Co, lamina cortex; La, lamina neuropile.

FIG. 9.16. A Golgi stained retinula axon growth cone entering the outer optic anlage (Ooa). Compare this figure with the schematic diagram (Fig. 19). (Bright field illumination.)

FIG. 9.17. The same growth cone is shown here under dark field conditions. Several short and one long filapodia are visible.

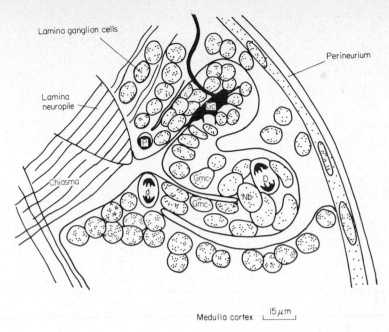

Lamina ganglion cells

Perineurium

Lamina
neuropile

Chiasma

Medulla cortex   15 μm

FIG. 9.19. This schematic representation of the outer optic anlage of *Schistocerca gregaria* reveals important details of the relations between the retinula axon growth cones (Gc) and the growing zone. The large neuroblasts (Nb) are situated some distance from the point of entry of the growth cone. By division (D) the large neuroblasts give rise to ganglion mother cells (Gmc). In turn these divide (d) to form lamina ganglion cells. The growth cone appears to make filapodial contact with immature lamina ganglion cells and it then grows along the inner surface of the anlage to the leading edge of the lamina. Pycnotic nuclei (P) of degenerating cells may be ganglion cells which have failed to receive appropriate retinula innervation.

or to travel along interfaces. There is little doubt that contact guidance plays a substantial part in directing nerve fibre growth in insects. A striking example is provided by Wigglesworth's (1953) experiment in which growing axons from sensory hairs in *Rhodnius* were deflected into a circular path by burning. The fibres formed a thick coil by growing continually around this restricted pathway. Because of the growth sequence in the compound eye new optic fibres always have an interface of pre-existing fibres to grow down (Meinertzhagen 1973). This applies to both embryonic and post-embryonic stages of development. In the fly, the eye discs originate from a pair of evaginations stemming from the dorsal wall of the pharyngeal cavity. The lamina anlage develops quite independently but is physically connected to the homolateral eye by the optic stalk. This consists of a bundle of axons derived from the larval light sensitive organs. The first fibres to grow from the retina to the lamina travel along the surface of this stalk (Trujillo-Cenoz & Melamed 1973). In Lepidoptera, the stemmatal nerve performs a similar function (Meinertzhagen 1973). In the post-embryonic growth of the retinula axons in *Schistocerca* I have found two growth stages (Shelton, unpublished). First the

FIG. 9.18. This photograph of another Golgi preparation shows four retinula fibres (only three axons are clearly visible due to the depth of field) with growth cones (G) so close together that they appear to have fused. To the left in the lamina neuropile (La) a retinula terminal (Re) has begun to differentiate.

axons have to establish contact with the outer optic anlage. Golgi studies show that adjacent fibres may take somewhat different routes. Here the developing axons have to grow through the lamina cortex between loosely packed lamina ganglion cell bodies and precise mechanical guidance is almost impossible in these circumstances. Once the fibres have reached the outer optic anlage they form expanded growth cones and their filapodia make exploratory contact with the newly formed lamina ganglion cells (Figs. 9.14, 9.16 & 9.17). They then enter the second growth phase and they grow down the clearly defined interface between the cell bodies of the cortex and the lamina neuropile and the extant fibres of the first optic chiasma. Presumably contact guidance facilitates directional growth of fibres here but there is no evidence that it maintains their perfect spacing.

Experimental evidence for contact guidance is minimal but after section of retinula axons in the locust *Chortoicetes* the regenerating axons form complex whorls of fibres similar to those described for the sensory axons of the epidermis (Bate, cited by Meinertzhagen 1973).

ESTABLISHMENT OF CONNECTIONS BETWEEN THE RETINA AND THE LAMINA NEUROPILE

There are several ways that the adult projection patterns could arise. The ingrowing retinula fibres may have positional labels and grow to second order cells with similar labels. Alternatively, the retinula cells may be labelled but grow to unspecified second order cells. Then by a process of induction the retinal pattern could be imprinted on successively more central layers of the neuropile. Finally, both retina and lamina may grow autonomously without reference to positional information. In this case connections would be established by a temporal sequence of growth resulting in particular neurons establishing contact by developmental mechanics.

The ingrowing retinula fibres keep themselves spaced out as they grow to the lamina. It seems unlikely that contact guidance alone could guide so many axons in so short a time, in so confined a space and still achieve the necessary precision. Particularly interesting in this context is the behaviour of the expanded growth cones of the fly as they enter the lamina. There is considerable exploratory activity and the filapodia of a particular growth cone sprout profusely both within its adopted cartridge and outside it to establish contact with neighbouring growth cones (Meinertzhagen 1973). This activity continues for a considerable period of time until finally most of the filapodia regress to leave a single terminal. There seems to be a similar exploratory invasion of the lamina by retinula fibres in *Schistocerca*. Here, Golgi preparations demonstrate the apparent coalescence of adjacent retinula growth cones (Fig. 9.18). Such competitive activity militates against a purely mechanical theory for the establishment of connections and it suggests that adjacent growth cones can recognize one another and maintain their spacing even though their filapodia interweave. In addition the searching behaviour strongly suggests that retinula terminals are attracted to preferred sites in the lamina.

If retinula cells do have positional labels and recognize specified sites then they should be able to reform the correct connections even when they are experimentally offered alternative sites in addition to the normal ones. There is some evidence that this is so. Mouze (1974) was able to deprive parts of the dragonfly lamina of its retinal innervation. Adjacent retinula fibres which were allowed to grow to the lamina did not invade this area but formed their correct connections. Other attempts to demonstrate specificity of retinula axons by regeneration have been less successful. In *Chortoicetes* regenerating retinula axons often form axonal whorls (Bate, cited by Meinertzhagen 1973). However the failure to reform an ordered projection may be due to the poor regenerative powers of locusts and it may not reflect a lack of specificity.

When retinal innervation is withheld numerous experiments have shown that there is a reduction in the size of the optic neuropiles (see Meinertzhagen 1973). This has been taken as evidence that lamina differentiation is initiated by the arrival of retinula axons at the outer optic anlage (Meinertzhagen 1973). Recent descriptions of eye development in *Daphnia* have been interpreted in the same way (Lopresti *et al.* 1973). Here it has been shown that outgrowth of lamina ganglion cell axons is subsequent to the arrival of retinula fibres. Whether or not there is a causal relation we do not know because descriptions of development rarely tell us anything of the underlying mechanisms. We are currently investigating this problem by withholding the retinula innervation and studying the effects upon cell proliferation and differentiation in the outer optic anlage of the locust. The idea that there is a centripetal imprinting of pattern upon the neuropiles by the inductive influence of the retina seems unlikely simply because developing centrifugal elements are invading the lamina at the same time as the centripetal retinula axons (Shelton, unpublished).

THE DEVELOPMENT OF THE RETINA/LAMINA PROJECTION IN THE FLY

In terms of positional information the eight retinula cells within a single ommatidium must have similar positional labels which are different from those in adjacent ommatidia. If connectivities are specified with respect to position it is easy to understand the simple retina/lamina projection of fused rhabdom eyes because here all axons from the same ommatidium terminate in the same optic cartridge (Horridge & Meinertzhagen 1970a). Until descriptions of the normal development of the fly projection appeared (Meinertzhagen 1973; Trujillo-Cenóz & Melamed 1973) it was difficult to see how its connectivity could be specified by positional information. This is because the retinula axons from a single ommatidium diverge to different optic cartridges (Braitenburg 1967). However, it is now known that during the initial stages of development, the projection of retinula axons passes through a stage resembling that of fused rhabdom eyes. Initially the six short retinula axons from a single ommatidium all project to the same locus in the lamina ganglion, together with the long retinula axons which pass through to the medulla. Somewhat later the short retinula axons develop lateral sprouts which grow across the surface of the lamina to their final optic cartridges (Trujillo-Cenoz & Melamed 1973). The long retinula axons remain in their original positions. It may be that the retinula cells in both types of eye are specified in a similar manner. In the evolution of open rhabdom eyes a new sub-routine has been added to the developmental sequence and this leads to the intricate pattern of the adult fly.

CONCLUSION

The anatomical precision of the adult eye arises from a programmed sequence which ensures that neurons are in the right place at the right time for forming appropriate connections. It is not clear whether those same neurons can still form appropriate connections if they are brought together in another context; for instance, in regeneration. If they can then neurons in the insect visual system must be able to recognize one another. There is a clear need to test their specificity during regeneration. Although much depends upon the programming of developmental mechanics a great deal depends upon supra-cellular organizing mechanisms which require intercellular communication. Thus both the organization of patterns within ommatidia (Shelton & Lawrence 1974) and the determination of polarity within the retina (Lawrence & Shelton 1975) occur by interactive mechanisms. As yet we have no idea of the extent to which positional information specifies neural patterning in the retina and optic lobes. Certainly none of the work which emphasises the importance of programmed growth excludes an important role for positional information. I am prepared to predict that its role is significant. Fortunately this prediction can be tested by direct experimentation. By changing the positional values of retinula cells in transplantation experiment we should be able to produce predictable changes in connectivity patterns.

Acknowledgements

I am indebted to Peter Lawrence and Ian Meinertzhagen for direct help and encouragement, to Chris Townsend for expert technical assistance and to David Sandeman and G. Adrian Horridge F.R.S. whose influence led me to consider this problem. Dr Mary Ross kindly supplied the cockroach mutants. Original research reported in this paper was supported by a Science Research Council Grant.

DISCUSSION

Palka: In many other parts of the nervous system, the animal is formed with the full complement of central neurons, but during development the number of sensory neurons at the surface may increase ten or twenty fold, and these cells have to enter the central nervous system, make some searching behaviour, and find suitable terminations. There are many cases in development where the two sets of neurons show no correlation in time, when establishing their connections.

Shelton: I should say that one of the critical experiments is to cut the eye off, and to study regeneration. Unfortunately, it is very difficult to get the insect retina to regenerate, because the retinular cells just degenerate after their axons are cut. In short, it is difficult to test neuronal specificity in the insect eye by regeneration experiments. Hopefully, one will be able to do rotation experiments and alter the gradient landscape in the retina so that one should be able to produce changes in the connectivity pattern between the retina and the lamina. This approach awaits the discovery of a suitable mutant or species in which one can actually trace the connections using a technique dependent on the light microscope. The electron microscope will be too laborious. Ideally, one needs to have a genetic mutation giving a cell autonomous marker and do grafting experiments.

Lees: It almost seems as if the ingrowing retinal axons are repelling one another. They clearly don't get tangled up.

Shelton: It's as if they are competing one with another.

Wilby: Does the ingrowing pattern of connections depend on function of the eye.

Shelton: No, this growth process can occur in the dark.

Ashburner: Payne (Biol. Bull, Woods Hole *21*, 297 (1911)) kept *Drosophila* in the dark for 69 generations with no ill effects.

Lees: It must have been very disappointing for him!

Ashburner: There is a Japanese paper in Biometeorology (Mori *et al.* Biomet. *2*, 550 (1967)) which contradicts the main finding.

Lees: Would anybody like to comment on Shelton's thesis that lineage mechanisms may not always be behind the determination of complex structures?

Sander: There is an important difference between the regulation and lineage systems, in the former case you may expect residual pattern elements to be left over, but in the latter not. In the case of cell lineage, each cell would produce the whole pattern, whereas with the spreading mechanism you would expect some cells not to fit into the developing patterns. This was one of the a priori arguments against this type of lineage specification in the eye. However in *Drosophila* a lot of cell death is found in the developing eye disc.

Shelton: In the cockroach you find very little visible cell death in the developing retina, but there is a lot in the optic lobes. We believe there are probably cells left over in the optic lobes. The secondary pigment cells may be a case in point. We know they continue to divide after the ommatidia are formed. These may be relatively unspecialized cells, and this process could account for the relative lack of degeneration that you see in the retina, I mean the secondary pigment cells may just fill in the remaining spaces around the ommatidia.

Gehring: I was very impressed with the experiments where you put epidermis in front of the advancing eye margin, and you get assimilation of this tissue into eye forming structures. What kinds of donor epidermis did you try, and from which stages did they come? Do younger stages integrate more easily than older stages?

Shelton: These operations are difficult to do, and to get successful incorporation. We had a good success rate in *Oncopeltus* but in other systems the rate is always low; so the problem here is that negative results are difficult to interpret. In cockroaches it has been claimed that prothoracic tissue can become incorporated into the developing eye. Hilary Anderson and I (unpublished) have tried very hard to repeat these experiments without success. Hyde (1972) used pigmentation as a criteria. However, we believe that the black pigmentation she observed may not have been ommatidial pigments as she thought, but rather melanisation due to wounding during the operation, caused by bacterial infection. She was misled perhaps over this because she did not cut sections of the eye, and this has generated some confusion in the literature. White, working on the mosquito, tried to transplant pieces of epidermis from elsewhere, and found that he could not get such epidermis to form eye. Experiments by Green and Lawrence in *Oncopeltus* have failed to get incorporation of thoracic tissue into eye. What happens is that the thoracic graft rounds up and gets sloughed off.

Lawrence: It sorts out. I am very happy to hear you give this explanation of Hyde's results. The claim that thorax could form eye was very upsetting.

Wolpert: The dreaded word induction would have had to raise its head.

REFERENCES

BENZER, S. (1973). Genetic dissection of behaviour. *Scient. Am.* (12), **229**, 24-37.

BERNARD, F. (1937). Recherches sur la morphogénèse des yeux composés d'arthropodes. *Bull. biol. Fr. Belg.*, (Suppl.) **23**, 1-162.

BOSCHEK, C. B. (1971). On the fine structure of the peripheral retina and lamina ganglionaris of the fly, *Musca domestica. Z. Zellforsch. mikrosk. Anat.*, **118**, 369-409.

BRAITENBURG, V. (1967). Patterns of projection in the visual system of the fly. 1. Retina-lamina projections. *Exp. Brain Res.*, **3**, 271-298.

BULLOCK, T. H. & HORRIDGE, G. A. (1965). *Structure and Function in the Nervous Systems of Invertebrates.* W. H. Freeman, San Francisco.

BUTLER, R. (1971). The identification and mapping of spectral cell types in the retina of *Periplaneta americana. Z. vergl. Physiol.*, **72**, 67-80.

CAJAL, S. R. & SANCHEZ, D. (1915). Contribucion al conocimiento de los centros opticos. *Trab. Lab. Invest. Biol. Univ. Madr.*, **13**, 1-168.

CAMPOS-ORTEGA, J. A. & STRAUSFELD, N. J. (1972). The columnar organization of the second synaptic region of the visual system of Musca domestica L. 1. Receptor terminals in the medulla. *Z. Zellforsch. mikrosk. Anat.*, **124**, 561-585.

EDWARDS, J. S. (1969). Postembryonic development and regeneration of the insect nervous system. In *Advances in Insect Physiology* **6**; pp. 97-137, eds. J. W. L. Beament, J. E. Treherne & V. B. Wigglesworth.

ELEY, S. & SHELTON, P. M. J. (1976). Cell junctions in the developing compound eye of the desert locust *(Schistocerca gregaria)*. (In prep.)

GAZE, R. M. (1970). *The Formation of Nerve Connections* Academic Press, London & New York.

GREEN, S. M. & LAWRENCE, P. A. (1975). Recruitment of epidermal cells by the developing eye of *Oncopeltus* (Hemiptera). *Wilhelm Roux Arch. EntwMech. Org.*, **177**, 61-65.

HORRIDGE, G. A. & MEINERTZHAGEN, I. A. (1970a). The exact neural projection of the visual fields upon the first and second ganglia of the insect eye. *Z. vergl. Physiol.*, **66**, 369-378.

HORRIDGE, G. A. & MEINERTZHAGEN, I. A. (1970b). The accuracy of connexions of the first- and second-order neurons of the visual system of *Calliphora. Proc. R. Soc. Lond.*, **B 175**, 69-82.

HYDE, C. A. T. (1972). Regeneration, post-embryonic induction and cellular interaction in the eye of *Periplaneta americana. J. Embryol. exp. Morph.*, **127**, 367-379.

KIRSCHFELD, K. (1967). Die Projektion der optisschen Umwelt auf das Raster Rhabdomere im Komplexauge von *Musca. Expl. Brain Res.*, **3**, 248-270.

KÜHN, A. (1965). *Vorlesungen über Entwicklungsphysiologie.*, Springer-Verlag, Berlin.

KURODA, Y. (1970). Differentiation of ommatidium-forming cells of *Drosophila melanogaster* in organ culture. *Expl. Cell Res.*, **59**, 429-439.

LAWRENCE, P. A. (1973). The development of spatial patterns in the integument of insects. In *Developmental Systems: Insects* (ed. S. J. Counce & C. H. Waddington), pp. 157-209. Academic Press, London & New York.

LAWRENCE, P. A. & SHELTON, P. M. J. (1975). The determination of polarity in the developing insect retina. *J. Embryol. exp. Morph.*, **33**, 471-486.

LOPRESTI, V., MACAGNO, E. R. & LEVINTHAL, C. (1973). Structure and development of neuronal connections in isogenic organisms: cellular interactions in the development of the optic lamina of *Daphnia. Proc. natn. Acad. Sci. USA*, **70**, 433-437.

MACAGNO, E. R., LOPRESTI, V. & LEVINTHAL, C. (1973). Structure and development of neuronal connections in isogenic organisms: Variations and similarities in the optic system of *Daphnia magne. Proc. natn. Acad. Sci. USA*, **70**, 57-61.

MEINERTZHAGEN, I. A. (1973). Development of the compound eye and optic lobes of insects. In *Developmental Neurobiology of Arthropods*, pp. 51-104, D. Young, ed.

MEINERTZHAGEN, I. A. (1975). The development of neuronal connection patterns in the visual system of insects. *(Ciba Foundation Symposium on 'Cell Patterning')* pp. 265-282.

MOUZE, M. (1971). Rôle de l'hormone juvénile dans la métamorphose oculaire de larves d'*Aeschna cyanea* Müll. (Insecte, Odonate). *C. r. Acad. Sci., Paris* (D), **273**, 2316-2319.

MOUZE, M. (1972). Étude éxperimentale des facteurs morphogénétiques et hormonaux réglant la croissance oculaire des *Aeshnidae* (Odonates, Anisoptères). *Odonatologica*, **1**, 221-232.

MOUZE, M. (1974). Interactions de l'oeil et du lobe optique au cours de la croissance postembryonnaire des Insectes odonates. *J. Embryol. exp. Morph.*, **31**, 377-407.

NORLANDER, R. H. & EDWARDS, J. S. (1968). Morphological cell death in the post-embryonic development of the insect optic lobes. *Nature, Lond.*, **218**, 780-781.

NORLANDER, R. H. & EDWARDS, J. S. (1969). Postembryonic brain development of the optic lobes in the Monarch butterfly *Danaus plexippus plexippus* L. II. Development of the optic lobes. *Wilhelm Roux Arch. EntwMech. Org.*, **163**, 197-220.

PANOV, A. A. (1960). The structure of the insect brain during successive stages of post-embryonic development. III. Optic lobes. *Ent. Obozr.*, **39**, 86-105.

PERRELET, A. (1970). The fine structure of the retina of the honey bee drone. An electron microscopical study. *Z. Zellforsch. mikrosk. Anat.*, **108**, 530-562.

ROSS, M. H., COCHRAN, D. G. & SMYTH, T. (1964). Eye-colour mutations in the American cockroach, *Periplaneta americana*. *Ann. ent. Soc. Am.*, **57**, 790-792.

SANCHEZ, D. (1919). Sobre el desarollo de los elementos nerviosos en la retina del *Pieris brassicae* L. (Continuación). *Trab. Lab. Invest. biol. Univ. Madr.*, **17**, 1-63.

SHELTON, P. M. J. & LAWRENCE, P. A. (1974). Structure and development of ommatidia in *Oncopeltus fasciatus*. *J. Embryol. exp. Morph.*, **32**, 337-353.

SHELTON, P. M. J., ELEY, S., ANDERSON, H. J. & TOWNSEND, C. (1976). Cell lineage relations in the development of the compound eye of the cockroach *Periplaneta americana*. (In prep.).

SKRZIPEK, K. H. & SKRZIPEK, H. (1974). The ninth retinula cell in the ommatidium of the worker honey bee *(Apis mellifica* L.*)*. *Z. Zellsforsh. mikrosk. Anat.*, **147**, 589-593.

STRAUSFELD, N. J. (1971). The organization of the insect visual system (Light Microscopy) 1. Projections and arrangements of neurons in the lamina ganglionaris of Diptera. *Z. Zellforsch. mikrosk. Anat.*, **121**, 377-441.

STRAUSFELD, N. J. & BLEST, A. D. (1970). Golgi studies on insects. Part 1. The optic lobes of Lepidoptera. *Phil. Trans. R. Soc. Lond.*, **B 258**, 81-134.

TRUJILLO-CENÓZ, O. & MELAMED, J. (1973). The development of the retina-lamina complex in muscoid flies. *J. Ultrastruct. Res.*, **42**, 554-581.

UMBACH, W. (1934). Entwicklung und Bau des Komplexauges der Mehlmotte *Ephestia kühniella* Zeller nebst einigen Bemerkungen über die Entstehung der optischen Ganglien. *Z. Morph. Ökol. Tiere.*, **28**, 561-594.

WADDINGTON, C. H. & PERRY, M. M. (1960). The ultra-structure of the developing eye of *Drosophila*. *Proc. R. Soc.*, **B 153**, 155-178.

WHITE, R. H. (1961). Analysis of the development of the compound eye in the mosquito *Aedes aegyptii*. *J. exp. Zool.*, **148**, 223-240.

WHITE, R. H. (1963). Evidence for the existence of a differentiation centre in the developing eye of the mosquito. *J. exp. Zool.*, **152**, 139-148.

WIGGLESWORTH, V. B. (1953). The origin of sensory neurones in an insect, *Rhodnius prolixus* (Hemiptera). *Q. Jl. microsc. Sci.*, **94**, 93-112.

WOLPERT, L. (1969). Positional information and the spatial pattern of cellular differentiation. *J. theor. Biol.*, **25**, 1-47.

WOLSKY, A. (1949). The growth and differentiation of retinular cells in the compound eyes of the silkworm *(Bombyx mori* L.*)*. *Expl. Cell Res. (Suppl.)* **1**, 549-554.

WOLSKY, A. (1956). The analysis of eye development in insects. *Trans. N. Y. Acad. Sci., Ser.*, **II, 18**, 592-596.

10 • Tissue interactions in the regenerating cockroach leg*

HORST BOHN

Zoologisches Institut der Universität
D-8000 München 2, Luisenstr. 14

INTRODUCTION

The first aim to which all developmental processes of insect embryogenesis are directed is the establishment of the main axial system, represented by the segmented germ band. Later new segmented axial systems are developing: the legs and similar appendages. The processes regulating their genesis and differentiation are almost completely unknown. The small size of the eggs and the position of the embryo within the chorion raises almost insuperable difficulties to the analysis of their development. But fortunately most insects during their larval life retain the ability to restitute lost or damaged appendages. The processes occurring during regeneration are, to a great extent, comparable with those occurring during embryogenesis; therefore regenerating larval legs may represent the development of embryonic legs.

Analysis of development usually involves analysis of interactions between the different parts of an embryonic system. In the following I want to point to three examples as illustrations of interactions occurring between different tissues during the regeneration of a cockroach leg (*Leucophaea maderae*).

I. THE INTERACTION OF DIFFERENT PARTS OF REGENERATION FIELD OF THE LEG

During embryogenesis a leg develops within an area which is called the embryonic field of the leg. If we analyse the regeneration of a leg we can, by analogy, discuss the 'regeneration field' of the leg. The problems are the same for both kinds of morphogenetic fields. We have to find out the temporal and spatial characteristics of the field. The spatial characteristics, which I have mainly studied, consist of the following two aspects:
1. The extent of the field, and
2. The organization of the field. A field, although structurally uniform, may have a latent organization consisting of different parts which act and eventually interact in a specific manner during morphogenesis.

The most proximal segment of the leg is the coxa. It is attached to the ventral surface

* The work has been partly supported by a grant of the Deutsche Forschungsgemeinschaft (Bo 453).

of the body by means of a few sclerotized elements, the largest of which are a triangular sclerite, the trochantin, and a chevronlike sclerite which I will call praecoxa (Fig. 10.3). A little more anteriorly lies the spiracle of the same segment. Adjoining the coxa posteriorly there are no sclerites but a membranous area which reaches to the basal sclerites of the following leg. Medially and laterally the leg is enclosed by the sclerites of the sternum and by the wing anlagen.

It has been shown in numerous investigations (Bohn 1971, Bullière 1967, Penzlin 1963) that regeneration in cockroaches takes place very quickly and completely, if the leg is cut at the autotomy plane, between femur and trochanter. The question was, how much of the more proximal parts can be removed without abolishing the capacity to regenerate a normal leg? In a first series of experiments I studied the effect of the removal of the *basal sclerites*. The whole leg (i.e. the coxa and the more distal segments) was extirpated in all experiments. Thus the posterior cut was made in all cases just behind the coxa. In addition various parts of the basal sclerites were removed. The results of these experiments are summarized in Fig. 10.1. The whole trochantin and even the major part of the praecoxa can be removed and yet a normal leg is regenerated in most cases (Fig. 10.4). But regeneration is almost absent if the sclerites have been totally extirpated.

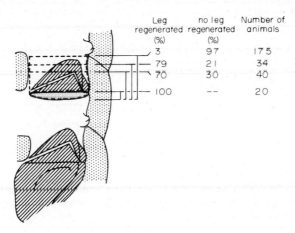

Leg regenerated (%)	no leg regenerated (%)	Number of animals
3	97	175
79	21	34
70	30	40
100	--	20

FIG. 10.1. Effect of extirpation of basal sclerites on leg regeneration. The left mid-leg (fine dotted area=cut surface between coxa and basal parts) and varying amounts (indicated by the brackets) of the basal sclerites are extirpated. For explanation of other symbols see Fig. 10.3.

From these experiments one can conclude that the regeneration field of the legs of *Leucophaea* extends anteriorly as far as the sclerites reach. But the experiments do not tell us, whether the sclerites are the only parts of the leg base which are necessary for leg regeneration. When after the extirpation of the leg the relatively large wound is being closed the cells from the anterior cut border will probably meet those from the posterior cut border, i.e. of the membranous part of the leg base. We have to find out, whether the membranous area takes part in leg regeneration. To analyse this the following series of extirpation experiments was made. Again the distal parts of the leg including the coxa had been removed. Now the basal sclerites were left intact, but the *membranous area* adjoining the coxa posteriorly was extirpated to a various extent (Fig. 10.2). If only a small part of the membranous area is extirpated normal regeneration occurs in all or nearly all cases. But the frequency of regeneration strikingly diminishes as the posterior

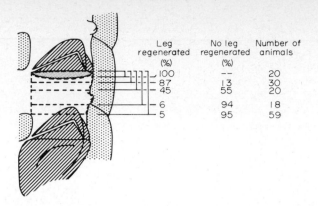

	Leg regenerated (%)	No leg regenerated (%)	Number of animals
	100	--	20
	87	13	30
	45	55	20
	6	94	18
	5	95	59

FIG. 10.2. Effect of extirpation of membranous parts of the leg base on regeneration. Brackets indicate extirpated area. For explanation of other symbols see Fig. 10.3.

margin of the extirpated area approaches the spiracle. Behind the spiracle leg regeneration is almost absent. It should be pointed out, that in those cases in which leg regeneration did not occur regeneration was not completely lacking. On the contrary, there was considerable regeneration, but always limited to the basal sclerites: The basal sclerites of the amputated leg were reduplicated symmetrically. Fig. 10.5 shows an example of this type of regeneration: A second set of basal sclerites was formed instead of a leg.

The results of the last experimental series indicate that part of the membranous area has to be included in the regeneration field of the cockroach leg. The regeneration field of the leg therefore consists of two parts: The sclerites in front and the membranous area immediately behind the coxa. A leg only develops when both parts are present at the same time.

The next question was: Where does the cellular material come from which builds up the leg? Does it come from the sclerites or from the membranous parts or from both together? To settle this question the tissues of two different species were combined which differ strongly in their pigmentation colour. In the one species (*Gromphadorhina*) the leg and all basal sclerites were extirpated and the remaining membranous area was combined with the basal sclerites of the other species *(Leucophaea)*. The leg arising from the region of contact between *Leucophaea*-sclerites and *Gromphadorhina*-membrane· has a clear cut chimeric appearance: The anterior half consists of lightly pigmented *Leucophaea*-tissues, the posterior half of dark *Gromphadorhina*-tissues (Fig. 10.6). The combination clearly shows, that each of the two parts of the regeneration field contributes the material for one longitudinal half of the leg.

The results of the experiments at the leg base are summarized in Fig. 10.3. Only the combination of the sclerites with the anterior part of the membrane area gives a leg. If the sclerites are combined with the posterior part of the membranous area a second set of sclerites develops. We therefore could call the respective membranes leg-inducing membrane and sclerite-inducing membrane. If, after the extirpation of the sclerites, the leg-inducing membrane is combined with the membranous parts lying anteriorly to the sclerites only membranes develop but no leg. Therefore the regeneration field of the cockroach leg consists of two parts which are both indispensible for leg regeneration: The sclerites at the anterior base and the membrane at the posterior base. Each of the two parts contributes the material for half of the leg, but neither of the two has the

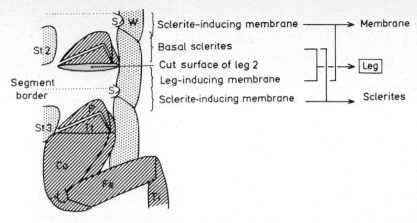

FIG. 10.3. Outline of the extirpation experiments at the leg base. The figure shows a ventral view of the left halves of thoracic segments 2 and 3. The mid-leg (leg 2) is removed at the base of the coxa; the left hind-leg is drawn, up to the proximal part of the tibia. Obliquely hatched areas: Basal sclerites (P=Praecoxa, Tt=Trochantinus) and leg segments (Co=Coxa, Fe=Femur, Ti=Tibia); W=Wing anlagen; St2,3=Sternal sclerites of 2 and 3 thoracic segment; S=Spiracle; clear area=membranes.

ability to build up its own half, when the other part is missing. Both tissues have to interact to allow the development of distal leg structures.

II. TISSUE INTERACTION DURING INTERCALARY REGENERATION

We have seen now the conditions which are necessary to give rise to a leg with its differently structured segments. But we do not know how the tissues interact; we do not know how the regeneration bud arising from the plain of the regeneration field gets its threedimensional structure, nor how the first unsegmented bud is further divided into the different leg segments. Regeneration in cockroaches takes place very rapidly; there is no gradually growing regeneration bud in which the processes of segmentation could be studied. Though the processes of segmentation cannot be studied we may analyse how the segments, once they are established, maintain and stabilize their segmental characteristics.

The experiments consist in combining various levels of the leg segments (Fig. 10.11). When the cut surfaces of transplant and stump have the same level the transplant heals in without any signs of regeneration. If, however, a distal level is combined with a proximal level, an intercalary regenerate is formed which seems to replace the missing levels in between. Combinations which are made between different segments, for instance, femur and tibia, follow the same rule. The results suggest that every cell within a leg segment is marked according to its position within the segment. And every cell knows its position within the segment by knowing its appropriate neighbouring cells, recognizing them by their positional markers. We may replace the normal neighbours of a cell by cells from another segment. As long as they are from the same level, i.e. the same position within a segment, they remain satisfied. That means that the positional markers for a given level seem to be identical in the different segments. But if we confront the cell with cells from a different level of the same or another segment regeneration processes are initiated with the view to giving every cell its appropriate neighbour. Thus all missing levels of a segment are regenerated; then, and only then, regeneration stops.

The proposed positional markers of the different levels may be different in quality; but the simplest model which fits all experimental findings is that of a quantitatively graded, i.e. gradientlike distribution of only one positional marker. Every level of a segment is characterized by an appropriate level of the gradient; the gradient reiterating in all segments of the leg (Fig. 10.10, bottom figure at the right).

The gradient model may be tested in one special combination. A long tibial segment is transplanted onto a distal level of another tibia thus producing a tibia of excessive length (Fig. 10.10, right top figure). The length of the tibia, though already greater than normal, was further increased by the formation of a long intercalary regenerate whose proximo-distal polarity was reversed. These, at first sight unexpected results, could have been predicted by the gradient model: The transplantation produced a sharp step in the gradient sloping away from distal to proximal; the step is filled in by an intercalary regenerate of reverse slope.

I will not discuss the possible physical or chemical nature of the proposed segmental gradients (Crick 1970, Lawrence *et al.* 1972, Goodwin & Cohen 1969, Wolpert 1971). At present the experimental evidence is not óf the kind to allow any founded assumptions. Instead I would like to touch another question raised by the experiments with intercalary regenerates. As with the experiments concerning the regeneration field we have to ask about the origin of the intercalary regenerate: Which of the two interacting tissues provides the material for the regenerate? Experiments in which differently structured or coloured segments have been combined show that in some cases the intercalary regenerate may have a composite structure, i.e. half made of stump and half of transplant tissues. But in most cases the regenerate consists almost exclusively of material of only one of the combinants. From which of the two it is made depends on the type of experiment. In the combination where a distal part of a segment is transplanted on a proximal level of a segment the regenerate is formed by the transplant. In the reverse combination where the cut surface of the stump represents the more distal level it is the stump which forms the regenerate. If it is accepted that the intercalary regenerates really represent the missing intermediate levels of the proposed gradients (and, consequently the structures relating to those levels) we must conclude that during intercalary regeneration proximal parts of a segment are formed from a more distal level.

This conclusion is surprising in the light of the results of innumerable regeneration experiments made with the appendages of the amphibia and insects which have led to the formulation of the rule that during regeneration from a given level only structures of more distal levels are regenerated (Rose 1962). But this rule is based only on experiments with terminal wounds, and in these cases cockroaches also conform to the rule, only more distal structures being formed. Nevertheless, once they are made, such rules are longlived (Shaw & Bryant 1975) and an overwhelming amount of evidence is necessary to repeal them again. Unfortunately none of the leg segments of *Leucophaea* and *Gromphadorhina* used in the transplantation experiments has structures specific for either proximal or distal levels that would allow identification of distal or proximal levels in the intercalary regenerate. In our search for such structures the fore-legs of *Blaberus* proved to be suitable. The femur at its anterior ventral edge has a row of bristles which increase in size from distal to proximal. In the proximal half the bristles are more scarcely distributed and, most important, between them there are 2-4 thick spines which are not found in the distal half (Fig. 10.7, 10.8). The same experiment was made with *Blaberus* as shown for *Leucophaea* in Fig. 9.10 (left bottom figure). A distal fourth of the femur of the fore-leg was transplanted to a proximal fifth of the tibia of a hind-leg. The intercalary regenerate which developed consisted of femur structures. The spines at the antero-ventral edge undoubtedly show that proximal structures had formed from more distal levels.

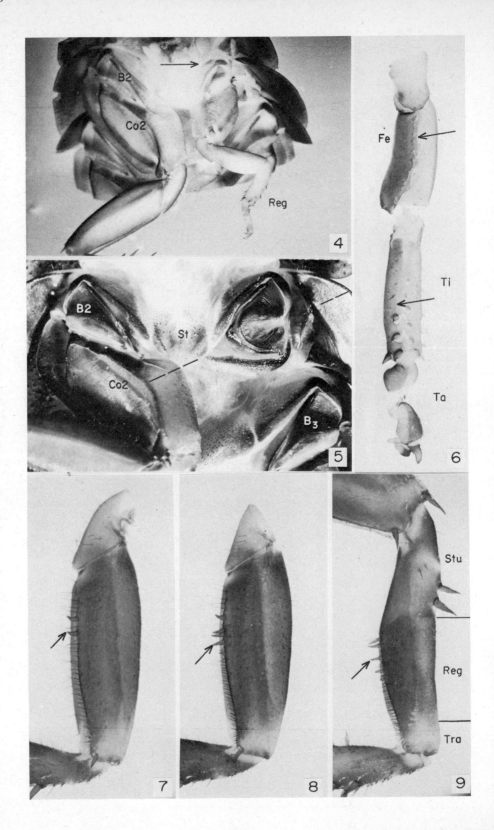

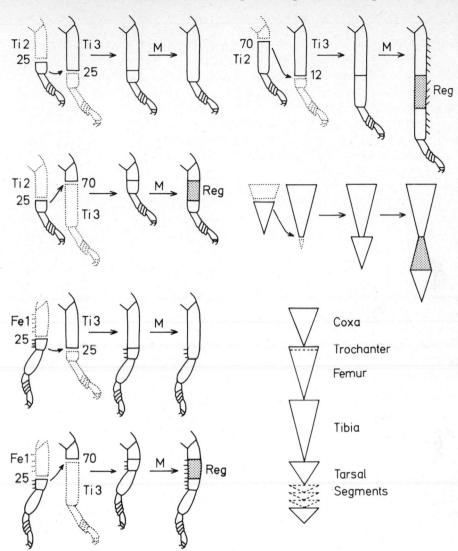

FIG. 10.10. Outline of the experiments combining different segment levels (indicated by the numbers beside the segments; 100=base, 0=tip). Ti 2,3=Tibia of mid- or hind-leg; Fe 1=Femur of fore-leg; M=Moult; Reg=Intercalary regenerate. Right bottom figure: Proposed segmental gradients of the leg; above: Production of an intercalary regenerate with reverse polarity and the interpretation of the experiment according to the gradient model.

FIG. 10.4. Regeneration of a complete leg (Reg) after the extirpation of the left mid-leg and most part of its basal sclerites (arrow indicates anterior border of the excised area). B2, Co2=Basal sclerites and coxa of the right mid-leg. Magn. 8x.

FIG. 10.5. Regeneration of a symmetrical set of basal sclerites (broken line indicates cut border and line of symmetry) after extirpation of the left mid-leg and the leg-inducing membrane. B2,Co2=Basal sclerites and coxa of the right mid-leg; B3=Basal sclerites of the left hind-leg. Magn. 15x.

FIG. 10.6. Regeneration of a mosaic leg after the combination of basal sclerites of *Leucophaea* and the leg inducing membrane of *Gromphadorhina*. Arrows point to the border between the dark *Gromphadorhina* and the lightly pigmented *Leucophaea* tissues. (The leg is cut into three parts to allow better reproduction.) Fe=Femur and Ti=Tibia in ventral view; terminal tarsal segments (Ta) in dorsal view. Magn. 14x.

FIGS. 10.7, 10.8. Structures of regenerated femora of *Blaberus*. Arrows point to spines at the antero-ventral edge, characteristic for the proximal half of the fore-leg femora. Magn. 16x.

FIG. 10.9. After the transplantation of the distal fourth of the femur of the fore-leg (Tra) onto a proximal part of the tibia of the hind-leg (Stu) an intercalary regenerate develops with proximal femur structures (spines, see arrow). Magn. 16x.

III. TISSUE INTERACTION DURING WOUNDHEALING

There is one assumption applying to any of the interactions of the different epithelia described in the previous two sections. The observed interactions obviously cannot take place before the two tissues are in intimate contact with each other. But any surgical manipulations as excisions or transplantations, are mostly followed by more or less extended cellular necrosis at the woundborders, which interrupts the epithelial continuity. This gap has to be closed by the two epithelia before they are able to interact and cooperate.

How important a rapid rejoining of the separated epithelia for the successful accomplishment of the repair processes is, may be illustrated by an abnormal leg which formed after the extirpation of the intermediate part of the tibia (Fig. 10.11). Instead of only replacing the removed parts of the tibia the animal regenerated excessive tarsal segments. Obviously because of difficulties during wound closure the epithelia of stump and transplant rejoined only after regeneration had already been initiated independently in both tissues.

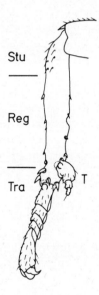

FIG. 10.11. Regeneration of excessive tarsal segments (T) presumably because of difficulties during wound healing. Stu=Stump, Reg=Intercalary regenerate, Tra=Transplant. Magn. 35x.

The migration of the epidermis over a wound, however, is not the first event in the process of wound healing. A wound almost immediately after its production is first closed by a plug of clotting blood, which avoids excessive bleeding and reduces the danger of infection. This preliminary wound sealing is after some time followed by the definite closure of the wound by the epidermis which in highly flattened condition seems to force its way through the aggregation of the hemocytes of the plug (Ermin 1939, Lazarenko 1928, Wigglesworth 1937). The importance of the blood clot for the *animal* is clear enough; but its role for the migration of the *epidermis* over the wound surface is uncertain. The following two extreme points of view are possible:
1. The haemocytes support the migration of the epithelia, in the simplest case for instance, by offering a mechanical substrate for them.
2. The haemocytes do not support, but by their dense accumulation actually hinder, the epidermal cells on their way over the wound surface.

To allow a decision between the two alternatives we should be able to observe wound healing without the participation of haemocytes. That is nearly impossible in living animals; therefore I tried to cultivate the epidermis of a cockroach leg *in vitro*. A piece of tibial epidermis is cut out of a regenerating leg 21 days after the amputation (Marks & Reinecke 1964) and placed with its inner surface down on the surface of a coverslip. A strip of cellophane (Rose *et al.* 1958) is laid over the explant to keep it in its position. The cut borders of the explanted tissue now should show processes of wound healing characteristic of wounded epidermis, i.e. outward migration of the marginal cells onto the free surface of the glass (in the *in vitro* experiment the glass provides the mechanical support normally offered by the haemocyte layers of the clot).

The epidermis, however, when cultivated *in vitro,* does not show any signs of outgrowth even after several days of cultivation. This absence of activity should not be very surprising in view of the difficulties in imitating the conditions which may be found in the living animal in an *in vitro* system. Certain observations, however, indicate that the absence of wound healing activities in the explanted epidermis is not attributable to general incompatibilities of the artificial medium (Landureau & Grellet 1972) but to the absence of haemocytes. In spite of thorough cleaning of the explanted epidermis in some cases haemocytes still adhered to the tissue. The haemocytes during the following day settled down to the glass surface and migrated out into the free area of the coverslip. When they were passing the border of the epidermis its marginal cells often attached to the moving hemocytes. Staying attached while the haemocytes moved away long projections were drawn out from the epidermal cells (Fig. 10.12). When more haemocytes were present outgrowth-like tongues with highly flattened and eventually dividing epidermal cells developed. We can conclude that outgrowth is in some way dependent on haemocytes.

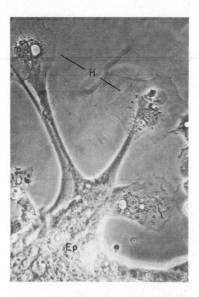

FIG. 10.12. Three haemocytes (H) moving away from the explanted epidermis (Ep) and pulling out attached marginal cells to long projections. Three days *in vitro*. Phase contrast. Magn. 312x.

To study the interaction of haemocytes and epidermal cells in more detail a monolayer of haemocytes was prepared to which the pieces of epidermis were added. Fig. 10.14 shows an experiment of this type. In the upper part the coverslip is covered by a monolayer of highly flattened haemocytes; in the lower part the haemocytes had been scraped away with a razor blade. The piece of epidermis was placed across the border between monolayer and scraped area. It is clear that the outgrowth of epidermis only occurred in the area of the haemocyte monolayer. The way the outgrowing epidermis takes is either over or under the haemocytes; in the latter case the haemocytes are pushed away by the proceeding epidermis and piled up to a prominent ridge at the front of the epidermis (Fig. 10.13). It seems that the haemocytes have substances on their upper and lower surfaces which are attractive to epidermal cells and which cause their flattening and migration. The substances do not seem to be soluble and diffusible since the outgrowth promoting effect is restricted to intimate contact with the haemocytes; the zone of outgrowth ends where the monolayer of hemocytes ends.

If we are allowed to correlate the results of our *in vitro* experiments with the *in vivo* observations of wound healing we could conclude that the blood clot not only serves as a mechanical support but also as a chemical guide attracting and directing the migrating epidermis. *In vivo* experiments have been done to establish whether this conclusion is right.

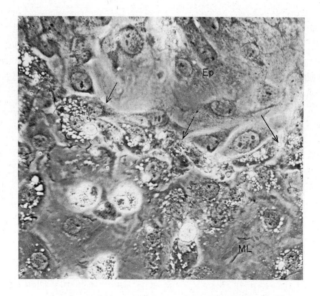

FIG. 10.13. Border of outgrowing epidermis (Ep) on a monolayer of haemocytes (ML). The haemocytes are detached from the glass surface by the advancing epidermal cells and piled up to a prominent ridge (arrows). Two days *in vitro*. Phase contrast. Magn. 312x.

A small strip of cuticle and epidermis (0,5×2 mm) was cut out of the coxa of last in-star larvae. The wound was artificially sealed with Nobecutan. Within 36 hours the gap between the cut edges of the epidermis is closed by several layers of highly flattened haemocytes (Fig. 10.15). At the same time the epidermis starts to migrate through the haemocyte layers. In connection with our *in vitro* observation it is interesting to see that the advancing epidermis seems to follow a line which is formed by extremely flattened haemocytes at the periphery of the plug just beneath the artificial sealing (Fig. 10.16, 10.17; Lazarenko 1928). Why does the epidermis not move along the inner surface of the plug instead of squeezing itself through the plug, between the hemocytes where they are most densely crowded? This route becomes comprehensible if we assume that the haemocytes, when they become flattened, are attractive to the epidermal cells and in an unknown way facilitate their movement over the plug. About four days after the wounding the gap is closed by the epidermis and new cuticle secreted (Fig. 10.18). It is known that heparin changes the clotting properties of the haemocytes (Gregoire 1953); my own experiments indicate that the adhesive properties and thus the surface properties of haemocytes are altered by heparin (Bohn, unpublished results). So heparin seemed to be a suitable means to analyse the conditions for wound healing *in vivo*.

Heparin was injected 24 hours before wounding (8 mg/animals). The plug of hemocytes which is formed after 36 hours looks different from that of control animals. The haemocytes are less flattened and not as densely layered (Fig. 10.19). The migration of the epidermis over the plug is highly retarded, the rejoining of the epithelia takes place 3-4 days later than in normal animals. The epidermal cells, on their way over the wound, no longer prefer the periphery of the plug—presumably because there are no suitably flattened haemocytes. The migrating cells often look disoriented (Fig. 10.20); they try to cross the haemocyte plug in diverse directions. The hemocytes obviously have lost their ability to attract and to guide the epidermis.

When the heparin is injected after the haemocyte plug has formed the epithelial wound closure is only slightly retarded.

The *in vivo* experiments confirm the conclusions drawn from the observations made *in vitro*: The haemocytes in the wound plug are important for a rapid closure of the wound by the epidermis. The flattened haemocytes obviously have surface properties which attract the hemocytes and facilitate their migration over the wound.

CONCLUDING REMARKS

I have tried to show in three selected examples that regeneration of a leg is not possible without interactions, at different stages, between the various tissues and cells. Such interactions start immediately after the wounding and—as the experiments with intercalary regenerates indicate—they do not stop even when the legs are fully differentiated. A steady control and feedback between a cell and its neighbours seems to be necessary to maintain the different structures of a leg.

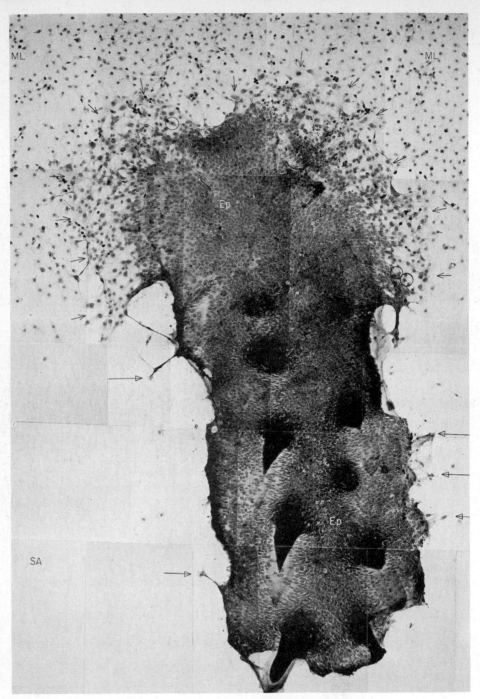

FIG. 10.14. Tibia epidermis (Ep) of a leg regenerate placed on a border between a monolayer of haemocytes (ML) and plain glass surface (SA, monolayer scraped away). Outgrowth only occurs on the monolayer area (→ point to border of the outgrowing epidermis). In the scraped area there are only a few projections (⇢) caused by scattered haemocytes leaving the explant. ○ indicates dividing cells. Four days *in vitro*. Tissues fixed and stained with haemalam. Magn. 58.5x.

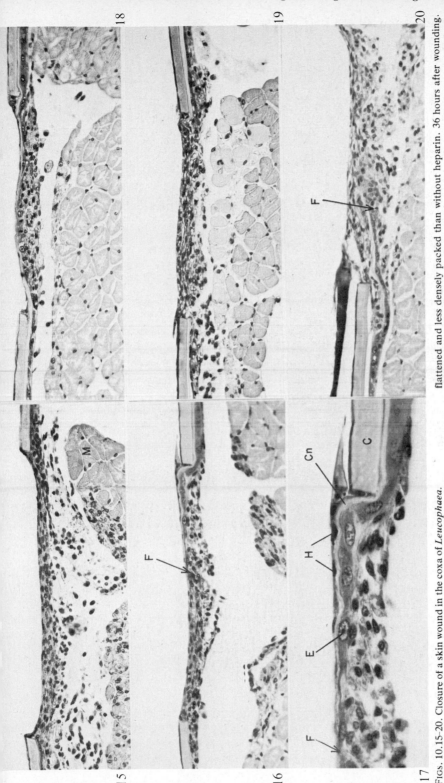

Figs. 10.15–20. Closure of a skin wound in the coxa of *Leucophaea.*
10.15. The excised gap is overbridged by a 'clot', formed by several layers of highly flattened haemocytes. 36 hours after wounding. 10.16, 10.17. The epidermis migrates over the wound in close contact with the extremely flattened haemocytes at the periphery of the clot. Three days after wounding. 10.18. The continuity of the epidermis is achieved. Four days after wounding. 10.19, 10.20. Injection of heparin one day before wounding. 10.19. The haemocytes forming the clot are much less flattened and less densely packed than without heparin. 36 hours after wounding. 10.20. The wound closure by the epidermis is strongly retarded and irregular. Seven days after wounding. E=Nuclei of the epidermis; C=Old cuticle; Cn=Cuticle secreted by the migrating epidermis; F=Front of the migrating epidermis; H=Nuclei of extremely flattened haemocytes at the periphery of the clot; M=muscles. Paraplast sections, stained with haemalam-eosin. Magn. Fig. 10.17 650x, others 260x.

DISCUSSION

Wigglesworth: Were the wounds open and sealed with a natural clot?

Bohn: No, the wounds were not open. They were covered with a proprietary compound, Nobecutan, 'new skin'.

Wigglesworth: It is a long time since I did this kind of experiment on *Rhodnius*, but I got the impression that as one sealed the wound with glass or with wax, it was the epidermal cells which spread directly over the surface and that the haemocytes spread later under the epidermis.

Bohn: In the cockroach, there is always first a layer of haemocytes of at least one cell layer thick.

Lawrence: What happens to the haemocytes when the epidermis has successfully joined under them—do they just degenerate?

Bohn: I haven't especially followed the fate of those haemocytes, but it seems that they disintegrate.

Lees: Could you explain why the cells don't spread under the haemocytes, that is, at the inner surface of the clot?

Bohn: The haemocytes at the inner surface of the 'clot' are less flattened than those at the outer surface. The heparin experiments support the assumption that only highly flattened haemocytes have those substances on their surfaces which are attractive to the epidermal cells. Thus following the most flattened haemocytes the epidermal cells spread along the outer surface of the clot and avoid the inner surface.

Schneiderman: Could we hear possibly from Vernon French about the kind of intercalary regeneration that he attained with strips of transplanted leg tissue in the cockroach. This is interesting to us because Bohn's and French's data describe fairly well what fragments of imaginal discs will do when you take two opposing ends of the disc and put them together. You get intercalary regeneration, generating the structures normally found between those two ends.

French: I'm talking about the position around the circumference of the leg, so that position can be defined to the monolayer of epidermal cells by two coordinates, one the proximo-distal axis and the other the position around the circumference. I have carried out grafts moving epidermal cells from one position to another and have followed the experiments to see whether any structures are regenerated between the confronting epidermal cells. We find that, in all cases, you form by a process of intercalary regeneration (exactly analogous to that about which we have heard from Dr Bohn) structures characteristic of the cells normally lying between the host and graft cell positions. Because the position of the cell is specified with respect to a circle, these intercalary regenerates could in principle go in two directions. In fact we find that the intercalary regeneration always goes in the shortest route between the positions of the graft and host. If you confront cells from opposite positions, in some animals the intercalary regeneration goes round the leg by one route, and in other animals it goes round by the other. You can make two points from this experiment. First, the position in the circumferential axis is analogous to that in the proximo-distal, and the second that because there appears to be a continuum round the surface, certain types of models are eliminated and certain new and interesting types of models are suggested. The continuous model for example, does not fit with the hypothesis that there might be a circumferential gradient with a sharp localized break from a high point to a low point.

Kalthoff: I would like to comment on the regeneration of differently labelled material that is from the sclerite and the coxal membrane. The regenerated leg reminded me of compartments. There were two very nice stripes all along the leg. Do these regenerates always look like the example you showed?

Bohn: Unfortunately I only have a few cases of this combination. The border was more or less exactly a straight line. In other kinds of experiments these lines can apparently be crossed during regeneration, that is a small marked piece at the base of the regenerate can expand to fill more of the regenerate.

Wilby: I thought regeneration in legs and in discs always went in one direction, that is from proximal to distal, yet you seem to have a case of distal to proximal regeneration.

Bohn: The direction of the main path of regeneration depends on the combination used. When you just make a cut, then the stump regenerates downwards, that is distally, but in intercalary regeneration it is quite the reverse. It is the rule that this type of regeneration goes upwards, that is, proximally, and I think that there is no doubt about this.

REFERENCES

BOHN, H. (1970). Interkalare Regeneration und segmentale Gradienten bei den Extremitäten von *Leucophaea-* Larven (Blattaria). I. Femur und Tibia. *Wilhelm Roux Arch. EntwMech. Org.*, **165**, 303-341.

BULLIÈRE, D. (1967) Étude de la régénération chez un insects Blattoptéroide, *Blabera craniifer* Burm. (Dictyoptère). I. Influence du niveau de la section sur la régénération de la patte métathoracique. *Bull. Soc. zool. Fr.*, **92**, 523-536.

CRICK, F. H. (1970). Diffusion in embryogenesis. Nature, **225**, 420-422.

ERMIN, R. (1939). Über Bau und Funktion der Lymphocyten bei Insekten (*Periplaneta americana* L.). *Z. Zellforsch. mikrosk. Anat.* (A), **29**, 613-669.

GOODWIN, B. C. & COHEN, M. H. (1969). A phase-shift model for the spatial and temporal organization of developing systems. *J. theor. Biol.*, **25**, 49-107.

GRÉGOIRE, C. (1953). Blood coagulation in Arthropods. III. Reactions of insect hemolymph to coagulation inhibitors of vertebrate blood. *Biol. Bull.*, **104**, 372-393.

LANDUREAU, J. C. & GRELLET, P. (1972). Nouvelles techniques de culture *in vitro* de cellules d'insects et leurs applications. *C. r. Acad. Sci., Paris* (D), **274**, 1372-1375.

LAWRENCE, P. A., CRICK, F. H. C. & MUNRO, M. (1972). A gradient of positional information in an insect, *Rhodnius. J. cell. Sci.*, **11**, 815-853.

LAZARENKO, T. M. (1928). Experimentelle Untersuchungen über das Hypodermisepithel der Insekten. *Z. mikr. anat. Forsch.*, **12**, 467-506.

MARKS, E. P. & REINECKE, J. P. (1964). Regenerating tissues from the cockroach leg: a system for studying *in vitro*.

PENZLIN, H. (1963). Über Regeneration bei Schaben (Blattaria). I. Das Regenerationsvermögen und die Genese des Regenerats. *Wilhelm Roux Arch. EntwMech. Org.*, **154**, 434-465.

ROSE, G. G., POMERAT, C. M., SHINDLER, T. O. & TRUNNELL, J. B. (1958). A cellophane-strip technique for culturing tissue in multipurpose culture chambers. *J. biophys. biochem. Cytol.*, **4**, 761-765.

ROSE, S. M. (1962). Tissue-arc control of regeneration in the amphibian limb. In: *Regeneration*, (Rudwick, D.ed.) pp. 153-176. New York.

SHAW, V. K. & BRYANT, P. J. (1975). Intercalary leg regeneration in the large milkweed bug *Oncopeltus fasciatus. Devl. Biol.*, **45**, 187-191.

WIGGLESWORTH, V. B. (1937). Wound healing in an insect (*Rhodnius prolixus* Hemiptera). *J. exp. Biol.*, **14**, 364-381.

WOLPERT, L. Positional information and pattern formation. (1971). *Curr. Topics Devl. Biol.*, **6**, 183-224.

11 • Juvenile hormone and pattern formation

V. B. WIGGLESWORTH

Department of Zoology, University of Cambridge

HORMONAL CONTROL OF METAMORPHOSIS

According to the usual description of the hormonal control of metamorphosis, the process of growth is initiated by a hormone secreted by neurosecretory cells in the pars intercerebralis of the brain, which is passed down the axons to the corpora cardiaca and there set free into the circulating blood. This brain hormone activates the prothoracic glands which then secrete the moulting hormone ecdysone. Ecdysone acts directly upon the epidermis, which is the chief agent responsible for growth in the insect, and sets in motion the sequence of protein synthesis, cytoplasmic growth, mitosis and cuticle deposition which lead ultimately to ecdysis.

The course of this moulting process, and the character of the cuticle laid down are controlled by a third hormone secreted by the corpora allata. Throughout the larval stages the corpus allatum hormone, the 'juvenile hormone', is present during the secretion of ecdysone—and the epidermal cells continue to build the larval form and pattern and the larval type of cuticle. In the last larval stage of a hemimetabolous insect, such as *Rhodnius,* juvenile hormone secretion ceases—and the epidermal cells now build the imaginal form and pattern and the adult type of cuticle. In holometabolous insects, such as *Bombyx* or *Galleria,* in the final larval stage, juvenile hormone is still secreted, but at a greatly reduced level—and the epidermal cells lay down the pupal form and cuticle. During the pupal moult juvenile hormone secretion is reduced still further—and the full imaginal characters are developed (Fukuda 1944; Piepho 1951).

Put didactically thus, the above outline provides a somewhat mechanical explanation of the complex control of growth and form in the insect. Many authors today tend to refer scornfully to this scheme as the 'classic theory'—which is no longer true; neither with respect to ecdysone nor to the juvenile hormone (Sláma 1975). I do not share that view. It is like pointing out that Mendel's inferences from the crossing of peas are no longer true because there are phenomena in the breeding of plants and animals which, by themselves, Mendel's laws will not explain.

It has always been recognized that the control of growth is subject to many modifying factors: genetic mutations, changes in temperature, nutrition, photoperiod etc; all of which can bring about disturbances in the normal balance of hormones. Recognition of these diverse factors does not invalidate the classic mechanisms; it merely expands them to embrace special cases. My contribution will consist largely in discussing a number of examples which are relevant to the subject of this symposium.

METAMORPHOSIS OF THE INDIVIDUAL CELL

Changes at metamorphosis are of two kinds: changes in form produced by the atrophy or the excessive growth and enlargement of certain parts (such as legs, wings, genital appendages etc.) and changes in the activities of individual cells. It so happens that in *Rhodnius,* which takes gigantic meals of blood at infrequent intervals, the provision for distension of the abdomen is quite different in the larva and in the adult. In the larval stages the entire cuticle of the abdomen stretches to give an increase of surface area of three-fold or more. In the larva the surface is thrown into stellate folds studded at intervals with plaques bearing tactile hairs. In the adult the cuticle of the abdominal wall is sclerotized and inextensible; stretching is provided for by a lateral pleat of soft cuticle set in the connexivum.

Consequently, when metamorphosis of the abdominal cuticle of *Rhodnius* is observed the features of the classic theory are particularly evident: the implantation of the corpus allatum from a young larva to a 5th-stage larva may result in a localized patch of larval cuticle in the resulting adult; or if extracted juvenile hormone is applied to a single abdominal segment of the 5th-stage larva, the resulting adult will show one larval segment interposed in the abdomen.

The abdominal cuticle has a different pattern in the larval stages and in the adult (Fig. 11.1). In the larva there are oval pigment spots at the postero-lateral angles of each segment; in the adult there are trapezoidal spots at the antero-lateral angles. In the adult there is a pattern of concentric ridges in the cuticle of the anterior tergites, of which there is no trace in the larva.

These patterns are not related with size. In the early experiments in which I joined a decapitated 1st-stage larva of *Rhodnius* in parabiosis on the tip of the head of a 5th-stage larva and obtained its transformation directly into a diminutive adult (Wigglesworth 1934) I was fascinated by the fact that the pattern of the new abdominal cuticle was identical with that of the normal adult, but the cells were of the same size and their nuclei equally spaced. Thus the pattern had been formed by less than 150th part of the number of cells concerned in the normal adult. That presumably means that the adult pattern is growing unseen throughout the larval stages.

Some years later (Wigglesworth 1940a) I found that if the epidermal cells over an extensive area of the integument are killed by high temperature, the wound is repaired by the inward migration of dividing cells from the undamaged epidermis around the injury; and that these migrating cells carry with them the characters of that component of the cuticular pattern for which they had previously been responsible. So that when such insects laid down a new cuticle it showed a centripetal displacement of the pattern in the area of the burn. If the burn was applied between two pigment spots they fused into one during the ensuing moult; and if a single pigment spot was burned out, it was replaced by unpigmented cuticle laid down by cells from the unpigmented zone around.

Does this displacement of the predetermined pattern during the healing of wounds affect the invisible pattern of the future adult in the same way as the visible pattern of the larva? We saw earlier that the adult pattern is the converse of that of the larva. The black spots of the larva are replaced by pale areas in the adult, and the trapezoidal black spots of the adult appear in areas unpigmented in the larva. In fact, when these treated insects suffered metamorphosis, where a pigment spot of the larva had been burned out there was a fusion of black spots in the adult; and where the black spots in the larva had fused, the black spot of the adult was missing (Fig. 11.2). Clearly the adult pattern,

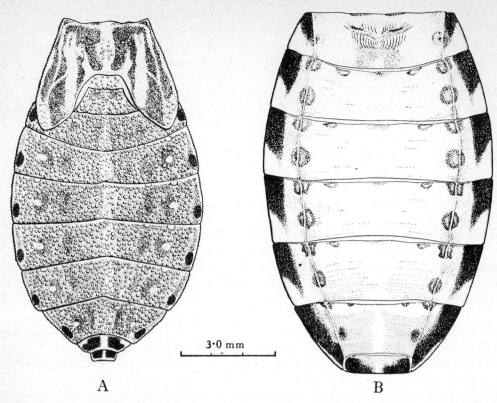

FIG. 11.1. A, dorsal view of meso- and metathorax and abdomen of 5th-stage larva of *Rhodnius*. B, dorsal view of abdomen of adult female.

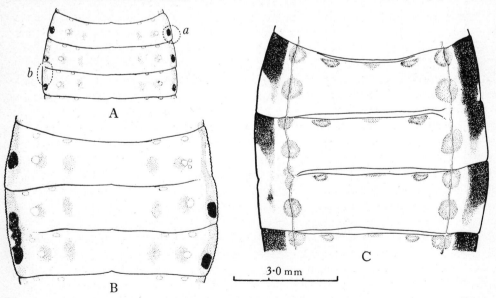

FIG. 11.2. A, abdominal tergites three to five of a normal 3rd instar larva of *Rhodnius*: the broken lines *a* and *b* show approximate regions burned. B, corresponding segments in the 5th-instar larva resulting. C, corresponding segments in the adult resulting.

growing invisibly in the epidermis, expands and spreads during mitosis in the epidermis just like the visible pattern of the larva.

The implications of the experiment are clear. The same cells which have been laying down larval cuticle turn over to laying down adult cuticle at metamorphosis. There are no 'embryonic cells' in the epidermis of the *Rhodnius* larva that are unoccupied in cuticle formation. So that, so far as metamorphosis of the *Rhodnius* abdomen is concerned the experiments exclude theories of metamorphosis which require the bringing into action of 'adult cells' which are supposed to have been dormant during the larval stages.

Cells determined for one function during the larval stages (for example, the formation of heavily melanized cuticle in the pigment spots or colourless cuticle in the intervening zones) are at the same time committed to carry out an alternative function during the adult stage (that is, for laying down sclerotized cuticle which is colourless where they have been laying down black cuticle in the larva or vice versa).

In the higher Diptera it is well known that there are pockets of epidermal cells, invaginated during the larval stages, which take no part in laying down the larval cuticle. Not until metamorphosis do these pockets become evaginated and their epidermal cells become active in forming the cuticle of pupa and adult. These are the well known imaginal discs of Weismann; but they are not a necessary feature of metamorphosis.

As Pearson (1972) has shown, even in the larva of *Calliphora* the histoblasts of the abdomen, which take the form of islands of small epidermal cells surrounded by the large polyploid cells of the larval epidermis, take an active part in laying down larval cuticle alongside their polyploid neighbours. At metamorphosis the polyploid cells break down and a new epidermis for the abdomen is derived from multiplication of the small histoblast cells. These cells behave like the epidermal cells of *Rhodnius*: during the larval stages they lay down larval abdominal cuticle; not until metamorphosis do they and their daughter cells turn over to secreting the latent pattern for the abdominal cuticle of the pupa and adult.

METAMORPHOSIS IN CELL SYSTEMS

Even in the abdomen of *Rhodnius* there are structures whose form depends upon the co-operation of multiple cells. The epidermal cells which form the general surface of the tergites during the larval stages, give rise to scattered plaques of smooth cuticle each of which surrounds a tactile seta arising from a socket (Fig. 11.3). The mutual separation of these sensilla is determined in some way by distance as measured by the number of cells intervening: when this gap exceeds a certain threshold one of the epidermal cells (during the moulting cycle) divides into four to produce a new sensillum in which a trichogen cell (forming the hair), a tormogen cell (forming the socket), a primary sense cell (forming the axon and dendrite) and a neurilemma cell (forming the nerve sheath) co-operate.

Along the margins of the abdomen sensilla and plaques of the same character are developed, but the plaques are densely packed to form a narrow band (Fig. 11.4). If the margin of a burn passes through this band the process of wound healing leads to the centripetal displacement of the zone with densely crowded plaques. This shows that the migrating cells carry with them not only the capacities for laying down a defined type of cuticle but also their co-operative capabilities—in this case the ability to form dense arrays of plaques.

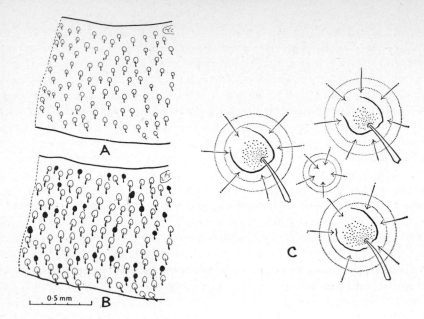

FIG. 11.3. A, part of an abdominal tergite in 4th-stage larva of *Rhodnius*. B, the same area after moulting to the 5th-stage, with newly differentiated plaques black. C, diagram to illustrate a gradient hypothesis for determination of new sensory hairs.

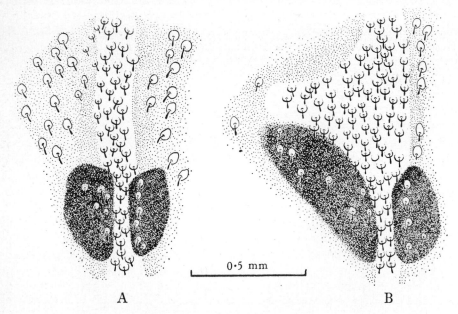

FIG. 11.4. A, marginal plaques and adjacent tergal and sternal black spots on abdomen of normal 5th-stage larva. B, corresponding region in a 5th-stage larva burned on the tergites in the 3rd instar, showing extension of the marginal plaques and of the tergal pigment spot.

When the larva undergoes metamorphosis the crowding of the marginal setae persists in the adult cuticle; but the plaques are absent and the form of the setae changes. The setae are laid down by trichogen cells which persist from one instar to the next. They afford another example of the single epidermal cell (the trichogen cell) changing its function in the absence of the juvenile hormone (Fig. 11.5). Over both tergites and sternites the plaques disappear in the adult. In the tergites the tormogen and trichogen cells undergo autolysis: thus absence of juvenile hormone leads to controlled death of specific cells in these areas. In the sternites the tormogen and trichogen cells persist; but the form of the setae is greatly changed and no plaques are developed around them.

On the first and second abdominal tergites of the adult *Rhodnius* there is a pattern of semicircular ridges in the cuticle. During the larval stages there is no sign of any such pattern: the cuticle is of the ordinary stellate type with plaques; when a burn through this area in a young larva is repaired, a new area of stellate cuticle with plaques is laid down, with no change in the visible pattern (Fig. 11.6). But when such an insect undergoes metamorphosis the ridged pattern in the resulting adult is found to be greatly distorted. This experiment serves to show that even an adult pattern which requires the co-operation of epidermal cells over a wide area already exists in invisible form in the larval stages.

These experiments on the cuticle pattern of the *Rhodnius* adult provide perhaps the clearest and simplest demonstration of the principle of the pre-formation of imaginal characters in invisible form, as adumbrated by Jan Swammerdam more than three hundred years ago.

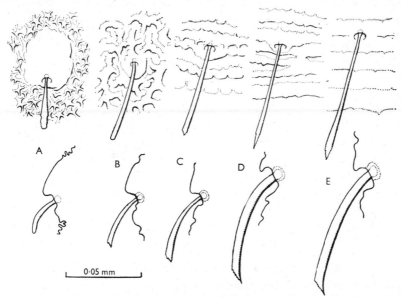

0·05 mm

FIG. 11.5. The change in form of cuticle surface and persisting setae in presence and absence of juvenile hormone: above, on surface of abdomen; below, from margin of abdomen. A, normal 4th-stage larva; D, precocious adult produced by depriving 3rd-stage larva of juvenile hormone; E, normal adult for comparison; B, and C, intermediate forms resulting from partial deprivation of juvenile hormone.

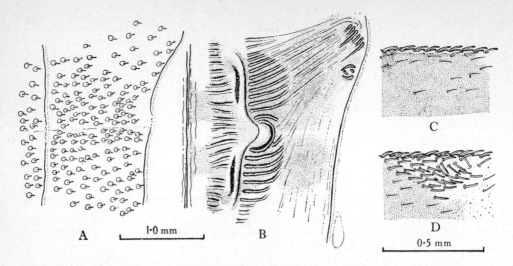

FIG. 11.6. A, part of mid-dorsal region of first and second abdominal segments in a 5th-stage larva which had been burned on the right side in the 3rd instar. B, corresponding segments in the adult resulting. C, marginal setae and part of a black spot in a normal adult *Rhodnius*. D, corresponding region in an adult which had been burned in this area in the 3rd instar.

THE TIMING OF DIFFERENTIATION

In the abdomen of the *Rhodnius* larva the ordinary epidermal cells have undergone 'differentiation' to form the various components of the larval pattern, while being at the same time committed or 'determined' to form various other components in the future adult pattern. Absence of the juvenile hormone permits this latent determination to be realized and allows the cell to manifest its new 'differentiation' to the adult form. At what stage in the growth process does this change-over occur? At what point does the formation of the adult pattern become inevitable?

That was tested by allowing a 5th-stage larva to start its normal moulting process, which (in the absence of juvenile hormone) leads to the appearance of the adult pattern, and then, after a predetermined interval, to expose the cells once more to the juvenile hormone in order to see whether the larval pattern could still be formed.

The moulting process is initiated by the large meal of blood; at the time I did these experiments (Wigglesworth 1940b) the culture was being kept at 24°C and the 5th-stage larva required about 28 days between feeding and ecdysis to the adult. At daily intervals several 5th-stage larvae were decapitated and joined in parabiosis each to a 4th-stage larva at 6–7 days after feeding (when the corpus allatum is producing abundant juvenile hormone). Alternatively extracted juvenile hormone can be applied topically to the developing 5th-stage larvae (Wigglesworth 1963).

For the first five days normal larval development was restored by the supply of juvenile hormone. From that time onwards some adult characters began to appear, first at the posterior extremity and the margins of the abdomen, but gradually spreading from day to day until by 17 days onwards the entire pigment pattern and cuticle structure were of normal imaginal type. The irrevocable determination of the epidermis to form imaginal cuticle proceeds at different rates in different parts of the abdomen.

Here I will concentrate on the simple system of stellate cuticle and plaques which

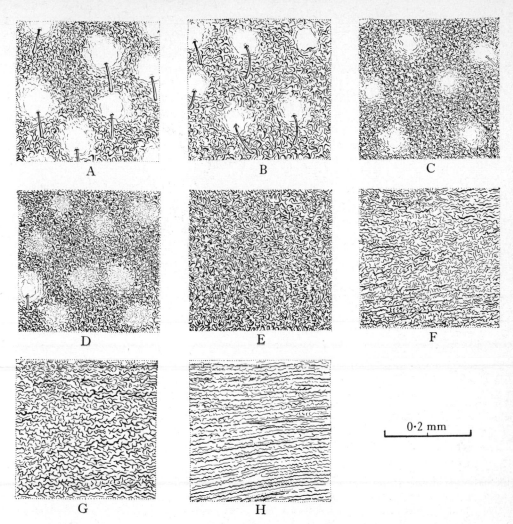

0·2 mm

FIG. 11.7. Typical areas of the cuticle in tergites of insects produced from 5th-stage larvae switched from imaginal to larval development at different times after feeding. A, 5 days; B, 7 days; C, 9 days; D, 10 days; E, 13 days; F, 15 days; G, 16 days; H, 17 days. All drawn over photographs and then bleached.

covers the central area of the tergites.

When juvenile hormone is supplied at five days the plaques and stellate folding is of normal larval type (Fig. 11.7A).

At 7 days a few of the plaques are abnormal or have imperfect setae (Fig. 11.7B).

At 8–9 days the stellate folding is larval but many of the plaques have disappeared in the central region of the segments. Where plaques are present many of them have defective setae or none at all (Fig. 11.7C).

At 10 days there are very few plaques, but numerous pale areas with unpigmented cuticle are visible where plaques had previously existed (Fig. 11.7D).

At 13 days the cuticular folds are of the larval stellate type but the epicuticle is melanized and grey throughout and plaques are virtually absent (Fig. 11.7E).

At 14 days the cuticle is still of larval type (but without plaques) in the central part of each tergite; but more laterally the cuticular folds are tending towards the adult type (Fig. 11.7F).

At 16 days, apart from a small area of intermediate cuticle in the central part of each segment (Fig. 11.7G) pigmentation and cuticle structure are entirely imaginal.

At 17 days onwards, the entire cuticle is of normal adult form (Fig. 11.7H).

The loss of setae after 8–9 days is correlated with the death of the trichogen and tormogen cells: chromatic droplets resulting from their cytolysis appear at about 10 days. The type of cuticle laid down is still capable of reversal two or three days before deposition is due to begin. Cuticle deposition begins at about 18 days; some larval features can still be produced at 15 and 16 days (Fig. 11.7F, G); but once cuticle deposition has begun neither form nor pigmentation can be influenced by the juvenile hormone.

It is particularly interesting to note that irrevocable determination can affect different characters manifested by a single cell, at different times: in Fig. 11.7D the cells at the sites of former plaques are laying down folded cuticle and not smooth plaques, but the cells retain the faculty of secreting an epicuticle that is unpigmented. In Fig. 11.7E the cells are now laying down a pigmented epicuticle, which still shows stellate folds. In Fig. 11.7F the epicuticle shows transitional types of folding, intermediate between larva and adult.

In the larva of *Oncopeltus,* in which, as in many insects, the area of cuticle laid down by each epidermal cell has clearly visible boundaries, Lawrence (1969) was able to demonstrate very elegantly the progressive change in the type of cuticle laid down by single cells as this process of switching goes forward.

THE SWITCH FROM LARVAL TO ADULT DIFFERENTIATION

From these results it was abundantly clear, as stated at the time (Wigglesworth 1940b) that 'each cell must contain the metabolic systems needed for the formation of both larval and imaginal cuticle. The role of the hormones is to determine which of these systems is effective. Since we have no knowledge at present about the internal organization of the living cell, we can of course only speculate about the nature of these intracellular systems which it is necessary to postulate'.

My speculations took the form of picturing two 'enzyme systems', the 'larval system' being activated by the juvenile hormone, acting perhaps as a 'co-enzyme' and taking precedence over the 'imaginal system' because of an increased rate of development inherent in the larval system.

The existence of these two 'systems' was regarded as an example of dual determination in a single cell. We saw, in the repair of a burn, how migrating and dividing cells retain their existing state of determination in respect to both larval and imaginal systems. At that same time (Wigglesworth 1940a) I wrote: 'in both cases the individual cell and its progeny are all-important in determination. It is therefore possible to look upon the first process of determination . . . (the progressive limitation of potency among certain groups of cells) as a process of orderly 'somatic mutation' resulting in strains of cells with specific characters, and to regard the organism as a mosaic of such mutant strains'.

Writing again on the nature of determination in 1953 (before the days of the double helix and the genetic code) with particular reference to determination in the migrating pigment spots of *Rhodnius,* I pointed out that 'one of the most familiar examples of a modification of this kind is in the 'transformation principle' (apparently a desoxyribose nucleic acid) which will induce a permanent inheritable transformation of unencapsulated variants of type II pneumococci into the fully encapsulated type (Avery, Macleod & McCarty 1944)' (Wigglesworth 1954).

Since those days molecular biology has taken over, and there is an immense amount of factual information which is bringing us very much closer to an understanding of the nature of determination. DNA in the nuclear chromosomes is still the efficient cause of all things; and ribonucleic acids are still the agents which translate the requirements of the genes into the enzymic and other proteins which build the visible structures of the body. But the RNAs are a complex association; it is messenger RNA (mRNA) which carries the coded instructions from nucleus to cytoplasm. These instructions initiate a specific pathway of development by evoking the formation of particular enzymes etc. and the cell suffers a corresponding differentiation.

But after reaching the cytoplasm these messenger RNAs may remain in an inactive or 'masked' state (mmRNA). According to the conception developed particularly by Tyler (1967) the formation of masked mRNA represents the process of determination; the activation of that mRNA results in differentiation. In accordance with this idea the epidermal cells of *Rhodnius* would carry two families of mRNA; one family maintained in action by the presence of the juvenile hormone, the other becoming activated in its absence; and, of course, other mRNAs which will be active in both larval and adult development alike.

THE SO-CALLED REVERSAL OF METAMORPHOSIS

We have seen that *Rhodnius* larvae in the 5th instar, after beginning their metamorphic moult can be diverted to a larval moult by the introduction of juvenile hormone. Since the 'larval system' in some of the epidermal cells can be re-activated in this way almost up to the time of cuticle deposition, the question arose whether such re-activation could be brought about even in the adult.

The adult *Rhodnius* can be induced to undergo a new moulting cycle and to lay down a new cuticle under the existing cuticle by parabiosis with a moulting 5th-stage larva (or by the injection of ecdysone). The characters of the new abdominal cuticle are wholly imaginal in sculpturing and pigmentation. On the other hand, if the moulting adult is supplied with juvenile hormone by parabiosis with one or more 4th-stage larvae (Wigglesworth 1939, 1940b) or by application of extracted hormone (Wigglesworth 1958) there is an increased multiplication of epidermal cells, the cuticle laid down shows stellate folding like that of the larva, and there is a hint of plaque formation around some of the surviving setae, which tend toward the larval type. To a small extent larval differentiation has again been evoked in the adult epidermis.

These observations have been confirmed in principle in the milkweed bug *Oncopeltus* (Lawrence 1966), in the earwig *Anisolabis* in which the moulting adult will lay down thoracic cuticle with an ecdysial line of weakness characteristic of the larva (Ozeki 1959), and in adult *Tenebrio* (Caveney 1970). But since such reversals of differentiation cannot be demonstrated in all parts of the body, or in all insects, the observations are rejected by some authors. What is quite evident is that the cells seem to acquire a certain 'inertia'; such that once they have begun to form pupal or adult structures, they resist the action of the juvenile hormone in causing them to revert to the larval state. That inertia seems to be eliminated during wound repair. That was very evident in the experiments of Piepho (1939) in which reversal of metamorphosis in implanted fragments of integument of *Galleria* pupae was most evident where wound repair had been most active. Cell division appears to favour the changing over of the gene function, presumably through the synthesis of new DNA.

The corpus allatum hormone was originally called the 'inhibitory hormone' because it appeared to inhibit metamorphosis by maintaining the *status quo* during the larval stages; it was these observations on the partial recall of larval characters under the action of this hormone which suggested that it would be more appropriate to call it the 'juvenile hormone' (Wigglesworth 1940b).

METAMORPHOSIS OF BODY FORM

Most of the spectacular changes in form at metamorphosis consist in the formation of elaborate outgrowths such as wings and legs and genital appendages. The formation of such outgrowths, and the consequent changes in the musculature and other systems, require more time for their completion than does the moulting of a larva to a further larval stage, which involves no more than the deposition of a new and larger cuticle. It was noted that whereas at 24°C the time interval between feeding and ecdysis to the adult, in the 5th-stage larva of *Rhodnius,* averaged 28 days, moulting of the 5th-stage in the presence of juvenile hormone to give rise to a 6th-stage larva required only 17 days (Wigglesworth 1934).

The first suggestion put forward to explain the hormonal control of metamorphosis was that the 'inhibitory hormone' from the corpus allatum accelerated the process of cuticle deposition and thereby halted growth and differentiation towards the adult form (Fig. 11.8A). This was an extension of Goldschmidt's idea of metamorphosis being controlled by the relative rates of competing processes (Wigglesworth 1936).

This effect was clearly shown when the moulting of decapitated male 5th-stage larvae of *Cimex* was induced by parabiosis with moulting 3rd-stage larvae of *Rhodnius.* The claspers and other cuticular structures in the genitalia of the *Cimex* so produced showed intermediate stages between those of the larva and those of the adult; and these stages agreed exactly with the form of the epidermal rudiments of the claspers during their normal differentiation as described by Christophers and Cragg (1922). Their form had been frozen by cuticle deposition.

At that time it was uncertain whether the hormone responsible for the inhibition of metamorphosis was distinct from the moulting hormone, or whether it was simply a higher concentration of a single moulting hormone that led to the acceleration of cuticle deposition and the consequent arrest of metamorphosis (Wigglesworth 1936). But when it was shown that moulting is initiated by secretion from the neurosecretory cells of the brain (Wigglesworth 1940b); that the actual source of the moulting hormone is in the prothoracic glands (Fukuda 1940) which are activated by the secretion from the brain (Williams 1946; Wigglesworth 1952a) it became possible to separate the action of the two hormones. It then became evident that in the original experiments in *Rhodnius* and *Cimex,* the accelerated deposition of cuticle was due to the moulting hormone and not the juvenile hormone.

Thus it is possible to restrict the growth of wing lobes in a *Rhodnius* larva by

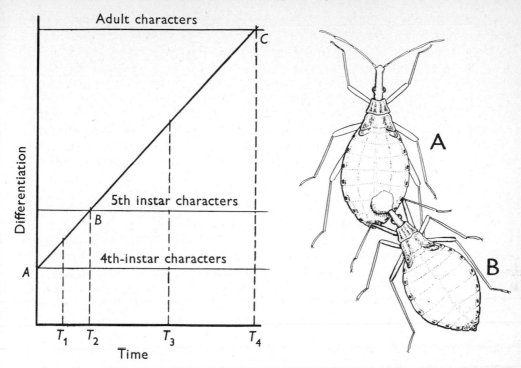

FIG. 11.8. To the left, diagram to illustrate the way in which differentiation towards the adult form can be arrested at different points by accelerated deposition of cuticle at times T_1, T_2 etc. To the right, accelerated cuticle deposition induced in the 4th-stage larva (A) by joining to it a larva (B) already at a more advanced stage in moulting.

accelerated cuticle deposition induced by parabiosis with a larva in the same instar (Fig. 11.8A, B) but at a more advanced stage in moulting (Wigglesworth 1952); or by implanting several prothoracic glands in *Locusta* (Halbwachs, Joly & Joly 1957). Indeed it is now generally accepted that an excessive dosage of ecdysone in the last larval stage can inhibit the full formation of all the characteristic outgrowths of the adult by acceleration of cuticle deposition. That occurs in *Rhodnius* (Wigglesworth 1970); in *Samia* (Williams 1968); in *Galleria* (Sehnal 1971); and in *Sarcophaga* (Zdarek & Denlinger 1975). On the other hand, whereas the application of juvenile hormone to a wing lobe of a 5th-stage larva will prevent its differentiation into an adult wing, such applications do not have the slightest effect on the growth of wing lobes in the earlier larval stages (Wigglesworth 1958): the treated wing lobes of a 4th-stage larva develop in the normal manner to the enlarged wing lobes of the 5th instar (Wigglesworth 1961).

LARVAL DIFFERENTIATION AND METAMORPHOSIS

At each larval moult in hemimetabolous insects, there is a small degree of differentiation towards the adult form: there is a progressive relative enlargement of the wing lobes, and progressive differentiation of the genitalia. If the 5th or last larval stage of *Rhodnius* is supplied with juvenile hormone by implantation of active corpora allata, or by the application of extracted hormone to the cuticle, it will give rise to a 6th-stage larva with a constant and characteristic morphology in the wing lobes and genitalia. In the male the future claspers are no longer in the form of a slight ridge on the cuticle surface; they form little conical outgrowths. If the supply of juvenile hormone is deficient, all intermediate stages in the genitalia are produced between the small outgrowths and the highly differentiated structures of the adult. But no increase in the dosage of juvenile hormone or acceleration in the timing of its supply will reduce the degree of differentiation below the stage at which they form little oval knobs (Wigglesworth 1973).

The question arises whether a large number of these larval moults in the presence of juvenile hormone would eventually lead to the full differentiation of the wings and genitalia. Since 6th-stage larvae have always failed to free themselves successfully from the old cuticle, the 7th-stage is the last that has been obtained. In this, wing lobes and genitalia are differentiated only a little more than in the 6th-stage; and the pigment pattern and cuticular characters of the abdomen are wholly larval even in the 7th instar. It appears unlikely that continued larval moults would ever lead to the adult form.

The same phenomenon is seen in the larvae of Lepidoptera: these go through a series of morphological changes characteristic of each successive instar; and these characters are barely influenced by the juvenile hormone (Staal 1967).

Two components are held dormant by the presence of the juvenile hormone in the larva of *Rhodnius*: (i) the pattern of cuticle structure, pigmentation and distribution of sensilla as seen in the abdomen; (ii) the pattern of intense local mitoses and collaborative outgrowths of the epidermis which will produce the adult form. But we saw that even in the abdomen there is collaborative activity between the epidermal cells in the development of the pattern of setae and plaques. The patterns of cuticle structure and the patterns of cellular outgrowth, differ only in degree.

MODE OF ACTION OF THE JUVENILE HORMONE IN PATTERN FORMATION

As always in the study of hormones we reach the conclusion that the juvenile hormone is creating nothing. It is merely the key which opens the door so that particular elements of the gene system may come into play. Its activity is in no way fundamental to the understanding of pattern as such. It has long been realized that the action of both ecdysone and the juvenile hormone depend upon gene activation, resulting in appropriate RNA and protein synthesis (Wigglesworth 1957); and this conclusion has been greatly reinforced by the visible effects of these hormones in producing 'puffing' of defined loci in the polytene chromosomes of Diptera (Becker 1962; Clever 1963).

Much research has been directed towards elucidating the mechanism of this activation. The standard material for endocrinologists in this field has been the action of oestrogenic hormones on the uterus of mammals. Here the oestrogen is believed to combine with a 'receptor protein' of high molecular weight, and it is this altered protein which enters the nucleus and acts upon specific loci in the chromosomes to give rise to extractable RNA, the application of which will reproduce the protein synthesizing effects of the oestrogen (Segal 1967; Jensen & De Sombre 1972).

In insects a 'carrier protein' has been found in *Manduca,* which is concerned in the solubilization and transport of juvenile hormone in the blood (Kramer *et al.* 1974); and a 'receptor protein' of high molecular weight has been isolated from the epidermal cells of the *Tenebrio* pupa (Schmialek *et al.* 1973) serving perhaps as an intermediary in the activation of the nuclear genes. Like the oestrogen-binding protein of mammals this receptor substance also contains RNA (Schmialek 1973).

DISCUSSION

Cell division and differentiation

One of the most spectacular forms of differentiation is differential division; where for example a single cell divides to give two or four daughter cells of different form and function. Perhaps for this reason a dogma has grown up which claims that cell division, that is DNA synthesis, is necessary for differentiation; 'that the cytoplasmic reprogramming of gene activity at mitosis may constitute a mechanism of general importance in cell differentiation' (Gurdon and Woodland 1968).

It so happens that many of the examples which I have selected in this account of the juvenile hormone suggest that this assertion may not be invariably true: the altered activity of trichogen cells, and other cells which persist from one instar to the next, in the presence or absence of the juvenile hormone; the changes induced in the activity of epidermal cells by exposure to the juvenile hormone late in the moulting cycle, when all cell division is over; and the partial restoration of larval characters in persisting cells of the moulting adult.

But it is self-evident that the differentiated outgrowths which are so prominent at metamorphosis, and indeed many other forms of differentiation, could not take place without cell division.

Position and differentiation

In most of the experiments described in this account, the cells which make up a given element in the surface pattern have been shown to carry their state of determination with them when they divide and spread during the repair of a burn. On the other hand there are many examples of new determination and differentiation being dependent upon 'position'. At some early stage in embryonic development almost all elements in the pattern of the future organism must depend upon position effects. A well known example of a late effect of this kind is in the integument of the pupa of *Galleria* where, as described by Marcus (1962) and by Stumpf (1968) implanted epidermal cells lay down cuticle whose character is controlled by their position in the body segment of their new host.

Position effects of this kind are commonly ascribed to gradients of some unknown nature in the environment of the cells. An example briefly mentioned was the differentiation of plaques and setae in the integument of *Rhodnius* at points where the existing plaques are most widely separated (Fig. 11.3). We saw that a burn passing through the margin of the abdomen led to the formation of a wide area of closely packed plaques and setae (Fig. 11.4). This is an example of the spreading of a determined structural character the manifestation of which depends upon a small-scale positional or gradient effect; but here again the morphology of the structure produced (whether larval plaques or adult setae) is controlled by the presence or absence of the juvenile hormone (Figs. 11.5, 11.6D).

DISCUSSION

Henson: I have made morphological studies of metamorphosis. I came to the conclusion that there was no such thing as imaginal cells that is, no imaginal organism embedded in the larval organism. My opinion, which I considered proved correct, is that you have a developmental process manifested for the first time in the egg, and reiterated from instar to instar during subsequent development. The result of this reiterated embryogenesis depended on the hormonal environment; under juvenile hormone it reacted differently to when juvenile hormone was lacking. I have listened I must confess with some difficulty of comprehension to the papers at this symposium and I must admit that old ideas are very resistant to change. I would like to remind you that in earwigs and in cockroaches you have a regrowth of Malphigian tubules at every ecdysis. In earwigs, you have a regrowth of antennae at every ecdysis, and in both groups of insects a regrowth of compound eyes. If my viewpoint is correct, there is a time in every stadium when the whole gamut of development is repeated, that is, determination is redetermined and it may be that conflicting results that I have sensed in some papers are due to this process, so that even apparent determination can be undone by another of these developmental cycles. I know nothing in this view which is contrary to Professor Wigglesworth's results, and indeed, much of it was suggested to me by his early work.

Wigglesworth: I only would like to remind Dr Henson that many years ago when he put forward this view I pointed out to him that it was quite true, and I entirely agreed with him, but that this had been pointed out earlier by Aristotle. Dr Henson had said that he never read the literature as far back as that!

Varley: What happens to the juvenile hormone when the nymph becomes adult? Is it excreted, or is it merely denatured in some way?

Wigglesworth: These hormones are dangerous things, and therefore have a very short life in the insect's body. The juvenile hormone, for example, is continuously being produced in small amounts and broken down rapidly. The enzymes responsible for this breakdown are known.

Schneiderman: Are there conspicuous differences in the kind of wound healing that one observes after a burn as compared to that after a cutting out of a piece and covering it with a plastic slip?

Wigglesworth: Yes, they are completely different. After a burn, the nuclei immediately adjacent to the burnt cells show activation and enlarged nucleoli, and these cells then later divide. But when you have a cut, cells are activated much further away and this is followed by tremendous migration so that they pile up around the cut area.

Schneiderman: What about the end result, that is, the pattern that appears. Is it different after the two kinds of experiments?

Wigglesworth: After a burn, or a cut, in my experience you never get a normal cuticle pattern in the following moult, although of course you do get normal patterns some moults later.

Nöthiger: Has anybody tried to play again and again with these cells? How many times can you go backwards and forward between larval and adult states?

Wigglesworth: The best work on this is done by Piepho on *Galleria*, but these experiments are completely disbelieved by our cousins on the other side of the Atlantic.

Schneiderman: I believe them and I am a representative!

Wigglesworth: Piepho claimed to have got the cells to go back from the adult to the pupa to the larva and then got them to go forward again.

Nöthiger: That would be very difficult to explain on the basis of your 'masked messenger' hypothesis, unless you have it resynthesized all the time.

Wigglesworth: Well this story that I have given about masked messenger is very hypothetical. I just put that in to show that I know the language!

Gurdon: To what extent can you compare these hormonally produced changes in insect cuticle to the effects of vitamin A on vertebrate skin? In the latter case, it seems to depend on what the basal cell layers do. It is not the differentiating cell itself which responds to the vitamin A but the underlying stem cell. In the insect case, is it the same cells that are changing in response to the hormone, or is it more like the situation in the vertebrate, that is underlying cells which produce progeny which go off in a different direction?

Wigglesworth: There is no doubt in these experiments that it is the same cells, but surely the process must be similar in character in both systems. In both cases in a single cell you are evoking different potentialities.

Gurdon: I wasn't clear whether it is really certain that the hormones are activating new genes.

Wigglesworth: Well it is certainly the same cell, but whether the hormones are getting at the genes is not clear. I thought the idea was that if you got these changes without mitosis or endomitosis then it was likely to be an effect directly on the cytoplasm. Is that reasonable?

REFERENCES

AVERY, O. T., MacLeod, C. M. & McCarty, M. (1944). Studies on the chemical nature of the substance inducing transformation of pneumococal types. *J. exp. Med.*, **79**, 137-158.

BECKER, H. J. (1962). Die Puffs der Speicheldrüsenchromosomen von *Drosophila melanogaster*. II. Die Auslösung der Puffbildung, ihre Spezifität und ihre Beziehung zur Funktion der Ringdrüse. *Chromosoma*, **13**, 341-384.

CAVENEY, S. (1970). Juvenile hormone and wound modelling of *Tenebrio* cuticle architecture. *J. Insect Physiol.*, **16**, 1087-1107.

CHRISTOPHERS, S. R. & CRAGG, F. W. (1922). On the so-called 'penis' of the bed-bug *(Cimex lectularius* L.) and on the homologies generally of the male and female genitalia of this insect. *Indian J. med. Res.*, **9**, 445-463.

CLEVER, U. (1963). Von der Ecdysonkonzentration abhängige Genaktivitätsmuster in den Speicheldrüsenchromosomen von *Chironomus tentans*. *Devl. Biol.*, **6**, 73-98.

FUKUDA, S. (1940). Induction of pupation in silkworm by transplanting the prothoracic gland. *Proc. imp. Acad. Japan*, **16**, 414-416.

FUKUNDA, S. (1944). The hormonal mechanism of larval molting and metamorphosis in the silkworm. *J. Fac. Sci. Tokyo Univ.*, sec. IV, **6**, 477-532.

GURDON, J. B. & WOODLAND, H. R. (1968). The cytological control of nuclear activity in animal development. *Biol. Rev.*, **43**, 233-267.

HALBWACHS, M. C., JOLY, L. & JOLY, P. (1957). Résultats d'implantations de 'glandes ventrales' à *Locusta migratoria* L. *J. Insect Physiol.* **1**, 143-149.

JENSEN, E. V. & DeSombre, E. R. (1972). Mechanism of action of the female sex hormones. *Annual Rev. Biochem.*, **41**, 203-230.

KRAMER, K. J., SANBURG, L. L., KEZDY, F. J. & LAW, J. H. (1974). The juvenile hormone binding protein in the hemolymph of *Manduca sexta* Johannson (Lepidoptera: Sphingidae) *Proc. natn. Acad. Sci. USA*, 71, 493-497.

LAWRENCE, P. A. (1966). The hormonal control of the development of hairs and bristles in the milkweed bug *Oncopeltus fasciatus*. Dall. *J. exp. Biol.*, **44**, 507-522.

LAWRENCE, P. A. (1969). Cellular differentiation and pattern formation during metamorphosis of the milkweed bug, *Oncopeltus. Devl. Biol.*, **19**, 12-40.

MARCUS, W. (1962). Untersuchungen über die Polarität der Rumpfhaut von Schmetterlingen. *Wilhelm Roux Arch. Entw Mech. Org.*, **154**, 56-102.

OZEKI, K. (1959). Secretion of molting hormone from the ventral glands. *Sci. Papers Coll. gen. Educ. Univ. Tokyo*, **9**, 256-262.

PEARSON, M. J. (1972). Imaginal disks and the abdominal histoblasts of *Calliphora erythrocephala* (Diptera) *Nature, Lond.*, **238**, 349-351.

PIEPHO, H. (1939). Raupenhäutungen bereits verpuppter Hautstücke bei der Wachsmotte *Galleria mellonella* L. *Naturwissenschaften*, **27**, 301-302.

PIEPHO, H. (1951). Über die Lenkung der Insektenmetamorphose durch Hormone. *Verh. dt. zool. Ges.* Wilhelmshaven, **1951**, 62-75.

SCHMIALEK, P. (1973). Ribonucleoprotein particle in epidermis cells as the receptor for juvenile hormone. *Nature, Lond.*, **245**, 267-268.

SCHMIALEK, P., BOROWSKI, M., GEYER, A., MIOSGA, V., NÜNDEL, M., ROSENBERG, E. & ZAPF, B. (1973). Ein Receptorprotein für das Juvenilhormonaloge 10, 11-Epoxy-6, 7-*trans*-2, 3-*trans*-farnesylpropeny-läther aus den Epidermiszellen der Puppen von *Tenebrio molitor* L. *Z. Naturf.* **28c**, 453-456.

SEGAL, S. J. (1967). Regulatory action of estrogenic hormones. *Devl. Biol.* Suppl. **1** (1967) 264-280.

SENHAL, F. (1971). Rôle de 'l'hormone de mue et de l'hormone juvénile dans le contrôle de la métamorphose de *Galleria mellonella* (Lepidoptera). *Archs. zool. exp. gén.* **112**, 565-577.

Sláma, K. (1975). Some old concepts and new findings on hormonal control of insect metamorphosis. *J. Insect Physiol.*, **21**, 921-955.

STAAL, G. B. (1967). Endocrine aspects of larval development in insects. *J. Endocrinol.*, 37, 13-14.

STUMPF, H. F. (1968). Further studies on gradient-dependent diversification in the pupal cuticle of *Galleria mellonella. J. exp. Biol.*, **49**, 49-60.

TYLER, A. (1967). Masked messenger RNA and cytoplasmic DNA in relation to protein synthesis and processes of fertilization and determination in embryonic development. *Devl. Biol.* Suppl., **1**, 170-226.

WIGGLESWORTH, V. B. (1934). The physiology of ecdysis in *Rhodnius prolixus* (Hemiptera) II. Factors controlling moulting and metamorphosis. *Quart. J. micr. Sci.* **77**, 191-222.

WIGGLESWORTH, V. B. (1936). The function of the corpus allatum in the growth and reproduction of *Rhodnius prolixus* (Hemiptera). *Quart. J. micr. Sci.*, **79**, 91-121.

WIGGLESWORTH, V. B. (1939). Häutung bei Imagines von Wanzen. *Naturwissenschaften*, **27**, 301.

WIGGLESWORTH, V. B. (1940a). Local and general factors in the development of 'pattern' in *Rhodnius prolixus* (Hemiptera). *J. exp. Biol.*, **17**, 180-200.

WIGGLESWORTH, V. B. (1940b). The determination of characters at metamorphosis in *Rhodnius prolixus* (Hemiptera). *J. exp. Biol.*, **17**, 201-222.

WIGGLESWORTH, V. B. (1952a). The thoracic gland in *Rhodnius prolixus* (Hemiptera) and its role in moulting. *J. exp. Biol.*, **29**, 561-570.

WIGGLESWORTH, V. B. (1952b). Hormone balance and the control of metamorphosis in *Rhodnius prolixus* (Hemiptera). *J. exp. Biol.*, **29**, 620-631.

WIGGLESWORTH, V. B. (1954). 'The Physiology of Insect Metamorphosis'. 152 pp. Cambridge University Press.

WIGGLESWORTH, V. B. (1957). The action of growth hormones in insects. *Symp. Soc. exp. Biol.*, **11**, 204-227.

WIGGLESWORTH, V. B. (1958). Some methods for assaying extracts of the juvenile hormone in insects. *J. Insect Physiol.*, **2**, 73-84.

WIGGLESWORTH, V. B. (1961). Some observations on the juvenile hormone effect of farnesol in *Rhodnius prolixus* Stal (Hemiptera). *J. Insect Physiol.*, **7**, 73-78.

WIGGLESWORTH, V. B. (1963). The juvenile hormone effect of farnesol and some related compounds: quantitative experiments. *J. Insect Physiol.*, **9**, 105-119.

WIGGLESWORTH, V. B. (1970). *Insect Hormones* 159 pp. Edinburgh, Oliver & Boyd.

WIGGLESWORTH, V. B. (1973). Assays on *Rhodnius* for juvenile hormone activity. *J. Insect Physiol.*, **19**, 205-211.

WILLIAMS, C. M. (1946). Physiology of insect diapause: the role of the brain in the production and termination of pupal dormancy in the giant silkworm *Platysamia cecropia. Biol. Bull., Woods Hole*, **90**, 234-243.

WILLIAMS, C. M. (1968). Ecdysone and ecdysone-analogues: their assay and action on diapausing pupae of the cynthia silkworm. *Biol. Bull. mar. biol. Lab., Woods Hole*, **134**, 344-355.

ZDAREK, J. & DENLINGER, D. L. (1975). Action of ecdysoids, juvenoids, and non-hormonal agents on termination of pupal diapause in the flesh fly. *J. Insect Physiol.*, **21**, 1193-1202.

12 • The role of ecdysone in the control of gene activity in the polytene chromosomes of *Drosophila*

MICHAEL ASHBURNER & GEOFF RICHARDS

Department of Genetics, University of Cambridge

Introduction

One of the most exciting discoveries in the field of insect development made in the early nineteen sixties, a discovery with important implications for wider areas of study, was that of Clever and Karlson who demonstrated the control of gene activity by the steroid hormone ecdysone. This discovery was made possible by the happy circumstance that the nuclei of many larval tissues in the Diptera possess giant, polytene, chromosomes whose bands may undergo a reversible morphological change, into puffs, when their DNA is transcribed into RNA. Only a limited number of bands of the polytene chromosomes actually puff and those that do show both tissue and developmental specificity. Dramatic changes occur to the pattern of puffed bands at certain stages in development. In particular the polytene chromosomes of larval tissues display intense puffing activity during moulting and during the early stages of metamorphosis. What Clever and Karlson (1960) demonstrated was that the changes in gene activity occuring at these times were, like moulting and metamorphosis themselves, controlled by ecdysone[1]. By injecting young fourth instar larvae of *Chironomus tentans* with ecdysone they prematurely initiated the changes in puffing activity that would have normally occured prior to the larval/pupal moult.

In this review we will discuss the present status of studies on the control of puffing activity by ecdysone drawing largely on our own analysis of this phenomenon with *Drosophila melanogaster* (Ashburner 1972, 1973, 1974; Ashburner & Richards 1976; Richards 1975, 1976). We wish to point to the usefulness of such studies for an understanding of both the fundamental mechanism of action of ecdysone and of the formal nature of the controls involved in the regulation of a complex temporal sequence of gene activity.

---

[1] We use the word 'ecdysone' in its generic sense. All our own experiments were with β-ecdysone unless we state to the contrary. This is probably the natural active hormone of *Drosophila,* at least, (for recent discussions see: King *et al.* 1974; Borst *et al.* 1974; Milner & Sang, 1974; but also, Mandaron 1973).

PUFFING PATTERNS DURING NORMAL DEVELOPMENT

The salivary gland chromosomes of young third instar larvae of *Drosophila* present a picture of relatively few large puffs whose activity is rather constant with time. The function of these puffs is unknown, although recent evidence (Kress 1973; Korge 1975) very strongly suggests that at least some of them code for proteins involved in the synthesis of what is, at this stage, the major secretory product of the salivary gland, its glue. The function of the glue is to fix the puparium to its substrate (Fraenkal & Brookes 1953). A dramatic change occurs to this pattern of puffs a few hours before puparium formation. Many of the pre-existing puffs regress and a complex sequence of changes in puffing activity, involving well over 100 puffs, is initiated. This change is a direct consequence of ecdysone. That this is so, in *Drosophila*, was shown by several experiments, particularly those of Becker (1962), and Berendes (1967) and, more recently, by those of Ashburner (1972), Kress (1972), Stocker and Kastritsis (1973) and Eeken (1974). As the background to the experiments we will discuss below Ashburner (1972) incubated salivary glands from young third instar larvae of *D. melanogaster* in the presence of hormone and showed that both the regression of the puffs active early in the instar and the induction of the complex sequence of puffs active late proceeded normally. The medium used for the incubation was fully defined and only a suitable concentration of ecdysone was necessary for these changes in puffing to occur. This *in vitro* technique has many advantages for the experimenter and all our subsequent work has utilized it.

During the part of *Drosophila*'s development that analysis of puffs is technically feasible two major sequences of puffing activity occur. The first begins, about six hours before puparium formation, by the regression of several of the puffs whose function is almost certainly to do with glue synthesis (e.g. 3C and 68C; Korge 1975) and the induction of puffs at such characteristic sites as 23E, 74EF and 75B. During the next 2–4 hours (depending upon the temperature) these three puffs increase greatly in size before, eventually, regressing. Coincident with their regression we see puffing activity at sites such as 62E to be followed, in order, by puffing at, for example, 78D, 63E and 82F. Each of these puffs is active for a characteristic time before regressing. By 3 to 4 hours after puparium formation all of the puffs of this larval sequence have regressed. The second puffing sequence starts about five hours after puparium formation with the simultaneous appearance of a group of puffs which includes 63E, 75CD, 69A, 52A and 52C. These puffs are active for about 3 hours and then regress. As they do so we see puffing for a second time at some (e.g. 74EF, 75B) but not all (e.g. 78D) of the puff sites active previously in the larval sequence whilst other puffs which are now active are so for the first time (e.g. 93F).

Fig. 12.1 summarizes, and Fig. 12.2 illustrates, the changes in puffing activity, at those sites that will be the subject of further discussion, during normal late larval and prepupal development. These changes in gene activity prompt many questions, not all of which can be fully done justice in this review. Before turning to the control of the temporal sequences themselves we will briefly touch upon two of these other issues.

One obvious question is that of the function of these changes in gene activity. Unfortunately we can only answer this in the most general terms at the moment. The common assumption that puffs are active genes has recently been strongly supported by experiments in several laboratories. These experiments have shown that conditions which alter the puffing pattern, such as heat shock, also alter, in a parallel way, the

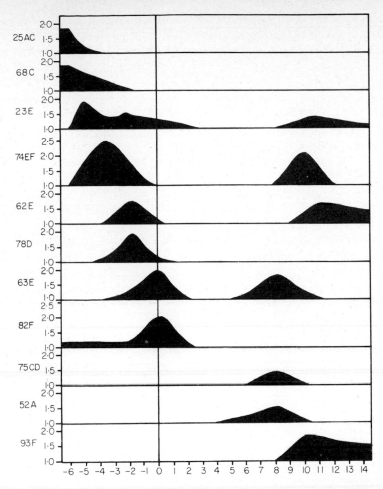

FIG. 12.1. The changing activities of selected puffs during late larval and 'prepupal' development of *Drosophila melanogaster*. The abscissa is time, in hours, at 25°C., before and after puparium formation. The ordinate is puff size (i.e. the ratio between the diameter of the puff and an inactive reference band).

pattern of salivary gland protein synthesis (Tissières *et al.* 1975). Moreover newly synthesized RNA extracted from heat shocked *Drosophila* tissues specifically hybridizes to the sites of puffs induced by this treatment (McKenzie *et al.* 1975; Spradling *et al.* 1975). *In vitro* this RNA translates into the same proteins that are made by heat treated tissues (Moran; McKenzie, personal communication). So we feel that we are on fairly firm ground when we state that the puffs code for particular proteins (see also references to Kress and Korge, above). Indeed a changing pattern of protein synthesis is seen in salivary glands as the pattern of puffs changes during normal development (Tissières *et al.* 1974; Ashburner & Lewis, unpublished); see Fig. 12.3. But, apart from the probable coding by puffs of glue proteins (see above) the physiological role of these proteins in unknown. Presumably some play a role in the histolysis of the salivary gland after puparium formation whilst others may be sequestered by developing adult tissues, as suggested by Ashburner (1967) and supported by more recent biochemical studies (e.g. Boyd & Logan 1972; Price 1974).

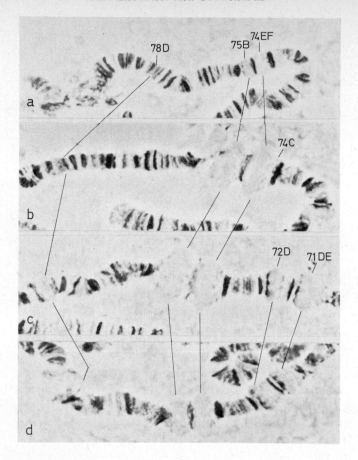

FIG. 12.2. Induction of two early puffs (74EF, 75B) and a late puff (78D) by ß-ecdysone in cultured puff stage 1 salivary glands. (a) unincubated control (b) after 2 hours with ecdysome (c) 4 hours and (d) 6 hours. From Ashburner, in *Results and Problems in Cell Differentiation* vol. 4, ed. W. Beermann, with permission of Springer-Verlag.

Although we are quite certain that ecdysone is the agent normally responsible for the initiation of the changes in gene activity that occur prior to metamorphosis (see below) we are quite ignorant of the molecular details of the hormone's action. Quite considerable progress has been made in understanding how many vertebrate steroid hormones may work and it is attractive to consider that perhaps ecdysone is not so different (for recent reviews see Jenson & De Sombre 1973; O'Malley & Means 1974 who discuss the mode of action of oestrogen and the female sex hormones respectively, and Yund & Fristrom, (1975) for a comparison with ecdysone). This would imply that ecdysone enters the cell, perhaps passively, binding to specific protein 'receptor' species within it. The complex of ecdysone and its receptor would migrate to the nucleus, the receptor protein perhaps first undergoing some transformation, or activation, and the nuclear form of the complex would then recognize specific genes and, thereby, influence their activities. Whether the recognition, by the hormone receptor complex, is of specific nucleotide sequences (e.g. King & Gordon 1972; Yamamoto & Alberts 1975) or of chromosomal proteins, themselves recognizing specific nucleotide sequences (e.g.

O'Malley *et al.* 1972), is still an open question.

Despite growing evidence that this scheme of events may be an appropriate description of how ecdysone works in insect cells (Emmerich 1969, 1960, 1972; Best-Belpomme & Courgeon 1975; Yund & Fristrom 1975, but see Gorell *et al.* 1972) it is speculative and quite different hypotheses may be entertained. These include, for example, the suggestion that the primary effect of ecdysone is on the ionic balance of the cell, the genes responding differentially to changes in intranuclear ion concentration (Kroeger 1968; Lezzi & Robert, 1972), that ecdysone may have secondary (or even primary) effects in altering the concentrations of metabolites which effect gene activity (see Kress 1973) and that ecdysone may act post-transcriptionally.

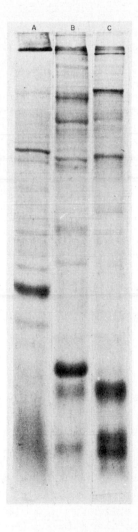

FIG. 12.3. Autoradiograph of a sodium dodecyl sulphate acrylamide gel separating salivary gland proteins labelled *in vitro* with ^{35}S-methionine for 20 minutes. (A) glands from late third instar larvae, (B) glands from 0 hour prepupae and (C) glands from 6 hour prepupae.

THE TEMPORAL CONTROL OF PUFFING ACTIVITY

Although the changes in puffing activity, from the mid third instar larva to the late prepupa, are continuous it is convenient to treat the control of the larval and prepupal sequences separately.

THE LARVAL SEQUENCE

Salivary glands from young to mid third instar larvae of *D. melanogaster* cultured in the presence of ecdysone complete the larval puffing sequence in 12 hours at 20°C or 9 hours at 25°C. Although the culture itself produces some changes in puffing the major features of the larval sequence *in vitro* are identical to those seen *in vivo* (Ashburner 1972). Confirming an important observation of Clever (Clever 1964; Clever & Romball 1966) we find that the puffs induced by ecdysone fall into two classes: 'early puffs' responding to ecdysone within a few minutes, and 'late puffs' which respond only after a lag period of several hours. In *Chironomus tentans* there are only two early puffs, in *Drosophila* there are more—six have been recognized and studied in *D. melanogaster*. By contrast the number of late puffs is much larger (of the order of 100). On the basis of the fact that the hormonal induction of early puffs does not require protein synthesis whilst that of the late puffs does Clever proposed that the appearance of the late puffs is a direct consequence of early puff activity.

The distinction between early and late puffs does not only depend upon their difference in time of response to ecdysone. In *Drosophila,* as in *Chironomus,* continuous exposure of glands to ecdysone under conditions in which protein synthesis is inhibited (e.g. by cycloheximide, anisomycin or puromycin) leads to normal early puff induction (though a failure of their regression) but to a complete failure of late puff induction (Fig. 12.4). Furthermore the shape of the curve relating puff response to hormone concentration is quite different for early and late puffs (see Fig. 12.10); the early puffs respond quantitatively over a wide (500 fold) concentration range, the late puffs respond over a very narrow concentration range (4 fold). Finally, and perhaps most interestingly, the activity of the early puffs requires the actual presence of ecdysone—if the hormone is removed the puffs regress—whilst late puff activity *may* occur normally in the absence of hormone.

The consequences of hormone withdrawal require further elaboration. An early puff, such as 74EF, is induced within minutes by ecdysone and increases in size steadily for a few hours before regressing. Cycloheximide, inhibiting protein synthesis, does not affect induction but does inhibit regression. At first we thought that the regression of the early puffs may result from the metabolism of ecdysone to an inactive product. This is not so (Emmerich 1970; Claycomb *et al.* 1971; Ashburner 1973). Yet the removal of ecdysone, by washing cultured salivary glands, during the induction phase of an early puff results in that puff's immediate regression. Significantly this hormone withdrawal caused regression is *not* sensitive to the inhibition of protein synthesis. The question naturally arises as to whether, having regressed as a consequence of ecdysone removal, an early puff may be reinduced by its re-addition. The experimental answer to this question (Fig. 12.5) is seemingly complex; after an hour or so initial exposure to ecdysone 74EF may be reinduced following an ecdysone washout caused regression but, as the time of exposure of the glands to ecdysone is prolonged, the puff becomes increasingly refractory to reinduction. Paradoxically this refractory period is brief—as the first period of exposure

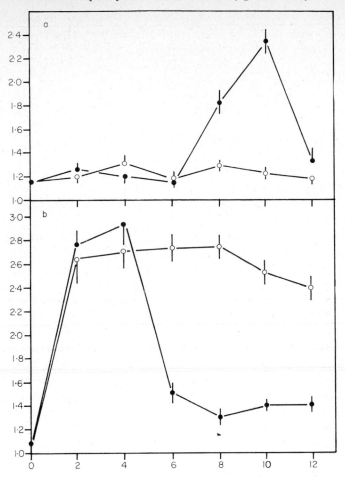

FIG. 12.4. The effect of inhibiting protein synthesis on the induction by ecdysone and subsequent regression of (a) the late puff 82F, and (b) the early puff 75B. Solid circles: β-ecdysone (2.5 x 10^{-6}M). alone, open circles β-ecdysone plus cycloheximide (7.0 x 10^{-4}M). Ordinate puff size, abscissa time in hours at 20°C.

to ecdysone is prolonged even further the puff becomes reinducible, following an ecdysone-free period, once again.

The effects of cycloheximide, to inhibit protein synthesis, on these processes are interesting. During the first period the drug inhibits or delays the early puff becoming refractory to reinduction. Later (after 4 hours in Fig. 12.5) the drug completely inhibits the re-acquisition of competence of the puff to respond to ecdysone.

With respect to the late puffs the consequences of ecdysone's removal may appear to be even more complex. Following an initial exposure of naive glands to ecdysone the hormone's removal at any time (or rather at any time up to the time these puffs would be active under continuous ecdysone conditions) results in the *premature* induction of most late puffs. The size of the prematurely induced puffs increases as the time of exposure to ecdysone increases. The induction of the late puffs under conditions of continuous ecdysone is inhibited by cycloheximide, their premature induction by ecdysone withdrawal is not.

Prematurely induced late puffs are inhibited by re-exposure of glands to ecdysone. Yet, following this initial inhibition, these puffs become active again as the second period of exposure to ecdysone continues (Fig. 12.6).

We will postpone a discussion of these results until we have considered the experimental analysis of the prepupal puffing sequence.

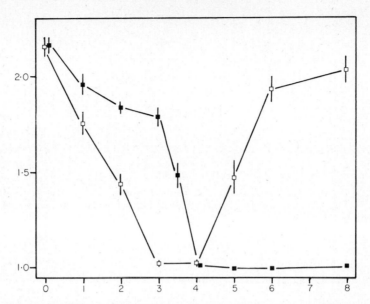

FIG. 12.5. The size of 74EF on re-exposure of larval salivary glands to ecdysone following an initial exposure of n hours in ecdysone and then a 3 hour ecdysone free wash. Open squares: control wash; closed squares: cycloheximide present (at 7.01 x 10^{-5}M) during wash. Ordinate puff size, abscissa time, in hours, at 25°C of initial exposure to hormone.

THE PREPUPAL PUFFING SEQUENCE

In prepupae rapid changes in puffing activity begin to occur five hours after puparium formation. As we will show the changes that then occur are not, like those of the larval sequence, under a single control (an increase in ecdysone concentration) but require more complex regulation.

Many of the puffs characterized as 'early' in the larval sequence are active again in prepupae. For example 74EF, which after its late larval activity has regressed by puparium formation, shows a second puffing peak 10 hours after puparium formation (Fig. 12.1). We have shown that these puffs are induced by ecdysone in larvae. Are they also under the hormone's control in prepupae? To answer this question salivary glands from timed prepupae, taken at hourly (or less) intervals after puparium formation were cultured for up to 14 hours either with, or without, ecdysone. The result of this experiment, shown in Fig. 12.7, was rather surprising. Glands from prepupae younger than $4\frac{1}{2}$ hours never puffed at these early sites even on prolonged culture with hormone. On the other hand glands from 6 hour prepupae gave a very rapid, and maximal, response to ecdysone. That is to say between $4\frac{1}{2}$ and 6 hours after puparium formation the glands suddenly become competent to respond to ecdysone at these puff sites. Note that this happens several hours before these puffs are active during normal development.

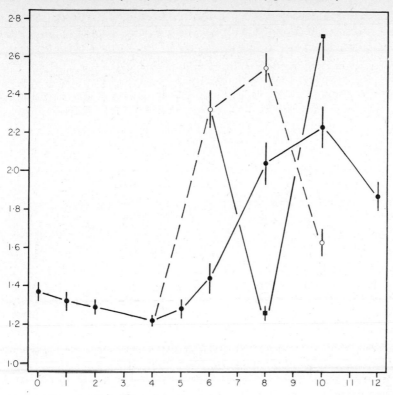

FIG. 12.6. Premature induction of the late puff 82F after an initial exposure to ecdysone for 4 hours and then culture without hormone for a further 6 hours (——O——); on re-exposure to hormone at 6 hours the prematurely induced puff first regresses (——■——) and is then reinduced. Also shown is the activity of the puff in the continuous presence of ecdysone (——•——). Ordinate puff size, abscissa time, in hours, at 20° C.

We are certain that this is a characteristically 'prepupal' response of the glands, rather than a replay of their larval response, since we see, along with such puffs as 74EF, induction of 93F (never active in larvae) and fail to see induction of a puff at 78D (which is only active in larvae).

   To study this acquisition of competence further salivary glands from 0 hour prepupae were cultured, in the absence of hormone, for various time intervals before being challenged by the hormone. We find that competence *can* be acquired *in vitro* but that a necessary condition is at least 3 hours culture without hormone (Fig. 12.8). Cycloheximide inhibits the acquisition of competence under these conditions as does actinomycin D. Once the glands are fully competent (either *in vivo* or *in vitro*) cycloheximide does not affect the induction of either 74EF or 93F. In fact, for the induction of 74EF and 93F by ecdysone to be completely insensitive to the inhibition of protein synthesis an extra hour without ecdysone is required (see Fig. 12.8). As is implied by the first experiment with prepupal glands described, ecdysone inhibits the acquisition of competence and a hormone concentration of 1×10^{-8} M or less is necessary during this period of three hours if even a 50 per cent response to ecdysone is later to be obtained (Fig. 12.9).

In fully competent salivary glands, i.e. glands from 6–8 hour prepupae, the response of 74EF to ecdysone is indistinguishable from its response in larval glands in terms of (1) sensitivity to hormone concentration (Fig. 12.10a), (2) relative sensitivity to α- and β-ecdysone and (3) in its insensitivity to cycloheximide.

The prepupal sequence also has its late puffs, such as 62E—also a late puff in the larval sequence. As in larvae the induction of 62E requires protein synthesis and the puff displays a very steep dose response curve to ecdysone (Fig. 12.10b). Whether or not ecdysone must remain present for the activity of the prepupal late puffs has not yet been studied.

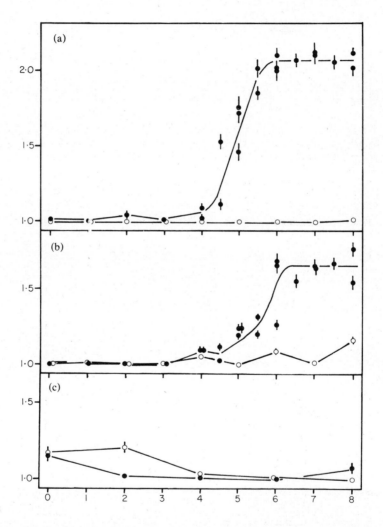

FIG. 12.7. Acquisition of competence to respond to ecdysone in salivary glands from prepupae of increasing age. Ordinate is puff size after 2 hours culture either with (•) or without (O) ecdysone (2.37×10^{-6}M). Abscissa is age, in hours at 25°C, after puparium formation. (a) 74EF, (b) 93F, (c) 78D.

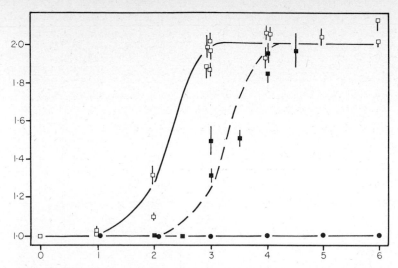

FIG. 12.8 Acquisition of competence to respond to ecdysone by salivary glands from zero hour prepupae cultured in ecdysone free medium (——□——), or in ecdysone free medium plus cycloheximide (——•——), for n hours before 2 hours exposure to ecdysone alone (——□——) or ecdysone plus cycloheximide (——□——). Ordinate is size of 74EF after the 2 hour ecdysone induction, abscissa is time, in hours at 25° C, of initial ecdysone free culture.

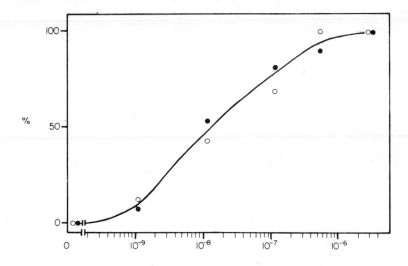

FIG. 12.9 The inhibition of acquisition of competence by ecdysone. Zero hour prepupal glands were preincubated for 3 hours in various ecdysone concentrations (abscissa) before being challenged with ecdysone at 2.37 x 10^{-6}M for 2 hours. The ordinate is the % inhibition of the induction of 74EF, (•) and 93F (O).

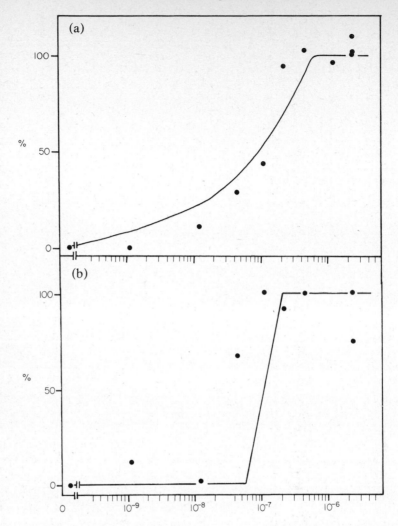

FIG. 12.10. Semi-log ecdysone dose-response curve for (a) 74EF, (b) 62E in salivary glands from 6 hour prepupae. For comparison the *curves* fitting the data points are the dose response curves of these puffs in *larval* glands. (From Ashburner 1973). Ordinate is % of maximum response, abscissa $\log_{10}$ ecdysone concentration.

Prior to the activity of such ecdysone responsive puffs as 74EF and 93F in prepupae, puffing is seen (from 6 to 8 hours after puparium formation) at several sites, notably 63E, 69A, 75CD, and 52A (see Fig. 12.1). Except for 63E, a late puff of the larval sequence, the activity of these loci is confined to this brief period. Their activity, in cultured salivary glands at least, requires the *absence* of ecdysone. Glands from prepupae of almost any age cultured without hormone show either an induction or, if the puffs are active on explantation, a maintenance of activity at these sites. Conversely glands cultured with ecdysone either never show puffing at these loci or, if the puffs were active on explantation, they rapidly regress (Figs. 12.11 and 12.12).

These results, give the clue to the explanation of why, when we start with larval glands, continuous exposure to ecdysone (even for as long as 24 hours at 25°C) *never*

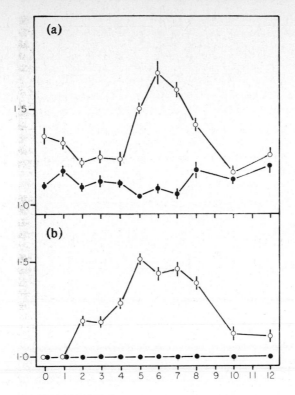

FIG. 12.11. The inhibition of (a) 63E and (b) 75CD by ecdysone. Salivary glands from prepupae of various ages were cultured for 2 hours either with (•) or without (O) ecdysone (2.37×10^{-6}M). Ordinate puff size, abscissa, age of prepupae in hours at 25°C.

results in the appearance of any puffs of the prepupal sequence. This is so since the puffs of the 6 to 8 hour prepupa require ecdysone to be *absent* for their activity and the later, ecdysone responsive, puffs require at least a 3 hour hormone free period to become inducible.

As a test of the correctness of this explanation salivary glands from puff stage 1 larvae have been cultured for 6 hours with ecdysone, then 3 hours without ecdysone and, finally, in ecdysone again. It is then possible to induce, in glands from *third instar larvae,* a normal *prepupal* puffing sequence.

This is a dramatic demonstration of the fact that merely by altering the ecdysone titre of our culture medium we can induce larval salivary glands to go through the complete spectrum of changes in gene activity that normally occupies a 20 hour period of development during early metamorphosis.

To elaborate these results we show, in Figs. 12.5 and 12.13, the behaviour of 74EF and 93F during the second period of exposure to ecdysone. The prepupal puff 93F only becomes inducible after the larval glands have suffered *both* at least 6 hours in ecdysone *and* at least 3 hours without hormone. This figure also shows that cycloheximide, present during the ecdysone free period only, inhibits the reinducibility of 74EF and the inducibility of 93F. The data for 93F also show one further point which emphasizes that we are still far from understanding just how, in detail, these puffs are controlled. A preincubation of *larval* glands with cycloheximide alone (i.e. in the absence of ecdysone) allows 93F to respond on later challenge with hormone (Fig. 12.14). Thus by this drug pretreatment we can allow 93F to be induced in a characteristically larval situation (this is reminiscent of the induction of the puff IV-2-B of *Chironomus tentans* by cycloheximide injection shown by Clever (1966)).

The behaviour of the 6 to 8 hour group of prepupal puffs, i.e. 75CD, 63E, 69A, 52A and 52C, in the 'three-phase' experiment confirms that larval glands must have at least a 6 hour exposure to ecdysone before showing a prepupal response. Only after 6 hours in hormone will hormone withdrawal allow the induction of these puffs (Fig. 12.15).

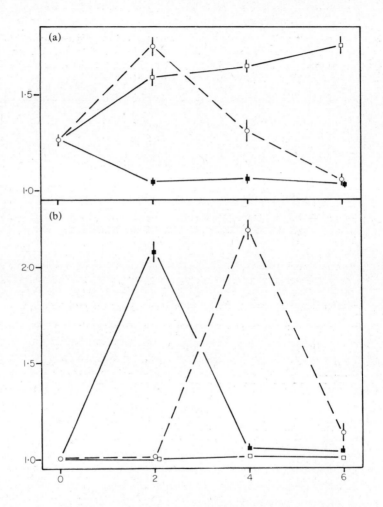

FIG. 12.12. The control of (a) 63E and (b) 74EF in prepupal salivary glands. Glands from 6 hour prepupae were cultured with (———■———) or without (———□———) ecdysone for up to 6 hours. The *in vivo* activity of these puffs in 6-12 hour prepupae is also shown (———O———). Ordinate puff size, abscissa time in culture (or prepupal age—6 hours) at 25° C.

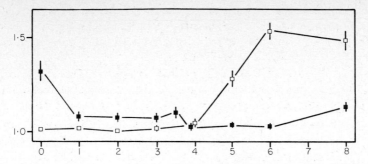

FIG. 12.13. The size of 93F on re-exposure of larval salivary glands to ecdysone following an initial exposure of n hours to ecdysone and then a 3 hour ecdysone free wash. Open squares, control wash, closed squares, cycloheximide present (at 7.01×10^{-5}M) during wash only. Ordinate puff size, abscissa time, in hours at 25°C., of initial exposure to hormone.

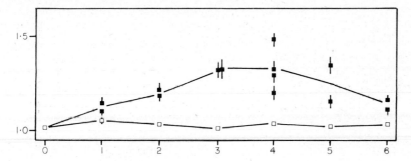

FIG. 12.14. Size of the prepupal puff 93F induced by 2 hours exposure to ecdysone in larval glands as a consequence of preincubation in cycloheximide (7.01×10^{-5}M) medium (■). Ordinate puff size, abscissa time in hours at 25°C of preincubation with cycloheximide before 2 hours in ecdysone. Controls (□) were incubated in medium without cycloheximide before ecdysone exposure.

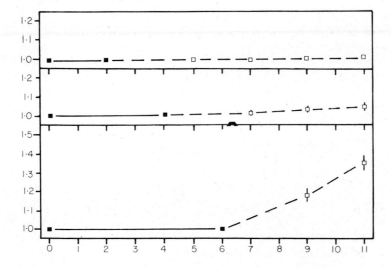

FIG. 12.15. Induction of the prepupal puff 75CD in larval glands during ecdysone free culture (——□——) following 2, 4 and 6 hour initial exposures to ecdysone (——■——). Ordinate puff size, abscissa time of culture in hours at 25°C.

Discussion

ECDYSONE TITRES DURING DEVELOPMENT

We will start our discussion by first considering the implications of our data for the changes in ecdysone titre during normal *Drosophila* development. Since, during the greater part of the third instar the early ecdysone puffs are inactive, yet will respond immediately to ecdysone, we must conclude that the effective ecdysone titre is, during this period, low (below 5×10^{-9} M). The rapid appearance of the early puffs six hours before puparium formation, and the regression of puffs active hitherto at this time, both suggest a rapid increase in effective ecdysone titre and it is probably this increase that is monitored by the determination, by ligature, of the critical period (Fraenkel 1934; Becker 1962; Kress 1974). This titre must remain high for the next four hours, at least, since during this time any marked drop in concentration would result in early puff regression. The rest of the larval sequence *can* proceed in the absence of ecdysone but we think, in fact, that the titre remains high until about three hours after puparium formation. We do so from detailed consideration of the regression of 63E after puparium formation and of the experimental behaviour of puffs active later in prepupae.

Between three and four hours after puparium formation the ecdysone titre must rapidly fall, if the experimental behaviour of puffs such as 63E and 75CD is a reliable guide. These puffs are induced not only as a consequence of events in the larval cycle but also of this fall in titre. The titre probably remains low (below 1×10^{-9} M) until eight hours after puparium formation. Another important consequence of this period is that it prepares the gland for the coming rise in ecdysone concentration by allowing puffs such as 74EF and 93F to become responsive. They do respond after eight hours as the titre increases again. Not only does this increase lead to the induction of 74EF and 93F (for example) but it also results in the repression of the prepupal puffs active earlier (i.e. 63E, 75CD, etc). How long the ecdysone titre persists high, after head eversion (at 12 hours after puparium formation), is not known.

We must emphasize that the previous paragraphs are speculations and predictions based upon the experimental behaviour of puffs. The radioimmune assay of ecdysone (Borst & O'Connor 1972) now allows the direct assay of ecdysone in a convenient and accurate way and one study of the titre in *Drosophila* has already been published (Borst *et al.* 1974). This study does indeed detect the fall in ecdysone titre we expect a few hours after puparium formation and the subsequent rise. However, the animals sampled in this experiment were too heterogeneous in age to allow a detailed comparison of the data with our expectations.

It is of great interest that the absolute ecdysone concentrations found, by these authors, in late third instar larvae are very similar indeed to those necessary to induce a normal larval puffing sequence in cultured salivary glands (about 1×10^{-7} M).

The relatively high dissociation constant for the binding of ecdysone to its (presumptive) receptors, previously implied on the basis of rather indirect evidence (Fristrom 1972; Ashburner 1973) and now measured (Yund & Fristrom 1975) may, as the last named authors suggest, be an adaptation to the need for very rapid changes in hormone titre during *Drosophila* development.

DETAILED CONTROL MODELS

The evidence that ecdysone plays an important role in the control of both larval and prepupal puffing activity is strong. Our data, however, show that this is not a sufficient answer to the question 'how are these puffs controlled?' To a certain extent our results support the conclusion of Clever (1964) that puffs late in the sequence owe their activity to the products of puffs early in the sequence. This may now seem to be an obvious class of model, *a priori,* but we must point out that other, very simple, models—such as each puff responding directly to ecdysone, the temporal sequence then being a sequence of decreasing affinities of the puff sites to the hormone—required refutation.

Although Clever's proposal that early puffs control late puffs is a correct description of our own interpretation of our data it is, in detail, quite insufficient. The formal model proposed earlier to account for the control of the larval sequence (Ashburner *et al.* 1973) remains unrefuted by any new experimental data. It is shown in Fig. 12.16 and describes, for one early puff and one late puff, how the larval sequence may be controlled.

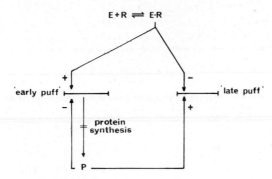

FIG. 12.16. A model for the control of an early and a late puff by ecdysone in larval salivary glands. See text for explanation (from Ashburner *et al.* 1974).

In essence we proposed that ecdysone's 'active' form is when it is bound to its receptor protein(s), a binding that is freely reversible and obeys the laws of mass action. The early puff of our model responds quantitatively as a function of the concentration of ER (and hence of ecdysone itself) and produces a product, P, which is either a protein or requires protein synthesis for its synthesis. P has two functions: it acts in a negative way on the early puff itself, to repress it, and positively to induce the late puff (we imply no parallels with negative and positive control as understood in prokaryotic systems). Thus in the absence of P, e.g. during induction by ecdysone in the presence of cycloheximide, the early puff does not regress and the late puff is not induced. The ecdysone-receptor complex (ER) also has two functions: in addition to inducing the early puff it represses the late puff. We envisage, during a normal induction by ecdysone, that the concentration of ER is constant with time but that of P increases. Eventually the concentration of P is sufficient to displace ER from both the early puff site and the late puff site leading to the former puff's regression and the latter's induction. If ecdysone is removed at an early stage in the proceedings then the early puff immediately regresses, since ER is necessary for its continued activity. This regression is independent of P and, hence, of protein synthesis. The extent to which the early puff may be reinduced on re-addition of ecdysone naturally will depend upon the concentration of P present at the time of re-addition of ecdysone and, therefore, on the time the early puff had previously

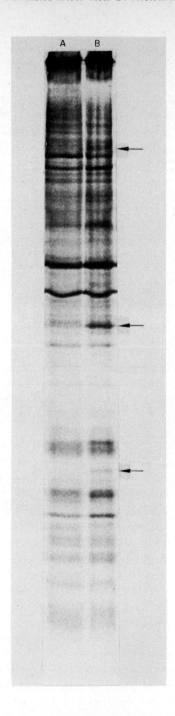

Fig. 12.17. Autoradiograph of a sodium dodecyl sulphate acrylamide gel separating salivary gland proteins labelled for 20 minutes after 1 hour culture without (A) or with (B) 1×10^{-6}M β-ecdysone. The arrows indicate polypeptides whose rates of synthesis are vastly increased as the result of ecdysone culture. The synthesis of the majority of polypeptides is unaffected.

been active. Similarly, ecdysone washout removes the repression of the late puff by ER and the puff is then immediately induced to a size determined by the P concentration at the time of washout.

Re-addition of ecdysone, before 4 to 6 hours, reinduces the early puff and represses the prematurely induced late puff. This is because the increase in ER concentration now counteracts the previously synthesized P. With renewed early puff activity the concentration of P increases again, eventually resulting in the (cycloheximide sensitive) regression of the early puff and the second appearance of the late puff under these experimental conditions.

With respect to the subsequent prepupal puffing sequence we have, at first sight, added greatly to the complexity of formal models required to explain its control. In fact a satisfactory explanation can be obtained by making one further assumption: the stability of P requires the continued presence of ecdysone (at least its stability after the completion of the larval sequence). The fall in ecdysone titre three hours after puparium formation thus allows the P concentration to fall (we note that this requires protein synthesis) and this is the event that is necessary for the process we have previously described as 'the acquisition of competence to respond to ecdysone'. This decline in P concentration takes three hours, and is very sensitive to ecdysone.

In fact we suspect, from experiments that we will publish in detail later, that the control of the prepupal puffing sequence is rather more complex than this, even at a formal level. Indeed we have hinted at one further degree of complexity when describing the fact that a prepupal puff (93F) can be induced in larval glands providing that protein synthesis has previously been inhibited.

Although our aim, in these experiments, has been to provide a formal model for the control of the sequential changes in puffing activity that occur subsequent to the initial induction by ecdysone in late third instar larvae this is but the first step in an analysis which must proceed using both genetic and biochemical techniques. As a start towards the biochemical study of these events we show, in Fig. 12.17, that a very early effect of ecdysone on larval salivary glands is to induce the synthesis of at least one (and probably two or more) proteins. The synthesis of these proteins is detectable after 30 minutes of ecdysone exposure and occurs long before any effect of the hormone on the gross rates of incorporation of labelled amino acids into proteins can be detected.

We have no evidence that the proteins induced by ecdysone have anything to do with P. We hope to show whether or not they are early puff products by studying their synthesis in genetic stocks of *Drosophila* which are aneuploid for early puff sites.

A similar induction, of a single protein, by ecdysone occurs between 2 and 5 hours after treating wing tissue of pupal *Antherea polyphemus* with relatively high (1×10^{-5} M) concentrations of β-ecdysone and, surprisingly, with α-ecdysone. This protein was detected by a double labelling technique (Ruh *et al.* 1974).

GENERAL CONSIDERATIONS

Although our biochemical results are preliminary they, and indeed the formal concept of early puffs playing a role in the subsequent effects of ecdysone, bear a striking similarity to the action of oestradiol on uterine tissue. Here a single 'induced protein' is synthesized within 40 minutes as a response to physiological concentrations of hormone with kinetics and dose-response relationships very similar to those of an early puff (Notides & Gorski 1966; Barnea & Gorski 1970; Katzenellenbogen & Gorski 1972; Baulieu *et al.* 1972).

This is a much more rapid response to oestradiol than had hitherto been suspected on the basis of relatively gross changes in macromolecular synthesis (Notebloom & Gorski 1963). The rate of 'induced protein' synthesis increases, after the 40 minute lag (presumably accounted for by the time necessary for transcription of its mRNA), until about two hours and then declines. The 'induced protein' is not reinducible after this decline.

The parallels in the action of insect and vertebrate steroid hormones, if they are anything other than wishful thinking, encourage us to think that the molecular mechanism of action of the classes of hormone may not be dissimilar. We are still a long way from fully understanding just what this mechanism may be and still further from knowing how a hormone such as ecdysone can control such a complex process as metamorphosis itself. Our hope is that, by a detailed study of one small facet of these events and by taking advantage of such fine material as the polytene chromosomes and their puffs, we can move from our present state of ignorance and wonder to one of real insight.

ACKNOWLEDGEMENTS

Original work supported by grants from the Science Research Council to M.A. and by a Medical Research Council Studentship to G.R.

DISCUSSION

Lees: It looks to me as if you have the makings of a biological clock in your system. I was wondering: your 3 hour period, is it temperature dependent or not?

Ashburner: We haven't done these experiments.

Illmensee: A few years ago, Emmerich showed that ecdysone bound to protein enters the nucleus. Are there any hard data as to whether ecdysone actually reaches the chromosomes?

Ashburner: No. There are, I think, three papers using autoradiographic techniques which suggest nuclear concentration of labelled ecdysone, but they can all be faulted on technical grounds. They may, of course, be right, but they do not give convincing evidence.

Shire: Do you know how ecdysone is inactivated? Are the enzymes that do this around at the right time?

Ashburner: There are several possible routes of ecdysone inactivation. There are three that are most popularly canvassed: One is a C20–C22 desmolase, another an ecdysone oxidase, and the third the formation of ecdysone conjugates. The isolated *Drosophila* salivary gland in culture does not metabolize ecdysone.

Gehring: Has it unequivocally been shown that a single isolated messenger RNA from heatshocked cells can hybridize to a single chromosome band?

Ashburner: Not as far as I am aware.

Gehring: So the evidence is not tight.

Ashburner: It is not as clean as you might like, but it is now almost impossible to argue out the evidence from the three laboratories that have done it, that specific heat shock puffs produce specific proteins.

Nöthiger: Can you antagonize the actions of ecdysone by providing juvenile hormone?

Ashburner: I am proud to say that I have *not* put juvenile hormone into this system. I have resisted doing so for many years, because there are as you know, in the literature, several reports of *in vitro* experiments in which substances which at best are juvenile hormone from *Manduca*, or one of the Cecropia juvenile hormones, and at worst are a horrendous miscellany of organic compounds, (which are rather thick and oily), and these reports describe inhibition of the *in vitro* effects of ecdysone. My own opinion of this is that I don't believe any of it. The question I always ask is, how can you believe results when everything is covered in oil, and the answer usually is that otherwise you can't get enough juvenile hormone in solution to produce the effect. John Law *et al.* (Proc. natn. Acad. Sci. Wash., *71*, 493 (1974) has shown that you can get an aqueous solution of Cecropia juvenile hormone up to 10^{-5} molar, so it is now clear that the solubility argument is just ridiculous. You can summarize all the juvenile hormone experiments by saying that they are all negative effects which you will get equally well, for example, by hitting the isolated salivary gland with a hammer, or using actinomycin D, dinitrophenol or sodium flouride. In no case, as far as I know, has anyone come up with a good control compound for doing juvenile hormone experiments. Of course for ecdysone we have a good control compound, such as 22 iso-ecdysone, which has very low bio activity, yet the gross physical properties of the molecule are very similar to the active compound.

REFERENCES

ASHBURNER, M. (1967). Patterns of puffing activity in the salivary gland chromosomes of *Drosophila*. I Autosomal puffing patterns in a laboratory stock of *Drosophila melanogaster*. *Chromosoma* (Berlin) **21**, 398-428.

ASHBURNER, M. (1972). Patterns of puffing activity in the salivary gland chromosomes of *Drosophila*. VI Induction by ecdysone in salivary glands of *D. melanogaster* cultured *in vitro*. *Chromosoma* (Berlin) **38**, 255-281.

ASHBURNER, M. (1973). Sequential gene activation by ecdysone in polytene chromosomes of *Drosophila melanogaster*. I Dependence upon hormone concentration. *Devl. Biol.*, **35**, 47-61.

ASHBURNER, M. (1974). Sequential gene activation by ecdysone in polytene chromosomes of *Drosophila melanogaster*. II The effects of inhibitors of protein synthesis. *Devl. Biol.*, **39**, 141-157.

ASHBURNER, M. & RICHARDS, G. P. (1976). Sequential activation by ecdysone in polytene chromosomes of *Drosophila melanogaster*. III The consequences of ecdysone withdrawal. (in preparation).

ASHBURNER, M., CHIHARA, C., MELTZER, P. & RICHARDS, G. P. (1974). Temporal control of puffing activity in polytene chromosomes. *Cold Spring Harb. Symp. quant. Biol.*, **38**, 655-662.

BARNEA, A. & GORSKI, J. (1970). Estrogen-produced protein. Time course of synthesis. *Biochemistry*, **9**, 1899-1904.

BAULIEU, E. E., ALBERGA, A., RAYNAUD-JAMMET, C. & WIRA, C. R. (1972). New look at the very early steps of oestrogen action in uterus. *Nature New Biol.*, **236**, 236-239.

BECKER, H. J. (1962). Die Puffs der Speicheldrüsenchromosomen von *Drosophila melanogaster*. II Die Auslosüng der Puffbildung, ihre Spezifität und ihre Bieziehung zur funktion der Ringdrüse. *Chromosoma* (Berlin), **13**, 341-384.

BEERMANN, W. (1956). Nuclear differentiation and functional morphology of chromosomes. *Cold Spring Harb. Symp. quant. Biol.*, **21**, 217-232.

BERENDES, H. D. (1967). The hormone ecdysone as effector of specific changes in the pattern of gene activities of *Drosophila hydei*. *Chromosoma* (Berlin), **22**, 274-293.

BEST-BELPOMME, M. & COURGEON, A. M. (1973). Présence ou absence de recépteurs saturables de l'ecdystérone dans des clones sensibles ou résistants de *Drosophila melanogaster* en culture *in vitro*. *C.r. Acad. Sci., Paris*, **280 D**, 1397-1400.

BORST, D. W. & O'CONNOR, J. D. (1972). Arthropod molting hormone: Radioimmune assay. *Science,* **178,** 418–419.

BORST, D. W., BOLLENBACHER, W. E., O'CONNOR, J. D., KING, D. S. & FRISTROM, J. W. (1974). Ecdysone levels during metamorphosis of *Drosophila melanogaster. Devl. Biol.,* **39,** 308–316.

BOYD, J. B. & LOGAN, W. R. (1972). Developmental variations of a deoxyribonuclease in the salivary glands of *Drosophila hydei* and *Drosophila melanogaster. Cell Differentiation,* **1,** 107–118.

CLAYCOMB, W. C., LA FOND, R. E. & VILLEE, C. A. (1971). Autoradiographic localization of 3H-ß-ecdysone in salivary gland cells of *Drosophila virilis. Nature, Lond.,* **234,** 302–304.

CLEVER, U. (1964). Actinomycin and puromycin: Effects on sequential gene activation by ecdysone. *Science,* **146,** 794–795.

CLEVER, U. (1966). Induction and repression of a puff in *Chironomus tentans. Devl. Biol.,* **14,** 421–438.

CLEVER, U. & KARLSON, P. (1960). Induktion von Puff-Veränderungen in den Speicheldrüsenchromosomen von *Chironomus tentans* durch Ecdyson. *Expl. Cell Res.,* **20,** 623–626.

CLEVER, U. & ROMBALL, C. G. (1966). RNA and protein synthesis in the cellular response to a hormone, ecdysone. *Proc. natn. Acad. Sci. USA,* **56,** 1470–1476.

EEKEN, J. C. J. (1974). Circadian control of the cellular response to ß-ecdysone in *Drosophila lebanonensis.* I Experimental puff induction and its relation to puparium formation. *Chromosoma* (Berlin) **49,** 205–217.

EMMERICH, H. (1969). Anreicherung von Tritiummarkiertem ecdyson in den Zellkernen der Speicheldrüsen von *Drosophila hydei. Expl. Cell Res.,* **58,** 261–270.

EMMERICH, H.(1970). Ecdysonbindende Proteinfraktionen in den Speicheldrüsen von *Drosophila hydei. Z. vergl. Physiol.,* **68,** 385–402.

EMMERICH, H. (1972). Ecdysone binding proteins in nuclei and chromatin from *Drosophila* salivary glands. *Gen. Comp. Endocrinology,* **19,** 543–551.

FRAENKEL, G. (1934). Pupation of flies initiated by a hormone. *Nature,* **133,** 834.

FRAENKEL, G. & BROOKES, V. J. (1953). The process by which the puparia of many species of flies become fixed to a substrate. *Biol. Bull. Woods Hole,* **105,** 442–449.

FRISTROM, J.W. (1972). The biochemistry of imaginal disc development. In: *Results and Problems in Cell Differentiation, Vol.* **5:** 'The Biology of Imaginal Discs'. H. Ursprung & R. Nöthiger eds. Berlin Springer-Verlag.

GORRELL, T. A., GILBERT, L. I. & TASH, J. (1972). The uptake and conversion of α-ecdysone by the pupal tissues of *Hyalophora cecropia. Insect Biochem.,* **2,** 94–106.

JENSEN, E. V. & DE SOMBRE, E. R. (1973). Estrogen-receptor interaction. *Science,* **182,** 126–134.

KATZENELLENBOGEN, B. S. & GORSKI, J. (1972). Estrogen action *in vitro*: induction of the synthesis of a specific uterine protein. *J. Biol. Chem.,* **247,** 1299–1305.

KING, D. S.,BOLLENBACHER, W. E., BORST, W. E., VEDECKIS, W. V., O'CONNOR, J. D., ITTYCHERIAH, P. I. & GILBERT, L. I. (1974). The secretion of α-ecdysone by the prothoracic glands of *Manduca sexta in vitro. Proc. natn. Acad. Sci. USA,* **71,** 793–796.

KING, R. J. B. & GORDON, J. (1972). Involvement of DNA in the acceptor mechanism for uterine oestradiol receptor. *Nature New Biol.,* **240,** 185–187.

KORGE, G. (1975). Chromosome puff activity and protein synthesis in the larval salivary gland of *Drosophila melanogaster. Proc. natn. Acad. Sci. USA,* **72,** 4550–4554.

KRESS, H. (1972). Das Puffmuster der Riesenchromosomen in den larvalen Speicheldrüsen von *Drosophila virilis:* seine Veränderungen in der Normalentwicklung und nach Injektion von Ecdyson. *S-B-Bayer. Akad. Wiss., Math-Naturw.,* **K1 1972:** 129–149.

KRESS, H. (1973). Specific repression of a puff in the salivary gland chromosome of *Drosophila virilis* after injection of glucosamine. *Chromosoma* (Berlin), **40,** 379–386.

KRESS, H. (1974). Temporal relationships between leaving food, ecdysone release, mucoprotein extrusion and puparium formation in *Drosophila virilis. J. Insect Physiol.,* **20,** 1041–1055.

KROEGER, H. (1968). Gene activities during insect metamorphosis and their control by hormones. In: *Metamorphosis, a problem in developmental biology.* W. Etkin & L. I. Gilbert eds., North-Holland, Amsterdam.

LEWIS, M., HELMSING, P. J. & ASHBURNER, M. (1975). Parallel changes in puffing activity and protein synthesis in salivary glands of *Drosophila. Proc. natn. Acad. Sci. USA.,* **72,** 3604–3608.

LEZZI, M. & ROBERT, M. (1972). Chromosomes isolated from unfixed salivary glands of *Chironomus.* In: *Results and Problems in Cell Differentiation,* Vol. **4,** Developmental Studies on Giant Chromosomes. Ed. W. Beermann. Berlin, Springer-Verlag.

MANDARON, P. (1973). Effects of α-ecdysone, ß-ecdysone and inokosterone on the *in vitro* evagination of *Drosophila* leg discs and the subsequent differentiation of imaginal integumentary structures. *Devl.*

Biol., **31**, 101-113.

MCKENZIE, S. L., HENIKOFF, S. & MESELSON, M. (1975). Localization of RNA from heat-induced polysomes at puff sites in *Drosophila melanogaster*. *Proc. natn. Acad. Sci. USA*, **72**, 1117-1121.

MILNER, M. J. & SANG, J. (1974). Relative activities of *α*-ecdysone and ß-ecdysone for the differentiation *in vitro* of *Drosophila melanogaster* imaginal discs. *Cell*, **3**, 141-143.

NOTEBLOOM, W. D. & GORSKI, J. (1963). An early effect of estrogen on protein synthesis. *Proc. natn. Acad. Sci. USA*, **50**, 250-255.

NOTIDES, A. & GORSKI, J. (1966). Estrogen-induced synthesis of a specific uterine protein. *Proc. natn. Acad. Sci. USA*, **56**, 230-235.

O'MALLEY, B. W. & MEANS, A. R. (1974). Female steroid hormones and target cell nuclei. *Science*, **183**, 610-620.

O'MALLEY, B. W., SPELSBERG, T. C., SCHRADER, W. T., CHYTIL, F. & STEGGLES, A. W. (1972). Mechanism of interaction of a hormone-receptor complex with the genome of a eukaryotic target cell. *Nature*, **235**, 141-144.

PRICE, G. M. (1974). Protein metabolism by the salivary glands and other organs of the larva of the blowfly, *Calliphora erythrocephala*. *J. Insect Physiol.*, **20**, 329-347.

RICHARDS, G. P. (1975). The hormonal control of chromosomal puffing in salivary glands of *Drosophila melanogaster*. Ph.D. Thesis, University of Cambridge.

RICHARDS, G. P. (1976). The control of prepupal puffing patterns *in vitro*: implications for prepupal ecdysone titres in *Drosophila melanogaster*. *Devl. Biol.* (in press).

RUH, M. F., RUH, T. S., DEWERT, W. & DUENAS, V. (1974). Ecdysterone-induced protein synthesis *in vitro*. *J. Insect Physiol.*, **20**, 1729-1736.

SPRADLING, A., PENMAN, S. & PARDUE, M. L. (1975). Analysis of *Drosophila* mRNA by *in situ* hybridization: Sequences transcribed in normal and heat shocked cultured cells. *Cell*, **4**, 395-404.

STOCKER, A. J. & KASTRITSIS, C. D. (1973). Developmental studies in *Drosophila* 7. The influence of ecdysterone on the salivary gland puffing patterns of *D. pseudoobscura* larvae and prepupae. *Differentiation* **1**, 225-239.

TISSIERES, A. MITCHELL, H. K. & TRACEY, U. M. (1974). Protein synthesis in salivary glands of *Drosophila melanogaster*: Relation to chromosome puffs. *J. Mol. Biol.*, **84**, 389-398.

YAMAMOTO, K. R. & ALBERTS, B. (1975). The interaction of estradiol-receptor protein with the genome: an argument for the existence of undetected specific sites. *Cell*, **4**, 301-310.

YUND, M. A. & FRISTROM, J. W. (1975). Uptake and binding of ß-ecdysone in imaginal discs of *Drosophila melanogaster*. *Devl. Biol.*, **43**, 287-298.

Index